Return to: Mo Langham

28 Days Behind Bars

Return to: Mo Bingham

28 Days Behind Bars

Harold Wagoner

*Graphics
by
Tish Wagoner*

Writers Club Press
San Jose New York Lincoln Shanghai

28 Days Behind Bars

All Rights Reserved © 2001 by Harold Wagoner

No part of this book may be reproduced or transmitted in any form or by any means, graphic, electronic, or mechanical, including photocopying, recording, taping, or by any information storage retrieval system, without the permission in writing from the publisher.

Writers Club Press
an imprint of iUniverse.com, Inc.

For information address:
iUniverse.com, Inc.
5220 S 16th, Ste. 200
Lincoln, NE 68512
www.iuniverse.com

ISBN: 0-595-20368-X

Printed in the United States of America

I dedicate this to my grandchildren.

Contents

Foreword xiii

Introduction xv

The Idea 1

My Least Favorite Ride 3

My Favorite Ride 5

The Planning Stage 8
    Letters 9
    Panniers 10
    Sleeping Pad \ Bag 11
    The Route 12
    The Calendar 14
    Tentative Plans 15
    The Bike 16
    What to Pack 18
    Clothes 24
    Shoes 24
    Helmet 25
    Tent 26
    Camera 26
    Computer 28
    Journal 28
    Tires \ Tubes \ Spokes 28
    Maps \ Books 29
    Chain \ Derailleur 29

Going Solo *30*
Protection *32*
Airline or Train? *33*

On The Train 35

Day One 44
   Riding from Seattle, Washington
   To near Leavenworth, Washington

Day Two 62
   From Leavenworth, Washington
   To Coulee City, Washington

Day Three 79
   From Coulee City, Washington
   To Spokane, Washington

Day Four 87
   From Spokane, Washington
   To Troy, Montana

Day Five 104
   From Troy, Montana
   To Columbia Falls, Montana

Day Six 123
   From Columbia Falls, Montana
   To Browning, Montana

Day Seven 146
   From Browning, Montana
   To Havre, Montana.

Day Eight 158
   From Havre, Montana
   To Malta, Montana

Day Nine 178
   From Malta, Montana
   To Wolf Point, Montana

Day Ten 192
   From Wolf Point, Montana
   To Williston, North Dakota

Day Eleven 204
   From Williston, North Dakota
   To New Town, North Dakota

Day Twelve 216
   From New Town, North Dakota
   To Harvey, North Dakota

Day Thirteen 232
   From Harvey, North Dakota
   To Cooperstown, North Dakota

Day Fourteen 244
   From Cooperstown, North Dakota
   To Barnesville, Minnesota

Day Fifteen 263
   From Barnesville, Minnesota
   To St. Cloud, Minnesota

Day Sixteen 276
   From St. Cloud, Minnesota
   To Hudson, Wisconsin

Day Seventeen 287
   From Hudson, Wisconsin
   To Eau Claire, Wisconsin

Day Eighteen 295
    From Eau Claire, Wisconsin
    To Wisconsin Rapids, Wisconsin

Day Nineteen 313
    From Wisconsin Rapids, Wisconsin
    To Eureka, Wisconsin

Day Twenty 332
    From Eureka, Wisconsin
    To Ludington, Michigan

Day Twenty-One 340
    From Ludington, Michigan
    To St. Louis, Michigan

Day Twenty-Two 354
    From St. Louis, Michigan
    To Sandusky, Michigan

Day Twenty-Three 365
    From Sandusky, Michigan
    To London, Ontario

Day Twenty-Four 375
    From London, Ontario
    To Niagara Falls, Ontario

My Day Off 383
    Niagara Falls, Ontario.

Day Twenty-Five 386
    From Niagara Falls, Ontario
    To Newark, New York

Day Twenty-Six 396
    From Newark, New York
    To Sangerfield, New York

Day Twenty-Seven 411
    From Sangerfield, New York
    To Hyde Park, New York

Day Twenty-Eight 428
    From Hyde Park, New York
    To New York City, New York

My Flight Home 445

Epilogue 450

Afterword 453

Conclusions 455

About the Author 457

Foreword

This is a love story. A love story with America, and it'll always hold an extra special meaning for me.

Unlike all the books I've read about cross-country bicycle touring, this isn't about the history of our country. If you're interested in that, I can only suggest that you read a history book. It's not about politics or towns (which I try to avoid at all cost). It's an emotional record of the tiny, commonplace adventures that I met with on the road and the feeling that arose in me at that time. It's about my tour across America, the scenery, my thoughts, emotions, experiences, and my opinions.

It's simply written and told, easy to understand with clear and realistic detail. There are no big college words in it (you know the kind that are only found in crossword puzzles). I believe college is a place that teaches normal people how to write books that are impossible to read by normal people. Even though a lot of what I write shouldn't be read by children, I believe that everything should be written in a way that a seven-year-old can read and understand. I think that it's more important that one's language be understood, than admired.

Please keep in mind that this is my first attempt at authorship. Writing this book was the hardest thing I've ever done. It was much harder than the ride itself. I burned a lot of midnight oil (well it was actually electricity) working on this book. It's taken me more than ten years, working in my spare time, to complete it. If you're a critic, and you're looking for the improper usage of the English language, you won't be disappointed; you'll find it in this book. I know it's not great, but it's the best I can do and I believe that's all that can be expected of anybody. I truly believe that there is a book in each and every one of us that should be written. And one thing is for sure, no one is ever going to write a book about me, except me. Just like the sports I do, this book isn't to be taken seriously. I don't believe you have to have all the details before you start to write. You can make a life's work of preparing and never get to the writing itself. Preparing is just like the pencil I'm using, if I put too fine a point on it, it'll break. I say use the talents you have, and use them now. Writing, like making chili, or making love, is one's own personal act. There is no one right way to do it.

My main purpose for putting this Journal…Book…Album…, or whatever you want to call it, together, is to furnish my grandchildren with some information in the hope that they will get a better understanding of their grandpa. If, someday, they were to ever say, "Grandpa, tell us about the good old days," these are the good old days.

Introduction

After my tour I read several books on bicycle touring. I'm glad I didn't read them before my tour, or I just might have abandoned the idea of riding across America all together. Every touring book I've read is so negative, all they seem to talk about is how bad the wind was, or how cold it was, or how hard the rain poured down on them for days at a time. I wonder why these people even wrote about their experiences (probably for the money). It's obvious that they hated their tour. In my book you'll also hear me complaining about the headwinds (they're a bitch, all right) but I can also see the positive side of things. You don't have to be a rocket scientist to realize that positive thinking is more productive than negative thinking. For one thing, a headwind forces me to ride at a slower pace and this is when I see all the small flowers hiding in the tall grass along the side of the road. I recall this one time in particular, when I had an especially strong headwind. I stopped and lay my bike and myself down in the fresh, new, spring grass and watched as the cumulus clouds drifted by overhead. It was wonderful. It made me feel like a kid again. I believe that on a bicycle tour, you have to have the right attitude and make the best of every situation.

* * *

Most people think I'm crazy to sit alone for hours...days...weeks...months...and even years working on a book that I never intend to publish. They say, "Why are you writing? Only fools write for fun. Sensible people write for money." Well, I'm writing because I believe that writing is just like painting, they are both putting your thoughts down on paper, or canvas, and I…for one…can't paint. I'm not writing to show off, but because I want to share a part of my life with my grandchildren. I've decided that I'm going to write as badly as I want to. After all, I'm not trying to make anyone believe that I'm any smarter than I am. No writing is a waste of time. With every sentence I write, I learn something. I also believe that you have to write for yourself, not for a teacher, a critic, or an editor. You can't allow yourself to worry about, "What will my friends think?" The minute you start to write to please someone, or not to offend someone, or to make big bucks, I believe you're doomed because you're losing sight of what is unique and true in you. If I were to write in a manner not to offend anyone, then it wouldn't be the real me writing. So if you don't want to be offended. Stop reading right Now…!

In this book I've told the truth, mainly. There are things, which I've stretched, a little, but mainly, I've told the truth. I've never seen anyone who didn't stretch the truth at one time or another. I find writing a much easier way to express myself than talking. After all, in writing it's much easier to go back and correct my mistakes. I tend to invent my own words, but that's all right…! After all, Mr. Webster isn't God.

Some aspects of my tour produced a stronger image then others. As I page through my album, I can look at a picture and recall exactly what was going on at that exact moment, years ago. The mind is a wonderful thing. You know what they say, the mind is the second thing to go, I forgot what the first was. The events in this book have been reconstructed from the very detailed tapes and pictures that I kept. I wanted to relate to you my experiences, not as I see them now, but as I felt about them then.

I'm pretty much a loner, a shy person. I don't talk to people when I can avoid it, so this book will pertain to my riding experiences more than to the local people. Isn't it nice that we live in a country that people like to write books about?

The Idea

Let's see, just how did this idea of a cross-country bike tour all come about?

Well, let's start at the beginning.

It is a warm summer evening in L.A., especially in the Valley, where I live. It is a Friday night so I call my girlfriend up on the phone. We decide to go on a *Sierra Club* hike, which we do quite often. She is all the time telling me to take a hike.

As the hike starts out, it follows along this dry streambed which is abundantly lined with trees. It's much cooler in this canyon than it is in the Valley, which makes it quite pleasant for hiking.

We socialize and stay with the group for about a half-hour. By this time, we are far enough up the canyon to be away from all the light and noise of the city. We slow our pace down a little, so we fall behind and hike alone, in the quiet of the night. (When hiking with the *Sierra Club*, the leader is allowed to lose 10% of the group.) It's nice to be out in nature, away from the hustle and bustle of the city, at night, with someone special.

Twilight rapidly changes into darkness. Pinks and golds streak the sky. The sun is an orange ball, so far away and cold that you could look straight at it. The ball moves toward the horizon, contacts it, then slowly disappears.

As we make our way up the trail, we hear the distant call of a coyote.

By now the moon is full and high, which furnishes us with sufficient light. As we round one of the many switchbacks we hear the hoot of an owl. We pause...An enormous tree hanging over the trail casts a dark shadow. Dark silhouettes of trees and branches line the trail. A cloud drifts directly in front of the moon, softening, but not diminishing its glow. As we look up into the trees, we make out an owl's silhouette against a sky filled with brightly shining stars, which look like an opened jewelry box, filled with diamonds, lying on navy blue velvet. As we hike on, the owl flies off into a nearby tree, where its mate is waiting.

When we finally reach the summit and are in need of a break, we come upon a panoramic view. To the north are all the city lights as far as the eye can see. We watch the electric signs come on, and the red and green stop-and-go traffic signals in the valley far below. To the east the San Gabriel Mountains form a neutral border. It kind of reminds us of the movie, *"Close Encounters of the Third Kind."*

Then to the south, is another spectacular view: the ocean, with all the city lights accenting the coastline.

We watch as a hungry fog rolls in off the ocean and creeps its way slowly up the valley toward us. The trees turn into ghosts and then disappear all together.

After taking in the outstanding views for a while, we start back down, which is much easier than going up.

It is another perfect Southern California evening.

At some point on the way down, I don't recall exactly where, but it really doesn't matter anyway, my girlfriend brings up the fact that I've been doing things for other people all my life, and it's about time I did something for myself. I had to agree with her. So I put a lot of thought into it. Just what would I like to do for myself?

My Least Favorite Ride

I've done a few 25 mile time trials, my best time being one hour, ten minutes, and thirty seconds, which is an average of 21.28 mph.

I've done a lot of centuries (100 mile rides). My average time is around six hours. Like they say, "Bicyclists do it for Centuries."

As a member of *The San Fernando Valley Bicycle Club*, I've also been on several, one to two week-long bike trips.

My least favorite ride would have to be the 300 mile ride I did (in one day) with *The Los Angeles Wheelmen Bicycle Club* (which I'm also a member of) on their so-called Grand Tour. The longest day ride I had done pier to this was a century. The Grand Tour consist of either a 100…200…300…or 400 mile ride in a 24 hour period. A lot of my friends were going to do the 200 mile ride. But for some unknown reason I decided to do the 300 miles. It turned out to be a very…very…hard ride. There were a lot of hills and I was riding into a strong headwind (down on my drops) for over 100 miles. The ride started at 6:00 a.m. and around 4:00 a.m. (with 22 hours in) the next morning the C.H.P. was going to call the ride off because of the fog along the coast. Luckily they didn't. I wanted to finish the 300 miles although by this time my left leg was so sour I couldn't peddle with it at all. All I could do was push down and pull up with my right foot. When I pulled my right foot out of the peddle at the finish line after 23 and a half hours I put my foot on the ground and my leg just collapsed and I fell over with my bike on top of me. After being helped up I had to wait several hours before I could even put my bike on my car and drive home. It was three days afterwards before I could walk normally again. But…, I DID IT…!

So, I thought about what I would like to do next?

Suddenly, it was as clear as a cloudless day. A solo cross-country bicycle tour. I believe that most of us cyclists harbor similar dreams but are a little scared of what might happen once we leap off that cliff into the unknown. It may be dangerous, I'll be the first to admit it, but then again, if dreams were safe and predictable they wouldn't be worth pursuing. And visions have to be followed by the venture. It isn't enough to stare up the steps…you must climb up the stairs. I would rather attempt to do something great and fail, than attempt to do nothing and succeed. So why not attempt to do the ultimate bike ride? For me, this would be a cross-country bicycle tour. In an automobile it would be a transcontinental trip, but on a bicycle, it's a cross-country bicycle tour.

So, that's how it all came about. I didn't want any sponsors. I didn't want to raise money for any organization. Cycling for fund-raisers would mean riding into all the larger cities and being involved with television, radio, and newspaper interviews. There would be no moving about in my country, quietly slipping in and out of towns unnoticed.

I wanted to do it, by myself, and for myself.

My Favorite Ride

I got into riding bicycles, as a sport, about four years prior to my tour, and I really enjoy riding. Living in the Los Angeles area and having beautiful weather all the time, I ride almost every day, year round.

Let me tell you about my favorite bike ride. It starts in the San Fernando Valley and goes over the Santa Monica Mountains down to the beach. Then, I take a 20-mile long bike path that's right on the beach, from Santa Monica to Redondo Beach.

I like to get an early start, while the air is still fresh and clean and before the roads and bike path get too crowded. This way I can ride fast and hard, all the way to Redondo Beach, which is 40 miles and my turnaround point.

Once I'm there I usually have a coke, a piece of pizza and a bowl of clam chowder, and take a little walk on the pier.

By this time, it's warmed up considerably, so I take off my shirt to soak up a few rays on my return ride. The bike path is getting crowded, with not only bike riders (most of which don't know how to ride) but also with roller skaters, and skate boarders who make very sudden turns and stops. There are always people walking across the bike path (of course) without looking either way.

It's very obvious that I have to ride a lot slower going back, but it's good sex-ure-size. I get to rest up a little, and the scenery is absolutely fantastic on the beach. This is where mothers read fat novels by women with three names, and fathers read the coed's damp T-shirts. I remember many a time when I lay on the beach for hours, watching the girls and getting sunburnt.

Riding this slowly, I can watch the sailboats in the ocean and people flying kites and playing volleyball.

Once I get to Venice Beach, the scenery turns a little bizarre. I quite often get off my bike and walk through this mile or so section, just to take it all in. There are bodybuilders lifting weights in the outdoor gym ("Muscle Beach") and skinny girls wearing (butt floss) bikinis watching them. I just love California, where you can wear (or not wear) anything you want.

There is an assortment of interesting people playing drums, keyboards, and guitars on the sidewalk. There are punk rockers hanging out and old ladies roller-skating. It's like a huge swap meet with all kinds of ethnic foods and outside shops. It's sort of like window-shopping, without the windows.

The girls down here live in their swimsuits. I'm really not a dirty old man, I'm not dirty and I'm not old, I just like to look at beautiful things, and girls just happen to be one of those beautiful things.

I usually stop along here and get another coke and piece of pizza.

There is free entertainment everywhere you look. My favorite is a guy who rolls his piano out on the sidewalk and plays requests. He's great. He can play anything. I really like his ragtime. One rule I have is to never go past a street musician without putting some money in his hat. These people have a wonderful talent and deserve to be compensated for it. I don't give bums money, though, because I'm afraid they'll just spend it on booze.

It would be easy for me to spend all day at Venice, but I still have a two-hour ride home, which takes me along San Vincente Boulevard. This is a popular jogging street…another good place to slow down, and take in the sights. What I say about runners is, anyone who says they run ten miles a day with their muscles aching, their heart pounding and their lungs on fire because it makes them feel good, will lie about other things as well.

From here it's up the mountain, through a tunnel and back down into the Valley, where I immediately stop and get a peanut butter malt, before I head on home.

It's Just a Great 80-Mile Ride.

The Planning Stage

I guess I came up with the idea of going on the tour close to a year before I actually did it. After all, you can't just take off on a cross-country bike tour on the spur of a moment...a lot of planning is needed. I did a lot of research on it, a lot of research. I believe that when you fail to plan, you plan to fail. I wrote to the *Chamber of Commerce* in every state I was riding through to get all the information I could about each state. I wanted to see everything there was to see, of interest to me. Nothing would be more frustrating for me than passing by some noteworthy camping place or natural attraction simply because I didn't know it existed. I wrote to the *Department of Transportation* in each state to see if it was legal to ride on the roads I wanted to ride on. These were the general rules I received:

(1) All vehicles that share the public roadways are subject to the laws of the state. That includes bicycles in the city as well as in the country. They are liable to traffic tickets and prosecution just like drivers of automobiles, trucks, and motorcycles are. Basically, the state and municipal codes, which may vary in detail from state to state and city to city, establish the same broad rules and regulations all across the country.

(2) Bike riders must always ride with the traffic (Pedestrians walk against the traffic). Therefore, bikers must ride on the right-hand side of the road as close to the curb or shoulder of the road as safety permits.

(3) Bicyclists must signal their turns with their left hand.

(4) Bicycles must not be ridden on sidewalks. Sidewalks are for pedestrians.

(5) Bikers must obey all traffic lights and traffic signs, including those that stipulate no bicycle riding on certain marked roads such as freeways and parkways.

(6) Bikes must not speed (no problem there).

(7) Bicycles have as much right to the road as cars, trucks, and motorcycles.

I wrote to the *Department of Parks and Recreation*, in each state, to see if there were any points of interest that I might want to see. It took close to six months to get all this information. I received a lot of very good information, and they sent me state maps which cost about $1.50 each, so that alone was worth my postage. I joined the *Bikecentennial Organization*, a move that made me feel like a pro and also enabled me to buy club maps of suggested coast-to-coast routes all over the United States. I even went so far as to get an almanac to find out the average temperature and see where the prevailing winds would be coming from.

*   *   *

Letters

Some of the return envelopes I received contained the usual form letters, maps, and tourist brochures, but many of them contained enthusiastic personal letters like this one;

Seattle
Engineering Department

February 21, 1989

Dear Mr. Wagoner:

- I have enclosed some maps, which will make your route planning easier. Here are some thoughts, in no particular order;
- I-5 in metropolitan areas is Not open to cyclists. That includes the entire distance between Seattle & Everett.
- Don't go to Everett unless you have a good reason. Intercept Hwy. 2 a little farther east.
- I have included a route sheet to Snohomish and Monroe. Go there for your first night. Both hotels and camping are available nearby.
- There is an *AYH Youth Hostel* in downtown Seattle: (206) 662-5443 , 84 Union St. Plan on taking your bike out of the box before walking or riding there.
- If you have time, Hwy. 20 is more scenic and less traveled by commercial vehicles. Use the route sheet to Snohomish, then Hwy. 9 to 530, then to Hwy. 20. It is my favorite route across the mountains.

Sincerely,
Benjamin Striker
Bicycle Program

*   *   *

Panniers

The *Sierra Club* was having a meeting on bicycle touring in Carson, which is 30 miles from where I work. It was on a Friday night and I knew the traffic would be heavy. So, I left for the meeting as soon as I got off work at 4:00 p.m. It was stop and go traffic (on the freeway) all the way. I got there right as the meeting was starting, at 7:00 p.m. I'm glad I went. It was a very interesting meeting. They had three bikes there all set up for touring, with the panniers all packed up and everything. The owners each gave a little talk on what they preferred to take along with them. Then afterwards, I had the opportunity to ask them questions. I asked a lot of questions, and got a lot of good answers.

This is when I decided I wanted the *Cannondale* panniers. One of the advantages they have over the others is that they have a plastic frame inside, so they keep their shape even when they are empty. These frames can be taken out so you can wash the panniers if needed. Also, they are guaranteed for life. The cyclist who had *Cannondale* panniers at this meeting said that on one tour he took, he hit a big pothole in the road and his tent, and other things he had strapped on his back rack, came down (hard) on top of his panniers, cracking one of the frames (which were five years old at the time). When he got home, he called *Cannondale* and told them that one of his frames broke. They sent him a new one, free of charge, no questions asked. Another big advantage to these panniers is that they unzip from the side. Most panniers unzip on the top and you have to take your tent, sleeping bag, and *Therm-A-Rest* off your back rack before you can get into the panniers. Then you have to put everything back and this is a lot of extra work, not to mention a waste of time.

*   *   *

Sleeping Pad \ Bag

All three bikes at the meeting were set up a little differently. Individual people have different likes and dislikes, thank God, but when I saw all three tourists preferred the *Therm-A-Rest* sleeping pad, I knew that was the right way to go. A bit expensive, but worth every penny. I'm a true believer in buying the best you can afford.

I also saw the advantage of a good goose-down sleeping bag at this meeting. They are warm, lightweight, and you can just stuff them into a very small stuff sack, instead of having to roll them up and trying to squeeze it into a sack that's always too small. I decided right then and there that was what I wanted. I checked around again to get the best sleeping bag I could buy. I only buy quality…it's always cheaper in the long run. I got a *BlueKazoo* (by *North Face*), which is really great.

*   *   *

The Route

Now that my preliminary planning was done with maps, suggestions, and letters, I had to plan my itinerary. Many travelers prefer to know what lies around the next corner but I personally enjoy traveling with a very loose itinerary. I spread out the brightly-colored maps of North America on my floor. They were huge beyond belief. And it looked almost impossible for me to ride from Coast to Coast. So I folded up all except the Washington State map. I figured I'd just take it one day at a time. My first plans were to ride from Los Angeles to New York City. So I sent away to *Bikecentennial* and ordered about $60.00 worth of maps for this route. When I received the maps, and looked at them, I decided that I didn't want to go that way after all. I didn't want to ride through the Mojave Desert and all those long hot miles in Arizona and New Mexico.

I took a week long bicycle tour in Utah last year and I saw the desert, with its sand and rocks, and scrubs, and sand and rocks, and that was all the sand and rocks I wanted to see for a while. I was ready for a totally different kind of scenery. I wanted to ride where there was green grass, and trees, and streams, and lakes, and an occasional mountain range. I wanted to ride in territory that was virgin to me.

Now, I had to decide, do I want the fastest, safest, or most scenic route? In a group of seven cyclists, there will usually be six different answers. Which route best fits my time frame? If I have limited time, I may have to take the most direct route, I thought about wind direction, rainy seasons, high-altitude, weather conditions, the extreme day and night temperatures. I know that towns can be 100 miles apart and I didn't want to plan such a tight schedule that I would have to ride through a storm, or cycle after dark (unless I wanted to).

I eventually decided on a northern route. I knew that while riding across the top of the country from Seattle, I would encounter rugged terrain almost immediately. About 100 miles inland from the Pacific Ocean lies the Cascade Mountain Range, an extension of the California Sierra Nevada. The Cascades extend through Oregon, Washington, and into British Columbia. They can't be avoided. They are a high, rugged range with peaks rising as high as 14,409 feet (Mount Rainier in Washington), although I would be biking through valleys. On the eastern side of the Cascades, arid, almost desert conditions exist. Then come the Rocky Mountains, the highest and longest mountain range in North America. The Rockies run through Idaho, Montana, Wyoming, Colorado, and New Mexico as well as into British Columbia and Alberta, Canada. Many peaks tower to 14,000 feet. There is no way I can avoid the Rockies on the northern route. In addition, the riding time through these high mountains is shortened by the relatively little snow-free time in the passes. Snow flurries sometimes come as late as the end of June, and as early as the beginning of August. Anyway, I decided that this was the route I wanted to take from Seattle to New York City. I decided to cross the Rockies at the most scenic spot which is on the "Going-to-the-Sun" road in *Glacier National Park*. I figured if there is beautiful scenery to look at, it wouldn't be so hard climbing the mountains. (I was wrong. It's hard riding up mountains, no matter how spectacular the scenery is.)

Also on this route, I could stop a few days, in Wisconsin and see my children and grandchildren.

*   *   *

The Calendar

After I finally decided on the route I was going to take, I had to figure out the best time of the year to go.

I had three weeks vacation saved up and I had two more weeks coming on my anniversary date, at the end of June. Company Policy is that I had to use the three weeks of vacation time I had saved up before my anniversary date, or I would lose them. Now, I don't plan on losing any vacation time. Vacations are not a luxury, but a necessary. So, I didn't have any choice of when I could take this much time off work. The company made that decision for me.

After reading an almanac and a lot of other books, and knowing that the "Going-to-the-Sun" road in *Glacier National Park* usually didn't open until the middle June (the exact time I could have off work) this was the perfect time of the year to do my tour. So, that worked out great.

This being my first long distance tour, I wasn't exactly sure how much time I needed. I proceeded to map everything out so I could get an estimate of how much time I thought it might take me to go all the way across the United States.

I also arranged for two additional weeks of Leave of Absence. I wasn't sure if I needed this extra time, but I thought, what the heck, I'll use it if I need it and if I don't need it I won't use it. It's always good to have extra time, and I didn't want to be rushed. Of course, my fellow workers would say to me, "You're crazy to take that much time off work, just look at how much money you are losing." I simply tell them that you can't lose something you never had.

*   *   *

Tentative Plans

My tentative plans were to ride approximately 80 miles a day and take one day a week off. As I mentioned before, I've ridden many 100-mile rides but I really didn't feel much like riding the next day. So, I wasn't sure if I could even do 80 miles a day, every day. I once read an article on touring which stated that if you can ride one hundred miles in a single day, on a bare bike, a fifty-mile day would be reasonable with gear on a long trip if you are riding over similar conditions. If the tour is in mountainous country and your trial runs are only moderately hilly, distances should be halved again. Thus, if a hundred miles make a good day on a rolling Sunday ride near home, fifty would be reasonable on a tour in similar conditions and twenty-five would be more realistic pedaling through the Rockies. Rain or headwinds will cut distance down still more. A high altitude requires some time before the body can be expected to function at all efficiently.

I arranged for plenty of time off work so if I wanted to, or needed to, I could take some time off from riding. As it turned out, I averaged 115 miles a day and I didn't need any days off. I discovered that when you ride along at a comfortable pace, enjoying the scenery, and not pushing yourself, it's amazing, and surprising, what you can accomplish and still enjoy.

*   *   *

The Bike

I have a racing bike, and for this tour I would need a touring bike. I did a lot of research on touring bikes to find out which one would be the best for me. I wanted to buy the best-made equipment I could because I knew it would be taking an incredible daily beating. I checked in the *Bicycling Magazine Buyer's Guide* and narrowed it down to two bikes. The *Miyata 1000* or the *Trek 520*. I phoned around to see where they had these bikes. Then I went and tried them out. I decided on the *Trek 520*. I don't think it was the best choice now, but that is what I got.

I knew that riding a fully loaded touring bike would be a lot different from riding my racing bike, so I wanted to get it early enough, so I could practice with it for a while before I started out on my tour. When I first got my new bike, I tried it out without the panniers on.

I have a long torso so I needed a longer stem. The only stem I could find that was high and long enough was a mountain bike stem. Seeing as how I would be riding over a lot of mountains, this seemed appropriate and the bike handled pretty well with this stem. I was considering buying Aero bars for this tour. But after taking a close look at them, I decided that they wouldn't be a very good investment: Number One, if I were to put them on I couldn't use my very much needed handle bar bag. Number Two, they are expensive, around $80.00 Number Three, I would have to rewire my computer and brakes and rewrap my bars. Besides that, I don't think they are made properly. Regular bars are supposed to be shoulder width, for better handling, and so it won't restrict your breathing. Aero bars are, at the most, six inches wide. Really Dumb…! Huh…! Try putting your hands six inches apart on your present bars and ride. Still, not convinced? Try it with a loaded touring bike, on a rough downhill corner. Besides, this was a new invention and I was still getting used to the old ones. Just like when I learned how to tell time, then they came out with digital watches. And as soon as I learned how to tie my shoes, they came out with velcro. So I figured, why bother with learning how to ride with triathelete handlebars, when they are bound to come out with something better.

So, I put my panniers on and loaded them up with books and rags (for weight). I did a lot of reading and found out that the best way to load panniers was to put 60% of the weight in the front panniers and not to carry more than 40 lbs. So, that is the way I loaded them up. Riding is a whole new ball game with loaded panniers. I practiced with them for about three mouths, until I felt quite comfortable with them on. I got a lot of comments during these practice trips, not all favorable. When you are riding a fully-loaded touring bike, everybody who rides catches up and passes you especially on hills. They usually have a comment but only a short one because they don't want to slow down to your speed. You get the usual, "Hi, how you doing?" and "Have a nice ride." Then there are the guys who ask, "Where you riding from?" or, "Where you riding to?" Or, "How far are you riding?" They expect an answer like, "I started in L.A. and I'm riding to N.Y.C." or "I'm riding 100 miles today." Then, when you tell them that you are only going about 15 miles, they seem to lose all respect for you and come up with comments like, "Do you think you've got enough stuff to make it that far?" or, "I think you need a few more pounds to carry," or "What you got in the bags? Food for all your rest stops." One guy politely said, "What are you huffing and puffing for? It's downhill. If you don't think so, just turn around and look."

I got really creative with my packing. I was trying every possible way to carry my camping equipment. This one particular time I had stood my tent up on its end on my back rack and, as this young rider passed me he said, "Your pack looks like it has an erection." After I'd had enough of their joking around with me, I told them the panniers are really coolers and they are full of cold beer. This gets rid of most of them but a few ride along with me, hoping I'll stop and share a cool, refreshing one with them.

* * *

What to Pack

When I was out on my training rides, people would often ask me, "What in the world do you need all those bags for?"

Well, here is a list. Besides this, I also needed room for souvenirs.

Bike

An *Avocet* seat
Specialized tires
Water bottle cages
Water bottles
Pump
Tail light / extra batteries
Front pannier racks
Rear racks
Front panniers
Rear panniers
A handlebar bag
A seat bag
Fenders
Look pedals
Cat-Eye computer
Waterproof seat cover
Cable / lock / key

Spare parts

Tire
Tube
Spokes
A rear derailleur
Chain
Brake cable

Tools

Tire irons
Patch kit
Needle nose pliers
Freewheel remover
Spoke wrench
6" *Crescent* wrench
Chain wrench
Screwdriver
Allen wrenches
Nuts and bolts
Grease rag
A pedal wrench
Chain oil

Camping equipment

Tent / poles / stakes / rope / stuff bag
Ground cloth
Therm-A-Rest / stuff sack
Sleeping bag / stuff bag
Hatchet
Flashlight / extra batteries
50 foot nylon rope
Pocketknife
An emergency blanket

Clothes

Helmet
Two short sleeve jerseys
Two pair riding shorts
Two pair riding socks
Lake riding shoes
Look riding / walking shoes
Riding glasses
Riding gloves
Windbreaker
Rain suit
Wool hat
Wool socks
Wool gloves
Arm warmers
Leg warmers

Long underwear
Blue jeans
A short sleeve shirt
A long sleeve shirt
T-shirt
Six pairs of underwear
Six handkerchiefs
Cycle cap
Sun glasses
Belt
Shorts
Watch
Sweater
Swimming suit

First Aid Kit

2" athletic tape
Sunburn ointment
Insect repellent
Band-Aids
Two rolls gauze 2" X 5 yards
Second skin
Six 4" X 4" gauze pads
1" adhesive tape
Snake bite kit

Other

Wallet
Cash
Traveler checks
Credit card
Drivers license
Birth certificate
Plane and train tickets
Address book
Social Security card
American Youth Hostel membership card
Bikecentennial membership card
American Automobile Club membership card
Camera / extra batteries
42 rolls of film
Tape recorder / extra batteries
10 recorder tapes
Compass
Thermometer
Radio / ear phones / extra batteries
Bungie cords
Wind and water proof matches
Duck tape
Zip lock bags
Baggies for my bike computer
Paper / pen / pencil
Stamps / envelopes
Dictionary
Tour books / camp books / motel books
Maps

Bag straps
Cough drops
Lock tight bags
Cycle wipes
Ear plugs
Granola bars / about 12
Tang / one large water bottle full
An alarm clock

Personal

Soap
Tooth brush / past
Comb
Shampoo
Razor / shave cream
Scissors
Wash cloth / towel
Mirror
Toilet paper
Vitamins
Sun screen
Chap stick
Aspirin
String
    Condoms (after all you never know what might come up. The old *Boy Scouts'* motto, Be Prepared, was never more appropriate).
    I was going alone so I had to be self-contained, kind of like a turtle carrying its house on its back.

I say, "Don't leave home without it:" a good route, adequate time and money, physical preparedness, proper equipment, and the right attitude.

Cannondale advertises their panniers as being waterproof. Well, no panniers are totally waterproof. I Scotch-Guarded mine inside and out. And I still put everything in clear, waterproof, zip lock bags. I even double-bagged some things, like my film. As it turned out, I had just the right amount of room for everything.

*   *   *

Clothes

If I have to say so myself, my new blue bike with red panniers really looks good. With my bike looking so nice, I had to go out and buy all new clothes, so I would look nice too. When riding you have to dress right, so, even if you are an amateur, you won't look like one.

I have six or seven pairs of riding shorts. The ones I like the best are my *Descente* touring shorts. Mine were all about four years old and worn-out. So I looked around until I found some new ones. Of course, I had to get a couple of matching jerseys.

*   *   *

Shoes

I have a pair of *Lake* racing shoes, which are broken-in (and they are very comfortable) but they are hard to walk in. So, I got a pair of *Look* riding shoes with recessed cleats, for easy walking. I rode with them, once in a while, but I mainly used them when I went out at night. I used the *Look* pedals, which I'm used to, and they worked out very well.

* * *

Helmet

I have a *Bell V1 Pro* helmet, which has seen better days, so I purchased a lightweight, *Giro* helmet for my tour, which was great. I believe that you should have a helmet at least as good as your head. Every year in the United States more than one thousand people are killed and an estimated 500,000 are seriously injured on bicycles. Head injury is the leading caused of death, 80 percent. Bicycle helmets reduce the risk of serious head injury by 85 percent. You say then, "Why don't more cyclists wear helmets?" Well, there are a variety of excuses like; "Helmets look foolish," "They're inconvenient," "They mess up my hair," and "Accidents happen to other people." Other say helmets cost too much. A well made helmet costs around $50.00. Measure that costs against the average lifetime care bill for a victim of a severe head injury-$4 million.

I also bought a new wind jacket, gloves, and a rain suit. Virtually everything I have now is new, and it matches my bike. I figured (in a way) I'd be out there representing the touring cyclist, and I wanted to look good, and I did. It's hard to be humble, but I'll try.

* * *

Tent

Since this was to be my first major tour, it took me quite a while to make a list of things that I was going to take along. I probably took a lot of things I didn't need but it's better to have it, and not need it, than it is to not have it, and need it.

I planned on doing a lot of camping, maybe camp out two nights and moteling it the next night. So, I checked around to get the best camping equipment I could. After all, my tent would be my portable home. I wanted a tent that would go up easily, even in the dark. One that was lightweight, and big enough to put my panniers inside. I did a lot of shopping around and ended up getting a *Tadpole* (by *North Face*). It was a very good choice. It's a freestanding tent, which is nice. When I got it home, I set it up right in my living room and sealed the seams.

*   *   *

Camera

I plan on taking a lot of pictures and all I have is an old 110 camera. Everybody tells me that a 35-mm camera would be a lot better. I figure that this will probably be a once in a lifetime tour, so I want the pictures to come out well. Knowing very little about cameras, I read a lot of literature so when someone would talk to me about a certain feature, I'd have some kind of an idea what they're talking about. Then, I asked my friends who have 35-mm cameras, to see what kind they would recommend. Next, I went to a lot of different camera stores and listened to their sales pitch. I didn't want to carry a camera with a big heavy zoom lens, or one I had to make a lot of adjustments on and chance taking a lot of bad pictures. Just for consistency in my pictures I wanted to take them all with 200-speed film and no telephoto, which would show mountains in a picture without the feeling of space the scene itself presented. What I wanted was for the pictures I took to illustrate my text rather than the other way around. So, I came to the conclusion that what I needed was a compact, fully automatic 35 mm camera. I wanted to find a camera that printed the time and date right on the pictures. This would save me a lot of time later, when trying to place them in their proper location. (I was anticipating problems and solving them before they occurred). As it turned out, I took almost 1,000 pictures and it would have been very difficult, if not impossible, to organize them without this feature.

I finally found a camera that I liked and I bought it. I took a roll of pictures with it, and compared them to some I had taken with my 110 camera. I was greatly disappointed. The 110's were much better. I immediately took the camera and the pictures to the camera shop and told the sales person who sold me the camera, that I was unhappy (to say the least) with the 35-mm camera. He compared the two sets of pictures and had to agree with me that the 110 pictures were better. But, he said, "You can't compare apples and oranges." The pictures I had taken with the 110 camera were taken on a bright, sunny day and the ones I took with the 35-mm camera were taken on an overcast day. He said that if I wanted a fair comparison of the two cameras, I would have to put the same make and speed of film in each camera, and take a picture with both cameras at the same time and place. And, he went on to say, "I'll guarantee you that the 35-mm camera will take better pictures." So, that's what I did and the 35-mm took much better pictures. I felt better about spending all that money on the new *Canon* camera.

My plans were to stop every 10 miles and take a picture (to show the difference in the terrain) which I did. At this time I would also record the temperature, the wind direction, the time, my average speed, and my total miles.

*   *   *

Computer

I have a *Cat-Eye Microcomputer* on my bike. It's smaller than a book of matches and it gives me my average speed, miles per hour, total miles, trip miles, maximum speed, cadence, and riding time. I wouldn't ride without one.

*   *   *

Journal

I also wanted to keep a journal of my tour. The best and easiest way I know of doing this is to tape record it. So I got a *Sony Micro-Cassette Recorder*. I put it on the outside of my handlebar bag and talked into it whenever I felt like it, even when I was riding.

*   *   *

Tires \ Tubes \ Spokes

I always thought the *Specialized Touring 2 Kevlar K4* tires were the best I could buy, so I replaced the *Matrix CD 3K* tires that came on my new bike with them. It turned out that the ones that came on the bike were the better choice. It just goes to prove that sometimes the most thought-out plans don't work out.

I took along an extra tire and tube, and some spare spokes.

*   *   *

Maps \ Books

I took maps and books on things to see and places to camp and where the motels were located. (These books were heavy and I shouldn't have taken them).

*   *   *

Chain \ Derailleur

Most touring cyclists carry a few extra chain links with them, just in case the chain breaks. I carried a whole extra chain, cut to length, so it would be fast and easy to replace, if needed.

Then I thought, "What screws up the most on a bike? And if it screws up or breaks, in the middle of nowhere, what would I do?" I would be in very deep Yogurt. Riding alone I must be able to fix any bike problem that arises, by myself. Of course, the worst problem would have to be the rear derailleur. So I thought, "Why not just take an extra one along?"

There are a lot of bike shops in the L.A. area. I called around, trying to find a derailleur, just like the one that's on my bike. It was very difficult to find one, even in Los Angeles...I would have never been able to find one, out on the open road, in any of the small towns and villages I would be passing through. So I carried an extra rear derailleur along, which I didn't need, but it was comforting just to know I had it.

I knew I would be riding in the rain, so I wanted to get some fenders for my bike. This wasn't very easy either. It doesn't rain in Southern California in the summertime. And it seems that, because nobody needs fenders, none of the bike shops stock them. I had to mail order them from out of state. I received them about a week before I was to leave on my tour.

*   *   *

Going Solo

When I told a few people in my bike club that I was going to do this tour alone, they said, "You're Crazy…!" Well, I already knew that. Sure, there are some genuine worries when traveling alone. You are open to attack, robbery, assault, and, my worst fear, dogs. It's a well-known fact that our roads are dangerous. But there is no use thinking about that. If I were to worry about everything that could hurt me, I would stay in bed all day with the covers over my head. I have to think about the good things, like the way the maple trees were leafing out along the road, or how the very small white clouds look. Sort of like they are painted on the very blue sky.

This was my vacation, and I didn't want any kind of a schedule to keep. When you ride with someone else, you have to have some kind of a schedule, and I'm strongly against that. Whether it is a party of two or twenty, you can only ride as fast as the slowest one in the group so it's comfortable for all. When riding with someone you need a schedule (there is that dreaded word again) of what time to get up, what time to start riding, what time to eat (and you have to enjoy the same kind of food) and what time to stop riding. You pretty much have to have a schedule and pre-arrange a very clear time and place to meet. If you get fed up with your cycling companions and decide to ride a little faster or slower than them so you can have the wide-open road to yourself, still at the end of the day, you'll have to find each other again. In other words, you have to live by the clock, and that's one of the reasons why I went on vacation in the first place, to get away from all that. I didn't want to set an alarm and have to get up at any specific time, day after day. When you ride solo, it eliminates this problem. You can travel at your own speed. You can make your own decisions about where to stop and which route to take. You'd be on your own completely.

I even thought about changing my route half way through my tour, I didn't, but I could have if I wanted to. When you ride solo, you can ride at your own speed all the time. When you're riding with someone, you tend to push a little harder (Ego) and that takes its toll on you. When you're riding at your own speed, you can virtually ride forever. You can ride as hard, or as easy, as you want to -except when you get too hills, then it doesn't matter if you are alone or with someone, it's still hard.

Also, riding solo allows you to practically do anything you want to. You can stay as long as you want in a nice restaurant, or you can stop at a fast food place, and eat fast, and be on your way. It's entirely up to you.

I must say, it was beautiful doing it by myself, and if I were to do it again, I would do it by myself, again. I could just wander all over the road admiring the natural wonders. And I don't have to hold up the ride if I want to stop and admire a wildflower. What was really nice was to be out there, early in the morning, just riding along and listening to the birds singing and not someone talking in my ear.

It's just peaceful and relaxing, very relaxing. All I could hear was the humming of my own tires, and the birds, and sometimes water flowing in the background, or maybe a gentle breeze blowing through the trees. It's just beautiful…!

* * *

Protection

Everyone I talked to said it wouldn't be safe to go it solo. I might get robbed, or hit from behind (by a drunken driver) and there wouldn't be anyone around to help me.

Well, I put a lot of thought into that. Just what would I do if someone tried to rob me? I took traveler checks, and a credit card along. I also carried a fair amount of cash with me. The best protection I could take with me would be a gun. I knew I would have to have a permit in each state I was riding through…probably each state would have different laws governing guns…not to mention all the red tape it would entail. If someone tried to steal something from me and I pulled a gun on them, they might leave, and call the cops, and have me arrested. So I thought it just might not be a good idea to take a gun along with me. My next choice would be a knife. A certain length knife would probably be legal, in most states. I could protect myself a little with a knife. So I talked to a guy at work who makes knives and he told me that if I didn't know how to use a knife to forget it. It would be more of a hazard than good for me. If I were to pull it on someone and they in turn, pulled one on me, and they knew how to use it (and they would or they wouldn't have pulled it out in the first place) and I didn't (which I don't) I would be history. I would be better off not to even have one. Besides, if I pulled a knife on them, they could legally protect themselves with a gun. So I decided that was out. There weren't too many options left. Most campers carry a hatchet with them and seeing as how I'm a happy camper, I went out and bought myself a really lightweight hatchet. Then I put myself in the other guy's place (like I do in most situations). If I saw a six feet, 185 lb., bearded wild man coming at me, with a raised hatchet, I would leave (fast).

Actually, I did take the hatchet out, once, when I was going up Steven's Pass but you will find out about that soon enough.

* * *

Airline or Train?

My ride was going to start in Seattle. So I had to get my bike and me up there somehow.

First I checked with the Airlines. A one-way ticket from Los Angeles to Seattle was around $300.00 and a round trip ticket was around $400.00. I asked them if they would consider letting me pay $100.00 to fly to Seattle, and when I got there, if I decided I wanted to come back, I would purchase a return ticket from them, for $300.00. They didn't see the humor in it.

I've ridden my bike down to San Diego, several times, and taken the train back, which is a nice and enjoyable trip. I've always heard that the train ride up the coast was very scenic. Besides, my girlfriend loves trains and she had planned on taking the train to Seattle with me. We had a silly argument about something and it didn't work out that way, but I decided to take the train anyway. So, I went to downtown L.A. to *Union Station* to check on their schedule and prices. I got all this information and took it home and looked it over. They had almost the same deal as the Airlines. A one-way ticket was about $150.00 and the return trip was only $7.00 more, which didn't make sense to me.

It seems like all the transportation companies make it hard for you to go anywhere and easy for you to return home. It seems like they want you to be home more than they want you to go anywhere. I wonder if they would be happy if everyone just stayed home.

Anyway, I decided that I wanted to go by train. They require that you put your bike in a box (one that you can purchase from them for a $10.00 fee). So, I went back downtown to *Union Station* a couple of weeks before I was planning on leaving on my tour and bought my ticket and bike box.

When I was at the train station, I observed them handling a boxed bike. "This End Up" meant nothing to them. I don't believe any of them could even read English. When I took my bike apart, I packed it up, very…very…carefully.

It seemed like I had been getting ready for this tour for eons. It was a proud feeling to know that all the pre-trip planning was behind me and another adventure was about to happen. I love it when a plan finally comes together.

On The Train

Now, there is a train stop about two blocks from my apartment but, of course, *Amtrak* wouldn't let me put my bike on the train there. They told me that I had to take it downtown, Los Angeles, to *Union Station*. So, now I'll have to find a way to get my disassembled, boxed up, bike to the station. Needless to say, it takes a very good size box to put a bike in. It's much too big to fit in any car, or even the trunk of most cars. So I thought I would tie it to the bike rack on top of my car, and take it to the station a day early. Then I could walk to the train stop by my apartment and board the train there the next morning. Well, *Amtrak* told me that I couldn't leave my bike at their station a day early, because they didn't want the responsibility for it. And after seeing the neighborhood the station is located in, I didn't blame them.

My daughter just happened to be moving out of her apartment at the same time I was going on my tour. So I asked her if she wanted to save a month's rent and stay at my place while I was gone. She did. Then I ask her if she would drive my bike and me to *Union Station*. I also told her that I would call her every couple of days while I was gone, just so she would know that I was alive and well.

I didn't sleep much the night before my departure. I guess I was too excited to sleep. I found that I couldn't read with the light on, and I couldn't sleep with it off. Things keep running through my mind.

On the day I was leaving I got up early, very early. I mean, it was still dark out. I had my bike tied on top of my car long before my daughter arrived to take me to the train station. We got there in plenty of time to have breakfast before the train departed. We said our good-byes and I was on my way.

After almost a year of planning, researching, mapping out routes, and purchasing equipment, I was finally on my way. God…It Feels Good…!

I think there is such a thing as over-planning. I know a few people who plan…and plan…and prepare…and prepare…so long that they never have time for the tour itself.

Being the shy, quiet person I am, my left brain yelled out to my right brain, "Hallelujah…! The hard part's finally over and the fun parts are about to start…!"

When I get on the train, I make sure I got a window seat on the ocean side, which has the best views. In the seat directly in front of me is a short woman with, beautiful features and rich chestnut brown hair.

About 45 minutes after the train leaves *Union Station*, it stops two blocks from my apartment. About five minutes later, it's going through a tunnel in the Simi Hills. Shortly after that, I am in the outskirts of Ventura, where I spot a field with a nice looking crop of plastic. Five minutes later and I am at the beach. One and a half-hours later, at 1:27 p.m. we are going through *Vandenberg Air Force Base*.

As the train goes through Guadalupe. I walk from car to car, and I can notice a big difference in their temperatures. One car is cool and the very next one is warm. But one thing they all have in common is the dirty windows. I later find out that the reason for this is, a long time ago, when the train stopped at stations, kids would run out and clean the windows and, of course, expect a small tip. This was fine. Everybody was happy. Then along came the Union, and for years and years the Big Brothers stopped the kids from picking up a little change for candy. And now the windows never get washed.

For weeks I've studied maps, large-scale and small, but maps are not reality at all. They can be deceiving and I use them only as a general guide. I know people who are so immersed in road maps on their vacations that they never see the countryside they are passing through. And there are others, who, after having traced a route, are held to it as tightly as the fanged wheels of this train holds me to the rails.

Whenever I go on a vacation, I try to stay awake as long as possible. After all, I don't see any sense in sleeping my vacation away. I'm too excited to sleep anyway. I watch out the dirty window until long after dark. Then, seeing as how I won't be driving for quite some time, I go into the lounge car to have a few beers. The first thing I notice as I enter the lounge car is the young girl with the beautiful chestnut hair. She's talking to this short, stocky, man. He has a thin mustache and black hair that sticks out at all angles. He looks like a flower child that hasn't been watered in fifty years. I have a few beers then I go back to my seat and listen to my radio for a while. Then it's back to the lounge for a couple more beers. Next, it's off to the dining car for a very late dinner. Then back to the lounge car, where they are showing a movie and serving beer.

About the time the movie is over, the train is coming to San Francisco. I watch the city lights go by the window, have a nightcap and go back to my seat for a nap. When I return to my seat, I notice that the guy from the lounge car is accompanying the girl sitting in front of me. Now, I don't like to be nosy but I can't help but overhear their conversation. After all, they're only about three feet in front of me. For an hour they talk about nothing important, the way travelers on a train do when they first meet.

It seems to me that he is spending half his time trying to be witty (you might say he was somewhat of a half-wit). He is sitting there, cleaning his fingernails with a pocketknife. I figure he's an "Off Duty" cop and intends to show it. He probably has good sense, but it sounds to me like he has it pretty well camouflaged. As I doze off at 5:52 p.m. near Gilroy in northern California, I receive two small items of information about him. One is that he rather enjoyed not having to play tennis, and the other is that he doesn't jog because he wants to be sick when he dies. The last thing I see him do before I doze off is kill a fly on the window with his finger. The gentle swaying of the cars and the clangety-clang of the wheels and, of course, the occasional whistle from the engine, is really quite relaxing

*   *   *

When I wake from my nap at 7:39 a.m., the train is near Fort Klamath, close to the southern border of Oregon. I overhear another conversation in the seat behind me. They are talking about the vacation they are taking. It seems they flew to L.A. and took this train out, and didn't see anything. All they are talking about are what hotels in L.A. boasted king size *Beauty Queen* mattresses, what restaurants in Ventura offered *Sweet and Low*, and how nice the *McDonalds* was in Santa Barbara. I take that back. They did see the rock at Morro Bay.

Shortly after Klamath Falls we go over the Cascade Summit in Oregon which is absolutely beautiful. As I take snapshots out the window, the trees look like sparrows frozen in flight. The mountains are full of tall pine trees, and there is a trace of snow on the ground. It is a long...slow...climb over the mountains, and the scenery is outstanding. I can't help but to think of my girlfriend as the train chugs its way up the mountain passes and through the many tunnels. She loves the mountains and trains. I see a few deer along the tracks. The train is a nice way to get to Seattle if you have the time, which I do. I'm getting a close up look at the backcountry of Oregon, which I couldn't have had if I had taken an airplane. Another thing that's nice about this train is that I can get up and walk around any time I feel like it. The one negative thing I've found is the food (although I'm not too crazy about airline food either). After a few meals, I mostly eat hamburgers, fruit, and beer nuts, washed down with beer. Even they can't mess that combination up too bad. I like to stick to the two basic food groups, beer and light beer.

At 8:56 a.m.: Cascade Summit in Oregon.
At 9:36 a.m.: McCredie Springs in Oregon.
At 10:23 a.m.: Black Canyon in Oregon.

At 11:45 a.m.: Corvallis in Oregon.

At 12:07 p.m.: Albany, Oregon.

One thing that's nice about this train is that it has a scheduled time to leave the stations, so, when it arrives early, you can get off and walk around if you want to. And I want to. This one particular stop is in Salem, Oregon. We arrive about 25 minutes early. I look out the window, and right across the street is a Saloon that serves sandwiches. After eating on the train for a day and a half, this place has everything I want. Beer and food. I get off and go over and have myself a steak sandwich and a cold beer. It is surprisingly chilly out. I talk to the proprietor as they make my sandwich. He tells me that he is originally from L.A. I ask him how he likes living up here? He says something like this; "There is lots of rugged unspoiled coastline, open spaces, and not many people here. Down south it's too crowded and filthy and noisy." He goes on to say that there's nothing but cement and asphalt and people down there. "Yep...!" He says, "I had my choice some years back. I could either rent a store in Los Angeles and live in that endless asphalt jungle and worry all the time about getting robbed or mugged and spend half of my time driving on freeways getting to and from work every day, or, I could buy this place here. I think I made the right choice."

After I leave the Saloon I have a little time so I walk around for a while. It feels good to walk on something that isn't moving, or at least you can't feel it moving. It's a refreshing break.

After sitting in my seat for a few moments the gal in the seat in front of me returns. She is chewing gum and holding hands with a different man. He is as black as the ace of spades. As they sit down, all I can see in front of me is short, black, curly hair. After listening to their conversation for a while, I think, "Boy...she sure knows how to pick'em." I overhear her ask him what he was majoring in, and he can't remember. He tells her that he studied law for an entire week, and then gave it up because it was too tiresome. He tells her that he could have been a lawyer but he failed the physical. I can't believe it...! She gives him her phone number anyway. Now for a collage grad I don't think she is thinking very well. He then tells her that she could call him and leave a message on his answering machine. He say's he never answers the phone because he doesn't like to be directly in touch with reality. As the afternoon goes on, he keeps digging in his left ear with a long fingernail on his little finger. A harmless act, I guess, but it irritates me nonetheless. It's like forever having to watch someone pick his or her nose.

At 2:10 p.m. the train is going through Portland, Oregon. I remember reading somewhere that the suicide rate in Portland is the highest in the United States, and that's because the sun almost never shines there.

At 3:16 p.m.: near Castle Rock, Washington.

At 4:50 p.m.: East Olympia, Washington.

* * *

It's 7:25 p.m. and I'm at the *King Street Train Station* in Seattle, Washington.

The train ride to Seattle was nice, but two days on a train is more than enough for me. Besides, I'm getting anxious to start riding.

As soon as I get off the train I go over to the baggage car and watch them unload my bike. And, sure enough the "This End Up" arrows are pointing horizontally. When they finish mishandling my bike, I go in the station to get my baggage and here is this same gal with the beautiful hair with her arms wrapped around this seven-foot tall guy that has apparently come to pick her up. One thing for sure, this gal isn't wasting her youth.

As I unpack my bike, I see it is really dirty, and dusty, from being in the baggage car. I carefully reassemble it as tourists watch. One guy tells me that my bike looks about as easy to assemble as an *IBM* computer. After it's together, I put one leg over my heavy bike, step on one pedal and began to turn the crank. I wobble my…what seemed to be…overloaded bicycle around the parking lot. It isn't shifting very well. It must have gotten bumped around more than I thought. I proceed to ride around and make some minor adjustments until I get it working a little better.

I start riding over to the *American Youth Hostel*, where I have reservations for the night. The Hostel is about two miles from the train station. So I ride north, until I find the street it's on. I turn left and about a half a block farther, down a very steep hill, the street ends. It just ends. So, I stop and look ahead to see why it ends and there is about a 20-foot straight drop-off. And right at the bottom is the Hostel. Well, now, I have to make a choice. I can take some steep stairs going down to the Hostel. Or, I can ride back up the steep hill I just rode down, make a right, and go one block, make another right, and ride back down a very steep hill on the next block over, make another right, go one block, one more right and climb up an unbelievable steep half a block to the Hostel. With me not yet being too comfortable with my heavy bike I decided to put my brakes to a test and walk my bike down the stairs. It's a little scary at first, but the brakes work fine and it is no problem.

At 8:23 p.m. I'm at the Hostel. I push my bike into the lobby. I check in and take my panniers up to my room. Then I go back to the lobby where the desk clerk is waiting to show me where to put my bike. It seems that they lock everybody's bike up in one big room, which I feel very comfortable with. So I go back to my room.

Now, if you've never heard of the *American Youth Hostel*, it's an organization (which I'm a member of) not only for the youth (obviously, if I'm staying here). It has reasonably priced rooms, usually around $8.00 per night. It's dormitory type housing for hikers and bicyclists.

The room I have has five bunk beds. There are eight other touring cyclists sharing the room with me, which is kind of nice. We talk and compare equipment and notes. The eight are on a *Bikecentennial* tour. They're taking six weeks to tour Washington State. When I tell them that I plan on riding to New York City in six weeks, I realize that talking to eight touring cyclists is like throwing a stone in a pond, you don't know what the effect of the ripples is going to be. For some unexplainable reason they aren't very friendly anymore.

*   *   *

Anyway, after two days on the train, I feel, and, I'm sure, I smell, like I haven't taken a bath since I fell in a creek back in 47. So, sure enough, after a shave and shower, I feel like a new man. It's 9:30 p.m. so I decide to walk down to the wharf to look around a bit. I see a sign that leads me to believe that things aren't too exciting around here. It reads, "All Day Parking (10 hrs) for 50 cents." The wharf is lit up like a cruise ship. All right…! There is a good old McDonalds…! I'm finally going to have some decent food. It's a nice warm night, so I'm going to walk around for a while. On second thought, I think I'll conserve my energy for the bar I spotted next to the Hostel. After all, if you really want to know all about a town, you have to find people that like to talk about it. And those types don't sit at home watching TV. They hang out in bars. So, I go in the cocktail lounge. The barmaid has a thick crust of powder, rouge, mascara, eye shadow, and lipstick on her face. A bushy blond mass of curly hair is swirling around her head and dropping onto her shoulders and down her back. She's wearing a white silk blouse that exposes a generous portion of her cleavage. I order a draft and ask her what the weather is supposed to be for tomorrow. She tells me that Seattle is where the rain starts. If it's not raining here today, it will be tomorrow. People up here have moss growing all over their bodies, and when they tilt their heads, water flows out of their ears. She tells me that I can pretty much count on getting very wet pedaling through Washington.

I can't help but to notice that sitting two stools down from me is another woman. Her oversize butt is hanging over her barstool as she sips her wine. She can still balance on the barstool but by the looks of her I'll bet she can't balance a checkbook. She looks as though she's never been in the sun…she's sort of pasty looking. She joins our small talk and says that it doesn't rain all the time. Sometimes it's just humid. She goes on to say that last week it was just beautiful, it only rained twice-once for two days and once for four days.

Although this is a nice bar, I can't stay too long because the Hostel locks its doors from midnight to six a.m. So I'll have a few more beers and go back to the Hostel. I want to get an early start in the morning anyway. Everybody wants to get an early start on his or her first day of riding. Later on, you don't really give a shit what time you get started.

Day One

Riding from Seattle, Washington
To near Leavenworth, Washington

It's 6:00 a.m. Monday morning the 12th of June. I'm just now getting up.

Yea...! My first day of riding...! I'm so EXCITED...!

I'm up and out early, leaving my bike and equipment at the Hostel where it will be safe, as I walk around looking for a little coffee shop. It's quite warm out already this morning, about 70 degrees. Ah...! There's one. I walk in the open door of the Coffee Shop which has a small U-shaped counter, and, much to my surprise, all the stools are occupied. I notice several of the customers have beers sitting in front of them. This is way too early for me. I take a seat at a small table for two overlooking the bay. It's quite nice. The waitress comes over. She's another woman who looks like she's never seen the sun. She's as white as a mushroom. As matter in fact, she sort of looks like one. She's pushing fifty, pushing it kind of hard I'd guess. As she walks toward me I think that she's looking at me but I'm not sure. It's hard to tell just where she's focusing. I order coffee, hash browns, eggs, and sourdough toast.

I watch the boats and the sea gulls, and the day, as they slowly come to life. The light over the bay slowly grows brighter and brighter. It's like someone is gradually turning up the dimmer switch on a lamp.

When the waitress brings me my check (by the way, why do they call it a check, when in reality it's a bill?) I ask her if she would take a travelers check? She says, "Only if you're 95 years old, and you're with your parents." She's way too sharp for me this early in the morning. So I pay with cash, and walk back to the Hostel.

Now, what the Hostel does, to help keep their costs down, is to have everyone that stays there do a 10-minute chore in the morning. My chore was to take some *Windex* and wipe off four pay phones. The guy that got his assignment right before me had to vacuum one hallway. So, you see, it's no big deal, unless you are in a big hurry to get on your way, since you can't do these chores until after seven a.m., to allow for the folks who like to sleep in.

Well it's 7:54 a.m. and absolutely beautiful out. I'm finally getting on my bike to start out on my adventure, taking off to parts unknown (at least to me). This is Day One of an unknown number of days or weeks, through unknown virgin territory. Let me tell you how it feels. It Feels Terrific…!

I'm going to ride down to the wharf. What I want to do is to get a picture of me with my bike's back tire in the Pacific Ocean. Then, when I finish my ride in New York City, I'll take another picture with my front wheel in the Atlantic Ocean.

I ride up and down the waterfront and there is no place in sight where I can get down to the water. So, instead of wasting any more time, I just have someone take my picture on Pier 57 and be on my way. I worry a little about handing my new camera over to a total stranger. After all, if everyone followed the rules, the Ten Commandments are all we would need. But, I guess I have to trust people more. The only person on the pier that I can see is this old man with an oval-shaped head and a face covered with white stubble. His head sort of looks like a fuzzy melon. There is a gray splotch on the brim of his hat where a pigeon or sea gull has done its business. I figure, what the heck…! If he takes off with my camera, I can easily catch him. He was kind enough to take my picture. Now it's time to, "Let the Good Times Roll…!"

*   *   *

I looked at my map (briefly), before I left the Hostel and saw that all I have to do is head straight east until I come to Lake Washington, and at that point and time I would get on the *Blake Gillmen Bike Trail* and ride north around the lake. I'm quite surprised as I immediately find out that Seattle, like San Francisco, is a town built on hills. I stop on the top of this hill and look around as the trees flutter in the sea breeze.

I'm at this intersection on Madison Street that has a road sign that impresses me. It reads, "Motor Vehicles Yield to Bicycles."

Two hours into my ride and…I'm not lost…but I can't find the bike trail. I figure it's nothing to get excited about though, after all this isn't the *Race Across America*. As a matter in fact, if I only get half way across the United States, it would be all right with me. I'd like to make it as far as Wisconsin though, so I can see my children and grandchildren. But I'm not going to push myself. I'm on vacation and I'm going to enjoy myself.

I ride around, climbing a lot of unnecessary hills, so I stop and ask a few people if they know where the bike trail is. Of course, they don't. It's amazing to me how people can live a block away from something and not even know it exists. I knew long ago, and just rediscovered, that the best way to attract attention, help, and conversation is to be lost. A man who wouldn't give his own mother the time of day, will cheerfully devote several hours of his time giving wrong directions to a total stranger who claims to be lost.

I even jokingly ask this guy with long dark hair hanging in his eyes (I'm sure his eyes were shooting daggers at me) if this was the way to New York? He say's, "No…! The airport is the other way."

After asking several people if they knew where the bike trail was I decided that if I don't want six different answers, I had better only ask the question once. So, I just ride around until I find the bike trail myself.

I ride along and catch up to, and ride parallel to, this beat-up old Chevy, late sixties I'd guess, chugging up a steep hill with a double yellow line. Hovering just above the wheel is a faded, wide-rimmed straw hat. Beneath the rim, a little old lady peeks over the steering wheel, hands together at the top, with her nose practically resting on her hands. She keeps her eyes on the road as I slowly pass her on the right.

I finally find the *Burke Gilman Bike Trail...!*

I follow this smooth bike path that's as wide as a small highway circling its way around Lake Washington. The absence of people even makes it nicer. There is a nice little breeze coming off the lake. Gulls are riding the winds on motionless wings and bumblebees dive from blossom to blossom with their hind legs full of yellow pollen balls. It's 70 degrees and it's just a beautiful spring day.

I've got 30 miles under my belt as I ride one mile east of Maltby. My bike still seems awfully heavy. It's sure a lot different from riding a bare bike. Ever since I got my bike off the train it hasn't been shifting right. I'll have to stop at a bike shop and get it adjusted before I get into the mountains. I've been told that it's easy to adjust. It's something anyone can learn in five minutes. But last time I tried it, five days later I was still making adjustments on it, and I just don't feel like messing with it.

No wonder it's so nice, I just rode past Old Glory a waving in the breeze. I've got about a 5 mph tailwind, the terrain is flat and I'm riding at a 15 mph pace.

At 12:18 p.m. I ride into Monroe. The mountains are getting closer, seeming to be almost within touch. The skylines of the Cascades are still snow-tipped in mid-June, but spring green colors cover all the country between me and the foot of the mountains. I'll have to find a bike shop pretty soon. This road looks like it goes up in the mountains, SOON...!

I have to make a little detour here so I can ride down Main Street until I find a bike shop. I have to get my shifter working right before I get into those mountains, because I know I'll need all the gears I can get up there. Ah...! There is a bike shop. I pull in and see if they can adjust my shifter without me having to wait too long. I lean my bike up against the front window and go in and talk to the owner of the shop. He's got hair and a beard the color of fire. I tell him what I need done. He says, "Bring it on in. We'll fix it for you right away." As he's working on my bike, I can't help but notice a sign hanging on the wall that reads, "We Do Precision Guess Work." When he finishes fixing my bike, I ask him how much for his labor (it didn't need any parts just adjusting). He says, "No charge for anyone that's pedaling all the way to New York City." I thank him as he gives me a pump-handle handshake and I'm on my way again, in less than 45 minutes.

He gave me directions for getting out of town (some of the few accurate ones I got on the whole tour). I'm riding back to Highway 522 then I'll follow it north until I pick up US Route 2, which will take me halfway across the Northern United States, all the way to Duluth, Minnesota. I'm turning east, riding into the sun, and beginning what looks like a long…winding ride through the Cascades. My bike is tuned and working smoothly. I touch my right gearshift lever and watch the chain flip effortlessly across clean cogs. And my brakes are trigger sensitive. Both wheels are shimmering in the sun that's rising over the Cascades.

I'm getting a strange, unfamiliar sound in the front end of my bike though. I think it might be the spokes on the front wheel. At 21 mph (going downhill of course) I get a lot of vibration in the front. I'll have to take a look at it and repack or something but not right now.

After a stop at a McDonalds to get something to eat I get on my way again. I've decided that, although I love McDonalds, I'm going to eat at some Mom and Pop's and where they advertise Home Cooking and All-You-Can-Eat-Possum…!

I stop to take a picture of this old shack next to a fast flowing river. With all this lush vegetation, the scenery is spectacular. I have a 10 mph tailwind now and it's just beautiful out here.

In the clean, clear air the BIG snow-covered mountains just ahead of me look like pale pink watercolors rising on all sides. At first glance I thought they were clouds. (It won't be long until I realize that these aren't the snow-covered, towering peaks that I'll glimpse later in the day. These are only the foothills).

I just saw my first logging truck. Luckily for me, it was going the other way. I've heard a lot of horror stories about the logging trucks. It seems that every year or so a touring bicyclist gets run over by one.

I stop at 48 miles to take a picture of this little Wayside Chapel. I pray that God will bless me as I set out across his land. This little Chapel has six pews and a pulpit with an open Bible on it. It also has stained glass windows. Now, it's not that I'm against organized religion, it's just that I'm a little burnt out on it. In my last marriage I went to church every Sunday, and Sunday night, plus every Wednesday night. Enough is enough.

I still have my 10 mph tailwind and I'm on Route 2, near Sultan, Washington. My bike continues to slice through the foothills that are rapidly growing into small mountains. That is, if there is such a thing as a small mountain. Now, I know that I prayed for a scenic route. They say to be careful of what you pray for. You just might get it. Onward I climb, hour after hour, tirelessly as a mountain goat.

If I keep stopping to take pictures I'll never get to New York City. Then again, who gives a shit? I stop to take a picture of this farm. It reminds me a lot of the farm I was brought up on in Wisconsin. It has a typical two-story house, a barn, corncribs, and other outbuildings, all painted white. The only thing that's different is the setting. This farm has lush green fields of hay and grass that stand at least two feet tall, surrounding it, and a very thick, absolutely beautiful, forest for a back yard.

It's 1:37 p.m. I'm near Sultan riding along at a leisurely pace enjoying the scenery. I'm just taking it easy. I'm not going to let life pass me by. I'm in no hurry to get to those mountains just ahead of me, anyway.

So far it's been a beautiful day. It's warmed up to 80 degrees.

Route 522 had about a seven-foot wide, smooth, clean, shoulder. And, after re-packing my panniers, my bike is handling a lot better. I took my sleeping bag out of my front pannier and put it on the back rack. I also put more weight in the back panniers.

I've discovered that the noise I was hearing wasn't the spokes after all. It's the hold down springs in my front panniers. I switched my two front panniers around and, for some unexplainable reason, it's quiet now.

My bike is still a little squirly. I don't know, I think it could be the tires.

I'm riding deep into this virgin forest to the little village of Startup. Startup…now that don't sound good to me and I see a lot of mountains up ahead.

I'm seeing a lot of oversize American Flags flapping in the wind, I think it's because its Washington's Bicentennial Year.

I can't believe all the beautiful trees out here some of whose buds are just beginning to open. Spring's first spikes of grass are poking through a mat of last year's pine needles.

At 54 miles into my ride I'm entering into the town of Gold Bear, elevation 192 feet. Excuse Me…! It's Gold Bar not Gold Bear. I like bars more than I do bears anyway.

It's 2:27 p.m. and I'm one mile west of Index, Washington. I don't like the looks of this. What I thought were white clouds ahead of me are actually snow-covered peaks. I see a lot of snow-covered mountains rising abruptly in the east. The only problem with that is that I'm riding straight east.

The Cascades are growing larger and larger as I ride. The hills are dominating the entire horizon. There is nothing but hills and they look BIG and COLD.

I've been riding through foothills covered with fir trees, and not much else. No towns for miles, no *Elks Lodges*, not even a *7/11* convenience store. In the clear pine-snapped air, Seattle is a distant memory to me now. Or at least I thought it was. I thought I might come across side roads with names like, "Apple Way" or "Evergreen Road." But, unbelievably, off to my right is a street sign that reads, "864th Avenue." My first reaction is that somehow, someone has misplaced at least 700 avenues, and no one in the entire state of Washington has noticed.

Onward I climb, hour after hour. It's still beautiful out here, but it's all uphill now.

I'm breaking-in my new shoes and my feet are getting a little tired, so I change into my racing shoes...not because I'm going to race...but because they are well broken-in and should be more comfortable. I'm still getting a little shimmy in the front of my bike. I'm going to switch my front panniers around and see if that'll help any.

I'm near Index. I've been following a fast-flowing river, off to my left, for quite some time now. Most of the time the dense forest has hidden it. But I can always hear it splashing and swirling over waterworn rocks as it makes small rapids. Once in a while, when I can get a glimpse of it, I stop and watch the glass-clear water, as it makes its way east through grassy banks. With the river, and the smell of the pine trees, it's like a whole new world out here. This is truly God's Country...!

*   *   *

I can hear what sounds like a large waterfall right next to the road. I stop to look for it. Well, it's a waterfall all right, but it's not right next to the road like it sounds. It's in the mountains about a mile away. Sound sure travels a long way up here.

I planned my journey for maximum observation. I wanted to stay, as much as possible, on secondary roads where there is a lot to see...hear...smell...and to avoid the wide...brain-deadening...heavily traveled Intestates. With the lack of traffic (which is really nice) it's easy to hear all of nature's sounds. Like the birds singing, the water flowing, and the sound of a gentle breeze softly blowing through the trees. It's truly beautiful out here.

At 3:12 p.m. I stop to take a picture of this absolutely beautiful swollen river near Baring. It carries the crystal-clear melted mountain snow to the valley far below. Sitting down at the farthest end of a half-submerged tree, I stare into the water. I watch as a large hollowed-out limb dances, like a feather in the wind, as it floats down the fast-flowing river. I'm really enjoying this time as I look upstream to where I've been and downstream to where I'm going.

I've ridden in other states and I have admiration, respect, recognition, even some affection for them. But with Washington it's true love. I'm in love with Washington and it's difficult to analyze love when you're in it.

I have a 15 mph tailwind (that is easy to love, believe me) and it's 77 degrees and everything is better than perfect.

There are some railroad tracks off to my right, paralleling the road. I'm riding through the village of Grotto, and I just can't believe how beautiful it is all through this area. If I'm using the word beautiful a lot, it's because I can't think of any other word that describes this part of Washington any better, and do it justice. I guess it's just something you have to see for yourself.

I have 75 miles on the old odometer and the road goes through a tunnel. I can't see how long it is so I'm going to stop and put my belt flasher on, just for safety.

Fortunately, it turned out to be a very short tunnel, and I really didn't need the flasher after all.

I've just got to stop and take a picture of these woods. A lot of the trees are just beginning to bud. Most of the woods along here have a lot of tall grass, and ferns, and moss growing all over them. It's so thick and dark I don't expect the picture to turn out, but I'm going to take it anyway.

There is a stream running through here but the dense forest hides it most of the time. It's like a tropical forest all along here. God…! It's beautiful. Heaven really can exist on earth.

*   *   *

I'm at a combination store…deli…and gas station…called the *Skykomish Deli and Liquor Store.* Next to the store is a tall pine tree that keeps dropping its cones on the hoods of parked cars. I go in and order a king-size turkey submarine sandwich, a couple of cokes, and some Reese's peanut butter cups, for dessert. I take them over to a picnic table, right next to the river, and have a pleasant dinner or supper (I'm not quite sure what the difference is).

Now, I had planned on camping out in Skykomish tonight, but, the pavement is good and the traffic is light and I have a beautiful 10 to 15 mph tailwind. It's only 4:20 p.m., so I'm going to ride on a little farther.

Three miles east of Skykomish I stop to take a picture of some of the many delicate wildflowers that grow abundantly right along the edge of the road. In the spring of the year, the hillsides are carpeted with wild flowers. It looks like a flowery sea and there is the smell of heaven in the air. I just wanted to show you that I take the time to smell the flowers…!

The road's beginning to climb steeply. I can't see the river anymore, but I sure can hear it, as its water flows over the rocks, making many…many…rapids. Damn…! I knew I was riding slowly, but this takes the cake…a butterfly just passed me…! Still, it just doesn't get any prettier than this.

It sure was a good idea to take two pairs of shoes along. My feet were getting tired with my new shoes on, so I changed into my other pair and now my feet feel great (as comfortable as an old shoe) just like they did when I started out this morning.

The sky is the color of wet cement now.

A white car coming down the hill toward me just stopped, and the driver is leaning her head out the window and telling me to be really careful, because there is a Big Black Bear in the road about halfway up Stevens Pass. Now, there is some good news and some bad news here. The good news is that now I know that this hill is Stevens Pass (a really steep hill) and the bad news is, there is a bear between the top and me.

I lost my tailwind as soon as I left Skykomish. I have 85 miles in, and I've got to stop and rest. It's been uphill for what seems like a long…long…way, and I'm BEAT…! After a stop where I drink a little Tang, I remount and go on my way up a very steep climb again. As I round a curve in the road, mountains still hoarding last winter's snow pop into view.

*   *   *

I think I see that black bear alongside the road just up ahead. Shit...! I'm afraid of dogs. I don't know how I'm ever going to get around a bear. I'm in second gear and I'm tired. This grueling climb is really starting to take its toll on me. I sure can't outrun him. Bears can run at speeds up to forty miles an hour for a short ways. And I'm sure not going to turn around and go back down the hill. He's just sitting there alongside the road. I'll ride on the other side of the road, to get as far as possible away from him. Maybe, just maybe, he won't come after me.

This reminds me of a joke I heard on a camping trip. These two guys were camping and in the middle of the night, they heard a rustling outside. As they looked out, they saw a bear coming toward the tent. One guy said, "Lets Get the Hell Out of Here...!" The other one said, "Wait a minute while I put my shoes on." The first guy said, "It's not going to matter if you got your shoes on or not. There's no way you can out run a bear." The other guy said, "I don't have to outrun the bear, all I have to do is outrun you."

Well, that wasn't a bear after all. It was a culvert that looked like a bear...I'm not paranoid!

I'm in low gear grunting my way up the hill. Another car stops and tells me that there is a Big Black Bear about halfway up the hill, and it looked awfully hungry and it has jaws large enough to take in an entire human being, bike and all. Now, that's really encouraging. Not only is the bear still in the road, but now I know I'm not even halfway up this hill yet. Damn...! My computer isn't working. The rpm's are but the miles aren't working so my miles won't be accurate. I'll stop here for a minute and try to fix it. My riding time is working so I can calculate my miles and average speed tonight. I haven't come to the bear yet but while I'm stopped I'll dig my hatchet out of my pannier and put it in the handlebar bag, just so I'll feel a little secure.

I have the feeling of being as much part of the landscape as the wild animals. I'm in the most natural of all possible elements, and all my senses are on the alert-hearing, sight and smell. My eyes dart from point to point, sizing up everything that moves. By the way, do you know how to tell a grizzly bear from a black bear? All you have to do is climb up a tree. A black bear will climb up after you. A grizzly can't climb so he'll just shake you out of the tree like a plum, if he doesn't tear it out by the roots first. Now that's reassuring, isn't it?

As long as its taking me to get up this Pass, the bear should be gone by the time I get to where it was anyway, I hope. A fairly large animal went leaping up the broken stone hill (or maybe it was a small animal). Anyway it made a little avalanche right behind me and it scared the shit out of me. Just because I had my hand around the handle of my hatchet, doesn't mean I'm paranoid. I don't want tomorrow's headlines to read, "Remains of a lone biker found..."

I'm shifting back and forth between first and second trying to get up this damn hill. I don't know where the top is. This #@&*%! hill doesn't level off anywhere. It's a steady climb all the way. I feel as though I'm riding up a down escalator and I'm almost out of water. Half the people that drive by look at me and think I'm crazy and the other half know I am. It's 6:40 p.m., and I've got to stop and rest again. It's 72 degrees out. The sun is just above the mountaintops on my left and it's still beautiful out but I don't think there is a top to this damn hill.

At 95 miles, I stop to take a picture of my bike up against a pile of dirty snow, right alongside the road. I don't know what elevation I'm at, but I must be getting up there. As I ride ever so slowly up this hill, I watch birds of prey chuckling overhead. Climbing Stevens Pass is a lot like being on a *Lifecycle* (a stationary bicycle). You pedal your ass off and get nowhere.

There is very little traffic on this road. It's really quiet and peaceful, and then, without any warning, a big ass rock rolls down a steep bank right along side me. The hair on the back of my neck rises, I think I'm going to have a heart attack, and I'm still not paranoid about any old bear…!

I stop to rest right next to a small waterfall. I'm going to get in the water and cool down a bit. It's so cool next to this waterfall I can actually see my breath. I splashed some cold water on my face, and get my hair all wet. It's cold as the Polar Ice Cap but it still feels good. Then I take my shoes off and put my feet in the icy cold water for a second…only a second. I think about lying down on the side of the road to rest, possibly to die…like some old noble Eskimo, but I've got to get moving again.

There is this very small stream, only about eight inches wide and one to two inches deep, flowing along the edge of the road, trickling its way down the mountainside. Crawling along at a snail's pace, I have plenty of time to observe it as it snakes its way around the larger rocks, sometimes creating a small whirlpool. I watch its crystal-clear water as it gurgles over a small stick lodged between two rocks, creating a small rapid. I watch as a leaf floats down, and I try to guess where it might eventually get lodged. Watching this stream helps to keep my mind off the long…long…long…grinding climb. I figure, with the water flowing this slowly in this small stream, the hill can't be too steep.

A car coming down the hill just pulled over and stopped at a turn-out on the other side of the road to take some pictures of the scenery. As I go by, I ask them if there is a top to this hill or not? One of them says, "Yea…! But you got a long way to go yet." Shit…! I knew riding my bike three thousand miles, alone, over every kind of road, would be hard work, but I didn't know just how hard.

Damn…! My odometer isn't working again. I'm not going to stop and try to fix it again. I want to get over this hill before it gets dark. I'll just calculate everything out tonight.

If it seems like I'm doing a lot of swearing, climbing this hill, it's not because I'm not enjoying my ride, because I am. (Although I would be enjoying it a lot more if it was downhill.) It's just that I feel like I have to swear at something and it might as well be this damn hill. I must admit it though…I don't particularly like (up) hills. But then again there are not too many bicyclists that do. Hey…! Maybe I'm normal after all. Nah…!

Climbing this hill brings to mind the children's story of the little train trying ever so hard to puff its way up a mountain. "I think I can…I think I can…I think I can…I know I can…I know I can." As I climb, the temperature drops. There are a lot of little waterfalls all along here, created by the melting snow. It's 7:24 p.m. and I'm stopping again. I'm BEAT…! There is a big black buzzard circling overhead, waiting…just waiting…

I see a ski lodge right up ahead of me, I hope that means I'm close to the top of this hill. My favorite part of skiing is taking off those heavy boots at the end of the day and getting some feeling back into my hands and feet. I guess ski instructors love it though…otherwise they would have to get a real job.

Fifteen minutes later I'm finally up this hill or mountain, or whatever it is. It has cooled down to 65 degrees. I cross the road so I can get a picture of this road sign that states the hill I just climbed was 6% grade for 7 miles…and let me tell you that it's a heart-pounding 7-mile climb. The way I see it, in hill climbing it's the grade, not the elevation that determines how difficult it is. I have little breath to spare by the time I reach the summit, but reaching the summit doesn't allow me time to catch my breath. The scenery is as breathtaking as the climb itself. Fluffy ribbons of clouds trace across the sky over a beautiful pine forest. I can't stay here too long though, I've got to get going before it gets dark on me.

*   *   *

I have 100 miles on the odometer and I'm one mile west of Merritt. When I started climbing this hill, hours ago…maybe days ago…I'm not sure, I thought the scenery was outstanding, but up here on the top, the crest view is worth every drop of sweat. The scenery is unmatched by anything I've seen yet. There are tall pine trees skirting the road, giving off a very distinctive, pleasant, smell. The air is fresh, and clean and crystal-clear. I can see for miles…and miles…in all directions. It was a hard mountain to climb, but it seems like the closer to Heaven I get the better things are. I would like to stay here and soak up the scenery some more but I have to find a place to spend the night. Speaking of soaking things up, I'm wringing wet, from perspiration. I'm going to dig out my wind jacket before I head on down this hill. I like that word, DOWN…! I've earned this DOWNHILL…!

Once over the 4,061-foot Stevens Pass, I descend through the jagged granite walls of Tumwater Canyon. I ride alongside the white-water Wanatchee River, through evergreen forest, through Merritt and Nason Creek.

I can see a light coming from over a stove in this little bitty country store in Coles Corner. It's a yellowish light that gives the appearance that it was left on only to create the illusion that the store is occupied. I roll to a stop and go in. I inhale some chocolate-chip cookies and I also chug down a couple of cokes. I suppose I look like a hungry bear to the storekeeper, but I don't care. I'm hungry and thirsty after that long climb.

I ask him if there is any place to spend the night.

He asks me, "Which way are you going?"

I tell him that I've just ridden my bike from Skykomish.

He say's, "Motorbike?"

I say, "No bicycle."

He say's, "I don't know that anyone's ever rode over Steven Pass on a bicycle before."

I'm sure they have, but it made me feel good just the same.

He says that there is a motel that might have a vacancy six miles on down the hill, and…if not there…there was a campground, four miles farther. I thank him, and head on down the hill. I guess you would say I'm cascading through the Cascades.

I'm savoring my reward…miles of downhill coasting. I take a long pull on my water bottle, shift up 20 gears, and pedal until there is no more point in it. The wind sends a chill through my sweat-soaked shirt and whistles through my helmet in a rage. It's delightful…! I'll tell you, this wind-jacket is worth its weight in gold. Even though I'm soaking wet, it still keeps me warm going down this hill. This is an excellent road, very lightly traveled and it has wide, sweeping curves. It's quite safe for a full speed coast.

It's too bad, though, that I can't go more than 20 mph because of this mysterious front-end wobble. It seems to vibrate all the time. It's frustrating because I can't find its source. Riding down this hill, the unsteadiness makes me especially nervous, particularly when I could have been coasting down at forty miles an hour if I didn't have the wobble.

I stop at a motel, which has a vacancy. They want $43.00 plus tax for a room for the night. I don't want to spend that much money for a place to sleep, especially with a campground only four more miles (downhill). Down, is the key word here. I know it'll be getting dark soon, so I jump on my bike and I'm on my way again.

How splendid this is…! I'm descending into a valley at twenty miles an hour with tears of joy flying out of the corners of my eyes. It's 9:52 p.m. I have 120 miles on the odometer as I arrive at Tumwater campground. Beat, but happy, I wheel into a campsite. I ride all through the campground, looking for a Ranger to give my campsite fees to and there isn't any. I stop at a bulletin board where they have instructions, referring to how to pay for your campsite if there isn't anyone around. It seems that you're supposed to put $6.00 in this little box. Well, all I have is a $20.00 travelers check. So I think I'll just wait and play the Ranger in the morning. It's 10.00 p.m. and there is still sufficient light to pitch my tent. I put my sleeping pad and sleeping bag in my tent, take my panniers off my bike and put them in the tent. Then I lock my naked bike to a picnic table.

I watch day turn into night. The river is glassy and twilight is stretching on for over a half-hour. Ducks are dropping in through a settling mist, and then they skid into the water among the skeletons of dead trees. Then purple slowly becomes the color of the night.

I take my soap, washcloth, towel, and a change of clothes and set out to find a shower. There isn't one, so I take a COLD sponge bath, which really wakes me up. Over at the river I sit down on a house-size boulder for a spell. I'm quite surprised, it's a warm night, with no breeze, and there aren't any mosquitoes out. It's so peaceful out here. There is no traffic noise. As a matter of fact, there isn't any type of man-made noise to disturb my thoughts. Just the sounds of the river, and frogs croaking, and crickets cricketing (or whatever they do) and an occasional bug buzzing around.

I'm exhausted but, as sometimes happens, I'm too tired to sleep. The day's events are hopping about in my mind like popcorn in a skillet as I think about what I've accomplished in just one day, just how far I've come, the hills I've conquered and the spectacular scenery I've seen. It's quite gratifying. I immediately develop an overwhelming sense of pride in what I'm doing. It isn't every day that one hops on his bicycle and takes off and doesn't come back for a month or so. I mosey back to my tent and crawl in. Being a warm night and no threat of rain, I leave the rain fly off. The tent I have is all open (except for the mosquito netting) without the rain fly on. This is really nice as I can just lie here and look at the moon and all the bright stars shining through the pine trees. I don't want this day to end. It's been a good day. But I'm tired and I finally close my eyes and go to sleep around 11:00 p.m. with the fragrance of pine, filling my tent.

*   *   *

Statistics for **DAY ONE** *Monday, June 12, 1989.*
120 miles of riding today, 10.4 average miles per hour for today.

Day Two

From Leavenworth, Washington
To Coulee City, Washington

It's Tuesday morning, the thirteenth of June.

It's just before the day is breaking (5:30 a.m.) and the birds are singing, "Good-Morning…" to me. I guess I'll get up.

Do you have any idea how wonderful it is to wake up to the lovely green trees and the blue sky and fresh, clean air, and not have a worry in the world? It's really nice to be woken by the singing of the birds and the trickling of water running over the rocks in the stream right next to my tent. It makes me feel like a kid again. It makes me want to go hopping on the stepping-stones across the river. But I know I'll fall in and wind up with a really cold bath. The winds dancing through the trees and the scents of flowers and pine sap and crisp clean air are abundant. It's quite a change from waking up to the alarm clock, smog, freeways, asphalt, and concrete.

I didn't see any mosquitoes last night but this morning I don't have to go looking for them…they're looking for me. There is nothing like the feeling of a mosquito walking around inside one's ear or nostril. One good thing about mosquitoes, only the females suck the blood out of you, the males don't. I guess that's where the term "Bloodsucking Females" come from. We don't have any flies or mosquitoes in L.A. I think the smog kills them off. But the *Environmental Protection Agency* assures us that the smog's all right to breathe-it hasn't killed any laboratory rats, yet…At least, they haven't told us if it has.

I must say my tent and sleeping bag worked out really well last night. It was quite pleasant out so I didn't need to zip my sleeping bag up and the tent was really nice without the rain-fly on. It was just like sleeping out under the stars, only better, no bugs could get to me.

Cobwebs covered with dew are glittering in the early morning light as I take down my tent. I just pumped up my tires and packed and zipped my panniers up. Now, I'm going to ride around the campground and look for a Ranger, so I can pay for my campsite.

Well, I rode all through the campground and there isn't any Ranger around. And I can't wait around until one shows up, so I guess it was a free night last night. "Thanks, Washington...!"

The motel I stopped at would have cost me $43.00 plus tax. The campsite would have cost $6.00 if I could have paid for it. So, in just one night, my camping equipment has saved me 43 plus dollars. At this rate, it won't take long for the camping equipment to pay for itself.

Well it's a brand-new day, and it's just beautiful out, and I feel great. I sure could use a cup of coffee, though.

At 6:22 a.m., I leave the campground. It's 60 degrees. I'm trying to get an early start this morning to take advantage of the early morning air and to avoid the traffic. I'm riding along catching whiffs of lilacs and freshly cut grass as an owl floats across the road right in front of me.

I think everybody goes to sleep with the chickens around here. After 8:00 p.m. last night, the traffic was virtually nonexistent.

I'm eight miles west of Leavenworth. I just heard a little Ping...! I immediately look back at my rear wheel, and sure enough, it's wobbling ferociously. I have a broken spoke. I'll pull over into this little roadside rest area where there are two picnic tables, next to this fast flowing river. What a nice place for a picnic, but of course, I'm not picnicking, I have to repair my rear wheel. Now, I've never fixed a broken spoke before, but just how hard can it be anyway?

*   *   *

Murphy's Law

Spokes always break on the freewheel side, that's because they are harder to replace on that side. Basically, this is what you have to go through to replace one on that side. First, you have to take your rear panniers off. Then, remove the chain from the freewheel. Then, remove the wheel from the bike. Next, you have to remove the freewheel from the hub. This alone is not easy, and you need two special wrenches to accomplish it. Next, you have to remove the tire and tube from the rim, and remove the broken spoke. Then, pull back the rim tape and extract the old nipple and replace it with a new one. Next, you need to feed the new spoke through the hole in the hub, twist and bend it around until you get it woven through the spokes (Right...!) then put a drop of light oil on the threads, and screw the nipple on. Next, you need to grease the freewheel and (carefully) thread it back on the hub. They are fine threads and very easy to cross thread. Now, you are ready to put the wheel back on the frame, minus the tube and tire (this comes later). Then, spin the wheel around and, using the break pads as a guide, tighten the new spoke with the spoke wrench you had better have remembered to bring along. When you get the entire wobble out of the rim, take the wheel back off the frame and put the tube and tire on. Put the wheel back on the bike, pump the tire up to its proper pressure, replace your chain and put your panniers back on and you're ready to roll again. Now, doesn't that sound like fun?

I was lucky, the spoke that broke this time was on the left side of the wheel so I didn't have to take the freewheel off. I just took the broken spoke out and put a new one in. I didn't even take the wheel off my bike, or even let the air out of the tire. God's law prevailed this time, not Murphy's. I was back on the road in twelve minutes. I knew it was going to be a good day.

*   *   *

I'm surrounded by unexpected beauty: timber, lakes, rivers, and mountains crowned by snow. The road is following along the Wenatchee River, which makes for easy pedaling. There are no steep climbs, and I have a nice tailwind.

I'm not sure if it's good for me to breathe all this clean fresh air or not. I'm sure my lungs have adapted themselves to heavy reddish-brown air. The kind you can sink your teeth into. You know, the kind you can see. Something with some substance to it. If you haven't caught on by now, you're not from L.A., the smog capital of the world.

I sure could use a cup of coffee.

Looking ahead in the distance, I can see that the road I'm riding on snakes along with the river. It's hard (no it's impossible) to explain just how beautiful it is out here. The pictures I'm taking might give you some kind of an idea, but they can't do this place justice. It's just unbelievable. It's like looking at picture postcard scenery all around me. I've never felt so in tune with the world before.

For the life of me I don't know why this river is flowing east. I thought all water on the west side of the *Continental Divide* was supposed to flow into the Pacific Ocean. Either the river or I am going the wrong way, and I don't believe it's me. I'll have to look at my map tonight and see what's going on here. I'm not complaining though, I'm glad it's flowing this way. That means I'm going downhill, and this is one time it feels good to go with the flow.

Boy...! There are sure some nice rapids along here.

It's 7:25 a.m. as I ride into Leavenworth and it's 64 degrees. I'm getting hungry and I need my morning coffee, I'm down about a quart.

I just saw this sign on the outskirts of this town that read: "Wilkommen zu Leavenworth" and I drop into the theme town of Leavenworth, with its authentic Bavarian atmosphere. The village stores are sporting gingerbread fronts and Swiss-chalet roofs. But, actually, the first thing that catches my eye as I ride into town is all the flowers. There are flower gardens everywhere and planter boxes full of flowers. More than

250 hanging baskets, full of flowers, line Main Street.

The village is ablaze with color. I ask this little old white-haired lady and am informed that the village sets out 16,000 red geraniums in the spring of the year, and the petunias are beyond counting. The whole village is only about two blocks long and, I have to admit it's a rather nice little town. I wouldn't mind living here myself.

This is going to be a little hard to explain, but I'll try. There is no stopping or parking on the main road that runs through this village. They have turnoffs that lead to a frontage road where all the stores are. Separating the main road and the frontage road are these large islands of the darkest green grass I've ever seen. They have small flowers planted all around the edge of these islands, and old-time (even for me) streetlights and benches in the center. It looks like a very well-maintained park.

As I ride through the village I spot this *Hansel and Gretel* pastry shop, so I stop in. I'm (past) ready for some coffee. I lean my bike up against the front window, so I can keep an eye on it even though I know it'll be safe in this town.

I'm surely glad I stopped in here. They've got the best cinnamon rolls I've ever tasted. I can't stop with just one. I have to have another and some more coffee. Now I'm ready to get out there in the fresh morning air and see what the rest of the day has in store for me.

I put a little more air in my rear tire and take a little out of the front one. I'm going to see if that helps my wobbling situation. I still can't ride more than 20 mph I'm even going to taper my front panniers in, and see if that helps. What I mean by tapering my panniers in, is this: *Cannondale's* front panniers have a feature, where you can zip them into a V shape, which makes them much more aerodynamic, but it also cuts down on the amount of stuff you can put into them. I'm also going to put a little more weight in my front panniers to see if it changes this front-end wobble. It's really slowing me down (not that I'm in a hurry) but when I get a nice straight, long downhill, it would be nice if I didn't have to use my brakes so much.

*   *   *

It's just another beautiful day. There is not a cloud on the horizon. There is a river that occasionally goes back and forth underneath the road. It's truly beautiful. I want to stop and take a picture every time I cross over it, but I guess I have enough pictures of it, so I'll just take a picture of the road up ahead.

It's nice to be out here this early in the morning where I can enjoy the sharp, clean smell of wood-smoke coming from the cottage chimneys. I think the sense of smell, almost more than any other, has the power to recall memories. I have many wonderful memories of sitting in front of a fireplace, and just as many, if not more, of sitting in front of a campfire.

In general this road is excellent and very lightly traveled.

My ride through Cashmere has been an easy, pleasant one. It's been a gradual downhill for a long…long…way now and I'm really a-cruising. I'm enjoying riding more than I had ever thought possible. I'm effortlessly flying along maintaining a steady average of 19 to 20 mph In only a few hours' ride I've pedaled through fragrant pine forests beside breathtaking rapids.

I have to tell you, I get in trouble at work all the time for not wearing my safety glasses, (which are mandatory) and now that I'm on vacation, I still refuse to wear glasses. Don't get me wrong. I'm not against safety. I would never ride my bike without my helmet on. Let me put it this way, the more brains you have the better helmet you should have, and my boss says I've got a lot of brains I haven't even used yet. I figure with it being an overcast day I really don't need glasses anyway. Well, I was wrong. This Big Ass bug just hit me right in the eye. Being June, I think it was a June bug. Man, it HURTS...! I stop to put my glasses on. I guess it's kind of like shutting the barn door after the horse is already out.

*   *   *

I must be close to the bottom of this hill now, because the river and I have both slowed our pace down. Route 2 going out of Seattle is one of the most scenic roads I've ever seen. I understand the northern route through the Cascade Mountains is equally nice, if not superior. Of all the countryside I saw on my tour, the one place I would like to return to and maybe do a week or two camping / bike tour of, is western Washington state. In my opinion, this is one of the most beautiful places in the United States.

It's 8:16 a.m. and I'm one mile east of Cashmere. And, judging by the American Flags flying, there is no wind at all out right now.

I'm following the road and the road is following the Klicketat River and the river is following the rocky valley down to the Columbia. Just east of the dam the land looks as though someone has drawn a north-south line forbidding any green life. West of the line is patches of forest and east is a desert with hills growing nothing but shrubs and dry grasses. It's Incredible...! The features of the country have entirely changed. The road just dropped into a dry, desert basin with high, barren hills nearly void of vegetation. The only green I can see now is along the Columbia River where there are lush vineyards and fruit orchards perched beside this barren, brown land.

I'm riding on a bridge that goes over the Columbia River. My riding conditions are ideal. It's overcast, accompanied with 66-degree temperatures. It's just a perfect day for riding. There is no wind at all.

With 30 miles on the odometer I stop at a fruit stand where I buy and eat a peach, a tomato, a pear, an apple, and I get some trail mix to take along with me. I fill my water bottles and reorganize my cargo again, putting a lot of weight in the front panniers. I guess no one can tell you just how to pack your panniers. It's a technique you have to learn. The way I'm learning is by failures. I also put a little more air in the front tire, still trying to get rid of the front-end wobble.

Just north of Wenatchee, away from the river, the features of the country are entirely changed again. Scrub brush and naked hillsides meet my eyes. I think that the most terrifying thought about mountain riding is the word "Mountain." For that reason you won't hear me use it (much). I tend to call the oceans, "Seas," and mountains, "Hills." Now, there are all kinds of hills. The Sierra Nevada, Cascades, the Rockies, and the Catskill Ranges are merely super hills. A slow, steady cadence will get me over any hill, that is, if I'm in good physical shape. Pedaling up a super hill is hard work, indeed. I have to set my goal as high as the hill top, but set my pace on a moderate, realistic time schedule. It is impossible to speed up a hill, but it is not impossible to inch my way to the top of any hill.

It's still overcast, and all the hills are brown and barren on Route 97 going north. There is a lot of traffic on this road. It's not nearly as nice as Route 2 was. I'll be getting back on Route 2 pretty soon.

I only had one little downhill since I changed my weight around. I got up to 22 mph and the bike seemed to handle a little better. I still have a little wobble, though.

It's 10:16 a.m. I reach Orondo, where Route 97 joins Route 2. There is a Post Office here, and that's about all.

"Shit…! I think I just broke another back spoke. Yep…! I did, on the left side of the wheel. I'm going to have to fix it.

Well, I tried to fix it the same way I did the other one but it didn't work this time. When I tried to tighten the new spoke, the turning of the nipple punctured the inner tube. So I had to take the tire and tube off and patch that sucker. Then I put a small boot inside so it wouldn't poke through the tube again. I wonder…is a person who builds wheels called a spokesperson?

I'm back on the road again. The normally flat to downhill terrain has turned hilly during the hottest part of the day. There is no breeze to take away the sweat that gushes out of me when I grind my way up the inclines. On my map the road looks straight. The map never told me that the road decided to go up a mountain for two or three or six miles at a time. I'm in second gear and I will be for quite some time. This looks like a long hill. There is a sign that says, "Rocks for the Next 6 Miles." That leads me to believe that it's going to be uphill for at least another 6 miles. "Shit…!"

I stop alongside the road to eat a granola bar and get something to drink and take a short rest. That was a good stop. I ate a few hands full of trail mix and drank about three-quarters of a bottle of water before proceeding on up the hill. It looks like it's going to be a long hill. I had put a little more air in my back tire hoping that it'll make peddling up this hill easier. (It didn't work). I've been in my granny gear (low gear) for the last mile.

I've ridden 46 miles today and I'm still climbing.

"How high is the mountain…?" "How deep is the ocean…?" No matter what you call it, a hill is still a hill. Have I mentioned lately that I hate hills? I need to stop and rest again.

As I pump my way up this hill my tongue is starting to drag on my front tire, and it's not because I've seen a pretty girl. I have to stop again and rest for a while. The landscape sort of looks like an artist's canvas before he or she adds the green grass and trees and the sparkling brooks and the birds and flowers. In other words, it looks pretty much like an unfinished painting. It looks like God created western Washington on the sixth day and eastern Washington was to be done on the seventh day but he rested instead. I look all around me for scenery that isn't there.

It's still uphill…granny gear all the way now. Even my eyelashes are in pain now. The meadowlarks are cheering me on. Sometimes I wish I were a bird. So I could fly up this damn hill. I'm glad I did Stevens Pass yesterday. I don't think there is any way I could do two of these passes in one day. When I stop, I can feel a very slight breeze. God…! It feels good on my sweaty body. It's a hard hill, but it's a beautiful day just the same. It's still overcast and about 75 degrees out, just perfect for riding. As I stop to rest again, I can hear a lot of birds singing.

I have about a 5 mph tailwind now. It's still uphill though.

After stopping for another well-deserved rest, I slowly…very slowly, continue on. It's been a steady 6% grade climb for a long time now with no breaks anywhere, no flat spots. It looks like it goes on forever. It appears to get steeper on up as I can hear the gear-grinding trucks shifting down. Cars pass by me slowly and the kids hang out the windows, waving and giving me the thumbs-up sign.

I've got a stomachache. I don't know if it's from all that fruit I ate or all this damn climbing. I spent the first 12 years of my life eating green apples and that never bothered me. I need another rest stop.

It's 12:48 p.m. and I'm on my way again, inching my way up this especially steep leg-burning hill. I guess these are the foothills of the Cascades. Boy, I can hardly wait to get to the Rockies…!

*   *   *

It's early afternoon and I'm finally on the top of the mountain. I'm pedaling through gently rolling hills and flat fields of wheat. Bicycle touring is so exciting. Every day, NO…! Every few miles, the terrain varies and over each hill and around every corner there is something new to discover.

It's nice now that the road has flattened out. It's flatter than Twiggy, and I'm riding through mile after mile of rolling grasslands, or maybe it's wheat, I don't know. I may not know the proper names of all the trees and plants and flowers or even if this is wheat or grass. But I can, and do, appreciate its beauty just the same. And, after all, isn't that better than knowing the proper names of things?

Ain't that ironic, I'm just riding past a sign that points to the town of Waterville (one mile down a side road) and it's starting to sprinkle.

It's stopped sprinkling now and as I top a slight rise, I can see a cluster of unpainted buildings up ahead. It gives me a feeling of relief, as I hadn't seen any buildings in a long time. They are snuggled in this hollow, as if they are trying to take shelter from the terrain.

At 57 miles I'm at the bottom of the holler and there is a sign. It's telling me that this is Douglas. I'm going to stop and get some water. You notice that I didn't say the town or village of Douglas. There are only five buildings here, all of which look as though a good wind would blow them down. I shift down to my lowest gear, set a calm pace, and listen to the gravel crackle under my tires, as I ride through the empty parking lot in front of the general store. I notice this unbelievably beautiful, I'd guess, seventeen-year-old girl, with big breasts, standing on the porch watching me ride in. I just thought, God…it would be embarrassing if I were to crash now. She goes inside as I approach.

I see no vehicles of any kind in Douglas. There is a weathered wooden porch, which I lean my bike against. And a BIG…black, lazy (thank God) dog lying in the doorway. As I walk up to him, he's doesn't even move. Then someone yells from inside, "Just step over him, he thinks he owns the damn place." So, I do. As I walk into the store, this man who's behind the counter greets me. His face is drooping with saggy flesh, his skin is the color of coffee (with two creams). His hair is bleached rust-red by the sun and it's as thick as wool. He's squinting his eyes, I would guess, from more than seventy years of tilling the earth in the bright sun. He's wearing overalls and a well-worn cowboy hat that looks as old as he is.

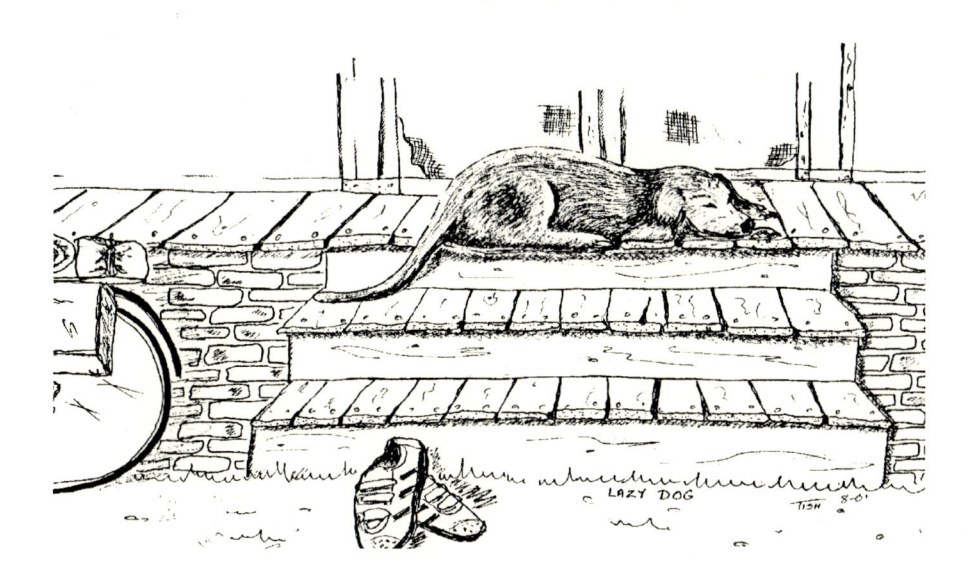

He's got a pot of coffee brewing so I have a cup and chat with him for a spell, while he fills my water bottles. The floorboards of random widths creak with my every step, as I walk around the store. They seem to sag under their own weight. All the canned goods, as a matter of fact, everything in the store, including the cowboy hat on the old man's head, and (I imagine) my coffee, is covered with a light coat of dust. I bought all the Tang and granola bars he had. He's extremely grateful. I think it might have been the biggest sale he had all day or all week or all month, who knows? Anyway he's a very nice, memorable gentleman. The girl had completely disappeared. Maybe she was a mirage. I'm not sure.

As I go back out, I have to step over the dog again. Then I sit down on the porch and change my shoes and take a couple of aspirins. I've got a headache, I think it might be from sperm buildup. Anyway, I'm on my way again.

Riding along, I often see hawks circling over head in the sky that always seems to be blue and warm. I'm surely glad they're not vultures. I feel so free…free enough to spread my wings and reach for the sky myself. As I ride along, I make up this little poem.

The road to life isn't always a flat road,
It has its ups and downs.
It isn't always straight,
It has its curves.
If it were flat and straight,
How boring it would be.
It would be too easy to figure out your destiny.
It's not always straight and true.
But, if you have perseverance,
You'll get through.

I'm learning a lot on this tour. I'm also taking a lot of pictures, mostly of the road. When you're on the road eight to 12 hours a day, that's what you see the most of. I am constantly looking out for cracks and potholes and debris. I realize now that I should take more pictures of the places where I stop. Like the restaurants and motels and the entire small towns and villages I go through. I also should take pictures of all the nice people I meet along the way. But I guess it's all right to make mistakes, as long as I learn something from them. I'll do better next time.

The sun's out now and I'm beginning to notice a change in the terrain. It's becoming drier and more desolate.

At 2:54 p.m. I'm thirteen miles east of Douglas. I stop and take a picture of a four-mile downhill and I don't like the looks of it. I know I'm going to have to climb out of this sucker. I've heard of people that study road and topo maps so much that they know where every turn and rise in the road is. That would take all the adventure out of it for me.

I stop and eat a granola bar. You know that granola bars are really a health-food hoax. They are actually leftover chunks of particle board that made an unscrupulous carpenter very rich.

I've got a very steep uphill climb again. There seem to be a lot of these rather steep downhills followed by a killer of an uphill, and I mean a long…long…killer of an uphill. This morning I was riding on Planet Earth, and this afternoon it looks more like Mars.

It's 80 degrees out as I start to ride up this hill.

Shit…! I know I was praying it would get flat out here, but I wasn't referring to my tire. I've got a flat tire in the rear. I have a card from one of those alphabet agencies, *AA* or is it *AAA*, anyway, I wonder if they fix bicycle tires? Most of the girls I've ridden bicycle with don't know how to fix a flat. But I guess they don't have to. If they are riding with me they know I'll fix it for them and if they are riding alone and have a flat all they have to do is sit on the curb and look at it. Some young feller will eventually come along and fix it for her.

I've heard that there is a video out on, *"How to Fix a Flat Bicycle Tire."* In my opinion anyone who can't figure out how to fix a flat tire sure as hell can't operate a VCR.

This morning it looked like what I would imagine the Garden of Eden would look like. This afternoon it looks like the Mojave Desert, or Mars or Utah. By the way, if it sounds like I don't like Utah, that's only because I took a bike tour there last year and for days…and days…and days…all I saw was sand…and rocks…and sand…and rocks…I'm not putting Utah down, I know it's a showcase for some of nature's most amazing works.

It's 4:16 p.m. I think I'm up the main part of this hill. It seems to be softening into a series of gentle rollers now.

Well, I'm up the big hill, but I can still see a bunch of rollers up ahead. And there is a little dust devil in the open field to my right. A road-weary Dodge is kicking up a rooster's tail of dust on a dirt road off to my left.

It's starting to sprinkle a little bit, real light. I'm almost out of water. The crosswind has switched around and I have to a 10 mph tailwind now. At 86 miles I stop and rest. The temperature has dropped down to 75 degrees. It's nice out. Great riding weather.

The afternoon has slipped by as I roll into Coulee City. There is a lot of brown grass and sagebrush all through this area. I stop to take two pictures, one of a canyon, and one of a lake off to my left.

I don't have many good things to say about the scenery out here, except that, once again, I'm glad I didn't take a southern route through the desert. A little of this is all I need. I sure wouldn't have wanted to ride through it for days and days. I suppose the desert does have its advantages. For one thing, my journal would be easier to write. It would be a lot shorter. There is not too much to describe in the desert. Also, I would save money on film and processing. Of course, if I wanted to save money, I wouldn't have gone on vacation in the first place. So, when you come right down to it, I really can't think of any advantages to this un-scenic, barren, wasteland, after all. I sure hope the plains states aren't like this.

*   *   *

I knew there was a reason why it cooled down, it's starting to sprinkle again.

It's 5:52 p.m. and I've ridden 94 miles today. It's starting to rain a little bit harder, well, sprinkle a little harder. I'm wet and the thought of camping grows increasingly unattractive. I'll just check into a motel for the night in Coulee City.

I see this neon sign advertising a motel about a block from Main Street. It's $23.00 for the night. Actually, it's not a room but a little two-room cabin, with a full kitchen, a refrigerator, stove, a television. It has a separate bedroom and bathroom. It's really a nice little cabin.

I unpack and take a relaxing shower and shave. Then I set out on foot to check the town out. This shouldn't take long, considering that the whole town consists of one street about four blocks long.

Well, this must be my lucky day. There are three taverns in the first block.

This is a really old western town, with wooden sidewalks and everything. It's modernized a little though. Instead of horses tied up to the hitching post (that's still in place) there are old rusted out pickup trucks and big new tractors, parked in front of the taverns.

I walk by and look in all three taverns to see which one has the biggest crowd, which consists of only four people. It's got a long western type bar, with the brass rail for a footrest. I pull up a stool and order a cold one.

There is a pay phone inside, so I try to call my daughter to let her know where I am and that I'm all right. I find that she isn't home, so I'll keep trying, consuming a beer in between calls. Well, I tried four different times and there was no answer.

They've got a jukebox in here, but there isn't any music playing. They have a pool table, but no one was playing.

I ask the barmaid (she is tall and bony, not a good-looking girl) if there was a restaurant in town. She says, "Yea…! Clear at the other end of town, but we have better food right here." I say, "Great…! Let me see your menu." She says, "We don't have a menu, we have hot dogs, hamburgers, and roast beef sandwiches." I say, "I'll have the roast beef sandwich." The sandwich and the few more beers I had to wash it down with were great. Now, seeing as how it's really dead in here, I'll walk back to my cabin and take a little nap to come back later when the place will be hopping.

Well, I took my nap; it's 10:30 p.m. as I walk back downtown. Two of the taverns are closed, but the one I was in earlier is open, so I go in. Well, I wouldn't exactly say the place is hopping. The same barmaid is still there, and the only other person in the place is the local sheriff, whose nose is somewhat red and swollen.

As soon as I sit down, the barmaid says, "I know what you did, you took a nap."

I say, "How did you know…?"

She says, "You looked awfully tired when you were in here earlier and you look rested now."

I say, "You're right…" and then I explained why I was tired.

They're both amazed that anyone could ride as far as I have on a bicycle.

It isn't long before the sheriff leaves. I have a few more beers, and ask the barmaid if she wants to play a game of pool. She says she can't because she has to do the dishes before quitting time. So I have a few more beers, and walk back to my cabin.

I just oiled my bike chain and then start to arrange things for tomorrow. I'll put everything in plastic bags, just in case it rains. I repatch my inner tube. The reason the tube went flat is that the hole was right on the seam, which makes it really hard to patch.

My bike is getting very dirty, so I clean it up a little. I have a reputation in my bike club as always having the dirtiest bike. Most of the guys in the club spend more time cleaning their bikes than they do riding them. Well, I didn't buy my bike to work on or to spend a lot of time cleaning. I got mine to ride and that's what I do. But, seeing as how, in a way, I'm out here representing the touring cyclist, I'll clean it up a little. I've learned to spend my time wisely, and I don't think it's very wise to spend two hours washing and cleaning my bike on a lovely day when I could be out riding instead.

I've got everything cleaned and pretty well packed now. It's 1:30 in the morning and I'm going to bed now.

I'm really surprised I haven't seen any wildlife, yet. I saw some deer on the train on the way to Seattle, but I haven't seen any while I've been riding.

* * *

*Statistics for **DAY TWO** Tuesday, June 13, 1989.*
94 miles of riding today, 12.1 average miles per hour for today, 214 miles of riding in two days, 107 average miles of riding per day.

Day Three

From Coulee City, Washington
To Spokane, Washington

It's 8:25 a.m. I get up and try to walk over to the door to see if it's raining and find I'm hobbling like an old man. The road is slightly wet, but it's not raining. It's clear and I don't see any clouds on the horizon. I'm still glad that I packed everything in plastic bags last night, just in case it starts to rain later.

I sure slept well last night. I wasn't quite sure just how I'd feel this morning, after the hard ride I did yesterday. But after walking around a bit I feel Great…! My little cabin has a coffee maker and enough coffee to make two cups. That should be enough to hold me until I can find a restaurant.

I love camping, but I have changed my mind about camping on this tour because, after riding 100 plus miles a day, I'm ready for a hot shower and a nice comfortable bed. There is nothing as pleasant as a good hot meal and a warm, soft bed waiting after a hard day's ride-and there is nothing quite so miserable as a poor meal and a cold, damp sleeping bag under the same circumstances.

Besides, I want to go to a local tavern and have a few beers and listen to the local gossip at the end of each day. This would be a little difficult to do if I were camping. Most campgrounds are quite a way out of town. I would have to leave all my equipment at the campsite, unprotected, ride into town in my long pants, leave my bike outside the tavern, again unprotected. Then, later that evening, I would have to weave my way back to the campground, in the cold night air, with an inadequate bike light, and hope everything was still there.

It's just much nicer to stay in a motel right downtown, take a hot shower, and walk to the local tavern, and know that my stuff is safely locked in my room. After last night, I knew that I would probably stay in motels all the rest of the way across the United States. But, I also want to carry all my camping equipment all the way across the United States, just to see if it's a problem or not. (It wasn't).

You might be thinking that I spent a lot of money on all this expensive equipment (and I did) just for one night's use. But, I plan on doing a lot of backpacking next summer and I made sure the equipment I bought could be used for that as well. So you see, I'm not as dumb as you thought I was.

It's 62 degrees out. The day has dawned gray and windless. It's as if the sky intends to hold its breath until it turns blue.

It sprinkled (very lightly) last night. I could have camped out all right, but the little cabin was worth every penny. It was really nice.

You have to be tough, real tough, if you want to ride, camp and cook. Pedaling long distances is only a fraction of it. You've got to get used to bugs in your food and shopping for food every day. And then, at the end of the day, when you're tired and hungry, you have to search for a good camping spot and cook your dinner on your little stove before you can eat. Nowadays most campgrounds are packed with the recreational vehicles with rumbling generators and blaring stereos and televisions that some people like to take with them when they go camping. And then, you've still got to wash the dishes before you can go to bed, and most of the time you're so tired you just go to bed without showering. And besides all that, in the morning you have to pack up your wet tent. Now that's what I call tough. I don't want to be that tough, at least not just yet.

On the outskirts of Coulee City, the road has about a four-foot wide shoulder. It's beautiful. I have to stop and take a picture of these huge John Deere tractors and combines. I just can't believe how big they are. You know you are in a small town when the biggest business in town sells farm machinery.

As I ride along in the early morning air, I'm a little stiff in the joints but well rested. Since movement seems to oil the joints, I'll keep riding, gradually becoming more and more flexible, receiving my daily massage from pedaling. I'm about two miles out of town, and I stop to take a picture of a wheat field with ripples of wind blowing in arcs a quarter of a mile wide across the field. There is very little traffic on this road this morning. There is a gray-blue cloud cover today, with a strong possibility of showers.

Uncertainties about road selections, pedaling a loaded bicycle, and camping has all rolled under my wheels by now.

It's been a gradual uphill climb for the last 10 miles. At 11 miles, I've come to the turn off to Hartland. I'm ready for coffee and breakfast, so I spin my wheels toward Hartland, only to find, to my surprise, there is no a restaurant in Hartland, only a farm co-op building. Luckily, it's only about a mile back to U.S. Route 2.

I'm riding in a slight drizzle now, nothing serious though. As soon as it hits the road it evaporates. A crosswind has picked up to about 10 mph and it's sprinkling a little bit harder, enough to keep the road wet. I've ridden 16.4 miles so far. It's 10:14 a.m. and I've got a light, steady rain, now. Of course, to a bicyclist there is no such thing as a "Light" rain. Rain is rain, and wet is WET...!

I have to stop and put a plastic bag over my sleeping bag. The plastic bag I have isn't quite long enough to fully enclose my sleeping bag, but it's better than nothing. I put my waterproof seat cover on for the first time. I also put my rain jacket on. It's a warm rain, so I didn't feel that it's necessary for me to put my rain pants on.

The drizzle has slowed down somewhat. It's not bad at all now.

I stop in a little restaurant in Almira to get something to eat.

Everything is looking better now. I had my coffee and a really good breakfast. Experts agree that breakfast is the most important meal of the day. I talked to some really friendly folks in the restaurant. You know,

Washington people give me a good feeling. It's difficult to describe but they seem real close to the earth itself. They seem to be content with where and what they find themselves to be. I left the farm when I was a boy, but the farm is still in my heart.

I'm on my way again now, winding through fields of freshly turned soil, which smells great. It's stopped sprinkling, and the road's even dry in spots. There is no shoulder on the road here, but it's a good road anyway. It's a slight, but steady uphill grade all the way now. The sun's trying to break through and the wet road is beginning to give off steam.

The crosswind today is from my right and there is a smooth, clean, two-foot wide shoulder on the road.

After 28 miles. I stop to take my raincoat off. It's rolling terrain and it's too warm climbing the hills with it on.

At lunchtime it's 70 degrees out as I stop at a hamburger joint in Wilbur. The dining room chairs in this joint are held together with electrical tape. The food is quite good and reasonably priced. I had a fried baloney sandwich, and a malt. Umm…! Sinfully Good…! I'm on my way again.

I'm riding along watching a few clouds build up in the east. After living in the "Big City" so long…maybe too long, I really appreciate all the spectacular beauty of the wide-open spaces. Riding a bicycle in Los Angeles, Seattle, or, I suspect, any other large city is not based on man against nature or man against himself. It's based on man against man.

I'm one mile east of Creston and I'm at the mercy of a prevailing 10 mph crosswind. For the most part of the day I've been in my middle chain ring. I don't know, this wind just doesn't give up, for a second. It's just hard going all the time.

It's 2:15 p.m., I feel like I've stepped back into history. I'm out here riding my iron horse, with the hot afternoon winds tumbling tumbleweeds across the road in front of me and into the barbed-wire fence that parallels the road. The crooked and eroded fence posts from years of blowing are casting long afternoon shadows.

I have to stop and take a picture of the blue sky. It's filled with cotton-ball clouds. It's very seldom you would ever see clouds like this above L.A. so this is quite a treat for me.

The terrain has really changed again.

I still have about a 10 mph crosswind.

Make that a 15 mph crosswind. It's a BITCH…!

I just rode into this rest area, for a well-deserved break. During the morning hours the sky was cloudless but this afternoon the intense blue sky is full of popcorn clouds. It's spectacular.

*   *   *

All Right…let's talk about saddle sores for a minute here. Just what is a saddle sore? Saddle sores are one of those things that many bike riders suffer from, but few talk about.

What causes saddle sores?

Cycling causes pressure and irritation at the crotch. This forces bacteria through the skin's protective outer layers into the sensitive inner layers. Once the bacteria penetrate the skin in this way, a saddle sore usually begins to form. And I think that's exactly what's happening to me right now, because I'm starting to get a pain in the ass.

I'm pedaling hard but making agonizingly slow progress. It's like swimming upstream against a heavy current. It's 3:55 p.m. I have 61 miles on the odometer as I stop one mile east of Davenport to take a picture of a sign that reads: "Have Any Kind of Day You Want."

A 15 mph wind is hitting me at a slight angle instead of straight on, but even so, it's still tough pedaling. It sure is wide-open space out here. There are no trees or bushes or not much of anything to block the wind.

I take a picture to show what the shoulder of the road looks like. It's about five feet wide, and clean. Totally absent of litter. It's been that way for most of the day.

I sure wish this wind would stop. It's fighting my every pedal.

Way out here in the middle of nowhere, if I need to take a leak, it's no problem. I can just stop and balance my bike with one hand and pee and be on my way. But if I want to take a little break, with no fences, or guardrail, or poles, or anything to lean my bike up against, I have to lie my bike down on the panniers. This bothered me a little at first. I didn't want to get them all dirty. But, after the first few times, I don't give it a second thought.

I'm going to stop and change my shoes and take a little break here. The wind has died down to maybe a 5 mph crosswind.

Riding along out here, looking up into the sky, I can make out a figure of a naked lady in the clouds, and I must say she looks awfully good. I think I had better call my girlfriend tonight.

I just rode through Reardan. It's about 69 degrees out and I put my windbreaker on as it's getting a little chilly. At 84 miles I'm passing through countryside of gentle rolling terrain.

The rolling terrain turns into small hills now. I stop to get something to eat at this little roadside stand in Deep Creek.

HOORAY…! The wind has stopped.

I ride into Spokane on the side streets to stay out of the business district of town. I just rode by a motel that advertised rooms for $19.00. I almost stopped, but I thought I would ride a little farther today. The location of a motel is important to me, especially in the morning. If I'm riding through a city, it's always better to find a motel on the far side of town. By basing myself there in the evening, I can avoid the incoming rush of cars and trucks the following morning. Since more people come into town than travel out of it in the morning, I find myself in a relatively traffic-free outgoing lane. I'm in the northern outskirts of town now. I have to get back to the main drag, and then find a motel.

Back on U.S. Route 2, heading north, I see a sign…Oh Great…! It says "No Bicycles…" Seeing as how it's this late (8:35 p.m.) and there is not much traffic, I'm going to stay on this road anyway. Oh Shit…! There is another sign, and a cop at the next corner. I think I'll pull in this driveway and ride on the sidewalk for a while. I ride on the sidewalk for about four blocks and I see a couple more "No Bicycle..." signs, but no more cops. So I hop back on the road and ride for about a mile, until I come to where Highway 2 comes to an Y. This is as far as I want to ride today, and, luckily, there is a motel right across the street. As I check into the motel the lady behind the desk (the owner) says that a lot of touring cyclists spend the night in this motel. It seems that her husband and herself do a little touring themselves.

Anyway, the room was $30.08. A little expensive. To get my bike into the room, I have to push it up some stairs. This isn't much fun, but I accomplish it satisfactorily. I lean my bike up against the wall of the room, and then I immediately go into the bathroom and put the toilet seat in its proper position, up. There is a right way and a not so right way of doing things, like putting toilet paper on its hanger. I unroll my clothes and lay them out on the bed. They're wrinkled but I figure they wouldn't be wrinkled anymore after a few weeks on the road than they are right now.

I take a relaxing shower and set out for the local pub. It's a typical early summer night, slightly cool with fat, full clouds shaped like potatoes filling the sky. The only pub that's within walking distance is a very nice establishment, not exactly my kind of place. I like to go to bars where the real local people hang out, not the phony, all dressed-up tourists. So, I have one drink and leave. There is a pizza parlor right next door, so I go in and have a pizza and a few more beers.

A little flashback here. Last Sunday evening when I arrived at the *American Youth Hostel* in Seattle, the first thing I wanted to do was to take a hot shower, which I did. After cleaning up I walked down to the wharf. I thought I would be smart and conserve on my clothes, so I didn't wear any socks or underwear. (The underwear isn't important to the point I'm trying to get across, but I thought you might want to know anyway.) When I walked to the pier, which was only about five blocks away, it proved to be a mistake because now I have blisters on top...yes on the tops of all my toes, on both feet. They don't bother me at all when I'm riding, but I can tell they are there when I'm walking.

I've ridden 107 miles today, with an average speed of 12 mph. Not too bad considering all the wind I had and the shimmying in the front of my bike. It's 11 o'clock and I'm going to go to sleep now.

*   *   *

*Statistics for **DAY THREE** Wednesday, June 14, 1989.*
107 miles of riding today, 12 average miles per hour for today, 321 miles of riding in three days, 107 average miles of riding per day.

Day Four

From Spokane, Washington
To Troy, Montana

At 6:00 a.m. I look out my window and see a sunless dawn, foggy and overcast and it looks COLD. It's not very conducive to getting out of bed. I'm moving kind of slowly this morning. I haven't packed anything yet. I think I'll walk over and get myself some breakfast.

After getting back from the restaurant where I had a good breakfast. I decide to rest a second. Then I get started packing. Sometimes it's hard to get started in the mornings.

I get on my bike. The owner of the motel told me that there was a bike shop about three miles up the road, but he didn't know what time it opened. I'm going to ride to the bike shop and see if they are open yet. It's not raining, but everything is wet. The clouds are hanging low and the rain feels very close.

Well, the bike shop doesn't open until 9:00 a.m. It's 8:30 a.m. so I'm going to ride on. I guess I'm sort of impatient. I hate to wait on anything. I'm sure I'll see another bike shop along the way, somewhere. It looks like rain.

It's 65 degrees and I'm in Spokane. I just rode past a freshly mowed cemetery with small American flags waving on the graves. It looks like I have about a 5 mph tailwind.

My bike is wobbling pretty badly so I stop to look at the front wheel. I'll have to stop at the first bike shop I see I just can't pinpoint why my bike has all this front end wobble.

I follow Route 2 out of Mead, heading due north toward Chattaroy in mild, partly clearing weather. I ride through an evergreen forest with tall pine trees lining the road. They go on for miles…and miles…and miles…

Let's see, what can I tell you about pine trees. Well, they are tall and shaped sort of like a dress. They move gracefully in the breeze and they smell awfully good. It's the kind of tree I would like to lie under and just take in its beauty. God…! I'd better call my girlfriend tonight. I'm feeling kind of romantic (if you know what I mean.)

I'd have a lot better average mph if I didn't have all this front end wobble. I can't ride over 17 mph and I can't seem to figure out just what the problem is. I put a little oil on the wheel bearings. I know they are sealed bearings but I do it anyway. Maybe, just maybe, it will help. I do a lot of what I call "simple fixes." Like taking the light bulb out of the oil light, when it won't go off, and turning the radio up when the car starts knocking. Sometimes they work and sometimes they don't. My motto is "If It Ain't Broke Don't Fix It."

I hate that sign I see just up ahead, "Passing Lane Ahead."

I have 20 miles on the odometer. I'm near Chattaroy. It's still overcast and I have about a 5 mph tailwind. It's early in the morning so my energy is at its peak. As the days pass I don't feel stronger or weaker, but I feel better every day.

There is a lot of traffic on this road.

There are miles…and miles…and miles…of green pines everywhere I look. And the air has a scent of pine in it. It's nice, really nice. The shoulder of the road is about three feet wide, clean and smooth. It's really nice, too.

I look across the road at this great looking log cabin. I don't think it matters a whole lot how good your house looks on the outside. After all, it's the house across the street that you'll be looking at all the time anyway.

I just saw a small kid riding a bike in his driveway. I remember when I was young and riding my first bike. I would coast down hills. I couldn't reach the pedals with my feet, so I would put my shoe on the top of the front tire and wedge it against the fork and that's what I used for a brake. I had to be very careful. If I applied them too much, I would fly over the handlebars. To this day, I believe that this is where the automobile industry comes up with the term, brake shoes.

I haven't seen any road signs since I rode out of Spokane.

There is no wind or cars. It's nice and quiet.

I'm climbing up what looks like is going to be a very long hill. The hills out here sort of surprised me since they are gradual and long…very long…

My girlfriend would like this hill. It's long and hard.

This is only my fourth day of riding and I've already taken over 100 pictures.

At 10:39 a.m., I'm two miles north of Milan and the road is very good. I have excellent riding conditions through some very pretty territory.

There is about a foot wide crystal-clear stream running in the ditch, right next to the road. Its narrow stream is constantly doubling back on itself. It's making little ripples and waterfalls as it rushes down the hill. It really sounds neat.

I recall how once, in a part of my youth, in the spring of the year when the snow was melting and running down our driveway, I would build little dams to divert it. I remember this one time in particular. It was down at the north end of our pasture where a creek funneled into a culvert and ran under the road. Well, when I dammed up a culvert, and the water got so deep that it ran over the road. The county had to come out to unblock it. The culvert was under ten feet of icy cold water. Needless to say, I got Hell for that one.

If there is one thing I'm for, it's the Wilderness. The more the better. Let there be more woods and fewer people. Oh Sure…! And where do I live? In L.A.

The people in charge of pollution control in California have decided that motorcycles ought to be smog-checked and proofed. They haven't gotten around to the big diesel buses and trucks just yet, but, Hey…! When you who get trapped behind one of those rigs and find that your clothing, lungs, and the front of your vehicles are bathed in a fine black, oily mist, take heart in the fact that a motorcycle will never bother you again.

* * *

Ah…! There is another small kid trying to ride a bicycle that's too big for him. I remember my first real bicycle. It was my cousin's first. He joined, or got drafted, I didn't know which, anyway, he went into the Army. So he gave me his bike. I was in the second grade at the time and the bike was way too big for me. I didn't care. I loved that bike. I couldn't wait to get home from school so I could take my bike for a walk. I can recall the very first time I actually rode that bike. I pushed it to the top of this (small) hill. Actually, all there is in Indiana, is flat or rolling terrain, but being a kid, it looked like a big hill to me. There was a small dirt road going into this field near the top of this hill and there was a wooden gate across it. I would lean my bike up against the gate, climb up on the gate, and get on my bike. Then I would put my right foot against one of the vertical boards in the gate and push-off as hard as I could. It would be just enough to keep me rolling until I got to the road, where I could coast down the hill. I would wiggle and wobble as my bike zigzagged at the slowest possible speed. I think that the hardest thing about learning how to ride a bike is the pavement. But you've got to start somewhere. I recall it was great fun for me. On weekends, after my chores were done, I would spend most of the day pushing my bike up the hill and coasting back down again. As I got a little older and taller, and could just reach the pedals with the tips of my toes at the top of the stroke, I would give them a quick little push ahead. It would be just enough to keep me going on flat ground. I would have to wear my shoes when I rode because the only way I could stop, was to put my foot on the front tire. Needless to say, the older and taller I got, the easier it was for me to ride.

* * *

The hills are actually very lush and green out here.

At 11:35 a.m. I've ridden 42 miles. I stop for breakfast or lunch or whatever you want to call it in the town of Diamond Lake. On an old pickup parked outside the restaurant is a sticker that reads, "Save a Tree, Eat a Beaver," which I thought was nice. I'm in favor of saving all the trees possible.

The waitress comes over to me with steaming hot buns. Her name is Mabel (I could tell by her nametag). She leans over the counter right in front of me. I think she likes me…! I can see her heart pounding faster…and faster…as I tell her all about my tour. She can't believe I rode my bicycle all the way from Seattle. She says, "I should think you would be very thin from bicycling all that way." Laughing, I replied, "I probably would be if I didn't eat everything in sight." She just smiles. I have another breakfast, biscuits and gravy and hash browns and, of course, my coffee. I love breakfast. It's my favorite meal, no matter what time of day it is.

I'm on my way again now. I just crossed the Pend Oreille River so I guess I'm in Idaho now. Crossing a State Line is a milestone for me. It's a time when I can put my old, beat up, map away, open a brand-new fresh one, and let my imagination run wild about the roads I'll be riding on in the upcoming days.

The shoulder of this road isn't nearly as smooth those in Washington.

I stop at the information booth in Newport and ask this girl behind the counter if there were any bicycle shops in town. She's all pink and perfumed and as cute as a button. She's wearing a tube top, but she doesn't have any tubes. Her jeans are very carefully torn in exactly all the right places. She answered me and says, "I don't know, I just started working here today." She's cute, real cute. If I were to be called into court my defense would be, at no time did my eyeballs actually leave my body. I'm riding through town, but I don't see any bike shops.

Just out of town I ride past a lake with a beautiful backdrop of pines.

I think I grew up in a time frame when girls clung to their virginity. There were a few girls that were a little freer than others and I thank God for Judy and bless her heart for being one of those girls.

Trucks as long as freighters are roaring by me. They are delivering a blast of wind that's like the blow of a fist. I like to keep my eyes on the road ahead. I'm not too worried by what is coming from behind me because I know that I'll soon enough see them out in front of me. I feel safe. Truck drivers are professional drivers and the safest drivers on the road. They pay attention to their driving; listening to their C.B.'s for road conditions, and of course, to find out where the Smokies are. They are not singing along to rap music (if you can call it that). They are not looking at the scenery, wondering all over the road. They are not stressed out from listening to kids fighting in the back seat. They are not arguing and shaking their fists at their wonderful wives sitting next to them.

Eighteen wheelers are BIG, as though they're the Goliaths of the road, and the tiny two-wheeled bicycles are the Davids.

Being a cyclist, I'm free to follow the lure of the open road at will, without significantly polluting the environment or taking up more than a fair amount of the earth's space.

Being out here in the fresh air for four days has cleared up my eyes so I can actually see without squinting. There is a lot of bark on the shoulder of the road that has fallen off the logging trucks going by.

It's 1:07 p.m. as I turn off the main road to ride through Priest River and see if there's a bike shop there.

There isn't.

I've still got my 5 mph tailwind.

I smell sawdust. I just love the smell of sawdust but I don't like what it represents. You may say we have to cut down trees to make lumber so we can build new homes and make paper. I'm not against that at all (if they replant). What I'm against is, I read somewhere, that 75% of all the wood cut in the United States was exported, mainly to Japan. I believe in planting trees not cutting them down. Woods make oxygen. Each tree planted absorbs 13 pounds of carbon dioxide every year.

I just saw an absolutely beautiful girl and my hormones are racing.

A little info here. After the male spider mates with the black widow, she eats him. Now that's gratitude for you. What's wrong with this picture? It seems to me that something is backwards here.

Just a few things I get pissed-off about: When you walk into a restaurant and there's a sign that says, "Please Wait to be Seated." You stand there for five minutes all alone and when the hostess finely comes over she says, "How many…?" Now is this girl blind or just stupid? Another thing that pisses me off, is when the hostess asks a guy or young lady carrying a child, "How many…?" and the parent answers two-and-a-half. These halfwits are surely talking about themselves as being the half because their life is half over and the child's has only began.

I've always considered myself to be a very easy-going person. But, actually, there are a few things that get on my nerves a little. Like when someone smacks their lips when they are eating, or when someone puts a fork full of food up to their nose and smells it before they eat it. And how about people who grab a hold of their fork like it was a baseball bat then they bend down close to their plate and scoop the food into their mouths. Why use a fork at all?

As I look across this lake, I can see a lot of heavy clouds washing across the sky and some of them are getting very dark.

I sometimes think of myself as a single current in a deep river. It's a wonderful feeling.

Trees, streams, and wildlife all surround me now, and I'm free to wander wherever I please. The freedom of bicycle touring feels good, so good that I'm starting to sing to myself. I only know two tunes, one of them is *Yankee Doodle*, and the other one isn't.

You ought to see all these beautiful green mountains out here. The hillsides are covered with a hundred shades of pastel green that are constantly changing from mile to mile.

I have 60 miles on the odometer. The sky, rivers and lakes are a deep blue as I ride on an open road that seems to slant down around the earth. The spokes of my shiny two-wheeler are slicing through the atmosphere as if I was sailing six feet off the ground. I'm on a machine, not in one, with the wind blowing in my face.

God, it Feels Good…!

This country road is becoming a little rough, but the sweet fragrance of pine makes up for it. As I ride out of Laclede, there are huge stands of forests all along the road. I feel as though I'm feeling the landscape rather than just driving through it and glancing at it through a car window.

There is no shoulder on this road, but traffic is virtually nonexistent, so it doesn't matter. Every once in a while I get an opening in the forest and I can see a beautiful, blue water lake, surrounded by tall pine trees.

I still have my 5 mph tailwind and it's 70 degrees.

I don't believe that there is any other setting as enjoyable for bike touring as the country with its fresh air, bright skies, trees, creeks, and birds that are all around me. The openness of long roads and the freedom of buildingless horizons combine to make this one of the most rejuvenating pleasures I could have.

It looks like it's finally starting to clear up a little…just another beautiful day. I've ridden through Drover and now I'm riding into Sandpoint to look for a bicycle shop.

These saddle sores I have are similar to a pimple. They don't bother me much, but they let me know that they're there.

*   *   *

It's 2:37 p.m. and I finally find a bike shop. As I walk in the shop, I can't help but notice this tall, bowlegged guy. (His legs are bent like a caterpillars). I imagine it's from being in the saddle for more than forty years, and I don't mean a bicycle saddle. He's got a head that seems to be much too big for his body. He seems bored as he stands behind the counter cutting an apple in half just to watch it turn brown. I tell him what my problem is (front-end wobble). He slowly answers and says, "Well, you got an awful lot of weight there." I say, "Yea…but it's not any more than the manufacturer recommends." Much to my surprise he holds the front brake on and there is enough give in the fork to rock my bike back and forth about an inch. It looks like an awful lot to me, but he says, "That's normal for this make of bike. They're just not built strong enough." He seems to know what he is talking about so I have him check the headset out. It is all right. Then he checks and tightens the front cone a little, but he says it is all right the way it is. Then he checks the spokes, to see if they are tight enough. They are. He looks the rest of the bike over and can't find anything wrong with it. I feel like I should buy something from him, so I ask him how much his spokes were as I wanted to replace the spare ones I had used. He says, "They're about fifteen cents apiece." So

I say, "Give me five for each side of the rear wheel." As he is getting them, he asks me about my tour and where I live, and work. I don't think he likes *Rockwell International* or maybe he thinks I made a lot of money or something, because as soon as I tell him where I worked his eyes light up and he becomes as happy as kids at the annual arrival of Christmas. He says, "You know there are a lot of different kinds of spokes. I'll have to look the price of these up in my book." Well, he decides they are 45 cents apiece instead of 15. He also overcharges me for his labor. But, I'm easy. I don't want to make a scene. So I pay the man and am on my way, with the bike handling the same way it was before. But I have a much better feeling about it now, knowing that there isn't anything mechanically wrong with it.

* * *

It's 3:21 p.m. and I stop at McDonalds. There are a few clouds floating overhead that look as if they might contain some rain.

I have 80 miles on the odometer and I'm four miles north of Sandpoint.

When I get a nice tailwind, like I have now, with my panniers protruding outwards, and me sitting in an upright position, I'm sort of like a sail in the wind. I feel like I'm flying along freely, much like I imagine the hawks feel, gliding through the sky effortlessly, not even flapping their streamlined wings.

It's so nice and peaceful out here. There is an unbelievable difference between being out here, and being in Los Angeles. Like there isn't enough noise in L.A. already, with all the busses…and trucks…and trains…and cars…and airplanes…now everyone's going out and buying alarms for their cars. You can hear these damn things going off all the time and nobody pays any attention to them. So what's the use of having them? A lot of these alarms are motion-activated, so you can just imagine what it sounds like in even the slightest earthquake.

There is no shoulder on the road now. Now answer me this: How come they have enough cement for miles and miles of highway dividers, but none to fill in the potholes?

It's great to be out here in nature, all by myself. I may not be sharing this with anyone at this exact moment, but it's something I'll never forget and I will share it with my closest friends, someday.

From the top of this knoll I'm on, I can look out over what appears to be an almost endless open area of perfect, unspoiled wilderness. Except for the road and its neighboring ribbon of railroad tracks there is no sign of man anywhere. The pine forest is unmarred by logging. It's spread out like a soft green comforter through the valleys and curled around the lakes and the waterfalls. I'm gliding down the face of this plateau and following alongside the Pack River. There is almost no traffic. The birds, waterfalls, wind, and the river are the only sounds I can hear as I cycle through all this natural beauty.

The railroad tracks parallel the road and, maybe once a day, I see a train go by. The engineer always blows the whistle and waves to me. I guess he's glad he's not in a car, or maybe he's a cyclist too?

I still have a 10 mph tailwind as I ride through Colburn. It's 68 degrees. The shoulder is about a foot wide and it's been flat to slightly downhill for the last 10 miles, so I've really been flying along. It's hard to get started some mornings but when I'm riding like this it's hard to stop. It's really nice.

When I was planning this tour, I purposely avoided looking at topo maps and elevation charts. Naturally, I had to study road maps in order to pick out a route that's safe and legal. But I think you can over plan a tour. I mean, if you know what's around every corner and over every hill, why bother doing the trip at all? It seems to me that you've already taken all the adventure out of it.

It's a green wonderland of pine trees out here.

There is a sign that says that I have a 6% down grade for two miles coming up just ahead.

At the bottom of the hill, I stop to put some more film in my camera.

I'm one mile north of Naples and I'm riding through what I believe to be the most unbelievable scenery in the entire west. As I stop at the top of this pass and look ahead, I can see that between the mountain passes are large, lush, lazy valleys that enchant me with their seemingly undisturbed calm.

I stop in Bonners Ferry to check out the camping and find that there is a *K.O.A. Campground*, but there is no tavern or restaurant close by and I need both.

I ride on through town and see what's there. I just coasted down a mile long 6% grade, right in town. It's just a series of never-ending climbs all through this area. I don't see anyplace I would even consider spending the night at on this end of town so I keep riding out of town. There is no way I'm going to ride back up that 6% grade to the *K.O.A.* The Cascades and the foothills of the Rockies are slowing me down a little with all of there up and down roller-coaster hills. I'm getting numb in places girls don't have places. It sure looks like rural America out here with half broken-down, knotty fence posts with rusty barbed wire strung between them.

I'm five miles west of Moyie Springs and I'm on this bridge overlooking what I would describe as the *Eighth Wonder of the World*. There is a fast flowing river far…far…below. And its banks are all lined with large trees of all shapes and sizes and colors. It's just a breathtaking sight.

As the mountains become higher…and higher…the climbs longer…and steeper…the woods becomes thicker.

It's 7:00 p.m. and I've ridden 115 miles today and I decide to stop at a little roadside park. I don't know if camping is allowed here or not so I ride over to another person that's camping here. He's wearing a cowboy hat that looks almost as old as he is. He's got a faded outline of a *Copenhagen* container in his back pocket. As I talk to him, he chuckles and says "I don't know if its legal or not to camp here and I don't care." Then he spat a shot of amber nectar on the road. I'm riding over to a spot at the far side of the park where I think I'll put my tent up. It's been a long day and I don't know of any other place to camp on up the road.

On second thought, I'm going to ride on. This place is full of ants and I have an uneasy feeling. Back in Bonners Ferry in a convenience store, I ask if they know of any place to camp. I suggest that no one should even bother asking directions of a Bonners Ferry native. Somehow they think its funny to misdirect people and they don't even smile when they're doing it. But they laugh inwardly; it's their nature. Anyway, they suggested this place, and at the time the store was full of a Hell's Angels type motorcycle gang, and they were looking for a place to camp, also. They know I'm planning on camping here tonight, so I think I'll just ride on into Troy. If I were to camp here, I just might wake up dead. The one I presume was their leader was a tough-looking guy wearing a studded leather jacket. One of the others had a leather headband, and they all carry knives. I wonder why you have to have a license to drive a car and to own a gun, but you don't need anything to carry a knife, which is capable of inflicting a wound just as lethal? Anyway, when I ask directions to the campsite they stare at me as if I was from outer space. I'm sure they were thinking, "He's wearing pretty little britches…Lets Kill Him…!" Even though I don't believe in evolution, the backs of these guys' hands were dragging on the ground. They were definitely a close descendant of apes. My Cycle-ology is to stay in towns anyway.

*   *   *

It looks like Troy's another 25 miles. God…! Another 25 miles. Oh Well, never say die. The sky is overcast and the wind is at my back

There are thin, low-hanging clouds in the sky and not a bit of wind. It's been perfectly still for the last 10 miles. It's getting a little chilly though, so I just put my wind jacket on.

I'm still riding toward Troy.

There is very little traffic out here, mostly pickups with gun racks in their rear windows. One had a bumper sticker that read; "Keep Idaho Green, Shoot a Developer."

I hoped I could ride at a leisurely pace and take it easy these last twenty-five miles. I figured wrong. Four miles out of Moyie Springs I come to the wall; (cyclists call a very steep, usually short hill, a wall). After riding 120 miles today, I really don't think all these hills are necessary. Anyway, I'm in my small chain ring climbing up another hill. As I wipe my tongue over my lips, they taste like salt. Oh Well…! I figure the difficult I can do right away…the impossible will take me a little longer. The sun is setting; the sky is blue, pink and salmon colored with the salmon reflecting on a nameless mountaintop.

I'm riding into Montana. This is where I ride out of the *Pacific Time Zone* and into the *Mountain Time Zone*. I'm not sure if I like the sound of that or not. I'm going to change the time on my watch and camera tonight. I've ridden all the way across Idaho today and I never saw a potato field.

My map tells me that it's about 14 more miles to Troy. The sun is fading fast. Happens every shittin' day about this time. It's still light enough to ride without a light, but I think it's too dark to take anymore pictures.

There is lots of beautiful country out here. The pine trees are growing straight and tall, right next to the road.

It's starting to drizzle a little bit now it's 64 degrees.

Jesus…! These trees are beautiful, I wish I could take more pictures.

It's sprinkling enough now that I'm going to put a baggie over my computer, put my camera away and put my raincoat on. Just goes to show that I should always stop riding before dark.

I'm sure sorry it's too dark to take my 130-mile picture.

It's 8:51 p.m. and it's still sprinkling very hard. When riding a bicycle there's no such thing as getting a "Little Wet." It's just like being pregnant, you either are or you're not.

I'm getting tired. I have to stop and rest a minute. There were a lot more hills in the last 15 miles than I really need. Let me tell you, the sensations resulting from sitting on a bicycle saddle for 12 hours just can't be explained. It can only be appreciated by someone who has experienced it themselves.

After riding in the dark these last few miles I've decided that a bicycle is a daytime vehicle. It should be used when the sun is up and parked when the sun goes down. Riding at night can be very dangerous. You simply can't see. You can't see the rocks and nails on the road or potholes filled with water. The potholes may be an inch deep or a foot deep. You can't tell which from their appearance. I have to stay clear of them or they may puncture my tube or even worse, bend my rim and I'll probably spill over the handlebars.

These roads are unpredictable. Some are well maintained, and others are left to rot in the weather year after year. It's impossible to tell from maps, which are which. Most country roads that I favor for unharassed riding are not the super roads that get all the attention. This means that I have to watch for such hazards as potholes and bumps. Rain, wear and tear, and lack of proper maintenance erodes the asphalt of country routes.

Worse yet, people have a difficult time seeing me at night. I don't recommend riding after dark for anyone. Bicycle lights are totally inadequate. A biker is a daytime animal. He's not naturally nocturnal. When he ventures into the night, he ventures into high risk. My visibility is narrowing as the rain increases, but I can still see the pine needles tipped with teardrops of rain. My rear wheel is sending out an arc of spray.

As the lights beam out from Troy into the night, they spoil the view of the sky, but they are a welcome sight just the same. It's 9:13 p.m. and raining steadily as I check into a motel in Troy with 140 miles on the odometer. It's raining enough to get everything soaking wet.

As I lean my bike up against a small tree, BIG, COLD drops shower me. I'm soaked.

I still have this pain in the ass. I've never had a saddle sore before, but I've read about them. Some of the things you can do to help prevent them are keep clean and wear clean shorts, which I do. I shower as soon as I finish my ride every day, and I put on a clean pair of shorts every day. I don't know why I got them, and worst yet, I don't know how to get rid of them. I have some *"Second Skin"* in my first aid kit. I'm going to put some of that on in the morning and see if that helps.

I go to my room and replace my wet suit with dry, warm clothes. Then, seeing as how there aren't any bars in sight and it is still raining, I run over to a coffee shop next door. Coffee has a special taste on nights like this, and the third cup is as good as the first. As I run in, I notice this sign above the counter that reads, "Buy one hot dog for the price of two and receive a second hot dog absolutely free."

This man with sunken eyes and a three-day growth of white stubble whiskers and a bright red handkerchief wound very loose round his neck was sitting at the counter. He looks like a character so I sit down next to him. As I talk to him, I notice that he has his shirt buttoned all wrong. We talk and I learn that there is a 15-mile stretch of road construction that's dirt up ahead and, seeing as how it's been raining, it's mud now. He doesn't know if I can get through or not. As I sit there talking to him, he picks something from his teeth, and then he wipes it through his greasy hair. He says that there is up to a two-hour delay. I'll just have to see what tomorrow brings.

It's 11:00 p.m. and I'm going to go to bed. I know it's going to be a rough day tomorrow. There is a sign just outside my room that reads, "Road Construction, bicycles take alternate routes." But I'm choosing not to.

*   *   *

*Statistics for **DAY FOUR** Thursday, June 15, 1989.*
140 miles of riding today, 13.7 average miles per hour for today, 461 miles of riding in four days, 115 average miles of riding per day.

Day Five

From Troy, Montana
To Columbia Falls, Montana

It's 6:42 a.m. The day has dawned clear and crisp.

I don't know about all this road construction. Last night a guy told me that they only escort cars through once every two hours and they don't let bikes through. Bicycles are supposed to take alternate routes, but I don't want to. This is the route I planned on taking and that's just what I'm going to do, one way or the other. I don't exactly know what I'm going to do. I'll just ride up there and find out, I guess.

At 7:20 a.m. I start to ride. All Right…! Here's my plan: I'm going to ride through town and keep my eyes open for a restaurant.

This road's rougher than a Bitch…!

I have my windbreaker on because it's pretty damn chilly out. This early in the morning I've got the road all to myself. The cool air, combined with the wind, quickens my pace. Steam is puffing from my mouth and nostrils and rising off my shoulders as I climb a rather large hill. I'm about three miles out of Troy now. I rode all the way through town without finding a restaurant.

I can see a girl standing in the middle of the road with a stop sign in her hand. She really didn't need the sign. I would have stopped anyway. She's about as pale as a ghost and she has no chin. Her neck starts right under her lower lip. But I've been on the road for a long time and she looks like a diamond in the rough to me. She isn't the friendliest girl I've ever met, though. The first thing she says to me is:

"Didn't you see all the Detour signs?"

"Well, yes…" I say, "I saw some signs that said that bicyclist Should…take alternate routes, not that they had to."

"Well, that's what it meant…" She say's "You can't get through here. You'll have to go back and take an alternate route."

"That would be at least a two-day Detour for me." I say, "How about if you just look the other way and I'll ride on through?"

"You would get a $200.00 fine, and I would get fired."

"Well," I say, "We sure don't want that."

Then she starts to soften up a little and she says, "The only way you can get through here is to find someone with a truck and put your bike in it."

There was a pickup with an Escort sign on the back of it right in front of me. So, I say, "How about if I were to load my bike in the back of that pickup truck?"

Then she started to turn ugly again, and says, "There's no way you can put your bike in that truck. We don't carry insurance to haul people's bicycles around."

With that I said, "Have a nice day," and turned around, and leave.

I have about an hour wait in the early morning frosty air before the next escort goes through. The cars are starting to line up already. I'm COLD to the bone (its only 54 degrees). I consider myself to be pretty much like an old bear, in the winter I like to hibernate. As I ride by the second vehicle in line, which was a camper, I see an elderly couple sitting behind the windshield. Their faces are old but beautifully lined, and their gray heads are almost touching. He looks to be about 70, and she is maybe a year or so younger. As I slowly ride my bike by, the driver rolls down his window and says,

"What's the matter, young feller? Won't they let you through?"

I say, "No…! I have to find a truck to put my bike in."

He say's, "Let's just throw it in the back of my camper and I'll take you through."

"Thanks," I say, and he opens the back of his camper and we push my bike in. He asks me all about my tour, and then he goes on to tell me all about himself. It seems his wife and himself are both retired and living in Canada. He tells me that they travel a lot since they began to enjoy their poor health. He asks me if I have had breakfast yet. And, seeing as how I hadn't, he climbs into the back of his camper and brings out some bananas, oranges, and apples, which his wife cuts up, and we all share. That is awfully nice of them.

As I stand around waiting for the escort to go through, the sunless morning wind slides down the mountain like an invisible river, engulfing me in COLD. I didn't know I would be standing around in the cold or I would have dressed warmer. All I have on is my jersey and shorts.

A guy dressed in faded jeans and a brown plaid flannel shirt in the car in front of us gets out and sets up their camp stove. He brews a pot of coffee for all of us. It sort of brings back my faith in people. The steam from my hot cup of coffee thaws the ice on my brows and the water runs down my nose and drips into my cup.

It's almost time to go through the construction now and there really isn't enough room in the camper for me. So, a guy in the car behind us say's, "Hop in, there's plenty of room for you in my car."

So I do. All the cars are lined up in the middle of the road. Off to the right in a large parking lot, there are about eight logging trucks, waiting. Then, when the escort leaves, the trucks are the first to follow. These logging trucks only have two hours to get through the road construction and get unloaded and get back in line, so they can get escorted back to get another load. If they are a little late, they have a two-hour wait until the next escort goes through. Seeing as how they get paid by the load, they stand to lose a lot of money and that's why they get to go through first.

As we start rolling there are some gray-black storm clouds blowing in from the northwest.

The guy I'm riding with, who, incidentally, lives in the next town, says we are lucky it rained last night or we would be going through this in a cloud of dust created by the logging trucks. After the first mile of construction, I can easily see why they wouldn't let bikes ride through. It would be impossible to ride or even walk a bike through this mess. The escorts are going through as fast as they can to accommodate the logging trucks. The road, if you can call it that, is unbelievably rough. I'm worrying about my bike bouncing around in the camper. In some areas, where it's dirt, now mud, it has deep ruts. In other areas it's solid granite with potholes big enough to lose a compact car in. Then, to top it all off, where they just blasted part of the mountain away, it looks like they only took one pass through with a bulldozer, to scrape the worst of the debris off. There are still very sharp, jagged, pieces of granite in the road. I tell you, I'm sure glad I'm not driving my car through here. It just beats the shit out of your vehicle. This isn't exactly my idea of a good time.

This guy I'm riding with is very tall. I would guess him to be about six foot-six. He has an oval face and his head isn't very big, but he's got big popping eyes (gray). His once-sandy hair has almost gone gray. After listening to him for a while I come to the conclusion that he is a college idiot. I mean, he's using big words, but he isn't using any common sense. I believe he was a professional student. He says that his house and farm are filled of all sorts of weird inventions, some of which actually work. He says that it's true that people either passionately love Montana or passionately hate it. Then he goes on to say that he's planted here as solidly as a church. As he adjusts his spectacles on his long nose that inclines to one side, he asks me, "Why did you take the northern route?"

After I explain that to him, he asks me, "What's your philosophy of life?"

I say, "My philosophy or cyclolosy is: Life is a journey, not a destination. I say, have fun. Eat, drink, and shift before you have to. See everything you can and stay in towns, and go to bars. I'm proving to myself that I'm tougher than I thought I was."

I go on to say that we're all individuals. Each one of us is different from the other. Our social and financial status, our education, our religious, and our political convictions are all different. Let's face it, most men find it threatening to leave their jobs for even a two-week vacation. They think,

"How will the company ever get along without me?" I have an Aunt that refuses her vacations every year in fear the company may learn the answer to that question. I don't want to be a normal, average, ordinary, a typical person. That sounds a lot like the setting on a washing machine to me.

He asks me if I have any fears. I tell him I have a fear of snakes. He tells me that I should fear the redneck ranchers, cowboys and farmers around these parts more than the rattlesnakes. He tells me not to tell anyone that I'm from California, that overpopulated strip of America, teeming with drug addicts, perverts, hot tubs, and super-slick real-estate agents.

Anyway, talking to this guy, as we bounce our way through the construction, I find out that it will take them another four or five years to finish widening this 15-mile stretch of road. That's because it's solid granite and it's very hilly. They have to dynamite their way through most of it. Then, to make things even worse, there's no alternate route close by so they have to shut down their operations every two hours and halfway clean the road off to let the traffic through. Plus, they can only work in the summer months, which are very short up here.

There is sure a lot of construction going on up here. Boy…! They use some big equipment. Where it's dried out a little all this huge construction equipment is generating enough dust to clog up any car's air filter.

Thank God…! We're finally through the construction area.

The guy I'm riding with says to me, "What if the guy in the camper, with your bike and all your equipment don't stop?"

"Well," I say, "In that case, I won't have to ride any farther, will I?" To that he answers with a grin on his face, "I'm sure you'll make it across the United States all right. You have a fantastic view of life."

I believe what I'm doing made him feel very proud.

Well, the camper does stop and we unload my bike and say our farewells and go our separate ways.

*   *   *

I stop in Libby for breakfast. I don't consider the bananas and oranges and apples I had earlier, breakfast, although they did hit the spot at the time. I don't believe it's a real breakfast unless it's been floating in grease.

At 11:40 a.m. I leave the restaurant. It looks a little like rain and I have a 10 mph crosswind. White popcorn clouds are spread across an incredibly beautiful sky.

The wind is whistling off the peaks that tower all around me as I climb another hill in low gear. Have you ever been on a roller coaster and you just can't wait for it to stop? Well, that's how I feel about this road. It's just a hilly roller-coaster ride, which seems to go on forever.

I can see this bicycle shop a little ways off the main road, so I ride over to take a closer look at it. Its called *Whiskey Hill Ventures*. Of course, it's closed, but it's kind of neat, being way out here, miles from anything. You know if people would pay more attention to the really important things in life, there would be a shortage of bicycles.

It's overcast, but it looks like it's clearing up a little, up ahead. I stop and oil my chain and put some more air in both tires. Maybe, just maybe, it'll make it a little easier climbing up all these hills.

There sure are a lot of hills out here, and some of them really get my attention. I go back and forth between my little chain ring and the middle one. With this crosswind, and all these hills, I haven't been in my big chain ring yet today. And it doesn't look like I will be for a while either. All I can see ahead of me is hills and wind-bent trees.

There goes a red fox across the road. That's the first wildlife I've seen.

With 14 miles on my odometer the headwinds have picked up to a gusty 20 mph and I feel that it's completely unnecessary…! The wind is semi-cool (62 degrees) and it smells like pine oil.

Riding through here I don't just see green. I can see at least twenty-two shades of green.

I'm in my small chain ring, down on my drops, battling sharp gusts of wind that are blowing back the leaves of the trees. The hills out here aren't to be sneered at. I'm just barely moving along. But, nobody said it was going to be easy.

Route 2 passes through green forest and fields and on occasion goes around a blue pond.

Whal…! You should to see this…! There is a herd of horses running with their tails stretched out behind them. It's a sight which, once seen, can never be forgotten. This is definitely the right way to raise horses. Running wild, in huge fields, with lush green grass, and a pine forest where they can go for shade and shelter. This is the way it was meant to be. They almost look like wild horses.

There is very little traffic out here and I feel as healthy as a horse myself.

I have a chilly headwind. I'm surely glad I've got this windbreaker. It would be mighty cold without it.

* * *

Seeing these horses reminds me of a date I once had. No, she wasn't a horse. I met this girl in a bar, and we made a date for the following Saturday night. I was to pick her up at her place and we were going to go to the beach. She gave me her phone number. I was planning on calling her before Saturday night, but I had a slight problem with that. You see, she lived with her parents and I had forgotten her name, and what if her mother answered the phone? So I just waited until Saturday night, and drove over to her house, in my off yellow 1978 Ford station wagon, with a caved in roof and hood. The roof and the hood got this way because I park it in the alley behind my apartment and the neighborhood teenagers like to use it as a springboard. They would get a running start and jump on the hood and spring onto the roof. It may have been fun but it sure caved my hood and roof in. Anyway, as soon as I find her place, I know she isn't in my league. The place is a mansion. It has a gated circle driveway. Fortunately, the gates are open. As I drive in, I notice a shiny BMW and a Mercedes parked in the open six-car garage. Now, money is second rate to me. I believe that the only good thing to do with it is to spend it right away. I'm tempted to drive right on around and leave. But, I'm thinking, what the heck, I told her I would be there, and being a man of my word, I slowly pull in and turn the motor off. I believe it's trying to tell me something, because even though I've turned the key off it continues to run, for a few minutes.

As I get out with flowers in hand, these two big, and I mean BIG...! Dogs come running toward me from around the corner of the house. They aren't Dobermans but they are huge. Without any hesitation I run back to my car, open the door and jump in and shut the door, and roll up the window. After a few minutes, which seemed like an hour, a Spanish-speaking gentleman comes around the corner of the mansion and calls the dogs off. They leave, so, I gather up the flowers, that are half-broken and half-deleafed now, and head for the mansion again. This time I make it. I ring the doorbell. No, there isn't a rope to pull like I thought there might be. This lady, dressed in what I would consider an evening gown (but of course it isn't because it isn't evening) opens the door. Now, I had had a few drinks (actually quite a few) when I made this date, and I don't exactly remember what my date looks like. This lady looks a lot like her but she looks a to be a little older.

So, not remembering my date's name, I say, "Is your daughter home?" Well, her answer to that is, "I don't have a daughter, but my sister is upstairs. You may go in the den and wait." I'm thinking, good show, Harold. Talk about making a good first impression.

She shows me to the den. The house contains rooms the size of airplane hangars with marble floors, like a museum or official building would have. Her mother and father are both seated in the den. This room has two vases of flowers that make mine look like weeds, sick weeds. The room is full of modern things, fancy things people don't really need. I see a gold cigarcase, made of something else, I'm sure. As I walk past the bathroom, I notice these gold trimmed towels, you know the kind used only for guest and decoration. We say our hellos, and then her father asks me where I met his daughter. I don't think I should tell him the whole truth that I had met her in a bar, so I just said I met her around campus. He's about to ask me another question, when luckily my date comes down the stairs and rescues me. I thought I was dressed nicely until I see her. She's dressed fit to kill, and I have clean underwear on. We can see right away our ideas of a date are totally different. I hate dating anyway. It's so intimidating. It's obvious that I'm underdressed or she's overdressed. She suggests that we take a walk out in her back yard, so we can talk a little.

Her back yard is unbelievable. It's landscaped like a Beverly Hills park. There are gardens, and a smooth green lawn that would make a splendid golf course. First, we walk past her Olympic-size swimming pool, with a high diving board. Then past an enclosed Jacuzzi with a full wet bar. Next, it's past the tennis courts and out to the gazebo, where we sit and chat a little. Now, I'm not good at making conversation, which she could pick up on right away. I used to stutter when I was in grade school, and the kids would tease me so I hated to talk at all. Once in a great while I still stutter so I don't talk unnecessarily to this day. As we chat, I find out that I've mispronounced one of my favorite words for years. After she finds out that I used to be a farm boy, she asks me if I would like to see her horse. I say sure...even though I don't especially care for horses. I don't like any animal that's bigger than me. As we stroll over to the far end of their property where there is a small barn, I have this funny feeling that I shouldn't be stepping on the grass. It's too well tended. She goes up to the middle double door, of which the top half is open, and calls for her horse to come to her, which it does. As it sticks its neck and head out the door, it towers over me. I reach up to pet it on the nose, and it lets out a big snort, blowing snot in my hair. By this time, it goes without saying, I have decided that this is the last straw. She (and I say she because I never did find out her name) isn't exactly my kind of girl anyway. I'm sure she has never been in a *K-Mart* or *Denny's* or even heard of a *"Blue Light Special"* or a *"Grand Slam Breakfast."* So, we say our goodbyes and I gladly leave. So, that is why horses remind me of a date I once had.

*   *   *

Back on the road at 1:04 p.m., I'm seventeen miles south of Libby. Off to my left is a crystal-clear mountain stream winding its way through the foothills, furnishing some horses with cool, clear water. I can smell the grass and trees and see the hills and ponds. This country is wild and beautiful and unspoiled.

This wind is just terrible though. I'm in my middle or small chain ring all the time. The sun is starting to break through the cloud cover. It sure feels good. I don't like being cold. That's one of the reasons I moved to California from Wisconsin.

The wind is blowing in my face, increasing my effort and cutting my speed down to a crawl. The two major factors in bicycle touring are hills and wind. No bike rider likes hills (except maybe a few skinny, lightweight, young, energetic kids). After you grow up and put on a few pounds you learn to dislike hills. At least uphills, the downhills are all right. When you're as big as I am and you are carrying 40 extra pounds in your panniers and another 20 in your mid-section, it's hard to climb up hills, let alone mountains. In the mountains I don't only have to deal with the steep grades but there is also the altitude factor. The air is thinner and it's harder to breathe. I keep looking at my tires, it feels like I have two flats, but, of course, I don't. It's just uphill and windy. The hills and the headwinds are making my ride very strenuous, but the road surface and all the spectacular scenery make it quite enjoyable.

There are some really thick, lush, woods all along here, with a large variety of trees and plant life in them. Spring is an outbreak of color. It's dominated by green because it's a new season. I'm falling in love with Montana, just like I did with Washington. I hope that's all right with Washington. These woods bring back memories of my childhood days, of when I was out in the field working and it would start to rain. I would get off the tractor and take shelter in the woods, much like these. Being in the woods during a rainstorm has a very relaxing, peaceful, safe feeling about it. It's just you, and all nature's little critters, taking shelter from the rain. As I recall, it would be pouring out, but I didn't get wet at all. I would sit there on a fallen tree trunk and look up and see all the leaves moving with every drop of rain that fell on them. They acted like a natural umbrella, protecting everything under them. Then, the fresh rainwater slowly trickled down the branches of the trees and gently dropped to the ground, watering the delicate wild flowers and other vegetation that wouldn't be able to withstand the harsh pounding of the rain. Just to be in the woods during a thunderstorm and witness the vast number of events taking place is…well…it's something you have to experience for yourself. I can't explain it. All I can say is that it's something everyone should make it a point to do, at least once in their lifetime.

When I get a strong headwind, like now, I tend to stop and take a lot of pictures. That way I convince myself that I'm not stopping to rest, I'm stopping to take a picture.

I'm riding into fierce headwinds all the way, but it's beautiful just the same. There is a line of pine trees that winds along the road as far as I can see. To the west I see nothing but the unbroken green forest stretching its way to the horizon. I'd say it's certainly worth stopping and taking a picture of a scene this beautiful.

It's uphill all the way, but at least with all the trees it gives me a little windbreak, every once in a while. This is some of the most difficult, yet still pleasant riding, on my tour yet. The fresh air is intoxicating and these bubbling mountain streams, and delicate wild flowers throughout this area, are fantastic. The smells of spring really dominate out here.

There are some buildings with tin roofs off to my right. It reminds me of when I was a kid, when I was outside playing, around the house, and it would start raining. I wouldn't run for the house. Another favorite place for shelter was in the corncrib. From there I could hear the rain pounding on the tin roof. And, as I looked out through the slots, I could watch the rain run off the roof, which would make a small stream that ran down our driveway. Then, as soon as the rain stopped, or let up a little, I would run out and dam it up, but I guess I've already talked about my dams.

These unfavorable headwinds are forcing me to stop and rest at a marvelous forest overlook. As I eat a granola bar, I wonder just what kind of wine goes well with granola bars? I eat slowly, listening to the gurgle of a nearby stream and to red-winged blackbirds talking to each other.

Bicycle touring is a great way to travel. I move slowly enough to see and hear things that to passing motorists must be only blurs of color and void of sound. I take in the textures and odors of the soil and the vegetation. And, because bicycling is such a quiet mode of travel, wild animals aren't frightened away when I ride up the road toward them. Deer, accustomed to seeing and hearing huge, noisy boxes of accelerated steel on the road, often just stand at the edge of the pavement trying to figure out just what I am.

The winds are continuing to slow me down. I have to take another break here. It's been a very hard day's ride so far. I'm twenty-six miles south of Libby. I haven't been in my big chain ring yet today. A 20 mph headwind has changed into a crosswind now. It's a lot better, but I still have to stay in my small chain ring.

Boy, I'm really tired, but I figure a hard day of riding is still better than an easy day at work.

I'm going to stop and take a picture here just to show that not everything out here is beautiful. The state of Montana has marked spots of fatal car crashes with small, pole-mounted steel crosses, one cross for every death. They should put up a huge cross here, because this forest is dead.

There is no telling just how all this got burned off, but it really doesn't matter. The fact is it's DESTROYED...! And that's a real shame.

It's 63 degrees out, which is very chilly for a southern California boy, even though I have my wind jacket on. I still have a 10 mph crosswind that's blowing a little on my back and a little on my side, I guess you would call it a back-cross-wind.

According to my map, there is supposed to be a town around here somewhere, but I sure didn't see any.

For days now I've been riding through heavily wooded land, abundant with lush green grass and wild flowers and birds and squirrels and rabbits and everything that goes along with nature in its natural habitat. And now I'm riding through this burnt-off area, and it's just heartbreaking.

I have about a 10 mph tailwind now. But it's rolling terrain so I'm only in my middle chain ring. I don't have much more to say about this burnt-off area, except I can only imagine how beautiful this little stream would have been flowing through a lush forest.

I'm learning to appreciate all life forms rather than merely those that are considered beautiful, remarkable, or useful. Even though I live (exist) in L.A. I really try not to insulate myself from nature or the weather. I say, go barefooted whenever possible and build a sand or snow castle (depending on where you live) and enjoy all that nature has to offer.

I don't know how many years ago this fire took place, but it's sure a shame how a fire of this magnitude can literally destroy a forest. A tree, a hundred years old, can be destroyed in just a few minutes. Just think about it. A century of surviving all the natural elements like the heat, and the drought, the rainstorms and lighting, and the wind, and disease, and the harsh winter storms. Then, after surviving for 100 years, it can all be destroyed in a few minutes by one careless camper, or by some idiot throwing a cigarette out the window.

I think it should be mandatory that everyone plants a tree, at least once a year.

As I ride through this nine-mile stretch of burnt-off trees, with overcast skies, I feel a little gloomy. The bright rays of sun help to change the atmosphere with a little ray of hope, and I'm finally out of the burnt-off area. Thank God…!

Riding along out here is so different from riding is L.A. The blue water is sparkling between the trees and the air smells fresh and clean. The birds are singing, the cows mooing, as squirrels scamper across the road in front of me. There are no noisy machines running out here. No loud speakers squawking and no air compressors running. It's really nice.

I just came across some road-kill, a porcupine. Contrary to what most people think, porcupines are perfectly harmless. They don't throw their quills, and they are edible. They are the only animal that an unarmed man can kill for food. They're so slow and stupid that they can be clubbed to death if necessary. No Intelligent woodsman would ever kill them for sport because he knows someday he may be in a spot where a porcupine could save him from starvation. Some states, Montana, for example, have game laws to protect the porcupine for this very reason.

I'm getting hungry and my water bottles are getting dangerously low. It's 3:36 p.m. and I have 45 miles on the odometer as I stop in a small town called Happy's Inn. At the Deli a man stands by the door, his weatherworn hands parked in his front pockets. I go in and have two big bowls of vegetable soup and a piece of apple pie a la mode and coffee. It's great.

I sure hope there are not a lot of hills up ahead, because it's getting late and according to my map there are no towns for the next 40 miles.

There goes a huge deer across the road, or maybe it was a moose or an elk. I don't know, it was obscured by the trees, except for its ass . . . and it sure was BIG. It's really good to see wildlife on display like this. I may not be walking on the wild side, but I'm riding on it.

I ride past Thompson Lake. I feel a lot better…now; it's warmed up to 65 degrees. There is very little traffic on this road. I'm in second gear riding up another hill. It seems like I've seen and ridden over a lot of mountains but I'm sure these are nothing but small hills compared to The Rockies that I have to cross over. I think the worst is yet to come.

The big blue sky couldn't be any bluer.

At 58 miles, I have to stop and rest. It's 4:58 p.m. and I'm ten miles east of Happy's Inn.

*   *   *

There goes another deer across the road. Being from Wisconsin, I know that the cutest, sweetest animal in the woods is a newborn fawn. They are not reddish-brown like their mothers; they are spotted tan and white. That's so, when they remain still, like they do in the presence of danger they look like just another patch of sun-dappled shadow. There is nothing quite as defenseless as a new little fawn, so Nature takes over its protection until it can at least outrun the more deadly of its enemies. Not only does a fawn become practically invisible when it stands still, but it has no scent whatever to betray its presence. A dog that can smell a deer a half a mile away will pass a fawn almost within touching distance and never turn its head.

This road sure has a lot of corners in it. Part of the time I have a tailwind, and other times I have a crosswind, then it turns back into a tailwind. After climbing my way up this long hill, I finally get a rewarding descent that's offering me a very impressive view. For the last 5 miles I've had about a 10 mph tailwind and it's been slightly downhill, so I'm making really good time. I'm riding along as swiftly as the wind itself. By now,

I've learned that when I get a tail wind, no matter how little it is, I take advantage of it. Like they say, "Make hay when the sun shines" and "Ride when you have a tailwind," because I know that within a matter of a few hours it could turn into a headwind. With my panniers creating a tremendous amount of extra aerodynamic resistance, fighting against a headwind can be really exhausting.

As I ride along and look up at the sky, there are unusually white clouds floating against a very blue sky. I notice that the conditions out here (out of Marion) are ideal for raising beef cattle, as well as horses. When I lived in Wisconsin, I used to raise Polled Herefords, as a hobby. Out here, with all this green grass to eat, and trees for shelter, and a stream for them to drink out of, they would practically raise themselves.

This countryside just goes to prove the old saying that the grass is always greener on the other side of the fence is true. I don't know how the winters are up here. They might not be too bad, seeing as how I'm still west of the Rockies. This pretty much makes up my mind for me. When I hit the lottery and retire, I'm going to buy a ranch and raise Polled Herefords again. Not necessarily here, but somewhere that has ideal conditions, like this. This is the way cattle should be raised, not in feed lots.

For the last 7 miles it's been slightly downhill and I'm riding on the wings of a friendly wind. The scenery is magnificent, and I'm a happy camper. This is a bent and narrow rural American two-lane road. The nature of the road kind of describes the nature of my travel. Only when a car goes by, or birds land nearby, is the silence broken. I never know what to expect around the next curve. I'm riding through beautiful valleys, and hills, past geese-filled lakes and through picturesque little towns with spectacular views. It just doesn't get any better than this.

The road winds through inter-mountain meadows where cattle graze and birds sit on the guardrails and watch me as I ride by. I don't think I've ever seen it more beautiful than this. On one side of the road are calm-looking mountains, and on the other, there are cattle grazing waist-deep in rolling grasslands that are full of wild flowers. Occasionally, a deer will cross the highway, emerging from a forest that looks like a haven for all wildlife. Pines and oaks and redwoods are surrounding meadows that are bright with poppies and other wild flowers. Hawks soar overhead, riding thermals and diving into the pastures below, which are filled with cows.

As you can imagine the cycling, and the scenery, are outstanding.

It's 6:55 p.m. I have 82 miles on the odometer as I ride out of Kila. The road, without warning, is rolling off a plateau of woods and entering into an enormous sea of green, broken only here and there by the rivers and streams that run through it. I'm wandering all over the road admiring the natural wonders. As far as my eyes can see, there is nothing but green rolling pastures. It's one big cow pasture as I see it, with a flowing stream at the foot of a gentle slope.

I'm four miles west of Kalispell.

WOW...! I just got a magnificent glimpse of the steep mountain rising abruptly in the south. It's covered with snow. It looks like I'll be riding in BIG Hills Tomorrow, HELP...!

The temperature has dropped to 58 degrees. A pickup, then a van pass me, very slowly. The van is covered with stickers from, what looks like, a 100 different attractions.

Is this beautiful or what? There is a combination of a rocky mountainside rising sharply out of a grass valley that's full of yellow wild flowers swaying in the wind like Kansas wheat. The pastureland has a few horses running free. I think I'll have a few horses, running free, on my ranch, also. It sure looks to me like the people and animals are living right out here. You know, there is a big difference between living and existing and I can see it all around me.

It's 9:00 p.m. as I ride down Main Street of Columbia Falls. It sort of looks like a ghost town. I look for a motel. If you find me to be short with words that's because I believe a person learns a lot more about things by doing them than by talking about them.

After 112 miles I find a motel on the outskirts of Columbia Falls. The afternoon sun is dropping behind the mountains, leaving the little hotel in a chilly shadow. I'm going to get cleaned up and get something to eat. The first thing I do every evening, after my shower, is wash my riding clothes out in the sink and put them on the heater to dry. That way I will be all set for the next day.

They've got a swimming pool here that's open until 11:00 p.m. I haven't been swimming yet, so that's in my short-term plans. I left a 5:00 a.m. wake up call at the office. That's because I have to get up the Going-to-the-Sun Road tomorrow. Bicycles aren't allowed on it between 11 a.m. and 4 p.m., so I have to get to the top before 11:00 a.m. I have to get up very early, eat breakfast, pack, get ready, and be on my way.

These saddle sores are getting to be a pain in the ass. I think where I might have gone wrong was that I always wear underwear under my cycling shorts. Old habits are hard to break, and my mother always made me put clean underwear on every day. She would say, "Just in case we get in a car accident," even though she knew we weren't going anywhere. I recall it was kind of disturbing because just when they were starting to fit well she would make me change them. Riding shorts are made in a way that you are never sitting on a seam, and underwear isn't. And when you sit on a seam, it causes extra pressure in that area and that's the main cause of saddle sores. The second skin I put on this morning seemed to help a little. I'm going to try riding without underwear tomorrow. The only draw back to not wearing underwear is that riding shorts are so tight that anyone can easily tell what religion you are, or aren't.

I've been carrying all this camping equipment with me. I only used it once so far, but that's all right. At least I have it if I need it and I know it's good equipment. I have a lot of cold weather clothes with me. After I ride over the Rockies tomorrow, I can mail some of them back to California. Hopefully, I won't need them after that.

I didn't have any problems with my bike today, except for a little front-end wobble. I've already taken more than 150 pictures.

My motel room was $38.00 for tonight, but let me tell you, it's worth every penny. It's got a restaurant that's open at 6:00 a.m. for breakfast, and it's warm. I got cold today and it sure feels good to be warm again. If I were camping out it would be very hard for me to get warm. And the bed has nice clean, white pillowcases and sheets on it. They've been washed so many times that there as soft as snow, but much warmer.

It's midnight now. I'm going to stay up a little longer and call my daughter and let her know that I'm still alive. I'm sure she's not home this early on a Friday night.

*   *   *

*Statistics for **DAY FIVE** Friday, June 16, 1989.*
112 miles of riding for today, 12.7 average miles per hour for today, 573 miles of riding in five days, 114 average miles of riding per day.

Day Six

From Columbia Falls, Montana
To Browning, Montana

I'm up with the sun at 5:15 a.m. As I pack my panniers, I find my gear is falling into all the familiar nooks. I'll be ready to roll soon.

I finally got hold of my daughter on the phone last night so she knows I'm fine.

I left the window open and I fell asleep with the smell of pine and fir entering my room. I push my bike out the door and onto the gravel parking lot until I reach the paved road. One hour and a half after getting up I begin to ride. I really don't know how cold it is out here but I can see my breath. It's like riding into a walk-in freezer, but I'm dressed for it. It's hard to enjoy a tour no matter how beautiful the scenery is, if you're not comfortable.

It's another 15 miles to West Glacier. As I ride beyond a ridge just east of Columbia Falls, there is a radiant gleam from the rising sun on the horizon. It's illuminating the tall grass in the fields with a golden glow.

The morning has dawned brilliantly clear. It's a beautiful crisp day. The early-morning sky is the color of a bluebird's egg. The dry, frozen air is coming out of my nostrils in plumes of steam as I ride along. It's COLD…it's really COLD…My thermometer says it's 45 degrees, but it's probably still dropping because I had the thermometer inside my room last night. Let me tell you, when I stepped out of my warm room into the cold, crisp mountain air, it woke me up, real fast.

It's dawn and the sun's casting its rosy, rising light on a fog blanket that's hanging over a small lake off to my left. I'm sure the fog is there because the water is much warmer than this COLD…COLD…morning air. As I ride along, it's, quiet, and damp. The road ahead looks like its going to be a long…long…long…uphill.

It's been a gradual uphill climb for the last three miles.

I'm one mile south of Hungry Horse. Boy…! I can really see my breath out here…! All the houses have smoke coming out of their chimneys. I just love the smell of pine burning. There is steam rising off the wood fences where the sun is shining on it.

I'm not kidding when I say I'm riding in the frosty morning air. It's damn COLD out here…! I haven't been this cold since I lived in Wisconsin, about 17 years ago. Now I remember one of the reasons why I moved to sunny southern California. I don't think there is anything I hate worse than being cold. In Wisconsin they have the four seasons, Early Winter, Mid-Winter, Late Winter, and Next-Winter. Winter is when the days are two hours and fifteen minutes long. The weather was more than enough to tell me that I was living in the wrong place. I remember that when the weatherman would say "Frostbite Warning" this meant, do not go outside with any part of your skin exposed. It was during this time that the lake would freeze, everybody's water pipes would freeze, the streets would freeze, the people walking on the streets would freeze, cars froze, even dogs and cats froze. I guess the birds had good enough sense to go find a condo somewhere in Florida (and you say, bird brain, I think not). I also recall that all the small towns in Wisconsin brag and say that their town is so safe they don't have to lock their doors at night. Well, that's because they are all frozen shut.

Anyway, back to my ride. Two beautiful deer just strolled across the road and stopped to look me over, as if they thought they might buy me. Then they seemed to agree that they could do better for less somewhere else and they strolled off.

The early morning hours of today are foggy and therefore, very quiet. I'm all bundled up here with a lot of warm clothes on. I have my riding shorts, leg warmers, wool socks, a long-sleeved jersey, a wind-jacket and these wool gloves on. My bike helmet is made out of part Styrofoam, but I don't think it's the best insulation there is.

There is no wind at all. The surrounding countryside is nice and quiet. I have 10 miles on the odometer as I quietly slip through Coram in the crisp air. You know, I don't think noisy men can hear God.

On early mornings like this the air seems even colder than it really is. The air feels almost icy as the stream from my nose hangs suspended in my mustache. As I ride into *Glacier National Park,* I stop to read a sign that tells me that in 1932, *Glacier National Park* in the United States and *Waterton Lakes Nation Park* in Canada were joined to form the first *International Peace Park* in the world.

I think I lost my radio somewhere, I didn't see it when I was packing up this morning. But it really doesn't matter, I don't think I'd use it anyway.

This early morning spin on my bike is a real treasure. I stop to take a picture of the peaks that have now leaped skyward. The mountains are very vertical now. They're standing up tall and proud. Only the snow is covering their nipples, Oops…! Tops. (I think I had better call my girlfriend tonight.) I just took the last picture on a roll of film, so I have to take off my gloves and change the film.

I'm going to ride on up the hill without my gloves on and see how it is…it's about 45 degrees.

Forget it…! I rode about a half a mile stopped and dug my gloves back out of my handlebar bag and put them back on. It's COLD…! My feet are a little cold but otherwise I'm keeping fairly warm. I'm convinced that it's obstacles like these that constitute a real adventure. As you can see, cycling involves more than just turning the cranks.

I'm riding alongside Lake McDonald. The lake is nine and a half miles long and 473 feet deep. It's a big lake. The sun has melted the morning frost and the earth is beginning to warm up a bit, but I'm not. I stop to take a picture of a tree as the light filters through the forest and makes the new leaves of the elms look a pale green. As I take the picture a car going by slams on his brakes and stops. I guess he wants to see what I'm taking a picture of. He's a little disappointed when he asks me what I'm photographing and I tell him "A Tree." I can't help it, I like trees.

I stop and take another picture…it's beautiful out here. I haven't started to really climb any major hills yet. I don't know if I'll ever get over this Pass if I keep stopping to take pictures. There are just too many Kodak moments.

I'm getting comfortably numb, now. My hands are so cold that I have a hard time grasping my handlebars and shifting the levers. I just reached down to shift into a lower gear and I couldn't feel the levers, so I reached a little farther and stuck my fingers into the spokes of my front wheel. I can feel my fingers now.

As I'm riding along, cutting my way through the crisp morning air, the sun is slowly rising above the snow-covered mountain peaks ahead of me. As the sun's soft ray's filter through the trees, they seem to pick up a greenish tint, from the pine needles. My girlfriend's eyes have this same greenish tint and they sparkle like the rising sun. God…! I miss that girl this morning.

There is a campground with a lot of tents in it. I feel sorry for them…they must have frozen last night. I can only see one campfire. I've got to say one thing about a campfire on cold morning like this, if you stand next to it, the flames warm one side of your body, but not the other. Then, when you move away a little, it's COLD. I have to admit it, though…I do like the smell of the redwood needles, the fresh sap, and the burning wood as it fills my nostrils. A peaceful feeling has settled over me as I listen to the sounds of the river and the crackling fire as I slowly ride by.

It probably feels so cold out here because I'm riding in the shadows of the mountains and trees pretty much all the time. As I ride through this deeply forested canyon, the light is slowly filtering through the needles of the huge shaggy cedars. The trees are growing very tall and they are right along the side of the road.

There is a fast flowing stream that really sounds bubbly as it winds its way through the hills, right next to the road. I stop just to listen to a stream running under the road and watch as the sunlight breaks through and reflects off rocks along the stream. The stream I'm paralleling is so clear I can see all the small stones in its bed. The water has a greenish tint to it…it's sort of a jade color.

A car with New York plates pulls up and a young man gets out and asks me, "What do they put in the water to make it that color?" I tell him, "It's natural that's the way our rivers are supposed to look."

This is one of those places where I really forget about all the climbing and just soak up the scenery. I'm riding very slowly but after all…some things just shouldn't be rushed.

It's 9:04 a.m. and I'm twelve miles east of West Glacier. I'm crawling along this valley with views of McDonald Lodge. I'm surprised to see that they have horse rentals at the Lodge. Riding through *Glacier National Park*, every view seems to be better than all the others. I can't believe how crystal clear the air is out here this morning. This two-lane country road I'm riding on is following a stream. In some places it crosses and recrosses it in others.

A sign back they're said, "Don't Feed the Bears." I'll try not to. I remember when I was riding my Harley from Wisconsin to California back in '69. While going through *Yellowstone National Park*, I came across a sign that read, "Don't Feed the Bears. Stay in your car with your windows rolled up." Well, I came to a spot where four or five cars were stopped on both sides of the road and one guy had rolled down his window just far enough so he could throw out a piece of bread, which the bear gobbled up in one bite. That was fine for everyone in the cars, but here I am sitting in a traffic jam with nowhere to go, with this hungry bear going from car to car…coming toward me…looking for food. The only thing I could think of was to get off my bike and lay on the ground and play dead. So I lay there, as still as my ex-wife used to in bed, but it didn't work. The bear killed me anyway.

This is proving to be an easier climb than I expected it would be. I've been in my middle chain ring most of the time, the small one only once in a while. There is no wind at all, but it's COLD…colder than the moon's backside. I just saw my breath freeze in front of my face. But, it's beautiful up here. There is a sign that says that the mountain peak off to my left is 8,900 and some feet above sea level. The road I'm riding on is still following a crystal clear mountain stream. It has long, rippling runs and emerald pools.

Living in southern California as I do, where the climate is near perfect all the time, I would consider this to be extremely COLD. It's only in the upper 40's. Believe it or not, there are people in California who get bored with good climate all the time. They prefer weather to climate and maybe, just maybe they are right. When most people retire from L.A.…they go to Oregon…Washington or sometimes…even Canada. I've never heard of anyone from Oregon…Washington…or Canada moving into L.A. to retire.

I've ridden 32 miles so far today, and it's 9:37 a.m. 9:37 a.m. Hell…! I didn't even start riding yesterday until 10:00 a.m. and I still got 114 miles in.

There is a bunch of little bitty flowers all along the road here. They're smaller than the tip of my little finger. There are blue ones, white ones, and yellow ones. You wouldn't even see these traveling by car because in a car you can only stop at designated turnouts where the overlooks usually consist of a view of the massive mountains. You miss seeing all of the smaller beautiful things of life. Riding my bicycle, I can stop any place and any time I choose and smell the flowers. Traveling by car, you get the big picture…traveling by bicycle you get the whole picture.

I see a big deer standing right in the road ahead. It could be a moose or an elk, I'm not sure. I have a thin sheet of ice covering my eyes and it's a little hard to see through. It's so cold I have to keep blinking my eyes so they don't freeze shut (or open) on me. There are a lot of ferns and little patches of wild strawberries with really small white flowers blooming, all along this section of the road.

The road just turned. Now I'm heading directly toward a huge wall of the mountain that looks impossible to ride up and improbable to ride around. In this land the mountains tend to hurl the rivers abruptly and savagely downward. But this river which feeds the lush forest on both sides is running along somewhat quietly. It's as if it's in no hurry to tumble through the Rockies to reach the sea, as if it were reluctant to leave such a secluded peace.

The river has turned into a fast flowing river again, paralleling the road.

I must be at a very high elevation by now, but the climb so far hasn't been too challenging. It's been a long gentle climb. I'm nineteen miles east of West Glacier. I have about a 5 mph tail wind and it's 52 degrees. This is a very nice road with very little traffic.

The trees line the twisted highway as I ride in and out of their shadows. Windows of light peek through the forest and through these openings I can get a quick glance of some absolutely beautiful snow-covered mountains.

* * *

At 36 miles I come to a horseshoe turn in the road and that's where the climbing really starts. I'm down in second gear now climbing steadily. From here the road ahead looks almost vertical…it shoots straight up from the flat riverbed and seems to disappear into the clouds. Traffic is creeping up and slowly passing me as I ride along at a snail's pace. One motorist with smoking brakes shouts to me as he comes down the hill; "It's much too steep to bicycle up."

I'm climbing this hill and working up a really good sweat, so I'm going to stop to take off my windbreaker and gloves and eat a granola bar.

A car, with a bike rack on top (but no bike) coming down the hill stops to asks me if I have plenty of water and food to get me over the Pass. He offers me what he has, but I don't need it, I have enough with me. He wishes me good luck and is on his way. It's reassuring to know that there are still a few of us nice guys left.

The narrow, shoulder-less road is squeezing its way through a narrow pass. The road looks as though it was made by an overturned pot of tar at the summit and it hardened as it ran a crooked course down the mountainside. As the road turns skyward, every muscle and all the weight and energy in my body is going into each slow, deliberate stroke of my legs.

Because the road is so narrow (it only averages 16 feet wide) bicyclists aren't allowed on here between 11:00 a.m. and 4 p.m. It's 10:40 a.m. and it's obvious to me now that I'll never get up this hill before 11 a.m. It seems to go on forever. I read somewhere that a park ranger comes along in a truck about 10:30 a.m. and picks up anyone that's not likely to make the summit by 11:00 a.m. but I haven't seen any.

This section of the road is called the *Garden Wall*, I guess that's because it was hacked, blasted and scraped out of a solid rock wall. It's low gear all the way up this sucker now. This roads so crooked it could run for the legislature.

I've got to stop and put my jacket back on, it's pretty damn COLD up here (55 degrees). As I continue to pump my way up this hill, I'm locked into my lowest gear, hunched over my handlebars, thinking of anything except the fun I'm having at this exact moment. I tell you, if I'm not in shape now, I will be at the end of this tour.

From my vantage point very high and picturesque mountains with secluded waterfalls surround me. I can see way down in the valley below, where I was riding earlier this morning. There were a lot of little birds, chirping and singing away down there, but up here only eagles dare to soar.

I guess it's hills like this that separate the real men from the boys.

It's 11:00 a.m. I'm twenty-five miles east of West Glacier.

I'm supposed to be up the hill now, but I'm not. From what I've read, most of the time it's cloudy or foggy and there is usually very poor visibility up here. That's one of the reasons why bicyclists' aren't allowed on this road between 11:00 a.m. and 4:00 p.m. when the traffic is at its heaviest. But it's a perfectly clear day today, and there is very little traffic, so I don't think the rangers will say anything to me.

Now that the morning is getting on, more and more vehicles are passing me.

Every once in a while I get a real COLD 10 mph headwind, and with me sweating, from the hard climb, the cool air makes me shiver. This seems to be a never-ending 6 percent grade. It doesn't slacken as I ride higher…and higher…

Take note of this, there is a sign that says, "Scenic View One Mile." Is this a motor vehicle-oriented world, or what? I mean, here I am riding along, and all around me is nothing but stunning, never ending, panoramic views that require no signposting. I relish my ability as a cyclist to savor it continuously. Being a cyclist, I don't just occasionally look at the landscape, I pass through it, all of it, not just at vista points.

There is a waterfall right in front of me, and a little further up the road I can see a second spring oozing out of a wall of rock. As I slowly…very slowly…ride along, I'm getting a magnificent bird's eye view of the stream and the valley far…far…below. All around me are high mountains and deep valleys and glaciers and the sky and clouds and the wind and sun and rocks and two thousand-foot drop offs. Everything is so massive that it sort of makes me feel a bit insignificant

I stop here for a while, hoping to cement the images, not only in my camera, but also in my mind. The filtered sunlight is accenting the many shades of green in the valley far below with soft, angled light and deep shadows. The blue sky is offsetting the mountain peaks. As I stand here, I'm trying to take it all in. But there is much too much beauty. I can make out the campground with its blue smoke curling up gracefully from the campfires against the darker hills. I stand here looking upon the mountain scenery for quite some time…it's a rare treat for me. I get back on my bike to creep on up the mountain. There are no clouds to obscure my view of the chain of mountains that tower over the left side of the road. Cars are slowing down and shifting into their lower gears, and creep along behind me through the twists and turns until it's perfectly safe to pass. Then they ease by, usually waving or calling out encouraging words to me. I've read somewhere that this is rated as one of the 10 toughest climbs in the United States.

It seems the higher I climb the colder it gets. It's dropped down to 52 degrees now. My legs are working like pistons as I strain my way upward…forever…upward. This is taking an all-out effort on my part. It's taking all the breath I have since the air at this altitude is thin and has very little oxygen. The trick to a two or three-hour-long climb is not to look too far ahead…the end is never in sight. I try to take in the scenery instead.

Am I having fun yet? Well, I would say this is almost as much fun as a tax audit.

I've got to stop and rest again.

As I crawl higher…and higher…the natural beauty of the landscape is overwhelming. I'm pedaling hard, taking in deep breaths of cold mountain air as I grunt my way up a series of switchbacks, riding at a snail's pace. The last 12 miles of this hill is going to be at a 4 mph pace. The views from the road are spectacular. The white peaks towering over the dark-blue ridges of the mountains seem to be piercing the unpolluted heavens. Snow is lying in all the shaded depressions.

It's 11:55 a.m. and I'm twenty-eight and a half miles east of West Glacier. It's 50 degrees. For what seems like an eternity, I've been inching my way upward at a rate that feels slower than a walk.

I have to stop here and change my film again. There is a waterfall right alongside the road, which, if it's not, should be featured in travel posters.

It's really chilly out and uphill all the way. I'm in my lowest gear. I can pick out white dots, which are either mountain goats or snow patches. If the dots move, they're goats. I just saw a buff-colored animal on a cliff, which I believe was a mountain sheep.

I know it's spring, but at this elevation the landscape shows no sign of it. I stop and lean my bike against a snow bank. It's cold, but I'm hot, so I'm going to rub my face, neck and arms with snow to cool down.

Now it's time to ride on. I'm breathing heavily and dripping with perspiration. I've got to stop again to catch my breath. It's just an all-out effort for me to get up this hill. I think it has something to do with the 40 lbs of equipment I'm carrying with me.

Only a mountain goat would consider this to be a road. It's a never-ending climb that actually goes up into the clouds. I know at this point and time I could walk faster then I'm riding, but I won't. Bicycles were designed for riding, not pushing. I used to walk my bike when I was a kid, and now that I'm almost grown up, I'll stop and rest if I need to, but I'll never…never…never…walk it.

Most of this road has little or no shoulder and no guardrails. Without guardrails, this is definitely photo album country. But, I'm afraid of heights, and where it's a straight drop-off, it kind of gives me a sensation like I'm riding on a tightrope.

I'm grinding my way up this knee-busting hill at no more than 4 miles an hour, pulling hard with my hands and arms on the handlebars to create enough pressure to move.

I'm stopping again, I'm BEAT…! Every inch of my body aches. In my opinion, this is carrying the "No Pain, No Gain" routine a bit too far. I can see by the road ahead of me, and it's a long way to the top yet.

It's so cold out here…my nipples are getting hard.

You have to be careful when you turn over a new leaf and go searching for adventure on a bicycle-it's easy to find in the mountains, especially the magnificent Rockies, the views are just awesome. But to enjoy them you have to pedal up some mighty steep grades. This one, I'm sure, has ruined many car engines and radiators in its time. Way off in the distance, I can see naked snow capped mountain peaks, just a-sparkling in the sunlight, against a crisp, blue sky. And there, right next to the road, is a small flower in bloom. I believe courage is not the towering oak that sees storms come and go, but it's this fragile blossom that dares to open in the snow.

It's COLD, but the snow is melting in the sunny areas and making spectacular waterfalls all over the mountains. Sometimes they are quite a way off, but they sound like they're right next to the road. As I climb and reach for the clouds I'm asking myself, how much further can the summit be?

I stop to relieve myself in the snow, with a hot stream. I try to laugh but my lungs can't supply the oxygen as I spell out **Alive**. I realize now that everything seems to shrink in the cold. When I was a kid, living in wonderful Wisconsin, I would write my name in the snow this same way. I remember once my mother saw my name written in the snow and scolded me for it. That, I believe, was the first time I took the rap for someone else, you see it was in my girlfriend's handwriting.

My muscles feel tired, but they don't hurt.

*   *   *

Thank God…! I've finally reached the windy summit of Logan Pass…! Mission Accomplished…! I guess you'd say that I'm on a natural high.

I'm standing on top of *The Great Divide*, the granite backbone of this continent. Water that falls on the west side of me flows into the Pacific…water that falls on my east rolls toward *The Great Lakes* or the *Gulf of Mexico*. I'm looking to the West to see if I can see California, and now to the East in search of the Atlantic Ocean. I'm COLD…hungry… and tired…and maybe I'm hallucinating a little.

Right here on the top is what looks like a resort.

I ride up a sidewalk, with snow two to three feet deep on both sides. I park my bike under an overhanging roof. I lock it up and walk up a flight of stairs, very carefully, with my cleats on.

As I enter the establishment, I can see that it isn't exactly the answer to my prayers. I was hoping for a roaring fire, antlers hanging on the wall, and some great food and coffee. Well, as it turns out, it's only a ranger station. Needless to say, I'm a little disappointed. They don't even have coffee or any vending machines. But they do have a fireplace, with a nice warm fire going. I go over and get warmed up and dried off a little. Then I go over to the desk and talk to a ranger for a while. He gives me a little history of the Going-to-the-Sun Road. He says the road was constructed between 1925-1933, at the then-unheard-of cost of three million dollars. He explains how the workmen were only able to work an average of 100 days a year due to the weather conditions. It took them years to blast, clear and pave the 16-foot-wide roadbed up the side of the Garden Wall. He went on to say that the top 12 miles of the hill, on the west side, the side I just climbed was a 6% grade. It's definitely a road that defies gravity.

After getting thoroughly warmed up, I'm ready to take, what I think, will be an easy ride down the other side of the hill.

I proceed to coast down, only to discover that it isn't so easy after all. It's cold and very windy and steep. I'm on my brakes almost all the time. The cold gusts of wind are very unpredictable. They are so strong that my bike and I are blown from the edge of the road to the middle and back again.

One concern I have on this twisting descent, which, by the way, conceals a number of off-camber turns, is not to get so overwhelmed by the scenery that I might become a part of it. Another concern I have is there just might be patches of snow or ice on the road.

My front-end wobble doesn't help any either. It's almost as hard coasting down this side, as it was climbing up the other side. Other mountain ranges may be higher, but I don't believe any are more beautiful. It's towering cliffs, cloud-piercing granite spires, crashing waterfalls, rivers clear as glass, dazzling fields of ice, turquoise lakes, all combine to create one of the world's great scenic spectacles.

It's 1:11 p.m. I have 50 miles on the odometer and I'm fifteen miles west of St. Mary. Because of the elevation, the air is refreshing and the sun is bright but it's extremely COLD (44 degrees). I think I'm suffering from "Scenic Overload," something I thought would be impossible. I'm not going to take any more pictures until I get down off this mountain. My hands are tired from constantly gripping the brakes and my legs are stiff from not pedaling and I'm cold again.

As soon as I round a curve, a gusty crosswind blows me halfway across the road before I can correct my balance and direction. There are no guardrails. Large stones along the side of the twisting road leave plenty of room for an out-of-control bike to become airborne and hurtle it into eternity.

I just had to stop and take a picture of a glacier. All I want to do now is get down off this mountain. The wind is gushing through the cuts in the hills battering me around like a ping pong ball. As I wipe my hand across my brow to clear the sweat from it I immediately find out that it has turned into ice and my fingers are rattling like ice cubes.

I'm going down this hill back-pedaling, with both hands on my brakes. My helmet is floating off the top of my head, not from going too fast, but because the gusts of wind are so strong. These gusts of wind are also unpredictable. I have to hold on and be ready at all times. I'm thinking to myself, this is wrong, going downhill is supposed to be fun. I'm zooming only inches away from rock fences, and certain death, but at this point I don't care, I just want to get down off this mountain as fast as possible. I want to be down where the climate is warmer and the air has oxygen in it. I have to watch out for loose sand and gravel on turns, chuckholes in the road, and motorists coming around blind curves on the wrong side of the road. The thrills of my downhill plunge have to be modified accordingly. It would be easy for me to obtain speeds of 50 or 60 mph on a good downhill, with this fully-loaded bike, but if I were to come to a turn and I miscalculate my speed, I may very well end up finishing the turn on the wrong side of the road, and I'd better hope that there are no cars coming.

It's 2:01 p.m. and I'm five miles west of St. Mary. It's 55 degrees.

Because of the cold weather, my knees and leg muscles are stiffening up as I coast down this long…long…hill. I have a view of a turquoise blue lake that I'm sure was formed by glacial meltwater. The sun's glistening on the lake as if God were skipping stars across the water.

HURRAH…! It's summer again…! The sun's beaming down out of the heavens. Finally, it's starting to warm up a bit. I don't think there is a better feeling than to be warm …well…maybe one, and you're warm when you get that feeling. I'm down the steepest part of the mountain so I can take my hands off my brakes and rest my tired fingers. I'm still riding downhill with a 10 mph tailwind.

There are very few cars on this road and no billboards to obstruct my view of the breathtaking Rockies, and I can say that literally. They really took my breath away.

I stop here to take one last picture of the bright sun glittering off the snow-capped Rocky Mountains. I'm not going to look back again. I don't care if I ever see them again. I'm hungry and I just want to celebrate being alive. I stop in this Deli in St. Mary to eat lunch.

I've found paradise in the shape of an overpriced hamburger, fries and a malt. My bill came to $6.20 but being in a town with a name like Saint Mary (my ex-wife's name, only the Mary part. Believe me she is no Saint) I knew I would get ripped off. I talk to this cyclist that had just come down the same hill I did. He told me that he rode through a patch of a wet road and his brakes got wet and didn't work. He claimed he had just found religion…at first swearing off profanity, cutting his vocabulary by half, and by the time he had reached the bottom he'd decided to enter the Ministry.

*   *   *

I looked at my map and it's only 31 miles to Browning so I'm going to try to make it that far today. I'm over the Rockies now, so, hopefully, it will be downhill all the way to Browning.

Well, it didn't take me long to find out it isn't all downhill. The road stayed level for only about a mile, then it took a skyward bend. I'm starting to climb already, and I'm in my low gear now, climbing what looks like a long hill.

PHEW…! I'm up the hill. It was a mile long 6% grade.

This place, surely, is God's handiwork. It's just unbelievable…! This place has all kinds of trees…flowing streams…waterfalls…lakes…green grass…flowers…Good roads…mountains…BIG mountains…HUGE mountains…and snow and wild animals. It's absolutely everything nature has to offer. This is one beautiful place! *Disney* couldn't have done it any better than this. This is my favorite view in a day full of spectacular scenery.

There are some ducks on a small pond, but they fly away before I get a picture of them.

I'm going to take my leg warmers and jacket off. On second thought, I'm going to leave them on…it's pretty damn cold out.

I'm still in second gear, riding uphill. I've got about a 10 mph crosswind, a very cold crosswind. If I had known this hill was here, I never would have ridden it today. This suckin' hill just keeps going on…and on…and on…I've got to stop and rest again.

I'm so tired even my eyelashes hurt.

Isn't it funny how people generally can do more than they think they can and they almost always do less? Well, I'm doing more than I ever thought I could. I'm really tired, but there's no doubt in my mind that I'll make it to Browning all right. I'm not beaten until I admit it, and I refuse to admit it.

It's 3:54 p.m. I have 70 miles on the odometer and I'm five miles south of St. Mary. The hills on this road aren't as steep as they were in the Rockies but they seem to be endless.

I'm at the top of the hill…!

Shit…! This is only a false top, and the road is still going up…! I'm in second gear climbing a long…long…incline.

I have two empty water bottles, I usually fill them when I stop to eat but I forgot to in St. Mary.

Finally, I can see it, one mountaintop that's higher than all the rest and maybe…just maybe…it could be the top of this man-eating mountain.

The sky is blue, and filled with fluffy white clouds, and the warm sunshine sure feels good. It feels wonderful to be warm again.

It's very hilly out here. I'm soon to realize that there is a vast difference between what I had imagined the terrain to be, and what the reality is. Looking at the map, I presumed that after I had reached the summit of the Rockies, the road would be downhill or at least flat, all the way to the Mississippi River. The map is very deceiving. In reality there is a long succession of hills that I'm climbing with tiresome regularity. I guess I'm still in the foothills of the Rockies. But I still get a sense of contentment that comes through accomplishment. I know that what I have achieved isn't important to the world. No lives will be saved, but it's important to me. It's my one chance to get happiness through achievement.

It's still very rough going, but quite satisfying, just the same. The scenery is fantastic with a lot of abruptly rising snow-capped mountains, which fall again into rolling desert plains.

I think that for many, the phrase *"Bicycle Touring"* brings to mind flower children munching on granola bars, and smelly bodies limping their way through stretches of North Dakota corn fields at a 10 mph pace. The lure of the open road. It's a romantic notion that lures most of us as kids, with thoughts of flowering fields, rugged mountain passes, the songs of birds, and the wind whipping through our hair. All I can say is they should try it sometime. It has everything...challenge...adventure...beauty...accomplishment...you name it.

That's what a tour is all about. Discovering new places and new people. You take your chances. Riding through unfamiliar countryside, crossing the Rockies on the Going-to-the-Sun Road is definitely challenging yet one of the most memorable highlights of my trip. I'll probably begin with telling people about my tour with this story. I knew crossing the Rockies on the *Going-to-the-Sun Road* wouldn't be easy, and it wasn't. But, I highly recommend it to anyone making a cross-country ride. I believe it's one of the last truly unspoiled areas in North America.

At 5:02 p.m., I'm five miles north of Kiowa. The scenery that greets me now runs a broad spectrum. From the snow-covered mountain ranges, to crystal clear rivers, to streams and lakes that boast some of the best trout fishing in the world. There are pine forests stretching to the rolling, emerald pastureland, with skies that are bluer than blue. If I seem to be repeating myself while describing this scenery...you're right. It is just so beautiful at every turn, I can't help myself.

As the road turns eastward at Kiowa I finally get a well-deserved downhill, with a 5 mph tailwind...I can really cruise, now. There really is a God...! It's amazing how a good tailwind and downhill can cure all your aches and pains.

Across the river and ahead, small flowers of white, yellow, and purple, blend into a half-grown grass, bright green with new life that extends to the horizon. The mountains run down the middle of Montana like the ridged back of a giant alligator's tail. White clouds in round balls circle the dark green necks of the mountains like strands of pearls.

I have about a 10 mph tailwind now. Things are getting better and better.

* * *

It's 58 degrees as I ride through the reservation town of Browning. It's a Blackfoot town and has been the headquarters of the tribe's reservation and government since 1895. It's a dirt-poor town. Locals, with seemingly little else to do, stare at me as I ride by. I don't think there's a skid row in this town. The whole town is overwhelming with poverty. As I ride down Main Street, I can't help but to notice all the unpaved side streets with trashy yards and neglected homes and deserted automobiles. I've finally come to a so-called motel. As I go into the office, this burly tattooed manager with short sleeves and no neck asks me if I want a room as he sits there picking his nose and flicking the fruits of his labor at his feet. I think I had better look at the room before I take it. Now, I've never looked at any room before but for some reason I just thought I'd better look at this one. And it's a good thing I did. It's awful…absolutely awful…There's no way I would ever stay here. No effort has been spared to make the rooms uncomfortable and ugly. The bed is lumpy and the walls are a dirty yellow. The curtains are a dark brown and torn. The room has a mixed aroma of mice, moisture, mold and old…old…dust. The sheets on the bed look somewhat clean but the place needs some airing to get rid of the memories of old inhabitants. A naked bulb hangs from the ceiling and the room is heated with a kerosene stove. The lock on the door has chisel marks all around it. I figure if I were to stay here I would probably wake up dead. So, I'm going to ride on through town.

Well, it looks like that was the only motel in town, so I'm riding on out to Highway 2 in hopes of finding a motel on the outskirts of town.

Thank God...! With 95 miles on the odometer I found one! It's also an aging hotel that's not a whole lot better than the last one, but a little. The evidence of poverty is everywhere. It's got a bar right across the road and that's one of the things that are very high on my priority list. So, I'll take the room. It's $30.00 for the night. A bit much, but what's a feller to do?

I've cleaned up and I'm going to a restaurant that's adjoined to the motel. It's Chinese. Just outside the restaurant, leaning on his truck, is a lanky and somewhat muscular man with long black hair. They are about to close, I guess I'm their last customer. There is an unsavory-looking character sitting at the counter cutting his food with a pocketknife. He's an old man the color of leather, an Indian. I finally get my order, which consists of Tofu, brown rice with soy baco-bits, carrots, and, I think, bird seed. I don't care, I'm hungry, and I'll eat almost anything. After a few bites, I figure food that tastes this bad has to be good for me (some kind of health food, I imagine).

*   *   *

After dinner, I walk on over to the tavern to get the healing qualities of beer, and see what's going on. As I cross the street, there are two hoodless muscle cars with their engines exposed. They're crusted with dirt, and they're burning circles in the dirt parking lot in front of the tavern. One is an old beat-up elephant-colored Pontiac and the other is a two-toned sedan, half lime green and half rust. Being as brave as a New York pedestrian I walk on through the dust and go on in the tavern.

It's as dark as the inside of a rock in here. Everything is tinted reddish-brown by the single light bulb that hangs down from behind the bar. Cigarette smoke is hanging like ground fog in the crowded saloon. Almost all conversation comes to a standstill as I walk in. After a quick look around I see that it's a rough and untrustworthy lot in here. This place is packed. With 99% Indians and 98% of them look as if they've been here all day, if not longer. I've always heard that Indians can't hold their liquor and this confirms it for me. Ninety-seven percent of them are carrying knives strapped to their belts, and this includes the females. Two guys are sitting at a corner table just staring at each other. When I walk up to the bar to order a beer, I have to squeeze in next to a guy who has a scar across his face and the seat of his pants is reddish brown and he smells like a yak in heat. A sign behind the bar reads, "No Guns in Bar," and another one reads, "A Criminal is Someone that gets Caught." While I wait on my beer, I overhear this guy and another (who was either stoned or has a brain that has a lot of room to expand) he said, "Do you know what's the best thing about life?" Then he answers himself and says, "It's almost over."

Everyone in here is looking at me like they haven't seen this much white meat since Thanksgiving. Needless to say, I don't feel too comfortable in here. Right now, I'd rather be juggling hot coals.

I was about to set my half-full bottle of beer down and leave. Now, this is against my religion. Beer is good to the last drop. I always order bottles in places like this, for several reasons. One being, I don't believe they clean their taps or glasses very well or often, and because I can always use a beer bottle for protection. I was about to leave when a huge potbellied Injun, named OX (his name really isn't OX, but it should be) comes over and put his arm around my shoulder, and says, "Buy me a Beer...!" Now he's drunk out of is mind. He's wearing tan brown pants and a matching, sweat and beer stained tan shirt that looks like it might have been new, once...but now it looks as if he had worn it to the bar and bed for a long time. The end of his belt runs way past the buckle belt loop, just like I remember my grandpa's used to do. He has missed one buttonhole in his shirt so his collar is all cockeyed, and the fly on his pants is at half-mast. His face is sunburned. He pops a wooden match alight with his thumbnail and lights up an unfiltered *Camel* cigarette. As I look at him in disbelief, he pinches the cigarette out between his thumb and forefinger and pockets it. An act to show me just how tough he is, I guess.

So, I buy him a beer and put my wallet in my front pocket so it can't be picked easily. (You know a wallet is a device that allows you to lose all your valuables at the same time). This Injun is wearing a knife on his side and he's got a scar that runs the full length of his left arm and another one across the back of his right hand. So, I figure he's probably been in a few knife fights. And he's acting as if he's looking for a scalp to add to his collection. I prefer negotiation to fighting, and properly so, since I'm very bad at fighting. Right now, I just want to be invisible. I know I have insurance in case anything happens to me, but insurance is just like wearing one of those hospital gowns, you only think you're fully covered. I can see down a hall, and across from the restroom there is a back door that's cracked open. As soon as I have the opportunity, I excuse myself to go to the restroom. I hurriedly walk down the hall and step over an Injun laying flat on his back speaking in tongues. The hallway is littered with half-burnt cigarette ends and dead matches.

As I push the curtain aside and step into the men's room, which by the way, stinks of stale beer and male sweat and dried urine, there is a big fat Indian sitting on the john with his pants down around his ankles. It's not a pretty sight, and it smells like he just might have died. I'm not hanging around to see. As I stand in front of the sink for a few minutes, just so it looks like I came in here for a reason, an old Indian, a large pile of beef on the hoof, comes in, and grins with a smile that reveals he has fewer teeth than he was born with. He pisses in the general direction of the urinal. As I head for the side door, a skinny woman that looks as though she's been able to get through life without working at all, is coming out of the other restroom. She's wrinkled…pimpled…pale…thin…and has a sharp fox nose…rotten teeth that are black and uneven. Her nose is dripping and she's got a sharp chin, and a long crane's neck. She's filthy, with scabbed hands and wrists and a crooked back. As she hurriedly walks past me, she breaks wind. Now I know women, don't sweat or fart. I just can't believe the old gal did that. And believe it or not, she's carrying a baby. It's definitely time to blow this fine establishment. I go out the back door and walk as fast as I can back to my motel. I know it wasn't Hell in there but I could see it from there. When I turn to look back toward the bar, there is a reddish-orange light from the setting sun on a nameless mountaintop. I figure it's some kind of omen.

I turn and go in the motel. It was a killer of a day. I rode 95 miles with a 9.9 average, not too bad considering all those stupid hills I did. I did a twelve-mile hill, a three-mile hill and a couple of one-mile hills, all with a 6% grade. I'm not doing too well on my camping. So far I've ridden for six days 668 miles 111 miles average per day. So far everything is going very well on my tour (I'm still alive). I just repacked my stuff. I did lose my radio and I'm getting into territory now that I could use it, but that's life. It's 11:00 p.m. now, and I'm going to go to bed.

*   *   *

Statistics for **DAY SIX** *Saturday, June 17, 1989.*
95 miles of riding today, 9.9 average miles per hour for today, 668 miles of riding in six days, 111 average miles of riding per day.

Day Seven

From Browning, Montana
To Havre, Montana.

It's 5:00 a.m. and dawn has come to Browning. It's sunny...cool...and windless. I guess I'll get up and pack.

After one half hour I'm ready to ride back into town to get something to eat. I figure that if I get an early start, I can ride before it gets too hot. I step outside and take in a deep breath of the fresh cool morning air. Yes, the morning has dawned clear, but icy COLD.

As I ride through town, I realize that everyplace has its advantages, but for the life of me, I can't figure out what it could be in Browning.

About half a mile out of town I check the temperature. It's actually quite nippy out here this morning (50 degrees). The sun is just starting to break over the horizon in the east.

I haven't seen many spectacular sunsets, but that's all right. Being out here all alone, I really don't want to get into a romantic mood anyway. I've seen some awfully nice sunrises, though. There is a myth going around that the moonlight belongs to the young in love. Not true, the young in love enjoy each other if there's moonlight or not. I think that to fully appreciate the moonlight or a spectacular sunrise you have to venture into it alone. The problem with that is if there are other people around and you gaze for more than five minutes at the moon or early morning sun, they'll judge you as some kind of a nut.

After a good breakfast (the usual: eggs...hash browns...toast and coffee...lots of coffee), I go across the road to a filling station to see if they have any granola bars. Then I hop on my bike and take off. There is no wind at all this morning but the coolness is closing in all around me. The sun's brightly shining so I have my sunglasses on as I take to the open road. There is a sign alongside the road that says, "Crosswinds". I sort of expected I'd have some through here anyway. I read that the wind usually whistles across these prairies. I don't have any yet, though but about a mile out of town I get a very cold 5 mph crosswind.

It's 6:30 a.m. and it's only 46 degrees. It's getting colder instead of warmer...! I didn't dress for the cold today. I thought it would be hot. I just have my jersey and shorts on. But let me tell you, again, it's pretty damn cold out here. I guess this morning dawned with an uncertain sun. The clouds are taking turns blocking the sun out completely. It peeks through the scattered clouds every now and then. The town of Blackfoot looks deserted.

After riding all those tough hills yesterday, I thought I might be tired or sore today, but I'm not. I feel like I could ride forever. I guess I'm in very good shape for the shape I'm in. I must have what they call "a quick recovery time." I haven't been to a doctor since I broke my hip some 20 years ago. All my friends said I should get a checkup before going on this tour. Well, I didn't, because I didn't want one of those "Routine Tests" that people die from.

There is no wind at all out but there's definitely a chill in the air.

There's a marker that says, "Historical Point One Mile." I just can't imagine what it could be other than somewhere...sometime in history an Indian stopped and took a piss or something. There it is. The sign says, "Camp Disappointment." I can believe that, to me history like this happened too long ago to matter.

Life has to be very harsh for the Indians out here. There is nothing out here but empty plains and the mountains, and the desert, which is as dry and colorless as an old man's beard. I have discovered that the difference between them and me is that, for me, hardship is an adventure, for them it's a way of life. Back in the shadows of time when I was a youngster, I remember that the Indians were always the bad guys when I would play cowboys and Indians. We would sign treaties with the Indians but they always got broken as soon as the white people wanted something from them. Our words on paper meant nothing. All the Indians really wanted was to be left alone.

In my opinion, it's no sin to be poor. I think it's a sin to be rich as, let's say, Donald Trump, and elect not to help the poor. Nobody needs millions of dollars, nobody. I just read where his new Casino in Atlantic City, has to take in one million dollars a day, just to make expenses. Talk about ridiculous.

I recall a movie I saw, maybe 25 years ago, where this billionaire was giving away a million, tax-free dollars to some lucky person. He approached this person he had selected at random, and asked them, "If you had a million dollars, just what would you do with it?" This one particular guy said he would buy himself a new car, pay off his mortgage on his house, and take a vacation. Then he would put the rest of the money in the bank. The billionaire proceeded to add up just how much it would cost for the new car, to pay off the mortgage, and to take the vacation the guy wanted. This all added up to be around $150,000.00 so the billionaire gave the guy a check for $150,000.00 and started to leave.

"Wait a minute," the guy said, "you were going to give me one million dollars."

The billionaire said, "I gave you the $150,000.00 you needed, I figured if you were just going to put the rest in the bank, you really didn't need it," and he turned and left.

Anyway, right from the very beginning the Indians have been mistreated. We took their land away from them, and put them on reservations. Just put yourself in their place and see how you would feel. Have you ever thought about helping the poor?

You might come up with the most common excuse not to, and say something like, "I would really like to help the homeless out…But…I only make enough money to support my own family."

Well, the L.A. Mission, in downtown Los Angeles, can clothe, feed, and furnish a bed for a person for $15.00 a month.

Think about it.

*   *   *

All Right…! Enough of that. Let's get back to the ride. I have 20 miles on the odometer. For the most part, it's slightly downhill riding here. The sky is cloudless now and the sun is bright. The air, however, still holds a coolness that doesn't seem to disappear as the morning goes by. I'm going to try something here. I'm going to take my windbreaker off and freeze up a little bit, so it feels better when I thaw out a little later. Good thinking, huh…!

I have about a 10 mph tailwind now. It's warming up a little bit and I can feel my toes, again. It's nice to be able to ride in the big chain ring. It's still a little overcast. The sun's hiding behind the clouds almost all the time. Just peeking out once in a while…just to let me know it's still there.

This isn't a very good road through here. It's rough and there is no shoulder. But there is absolutely no traffic on it.

Riding from the West to the East the land changes a lot. I could see the grasslands for the first time from several thousand feet up in the Rocky Mountains. Up there, there were pine trees, rocks, and fast-running water all around me, but far below me, though still probably fifty miles off, was the flattest, smoothest, most treeless stretch of land imaginable. I'm riding in that land now.

There are a lot of tumbleweeds in the fencerow alongside the road. In L.A. at Christmas time, I would go out in the Mojave Desert and collect three tumbleweeds. I'd take them home and spray paint them, white, then stack them up, and Presto…! I had a Snowman…!

It's actually kind of pretty out here. It's all green. The color of my girlfriend's eyes. She's pretty, too. I'd better call her tonight.

Every 10 yards or so there is a crack across the road that's over-filled with black top making a two-inch high bump. It's jarring me all the way. It's just a steady pounding on me, NO FUN…!

I guess things have always moved across these plains. Like the geese, the ducks, the Indians, the buffalo. The buffalo were killed off. For what, you say…trespassing? The buffalo provided the staples for tribal life. Its flesh was the Indian's basic food, and its hide was used for both clothing and shelters. The Indians only killed buffalo as needed, and no part of the animal was ever wasted. Here's a fact that you may not know. The killing off of the buffalo was part of a government policy to dispose of the Indian "problem". Now, only the birds still move across the plains, on the migrations that take them thousands of miles south in winter and thousands of miles north in summer.

People travel this highway by the thousands but seldom stop in the grasslands for anything other than food for themselves and fuel for their cars. They travel mostly in the summer. Carloads of families cross the grasslands only to get somewhere else. They are on vacation heading for the mountains or the coast, telling themselves that the crossing won't be that bad. They'll probably stop at Cut Bank or Shelby for gasoline and cowboy hats for the kids. But they won't stay out here any longer then necessary.

I've ridden 36 miles so far. It's 8:23 a.m. as I ride into Cut Bank. It sort of looks like a living ghost town with forty percent living, fifty percent ghost, and ten percent not yet decided. I ride by an old house with a porch that I'm sure hasn't been painted in twenty years.

My loaded bike has, by now, become a part of me. Riding straight has become second nature to me, which is good because the road is as straight as an arrow.

Riding along out here, alone, through all these desolate miles…sometimes riding for miles without seeing so much as a car…I have plenty of time to think. I honestly believe that the physical condition of the majority of the people today is going downhill. A generation ago most men who finished a hard 10 to 12 hour work day, needed rest. However, today for most people a typical day consists of sitting in front of a computer for seven or eight hours, then they go home and sit in front of a television for the remainder of the day and evening. These people are, as you know, called couch potatoes. Back when there wasn't any TV, only radio, you at least got to use your imagination a little.

I think of George Burns as a couch potato. He once said that he used to watch golf on television, until his doctor told him that he needed more exercise, so now he watches tennis. I don't like to watch any sports on television. I would rather be doing it, instead of watching someone else do it.

It has warmed up to 58 degrees. The lack of civilization out here isn't all bad. It gives me some quiet time for myself, and I believe everyone needs quiet time by themselves.

You know that anyone can throw their stuff in a car and drive across America. But, I believe riding that same distance on a bicycle, a little at a time, is much more gratifying. Our pioneer ancestors took that for granted. They would walk or ride to their destinations and expect it to take days or even months. They had a different understanding of time, not rushing anywhere. They would simply rise and bed down with the sun. They watched the growing plants mark the seasons and looked up and saw the stars at night. When is the last time you looked up at the stars?

I ride into the town of Ethridge. I have to stop and change my shoes…these don't feel quite right. Maybe the cleats came loose and moved a little or something.

Problem fixed. I eat one of the granola bars I bought back in Browning. It's cinnamon flavored and it's really quite good. It's still overcast and I have a dry wind, which isn't bad for riding. After looking at my map, I see that once I get to Selby, the road makes a little turn. Then I should have a 20 mph tailwind. That would be nice.

While touring, I've come to appreciate this lands vastness and realize there is a place in it for me. Just like a little blade of grass in the cracks of the pavement pushing its way up toward the light. It knows it has its place in this world, and it's not going to let anyone or anything stop it from having that place. Being a bicyclist, I have an appreciation of the great outdoors, and of the little things in life.

I have 60 miles on the odometer as I ride into Shelby. The towns out here are few and far between. Shelby is a good example of what towns looked like before shopping malls. I just saw a sign in the window of a Barber Shop, which said, "Free Haircuts Tomorrow." It is a good joke because tomorrow never comes. And that's why I try to live every day to it's fullest.

I stop at Shelby's only restaurant and go in to sit down at a window seat. The waitress comes over and hands me a sticky handwritten menu, sealed in plastic. I begin by enjoying an endless stream of hundred proof hot coffee…my second favorite beverage…and a cinnamon roll about the size of a bicycle wheel. This restaurant is not exactly a showcase of the *County Health Department*, but it sure has good cinnamon rolls. I ate my fill and it the road again.

At 11:03 a.m. I'm one mile east of Dunkirk. I have, what I hope to be, a never-ending gradual downhill accompanied with a 20 mph tailwind. This makes for an extremely fast, easy, wind-blown ride. The wind blows me away from the Rockies and through Dunkirk. There is nothing out here but the wind and the grass. My singing tires are carrying me eastward over a foot-wide shoulder with no traffic or cracks. I can cruise in high gear at a 20 mph pace easily. I can't help but say to myself, as I fly through Devon, "This is a biker's dream."

As I ride through the grasslands of North America, I get a funny feeling that the whole world can see me but no one is watching.

It's still overcast and I still have my wonderful 20 mph tailwind as I cruise through Galata. I try to take advantage of a good tailwind when I get it. I sit up straight in my saddle, catching as much of the wind as I can. A sail would be nice for times like this. I've been averaging more than 20 mph for the last 10 miles.

It's just a glorious day with ideal riding conditions. After riding out of the Rockies my view has expanded from a few miles in every direction to more than a hundred.

I have 90 miles in and I'm near Lothair. The road is board flat (even with a little downhill). After riding through Lothair there's nothing out here except native grasslands zippered together with old railroad tracks.

Deep down in my heart I feel that anyone can lead a normal boring life, or they can do something out of the ordinary (like this tour) and have a full exciting life. The choice is ours. I know a few people that get up in the morning, drive 50 miles in heavy traffic, work 10 hours, drive back home (in even heavier traffic) go to bed, and start all over again the next morning. To me that isn't living, it's existing.

My philosophy is work to live, not live to work.

Riding along out here there is a silence as if civilization has disappeared. Some people might think it would become lonely…riding all alone…but I really enjoy cycling…undisturbed by hills…traffic and noise. I guess I've been a loner from the very beginning. After all, I was born alone. I think I was born lost and I take no pleasure in being found.

I really enjoy riding. At the completion of my tour I should be slim, trim and suntanned. The sun's hitting the spokes of my wheels as I ride along. My cyclometer reads 100 miles and it's only a little past noon.

Someone once asked me if I liked life. My answer was, "It's much better then the alterative." But to be truthful, "I Love Life…!"

I stop and lean my bike up against the front of a huge John Deere combine, for a picture.

At 1:06 p.m. I am hungry so I stop at a restaurant in Chester. As I eat my B.LT. this tall, graying man with sharp blue eyes comes over to ask me all about my travels. As I put a cold french fry in my mouth and finish my liquid malt he finally leaves. Then, after satisfying my hunger, I jump on my bike and roll on.

The sun's finally breaking through the clouds so I'm going to put my sunglasses on. It's kind of warm out here now so I put on sun block. I also put a little more air in my back tire.

The sky is a beautiful dark blue. Only a few distant clouds mar the crystal clarity of the early afternoon sky. I have 110 miles on the odometer as I ride out of Joplin. It's warmed up to 74 degrees and I still have my 20 mph tailwind. It's GREAT…!

I truly believe that anyone bicycle touring from coast to coast should ride from West to East. Aside from the prevailing winds, traveling from the West also gives you more downhills. On the central plains (where I am now) there is a gradual slant toward the Mississippi River.

It's nearly three in the afternoon on a beautiful summer day. It's 82 degrees as I ride through Rudyard. U.S. Route 2 is as straight as an arrow. I ride along out here and all I see is a bunch of grass, sort of like what you would see through a car window. It doesn't look like much. But, when I stop and look really close in the tall grass, there are all kinds of little yellow and blue and white flowers. There is really a lot of hidden beauty in the grass. I'm so delighted with the season. Spring has always been my favorite time of year.

I have learned not to take any of this for granted. Every day I'm reminded of just how privileged I am. Privileged to live in such a beautiful place and privileged that the circumstances of my life allow me time to enjoy it from the seat of my bicycle.

I'm riding out of Hangham. I can't help but notice how little traffic there is…it seems like I'm on a two-hundred-mile bikeway. After taking my vacation in Utah last year with all the rocks, and sand, and desert, just the tall grass along side the road (it's all at least a foot tall) is beautiful.

Am I having fun yet…? You can bet your bippy on it…! It's so clear out. I'll bet I can see for 100 miles in all directions.

You know, it's amazing just how much energy we waste at work. I've already ridden 130 miles and I feel great. It's 3:35 p.m. and I'm two miles west of Gildford. I have about a 15 mph tailwind now.

I haven't seen any garbage along the side of the road since I started way back in Seattle. No beer cans, no broken glass on the road or anything. It's really nice when I can ride along and look around and see things, instead of having to watch the road all the time for glass and debris.

By now I've ridden over a large part of Montana and I realize that within its borders I've seen a lot of different kinds of country and climate. The north winds bring their icy breath down to the wooded hills and fast-flowing streams in the Rocky Mountains. In the sagebrush grazing land of Eastern Montana, the unfenced plains stretch to the horizon. The hot and humid air of the Eastern Montana has no likeness to the cool crystal air in the Western Montana. What I am trying to say…is…that there is no similarity between Western and Eastern Montana.

They must grow a lot of grain around Gildford because I'm riding by a lot of granaries.

I think it's safe to say that I get my maximum efficiency by pedaling at around 60-70 revolutions a minute. I try to keep my rpm's between 60 and 70 all the time, and between 60 and 65 most of the time. Racers keep their rpm's over 100 all the time. I guess I'm not a racer. My pace is just as important as my cadence. If my pace is too slow, I tend to feel sluggish and tired, as if my muscles are bored. I like to maintain a brisk pace. But racing across the country would exhaust me, and poking along bores me. The solution I've found is to find my own particular pace and cadence and try to stick to it.

The road is as smooth as silk but the shoulder of the road has these ribs running perpendicular to it, so cars get a deep rumble if they ride on them. Bikes get even a deeper rumble. The road ranges from gently rolling to table flat. There is still very little traffic. I saw a sign, just out of Kremlin that said the mountains I see in the background are the *"Bear Paw Mountains."*

The land isn't ironing board flat anymore, it waves like a sheet in a breeze. I think I'll ride until I see if the world is really round. I feel as though I'm as free as the air itself as I glide through Fresno. It's really nice to have a 20 mph tailwind. I spin along effortlessly, and enjoy my afternoon ride. It's flatter than a pancake out here and so quiet I can hear cars coming miles away.

I just took a picture of some antelope that crossed the road right in front of me. You can indeed see the antelope play and you won't hear a discouraging word. That's because there's no one around to speak them.

When I resume pedaling, I notice a hawk drifting above me. You know hawks can see 25 times better than a human and antelope can see seven times better. Four miles east of Fresno I have 150 miles on the odometer and it's 4:50 p.m.

Time seems to lose all its importance out here. After all, what does time matter to me now…? It may be helpful at work and at church services. But what does it matter out here…? I'm thinking just how much more efficient it would be to work when a person feels like it, to eat when a person's hungry, and to sleep when a person's sleepy, instead of when the clock tells them to.

Here I am, riding along up this small hill, really slow, looking around enjoying the countryside and what do I see…? These black spots (about the diameter of my wheels and about at handlebar height) moving across the road. I can't make out just what it is yet. As I ride closer, I can make out that it's swarms of gnats or mosquitoes, I don't know which. Naturally, I try to dodge them, but there are so many that…every once in a while…I run right into a swarm of them. The gnats are getting in my hair…in my beard and mustache. They're crawling all over me...in my ears and even up my nose. Ugh...! About the time I get one batch brushed off, I hit another swarm. At least I have enough sense to keep my mouth shut. I don't think I've ever seen so many gnats before...They're all over the place. I pedal fast, trying to create enough wind to keep them out of my nose and ears. This will be a good excuse for me to get a motel room, instead of camping out. As you may notice, I don't need much of an excuse.

At 5:50 p.m. after 163 miles I check into a Super 8 Motel in Havre. It's $28.00 for the night. There is no restaurant, no lounge, and no place to eat dinner or breakfast. The desk clerk said he would furnish me with transportation to a restaurant, if I wanted it. I've wheeled a hundred-sixty-three miles without seeing one tree today. If there was anywhere else to stay on down the road, I would still be riding.

By looking at my mileage for today, one might think that I'm "Mileage-Crazy" (that's placing more importance on how many miles you're riding, than on the real reason for riding). Well, I'm NOT...! It's just fun to ride with a slight downhill, and a 20 mph tailwind, and, of course, the excitement of the never-ending, unexpected. You never know what's right around the next corner until you get there (of course there weren't many corners today).

After cleaning up, I step out the door and sit on the steps just as the rocks are changing from white to orange to pink and finally to purple. I sit there reflecting on the day's ride until the sky's giving way to the first twinkling of stars overhead.

* * *

*Statistics for **DAY SEVEN** Sunday, June 18, 1989.*
163 miles of riding today, 16.7 average miles per hour for today, 831 miles of riding in seven days, 119 average miles of riding per day.

Day Eight

From Havre, Montana
To Malta, Montana

It's 5:15 a.m. Time for me to get up and greet this gorgeous day. The sun's up and it's a clear, bright, sunny day. There's not a cloud in the sky. I'm going to look for a place to eat in this town. I have about a 10 mph headwind already this morning.

Twenty minutes later I finally find a little restaurant that's open. It's right at the edge of Malta. I'm going to stop in and grab a bite. As I walk into the restaurant, I'm greeted with a, "Hi." A little old man says, "I'm your waiter today, I'm also the cook and the owner."

He has a half-smoked cigarette hanging out of his mouth and his clothes, shirt, and skin are all the same color. He asks me where I'm from and when I tell him L.A. he wants to know if I knew his brother-in-law that moved to L.A. in the winter of '76. He asks me why I'm dressed the way I am and I tell him that I have just ridden my bicycle over the Rockies.

He says, "Yea they've been there as long as I can remember. But how in the world could you ride up those mountains?" he asks.

Being an experienced rider now, I know that it's not the hills but headwinds that I dread the most. The hills may be steep, sometimes very steep, but all hills have summits. I can and do ride uphills slowly, and they're usually only a few miles in length (the Rockies being the exception) and then I can coast down the other side (the Rockies being the exception again) to make up for the time and effort spent climbing them. But headwinds, if strong are constant, give me no chance to rest. They're a continuous force that I must constantly overcome in order to move forward. They're a lot like child support.

Anyway, I ask him if it's always this windy around here.

He says, "I've never heard of a bicycler catching a tailwind in Montana. Everyone has headwinds no matter which direction they're pedaling. They have headwinds and nothing to look at and lots of mosquitoes. After all, mosquitoes are our state bird you know."

I've got to admit it though, he sure knows how to cook. I had myself a good breakfast (except for the coffee that tasted like rocket fuel). The restaurant is a typical little mom and pop cafe. With only two customers, thank God. It seems like they spent more time visiting, mainly with me, than they did getting the food ready.

It's 7:17 a.m. as I ride out of Havre. It's 65 degrees. I can't believe I have these winds this early in the morning. These headwinds are a bitch. Boy, I'm surely glad I did all those miles yesterday. The wind is as strong as the coffee I had back there.

Oh Yea...the owner of the restaurant told me that he went to *Zion National Park* and he loved it. But when he went to *Grand Canyon* he didn't like it. I asked him why. He said, "I liked *Zion* because I could just drive through it, but at *Grand Canyon*, you have to get out of your car to see anything."

I'm three miles west of Lohman. I have at least a 10 mph headwind which keeps me down on my drops in my middle chain ring. After only 15 miles I have to stop and rest. The wind is a major factor when I ride a fully loaded touring bike. My panniers sort of act like sails in the wind and I am forced into my middle chain ring.

*   *   *

Let me try to explain how the wind effects my pace.

I can ride along on flat terrain, through calm air, comfortably, at a 15 mph pace. When I have a 10 mph headwind, pedaling with the same amount of energy, my speed is cut down to 7 or 8 mph. So, with a 10 mph headwind for me to maintain a 15 mph pace, I have to work twice as hard. Crosswinds also have an effect on my speed as a 10 mph crosswind will cut my pace down, from 15 mph to 10 mph A tailwind (this is the good one) of 10 mph will increase my speed from 15 mph to 18 or 20 mph with the same effort expended. Too bad this is the one that I don't get very often on a flat surface.

My body accounts for approximately 70 percent of the wind resistance and my bike the other 30 percent. So, I have to get down on the drops to make myself as aerodynamic as possible and, of course, I have to work twice as hard, just to maintain a 15 mph pace. You can bet I've learned to take advantage of a tailwind, no matter how little it is.

Here's the punch line. If I were to ride 120 miles in a day, everybody would say, "Good Job…!" "That's Great…!" Of course, I forgot to mention that I had a 10 mph tailwind all day. Then, on the other hand, if I were to ride 50 miles, into a 10 mph headwind all day, everybody would say, "Is that all you rode today?" "What did you do, stop at noon?" When, in actual fact, it took more energy (and the same amount of time) to ride the 50 miles, with a 10 mph headwind, as it did to ride 120 miles with a 10 mph tailwind. But needless to say, you don't get much credit for only riding 50 miles.

*   *   *

Just outside of Lohman I stop and chat with a touring cyclist who is going the other way. His clean-shaven face is the color of old ivory. He's from the Texas Panhandle. He rode straight up here to Route 2. Now he's riding over to the West Coast, then down the Coast, and back to Texas.

He says it's going to take him all summer to complete his tour. He gave me some discount tickets on meals at a small restaurant up the road a little way. It seems that they are giving a 10% discount to every cyclist that comes in.

I have a 15 mph headwind and I'm down on my drops in my middle chain-ring all the time. If this headwind were any worse, I would have to shift into my small chain-ring.

At 8:51 a.m. I have 20 miles in as I stop at the Chinook Post Office. The Post Office doesn't open until 9:00 a.m. So I go across the road to a grocery store to get a little box to put the stuff in that I want to mail home. It adds up to about 4 pounds of cold weather clothes. I sure hope it doesn't get cold again.

After riding a few miles I stop to see if I can repack to cut down on my wind resistance a little. I put my sleeping bag and air mattress inside my panniers, and put my tent length ways, on the back rack. I also have a granola bar. Oh God...! I'm starting to like these bars...! Of course, I haven't found a bar yet that I haven't liked. Anyway, I've never seen a *Surgeon General's Warning* on any granola bars, so they must be good for you. I've never heard of anyone dying from eating them, either.

I don't know if the repacking helped that much or not, I'm still in the same gear. The headwind has increased to about 20 mph now. I stop in Zurich (it does feel a bit like Switzerland...!) to change my shoes. My feet are getting tired from having to push so hard on the pedals with this headwind.

There's a little creek running through here. It's really muddy. Quite different from the crystal-clear ones that were up in the mountains.

It seems like everybody around these parts wears a cowboy hat.

There's a sign, lying in the ditch, flatter than a cow pie that's apparently been blown down...It reads: "Dangerous Winds."

There are little gophers or ground squirrels or prairie dogs coming out of their burrows by the hundreds, and standing perfectly erect on their hind feet. They seem to be laughing at me as I ride into this strong headwind. Cute, really cute.

Laughing Prairie Dogs

There's nothing worse than being forced into one of my lowest gears while riding on flat land pushing my hardest, only to reach the ridiculous speed of 10 mph. In spite of all my efforts, my average speed is very low, and it's getting lower by the minute.

I've got to stop and rest more frequently than I like.

There's an L.B.J. bird (little brown job). This headwind slows me down enough so I have plenty of time to see all the birds and wild flowers growing along the edge of the road. This time of the year around the L.A. area, all the grass is starting to turn brown. Out here everything is just starting to come to life.

I like the feel of the wind in my face, but this is ridiculous. Most people believe that the wind blows, let me be the first to tell you, "It Sucks…!" I've got to stop and rest, again.

I'm really trying not to complain, but this wind is a real Bitch…!

There's a nice fragrance in the air though. It would be beautiful out here, if it weren't for this #Z&@! wind…! When I get this strong a headwind, I switch my computer from mph to cadence. I really don't want to see how fast (or slow) I'm going. It's a little discouraging.

The air's fresh and clean and clear. I think I can see for a hundred miles in all directions.

In calculating temperatures in the winter, the *Weather Bureau* takes the wind into consideration. Thus, the wind-chill factor. I don't see any reason why I can't do the same, in the summer. Let's see my speedometer reads 11 mph and I have a 20 mph headwind, so, calculating this out, I'm really flying along here at a 31 mph pace…!

At 11:02 a.m. I have 40 miles on the odometer. I'm two miles west of Harlem. I've ridden 40 miles today into a 20 mph headwind. If the prevailing winds prevail, I only have 960 more miles of headwinds to contend with. That should be fun. If the headwinds were any stronger, I would be going backwards.

Montana is starting to look like a Really BIG State.

I'm going to stop and put some *Chap Stick* on. My lips are starting to dry out.

When I look at the bright side of things, at least I know, that with this strong headwind, I can't go fast enough to get any front end wobble…!

I stop at a greasy diner called Deb's for they're advertised special (it's right in their window): some beef, spuds, string beans and gravy. Fatigue and hunger are directly related to my attitude.

This sure is cowboy country. There are pickup trucks with guns in their rear window racks parked everywhere. I haven't seen any Appaloosa stallions tied up to any hitching posts, yet.

The first thing I notice, as I walk in, are the pictures hanging on all the walls. A local artist probably paints them. One painting is of a group of cowboys singing beside a campfire. Another is of a buffalo being chased by Sioux warriors. There are oils of pheasants flying over cornfields. They're all for sale. Everything is for sale.

A woman who seems unhappy to be alive is escorting me back to my table. She has fat ankles and a bruise on her leg. Truckers at a table are talking in loud voices…but as I cross the floor…the busy clatter dies and is replaced by a tense silence. One of them is a large-bellied man wearing a somewhat soiled shirt. He's sitting there with a loaded fork halfway to his mouth while his neighbor, grasping a huge mug of coffee in his oily hand, is staring with bulging eyes at me. Yet another, is wearing a light red jacket with the emblem of the *National Rifle Association*. He poured syrup on a pancake, rolled it up, and ate it with his fingers. Once I'm seated, they start talking loudly again. It seems that their basic philosophy is simple enough: all roads are constructed solely for motorized vehicles, therefore, bicyclers have absolutely no right to use them. They all hate bicyclists. They would like to eliminate them. Many bicyclists feel the same way about trucks and cars. I feel a little uncomfortable, much like the feeling you get when you're wearing a shirt that's too small for you.

As I leave I turn to close the door and notice a sign on the door: "No shirt, No shoes, No service." One thing is for sure, I got the "No service." I've never had a really good lunch or dinner (or a really bad breakfast) at a roadside restaurant before.

I was hoping that the wind would have died down a little while I was eating but no such luck. I'm eight miles east of Harlem and it's warmed up to 90 degrees.

*   *   *

As I ride along, I'm kind of keeping my eye out for those truckers from the restaurant. I'm sure they would like to kill and skin me. I find that most truckers are nice people. Hell…if it weren't for cars and trucks there wouldn't be any roads for me to pedal on. Nevertheless, right now I feel a little uneasy when I hear a truck approaching from behind. (No, I'm not paranoid.)

The birds are having almost as hard a time flying into this 20 mph headwind as I am. I stop and put some sunscreen on. It's quite warm out and I don't want to get burnt. It's 1:00 p.m. and I'm on my way again. This wayward wind is a restless wind so they say.

I keep looking for a tree or something, anything, that's been blown over but there's nothing out here to blow over. I guess a 20 mph wind really isn't much, unless you're riding headlong into it all day.

I watch very carefully as a two-ton American-made pickup with a gun rack mounted in its rear window eases past me. Then, it pulls off the road in front of me. I'm sure the man inside wearing a cowboy hat has decided to personally decrease the bicycling population by one, or at least he's going to blast a few holes through my panniers just for the hell of it. I wrap my hands around my brakes as he jumps out with his rifle in hand. Thank God he aims out in the prairie and shoots. He apparently missed whatever he was shooting at because he jumps back into his pick-up and speeds off.

My hands are trembling a little so I lie my bike down on its side and say a word of thanks to God…Benjamin Franklin…Albert Einstein…Edgar Allen Poe…Mark Twain…Tom Sawyer…Huckleberry Finn…anyone and everyone I can think of…

I just rode out of the cowboys' country and into Indian territory. This land belongs to them. I'm on an Indian Reservation.

This headwind feels like I'm getting a blast from a giant hair-dryer. It forces me to stay in my middle chain-ring all the time. I'm not riding that fast but the wind is so strong that its lifting my helmet up so much that the chin strap is choking me.

There is no shoulder on this rough…rough…road and I need some relief so I gear down and get off the drops for a while.

Summer is a few days away, but the heat isn't. It's 91 degrees. It's so hot out here that even the lizards are resting behind cactus plants that provide them with ample shade from the desert sun. They won't even venture across the road because they know they'll fry their little feet.

It's Monday but it feels more like Fryday.

The sun's in the center of the sky and there is no shade to be found anywhere and I need a break. I'm as dry as a bone I could easily drink all my Tang as I bake in the afternoon sun. The road's not too rough now, but this Damn wind just never lets up. I guess there's just nothing to stop, or slow it down, for a thousand miles in any direction.

I have a little trivia question for you here. If I'm riding along at a 15 mph pace and all of a sudden I was to get a 30 mph headwind, how fast would I be going?

Wrong…! I would be riding at least a 30 mph pace. You see, I made a quick U-turn to head back to the closest tavern. My mother didn't raise any fools. Of course I don't have a 30 mph headwind so I can't go to a tavern. Not quite yet.

I can feel the dry air in my throat as I ride through, what I believe to be, the world's largest microwave oven. I just took a picture of a discarded beer can glittering in the sun. I'm dehydrated and I believe this to be foreplay. Now, aluminum cans sell for two-and-one-half cents apiece, so if I were to drink seven six-packs a week (that's only one a day) I could make $1.00 on cans alone.

My favorite beverage is Not 92-degree water or Tang, especially when I have to drink it out of these hot plastic bottles. Right now I would give anything for a nice cold beer, in a large frosted mug.

I still have this 20 mph headwind. This is undoubtedly the worst blowjob I've ever had…! The wind seems to be switching around a little bit now but it's still sunny and HOT…! It's coming a little from my right and a little from the front. It's what I would call a cross head wind. It's much better than a straight headwind but I still have to stay in my middle chain ring.

At 2:08 p.m. I have 63 miles in and I'm ten miles west of Dodson. I've ridden all day into this strong headwind. I haven't made much distance as I fight for yardage like a football team.

I have to stop for a while. I'm BEAT…! There is a herd of long-horned cattle, which look like they have bicycle handlebars on their heads.

Oh Yea…I found my radio, last night, when I was unpacking my stuff.

*   *   *

The idea of riding across America was spawned on a completely different kind of day from this. It was warm and sunny, but not too warm. I was very comfortable riding along getting tanner by the hour. I enjoyed riding along the Pacific Ocean admiring its whitecaps and waves. The sandy beaches beckoned me to ride on. A tailwind pushed me southward at an unhurried pace. Restaurants and campgrounds were plentiful and I was having fun. I said, to myself, "Wouldn't it be fun to ride all the way across the United States?" You know, it's easy to get carried away with the romance of it all. My mind conjured up scenes of lush, green valleys with a sparkling stream paralleling the road on one side, and perhaps a rail fence on the other. In this vision the road is smooth and there are no bugs or dogs. And, of course, no traffic. In my mind's eye I could ride for ever through the countryside of great beauty. I never gave any thought to the lung-searing climbs up the steep grades that seem certain to burst my chest if my leg muscles don't play out first. And I certainly never imagined being overtaken on a two-lane road by a huge truck that, as it passes me, is, in turn, meeting another truck going the opposite direction, and the three of us meet and there is no shoulder…nothing but a drop-off of three inches onto the gravel.

I guess I'm riding along here a day dreaming or hallucinating. It's so HOT and dry I can't even spit. I stop and put my radio on and see what kind of music they listen to out here. All Right…! Shit-kicking music.

I just heard on the radio that it's 90 degrees out and there are southeast winds at 21 mph. Well, I'd say I'm a quite good guesser when I said it's 20 mph.

There is a bunch of clouds forming behind me. They don't look like rain clouds though, they're white. This hot sun is sapping the energy out of me. I keep taking small sips of hot Tang because I'm not quite sure where I'll be able to get more water. I'm drier than dust.

As I ride along with the sunshine on my shoulders, a mad whirlwind of hot red dust spins across the road and slaps me in the face. There's absolutely nothing in any direction out here to slow the wind down. The spring grasses extend over the rolling landscape, which seems to keep the horizon at a great distance.

*   *   *

So far today I've ridden 73 miles in the searing heat and blistering winds, which, of course, are blowing the wrong way. You know, a man could die of thirst out here. Wait, is that a town up ahead? Sweet Jesus, I may be saved. I ride into Dodson past a grain elevator, grocery store, a boarded-up school, and a church. What I'm looking for is a rustic welcome place where I can belly up to the bar and slug a few cold ones down.

And what do I see? Right in front of me? A TAVERN…! And there are two tandem bicycles leaning up against it…! Most people have nothing against bicycles built for two, but personally, I can't tandem. This is just too good to be true…! I figure it's either a mirage, omen, or a miracle. I'm not going to hesitate to find out.

There's a BIG dog with eyes that look like glistening honey. His tongue is smacking at his lips. He's lying by the door, but nothing…absolutely nothing…is going to stop me from going in there. I ride right up to the front door. I put my bike next to the tandems, take my handlebar bag off my bike and proceed to go in, where I know it'll be cool. Well, I thought it would be cool. I open the door and step in, out of the blazing sun. It's dark inside, as dark as midnight in a coal bin, at least until my eyes grow accustomed to the dim light, but it's a little cooler than it is outside. There's two "Budweiser Lite" lights hanging over both of the pool tables. A single light bulb hangs from a ceiling fan that's circulating the hot air. This looks like home to me.

At the far end of the long straight dark oaken bar sit the other cyclists. I think they're happy to see someone come in who looks worse then they do. I say, "Hi…" to them and pull up a stool and order myself a tall cool one. This sort of surprises them. They are drinking cokes. I guess I'm violating a cardinal rule of bike touring. You don't drink during the day. But I call this productive idle time. We exchange stories about our adventures on the road. They tell me that with no trees or shelter of any kind to furnish them with any shade, they would stop and take turns sitting in each other's shadow.

The bartender (a tall, lean woman with swept-back iron-gray hair) comes over and I ask her if the wind always blows this way? She says, "No…sometimes it blows the other way." She says, "It pretty much blows all the time. One day it stopped and everybody fell down. "They have a log chain fastened to a post out front and if the wind lifts the chain and blows it straight out, then it's considered a strong wind." She went on to say that one day it blew so hard that it defeathered all the chickens.

After a couple more cokes and jokes (and three or four more beers for me) the tandem cyclists were on their way.

There are no windows in this bar, at least none I can see out of. The back door is open and I can see that it's getting awful dark out, so I ask the barmaid if I could bring my bike inside. She says, "Of course." So, I do and…after another bucket of beer, an unusually loud clap of thunder rattles the doors, and every light in the place goes out. The sky opens up and the rains come down in sheets. Then, at precisely 4:30 p.m., a flash of lighting and heavy machine-gun drops splash onto the pavement faster than the water could run off. Then the rain turns to hail. The entire bar (all four of us) go to the open door and watch as the hail bounces off the sidewalk and cars and piles up on the edge of the road.

I sure hope that the tandem bikers made it to their destination all right. Anyway, I decide that this isn't a good time to leave so I drink in assembly-line regularity. I talk to, and play pool with the two gentlemen that are also smart enough to stay in out of the rain and hail. One of them, a very fat, red-faced, elderly pipe-smoker with pale watery eyes and mud-colored hair, says that he was once the mayor of this town. He goes on to say that it's a corrupt little town because he personally bought 50 votes and he only received 37. I could easily see that he has had enough to drink so I ask him if he was worried about getting a drunk driving ticket. He says, "No, I have five different drivers' licenses." I shoot him a game of pool and find out that he knows about as much about pool as I know about God. The other guy, his friend, is about the same height and possibly the same age but much thinner. His face is nearly the same color as his hair, though perhaps a little redder. He's a much better pool player than his friend. I buy a pizza and share it with my newfound friends. This may not sound like a healthy diet but I am thinking of my health…my Mental health. The beer and conversation are flowing freely. I'm drinking a lot of beer, a lot of beer. But, hey, real men don't sip beer, they drink it. This is the only and best bar in town.

I try to call my daughter a couple of times, but no answer.

I go to the door to see if someone has turned the water and wind off, and the sun on, but they haven't.

*   *   *

It's 6:04 p.m. (three hours after entering the bar) and I'm just now leaving. As I point my front wheel toward Malta, I can see massive thunderclouds ahead of me. The hail is all melted now, and I have a hell of a tailwind…I mean I have at least a 30 mph tailwind. Now, I know I've had way too much to drink. I'm about as stable as a newborn giraffe. But it's only 18 miles to Malta, I think I can make it that far all right. The skies are really dark and heavy. It's cooled down about 20 degrees since three p.m. It's only 77 degrees out now.

I had a good time in the bar. I shot some pool, had some pizza, and drank about 500 beers. I really had too much to drink and ride, but I'm going to try to make it to Malta anyway. It's only 17 miles now.

The skies are really dark up ahead. It looks like rain. I think it's the storm front that just went through Dodson. Thank God there's nobody on this road. I'm properly stoned. I'm riding all over the road. I stop and take a picture of the storm front. It's right ahead of me. I can see it hailing just ahead of me.

Hey…! It's cooled down to 74 degrees. I'm going to ride on into Malta. It's only 16 more miles. And I will keep an eye on the storm just ahead of me. I can see it's pouring down rain just a little way ahead of me and I'm riding along behind it.

The skies are filled with purple-gray clouds.

I've got a beautiful tailwind and it's very chilly out now.

I can't believe this…! This is fantastic…! I can slow down just a little bit and I'll be in the sun, riding in the sunshine, or I can go a little bit faster and I'll be in the shade where its cool. I'm right on the edge of the storm front, and it's moving the same direction I am. It's pouring down hail just up ahead. I've heard of the calm before the storm, well, this is the calm after the storm.

I must have at least a 30 mph tailwind. Speaking of the wind, I'm three sheets in the wind. The sky is so beautiful, but I definitely have had too much to drink. Where they've got a white line painted alongside the road, I can see two lines. Thank God, there's no traffic. I'm out in the middle of the road half of the time. But it's all right, the only black and whites I've seen are a few Holstein cows.

I really thought I could piss without getting off my bike. But it's hard to judge wind direction when you are drunk. I remember as a kid when I went out to the fields to spread manure I had to watch the wind direction also. I'm surely glad there is no traffic out here today, because I'm not too stable on this bike.

I read somewhere, sometime, that 72 per cent of the human body is water. In my case it's beer.

It smells good out here. That's the one thing I can't capture on a camera or video camera. I can get color and sound, but I can't capture aromas. I stop by this field to photograph some bales of hay that look like huge Jellyrolls to me.

I have about a 30 mph northeast wind (a fierce wind) as I pedal in a state of semi- or maybe total intoxication. I'm just staying behind the storm front, watching the drizzling rain.

It's late in the afternoon and the sun is sinking in the sky making a reflection against a dark red curtain of clouds hanging out of the sky. There are a few heavy drops falling like lead to the ground, making perfect conditions for a rainbow. WOW...! I am witnessing a magical double rainbow, just ahead of me...! I have to take a picture of it.

There's a "No Trespassing-Private Property" sign. I guess somebody really does own this land.

Hey...! I have at least a 30 mph wind now. It's coming a little bit from behind and a little from my left-hand side. If I wasn't drunk, I could really be hauling ass. Damn, I just pissed twenty or thirty minutes ago and I've got to go again. Shit...! I thought I had it mastered (to piss with the wind) without getting off my bike, but a 30 mph gust of wind switched around and I splattered all over my front panniers. Now that really pisses me off.

I'm watching thunderheads build up rapidly in the clouds on the eastern horizon. It's really pouring down ahead of me, I mean really coming down! I'm going to slow down and stay in the sunshine. The road's all wet now. The clouds streak across the sky, totally obstructing the sun, so the brightness is alternated with darkness.

Well, I didn't put on a whole lot of miles today, but it was quite an experience. I'm really glad I stopped in that bar. I had a lot of fun. After I check into a motel, in Malta, I'm going to meet up with the guys that were in the bar in Dodson. We'll shoot some more pool. It's going to be a lot of fun.

You wouldn't believe this. It's like a three-ring circus out here. All going on at once. Straight ahead of me, in the main ring, are some really dark thunderclouds with streaks of rain falling to the ground. Behind me, the sun is shining bright...seemingly casting its rays on one particular cloud overhead, turning it a brilliant white against a dark blue sky. It's just a gorgeous sight...almost too good to be true. A real Kodak moment. It's warmed up tremendously...to 90 degrees!

Boy...! I've got amateur marks (you know, the grease print from your chain) all over my right leg...!

I'm not riding too far today, but who gives a shit? It's only 18 miles from Dodson to Malta or whatever the name of the next town is. The guys I was playing pool with in Dodson said, "Don't worry about how much you've had to drink. We'll just load your bike up in our pickup and take you to Malta." I said, "No Way...! I'm going to ride. It's beautiful out now." So they said, "All Right..." They would just meet me in Malta, later.

I'm getting better, I only vary from the line about a foot now. I guess I'm still high as a kite. Speaking of kites, wasn't it Charles Dickens, or was it David Copperfield that flew a kite in a thunderstorm like this and allowed it to be struck by lighting, to demonstrate that lighting was electricity?

You know, I shouldn't even be mentioning about how much I've had to drink, my girlfriend thinks I'm a alcoholic anyway. But, Hey...! I'm on vacation and I can have a drink once in a while if I want. I can have fun...Nobody can stop me.

It's a wild and stormy night on the east coast. This, however, has nothing to do with me. I have a 30 mph tailwind, and it's absolutely beautiful out here. The air's always really fresh right after it rains. There are rolling oceans of grass as far as I can see in all directions. It's raining ahead of me, the sky is a dark blue with some very bright white clouds and the sun is still shining behind me.

I'd say I have a 30 mph tailwind. Lightning is dancing across the horizon, accompanied by low, rumbling thunder. The afternoon sun has found a few ragged holes in the clouds, which immediately close as if it had been a mistake to allow me even a short burst of warmth. The overcast skies are dropping lower, like a gray ceiling. If I hold back and ride slowly

I can stay in the sunshine. I can see the sunshine line, where the storm front is.

Even though I'm weaving all over the road, it's such easy riding with this 30 mph tailwind…I just keep right on a-pedaling. I have to spend the night in Malta because there's no place to camp and there are no motels for the next…oh…I don't know, probably 50 miles or so. So, I don't have any choice. That's one of the problems I have with the towns being so far apart out here.

I stop for no other reason other than that I have to take another leak. I recall as a kid us boys would line up and see who could pee over the hot wire without getting a shock. (Funny, the things that come to mind…).

It's 7:00 p.m. I just took a picture of the sky using the last picture on the film. I have a 30 mph tailwind and it's downhill. There's no way you can beat that. I only wish that I were in a little better shape. I forgot to turn on my computer for that little stretch of road.

So far it's been one hell of a day. Ranging from hot…very HOT weather…to rain and hail. It cooled off a little and now it's hot again. I don't know where my thermometer is anymore but I'll look for it.

I can't believe how much grease I have on my right leg…I mean that's just another reason why you shouldn't drink and ride. I've got more grease on my leg then I have on my chain.

The wind is blowing at 20 mph out of the north, northeast, now. The opposite of what it was all afternoon…all afternoon…all day. Now it's back to a 30 mph tailwind again. The wind is actually a little to my back and a little to my left side.

Man, when these BIG trucks come along and pass me, the wind they create really blows me around. They almost blow me off the road.

The sun is dropping down behind me. It looks like a big yellow-orange ball sitting on a cloud. It's softening its rays. It seems to be apologizing for being so hatefully HOT all day long.

At 7:45 p.m. I have 92 miles in as I ride in a slight drizzle. It's a welcome relief from the heat.

*   *   *

I check into a motel at the edge of Malta for $25.00 for the night.

The two couples on the tandems flagged me down as I rode into Malta. They're staying in a motel across the road from mine. They said I could share a room with them if I wanted to. I said, "No, thanks." Men have to have private places where they can go and scratch what itches. Besides, I have my most inspired moments in bed. Also, someday when I get famous and they hang out a sign in front of this motel that reads, "Harold slept here," I don't want any rumors about me sleeping with two other guys. Anyway, they told me that they had a hard time getting here. They had to fight the headwinds all the way. It robbed them of the downhill coast. They had to pedal on the descents to avoid being stopped in their tracks. Then the thunderclouds broke and a heavy downpour drenched them. I didn't even realize that there were any downhills…!

I told them that I waited for the storm front to go through and I had a 30 mph tailwind all the way. I practically coasted into town. I told them that I followed right on the edge of the storm front and even got a picture of a double rainbow. They said they were really sorry that they didn't wait the storm out, like I did.

These guys I met at Dodson said they were going to be in a tavern across the road from where I'm staying tonight. They wanted me to go over and shoot some more pool with them. I was really relaxed and shooting good pool in Dodson. But now I think the beer has caught up with me. I don't know if I'm going over or not.

My log entry for today should be written in fine print because nothing in fine print is ever-good news. In spite of the headwinds, I rolled my two tires across 92 miles of Montana pavement today, and the eleven hours required to do that has installed an aching numbness in that part of me that contacts the bicycle seat.

As I step outside to watch the sunset, the sun is a dark crimson ball hanging over a misty field. The blue and pink light of the sunset has fallen now and the earth is swept in shades of amber, rose and yellow.

I go back in and have no trouble at all falling asleep.

*   *   *

*Statistics for **DAY EIGHT** Monday, June 19, 1989.*
92 miles of riding today, 11.1 average miles per hour for today, 923 miles of riding in eight days, 115 average miles of riding per day.

Day Nine

From Malta, Montana
To Wolf Point, Montana

It's 6:00 a.m., 55 degrees, and I'm going to get up and pack my stuff.

After half an hour I ride into the town of Malta under cloudy skies. It's overcast, but it looks clear in the direction I'm heading. As usual, I'm going to ride downtown and look for a restaurant.

I found one and everybody in here (most of whom are eating without taking their Stetsons off) are talking about the golf-ball size hail they had in Dodson yesterday. They weren't quite golf-ball size, but they were marble-size. You see, everybody likes to exaggerate a little. There are 17 customers in the restaurant (I know because I counted them) and only one waitress, and let me tell you, she's busy. She has golden hair with streaks of silver. Her measurements appear to be 18-18-18. She comes over to my table and I ask her if she would mind warming up my coffee. She takes it and puts it in a microwave for a few seconds and brings it back to me. I say, "It looks like rain…" She say's, "It taste like it too…" Actually, it tastes more like tea made with sulfur water. She's so busy I think I'll only have the one cup and be on my way. One is about all anyone could handle anyway. It's guaranteed to open up a dead man's eyes and make him talk about his illnesses.

Malta (population, I believe, to be around twenty) consists of a rustic coffee shop on one side of Route 2 and a one-room volunteer fire station on the other. Now, if a fire were to break out in the coffee shop, the Simons (the middle-aged couple who run the coffee shop and live in the cottage connected to it) would…I suppose…dash across Route 2, jump into the fire engine, drive it back across the road to the coffee shop, and put the fire out.

I leave the restaurant. It's really dark and gloomy out, but it still looks clear and light up ahead. Riding east on U.S. Route 2, I have about a 10 mph tailwind…it looks like it's going to be a good day. It feels good to be in my big chain ring again.

It's just a beautiful day out. I feel like I'm as free as the birds that are singing "good morning" to me.

"Good Morning, America." I'm on the road again, seeing things I may never see again, (thank you, Willie Nelson).

I don't know if those tandems are ahead of me or behind me. They told me yesterday that they had started out really early in the morning, and if they do the same thing today, they're probably ahead of me. Not to worry, I'll catch them. They told me that they had started up the Going-to-the-Sun Road at 4:00 a.m. so they would be sure to get to the top by 11:00 a.m. and it was so cold that they felt like they were contracting. I didn't ask them, how long it took them to get to the top but I know it's very hard riding a tandem up a steep hill. They may have had to push it most of the 12 mile 6% grade. I told them I didn't start riding until 8:00 a.m. and I didn't get to the top until 12:50 p.m.

There's a little lake off to my right. There goes another antelope across the road. By the time I get my camera it's too far off to get a picture. All the flowers are open already this morning. It's only 55 degrees out so I have my wind jacket on.

After recording and listening to my tapes from yesterday, I think that if anyone is remotely thinking about giving up drinking they should make a recording of themselves when they've had too much to drink. It just might be enough to convince them that it's time to stop. I mean, I babbled on…and on…and on…about nothing. A lot of what I said I didn't include in this book, because it just didn't make any sense at all. I also repeated myself a lot. Granted, I did have fun yesterday, but I could have had just as much fun, probably even more, if I had drunk cokes instead of beers.

I'm riding through a vast area of gentle rolling countryside. It's a mile or two up and a mile down…really a gradual uphill climb. It's nice because I can stay in my big chain ring all the time.

Once you're in Montana, it seems to take forever to get out, and I understand some people never make it out. I don't understand this. It's only about six inches across the state on my map…!

I'm pushing it, riding hard, trying to get out of this cloud cover and into the clear skies just up ahead before it starts to rain. There is very little traffic out here this morning.

The Plains seem to begin at Browning. From that point on the land slants down toward the *Mississippi River Valley*, about 1,000 miles to the east. I know that the country is relatively flat in Wisconsin and the *Great Lakes* states. But with my destination being New York City I must face the *Catskills*, or the *Appalachian Mountains* sooner or later. The *Appalachians* rise no more than 6,900 feet, but I'm sure there will be some hard riding coming my way again. They shouldn't be anything compared to the Rockies, though.

If you are reading this to try to decide on whether or not to bike the northern route, I'll guarantee that if you decide to, you'll have breathtaking scenery, especially in the west near *Glacier National Park*. Also, be aware of the rough country you are to face. You have to prepare yourself both physically and psychologically or you'll be defeated quickly.

It's perfectly calm down here in these grasslands. There's not even the slightest little breeze. It's all green and there are lots of birds all around. I have a five foot-wide shoulder with very little traffic.

* * *

At 8:57 a.m. I have 20 miles on the odometer as I stop in a local watering hole that also features food in the little town or village of Saco.

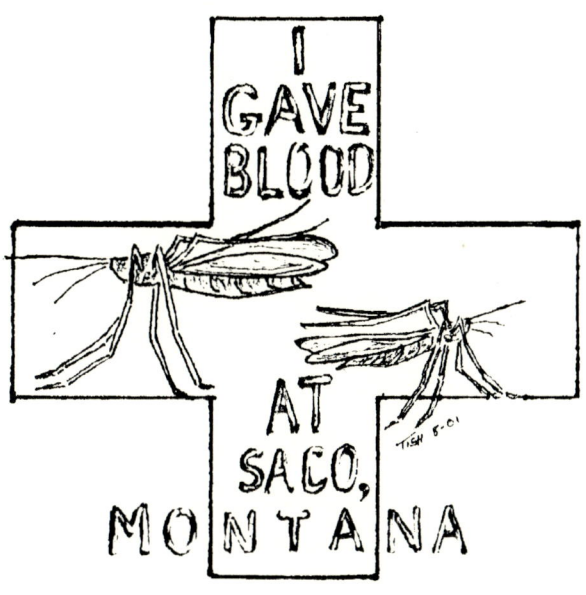

I'm sitting here in a restaurant enjoying a cup of coffee, looking out the window and what do I see? The two couples on the tandems are rolling up and coming in. We visit a while and I notice that mosquitoes are abundant and unmerciful. With every swat I take, I splatter two or three bloody bugs on my arms and legs and this is indoors! As the waitress greets me by saying, "Welcome to Saco, the mosquito capital of the world," I notice her lingering fragrance of insect repellent. Now, isn't that something to be proud of?

I eat breakfast while the mosquitoes eat me. I'm sitting on a stool at the counter next to this rancher. He's very tanned and is as thin as a pitchfork handle. He has a rust-colored beard that blends in nicely with his red face. He's dressed in faded jeans and a blue plaid western shirt. He has a silver belt buckle shining from the middle of his lean body. As I sit there next to him, I notice his worn cowboy boots that are covered with cow dung. Don't ask how...I just noticed...it wasn't hard. His hat looks like it had been eaten by a bunch of mice then glued back together, or buried in a silage pile for a decade then dug up, dusted off, and put back on. I'm sure he loves that hat I must admit it does have a lot of character.

As I talk to him, I learn that he has a ranch around these parts and on his ranch he has some all white horses. "But," he says, "If you were to see them from a distance they would look like they are a dark brown or reddish, because there's not enough room on these horses for another skeeter." He goes on to say that the mosquitoes aren't too bad this year, yet. He says on a normal year I wouldn't have had to pedal my bike through the grass lands at the west edge of town, the mosquitoes would have carried me across. He goes on to say that last year at this time, if he were to stand outside for a few minutes, there would be 50 to 100 mosquitoes on his arm at anyone time. He would sweep over it with his hand, and catch a whole handful of these swamp vampires. Then, he would make a tight fist and when he opened his hand, it would be a bright red. He says the kids around here enjoy doing this, then they'd smear the blood all over themselves and run to their mothers pretending to be hurt. He tells me that the Indians used bear fat to keep the pesky bugs away. But it's kind of hard to get a hold of bear fat these days.

The door and windows of the restaurant are covered on both sides with these blood suckin' insects. I'm not quite sure if they are trying to keep them in or out.

I step outside, and another squadron of bloodsuckers come after me. One giant skeeter sets herself up on my nose as an air traffic controller. She doesn't draw any blood. She just waves in her buddies in for landings on my neck, arms and legs. Then she sinks her drill in and starts pumping blood. I believe the guys who designed oil derricks must have been thinking of mosquitoes because they look just like them. It's trouble when, even in the daytime the mosquitoes are out and biting. I put my wind jacket on to keep the mosquitoes off my arms.

I have about a 10 mph tailwind. They say mosquitoes can't fly faster than…10 mph…they lied…!

I stop for a few minutes and the mosquitoes are eating me alive. I've got to get out of here. I must have ten mosquitoes on each leg right now. God, I itch all over.

I asked the rancher in the restaurant why they don't spray them. He said that it's such a large area they can't afford to. Besides, mosquitoes really are Montana's state bird.

I just went by some horses standing in the corner of this field. They had their tails going all the time, swatting clouds of smiling mosquitoes that are in hot pursuit. They're even shaking their skin trying to get some relief. I can see large clouds of mosquitoes swarming around them. I feel sorry for the horses, I can ride out of here, but they can't.

This is in the daytime with a 10 mph breeze. Mosquitoes aren't supposed to be out when there's a breeze and they aren't supposed to be out in the daytime. They're not living by the rules out here.

There are these birds swooping right down by me. I mean, they're coming within a few inches of me. They are following along…hovering over me…hoping to eat either the fresh blood-filled mosquitoes or trying to lead me away from their young. I'm not actually sure which, but they are fun to watch and listen to

These swamp vampires don't just bite where I have exposed skin; I've got many bites on my ass. It must look like a huge pincushion to them. I'm itching even as I write about it now.

I have 40 miles on the odometer and I'm two miles west of Hinsdale and out of the mosquito-infested area, thank God. I turn my radio on, but I can't get very many stations. No FM stations at all.

It's surely nice not to have to ride on my drops fighting a headwind. By now, the forces of nature are a reality to me and I know I haven't a Chinaman's chance of controlling them. I just hope I can outmaneuver them. It's a beautiful overcast day. I see a lot of red-winged blackbirds out here and a lot of black birds with a yellow breast. I don't know what kind they are but there really a pretty bird.

It is time to stop and have a granola bar.

I'm presently riding in what I would call filtered sunshine, as there is some clouding over the sun.

All these huge ranches are somewhat scenic and the towns out here are few and far between. Montana just seems to go on...and on...and on...On the horizon I think I can actually see the curvature of the earth. I ride along out here in the desert flatness and the road begins twisting for no apparent reason. Why...I wonder...? I don't have the slightest idea. I mean just what do you suppose they had to go around out here...? It's one of those rare points of interest of eastern Montana, a turn in the road.

At 11:27 a.m., I'm eleven miles west of Glasgow. It's 61 degrees and as I ride along, I seem to have left all civilization far behind me. I can see for miles and miles in all directions out here. And it's nothing but a large flat area, devoid of trees, bushes, or any roadside settlements.

*   *   *

A thought just crossed my mind. I know a few people who are very good at what they do and they've found their comfort zone. I believe the problem with that is they are afraid to venture out of that zone. They're afraid they might fail and quit altogether. In my opinion (and it should be yours) this is wrong. You sure don't have to be a rocket scientist to figure that out. I wonder how many times Thomas Edison failed before he invented the light bulb, or how many times the Wright brothers failed. Alexander Graham Bell, was working on an apparatus to aid the deaf when he invented the telephone...Edison was tinkering with the telephone when he invented the phonograph. You see, failing isn't all bad if you learn something from it. When I started this tour, I had no idea if I could finish it or not, but I gave it a try anyway and I'm sure I'll succeed. This will gave me the confidence to write a book, even though I know nothing about writing, or composing, or typing. And I sure as the hell can't spell. I'm looking forward to whatever I decide to try next.

I'm going to look for a place to eat in Glasgow, (No, not Scotland...!) I ride all the way through the town and now I have to turn around and ride back through to look a little harder for a place to eat. I see a graveyard of rusted automobiles but no restaurants.

I've finally found a restaurant.

My food tastes bad enough to cure something. I have a turkey sandwich. It's really bland. I have some soup and it's tasteless. The only thing that's halfway decent is the coffee, and it has an oil slick floating on it.

At 75 miles I stop to eat a granola bar...something that tastes good...to kill the lack of flavor of that lunch. I also put my radio back on. My odometer just turned over to one thousand miles.

The road is ironing board flat. It's overcast and cloudy and in the low 60's. It's just a perfect day for riding. This is definitely Rural America. It's early afternoon and half of Montana still lies ahead of me with the ever-flatter plains of North Dakota yet to come.

The awful aftertaste of the coffee I had in Glasgow, keeps me awake as much as its caffeine does.

*   *   *

One of the first things I have to do, when I start out riding in the mornings, is to make a mental note of my starting point. This might sound ridiculous, but one of the first questions curious people ask me is, "Where did you start riding from this morning?" and "Where are you riding to today?" Sometimes, when I'm asked that, late in the afternoon, after riding through so many small towns and villages, it's kind of hard to recall if it was last night or the night before that I stayed in such-and-such town. It really isn't important to me but it seems to be to them.

Yesterday someone said to me, "You were that close to *Yellowstone* and you didn't go." I replied and said, "If I want to see an old Geezer I'll just look in the mirror."

It's blissfully flat out here. There is a 30% chance of rain today. That means there's a 70% chance that it won't rain and those are very good odds, I'd say. I'm riding through the small village of Nashua.

Oh Yea...! When I was in the restaurant in Glasgow, a young gentleman was asking me all about my tour. He was wondering what kind of a work out schedule I did in preparing for my tour. I told him that I pretty much stuck to the same schedule year-round. I increased my riding a little, but not much. I believe that if you stay in shape all the time, you'll be ready for anything. Anyway he wanted to know just what my schedule was like, so I told him.

Monday: I ride my bike 40 miles after work.

Tuesday: I play nine holes of golf in the wintertime and eighteen in the summer, after work. Then I go to the gym and work out for one hour.

Wednesday: I ride my bike 40 miles, after work.

Thursday: I play tennis for one hour, after work, then I go to the gym for a one hour work out.

Friday: This is my easy, pleasurable day. After work I go for a four to six-mile hike with my girlfriend.

Saturday: I play 18 holes of golf. Of course, I don't use a cart. I walk and carry my clubs.

Sunday: I ride a century, (100 miles) on my bike.

He said to me, "I ride bicycle, do you think I could do a tour like you're doing?

I said, "I don't know. What's your work out schedule like?"

So he tells me, It went something like this:

Monday: He pumps his bike tires up.

Tuesday: Is his rest day.

Wednesday: He gets a massage, to work out the kinks in his sore muscles.

Thursday: He spins easily for 30 minutes.

Friday: He hoists a few beers.

Saturday: He talks about bicycling for 15 minutes, then he catches a movie.

Sunday: He unwinds.

By this time I was finished with my meal so I politely excused myself and left, without giving him an answer he really didn't want to hear anyway. He was such a blockhead. He probably gets splinters when he scratches his head. In my opinion he's not even qualified to wear a sports watch.

*   *   *

Speaking of work out, probably the fastest growing "Sport" for the over 40 group, is one that gives you a good cardiovascular workout with the disadvantages of looking like you have some kind of disorder. I'm referring to walking like a jerk. It's popular among people that used to jog but can no longer afford the knee surgery. The object of jerk walking is to make a simple, everyday act, look extremely complex and strenuous. To do this, you need to wear a special outfit, which includes color-coordinated shorts and sweat clothes and a headband and wristbands and a visor and a *Sony Walkman* tape player. You also need special walking shoes that cost as much as a round-trip air fare to Zimbabwe. After you get all this you have to make your arms and legs as stiff as possible and swing them back and forth in an awkward, Richard Nixon-like manner. It's a great spectator sport.

*   *   *

I have to tell you, when I was watching the L.A. Marathon this year I saw this competitor. He completed the full 26.2 miles, even though he had lost both his legs in the Vietnam War. No, he wasn't in a wheel chair. He struggled along using nothing but his own power and determination. He had pads on his hands and the stumps where his legs once were. He started a day early and finished a day after everyone else was through. The point is that he did it. I also witnessed other athletes giving up at the five and the ten and the fifteen and the twenty-mile mark. In my opinion the man with only stumps for legs wasn't a cripple, but I'm not too sure about the so-called athletes that give up.

I still have my 10 mph tail wind and it's overcast. There's been very little traffic on this road all day. The radio is playing shit-kicking music.

I watch as red-winged blackbirds, robins, and sparrows fly above the flowering prairie grasses. You know, birds always seem to be cheerful.

A couple of elderly people in a camper going the other way had a loud speaker and as they went by, they said, "Good going there, good going," and they waved and smiled to me. After my retirement (separation) from my second wife I wanted to see how the less fortunate people lived in L.A. So, I bought an old pickup truck with a camper and I lived in it for about six months. It was an experience I'll never forget, but that's another story.

I see an occasional small flower now and then.

At 2:34 p.m. I have 100 miles on the odometer and I'm one mile west of Frazer. I'm riding past a very old stone house, minus its roof. It brings to mind that a house takes everything from nature but eventually they'll crumble and fall and return everything back to nature. Everything man builds will eventually crumble and fall, but what God creates will stand forever. That is, unless man destroys it.

Surprisingly, I don't feel myself getting any stronger or weaker as my tour progresses.

There is bare, treeless land all around me. I stare blankly at the ribbon of asphalt that stretches on…and on…and on…to the horizon without making a single turn and without passing a single tree. I guess this is the flattest flat I'm going to see, at least until I get into North Dakota.

I think I appreciate nature more now that I've lived both in the country and the city. You really can't make a fair compassion if you haven't done both. I think that when I lived in the country I sort of took it for granted. It's just like the old saying goes, you can't see the forest for the trees. Out in the country, at night, with the absence of lights, the stars shine unbelievably bright. And because it's that way almost every night, you forget to look up and appreciate them.

My dad always told me not to live anywhere you can't walk out your back door and take a piss.

It looks like a flat, arid desert out here. With barren fields, there's not even any sagebrush growing here. There is no kind of shelter of any kind. As I ride along, I watch as a dust devil makes its way across this flat, open prairie.

I still have my 10 mph tailwind and it's 68 degrees.

*   *   *

Some people would say that I'm on my back nine of life and that's just fine with me. The back nine has always been the best nine, for me. I consider the front nine a learning and practice section and the back nine is the one that really counts. I started playing golf as a hobby to relieve my desire for sex, about three years ago. Golf is similar to sex in a way. You don't have to be very good at either one to have fun.

Speaking of golf let me tell you a little about the game. I believe it's the ultimate sport that requires very little physical activity. To play you have to go out and buy the most unattractive pants that money can buy. Pants so ugly that they had to have been manufactured in Mexico. Next you have to buy a $1,000.00 set of *Ping* golf clubs. For the life of me I don't understand just why you need a full set of clubs. I've been playing for years and I've never use all of mine. I honestly don't believe it would make any difference if I were to use a five-iron or a six-iron on a 130-yard shot. Maybe you need extra clubs for when you throw one in the rough and can't find it, or when you rap one around a tree (accidentally of course) or maybe for when one disappears in a pond, or maybe for when you lay one down by the green and you don't miss it until after you have played three more holes and you reach in your bag for it and it isn't there. Next, you need at least a dozen balls, which sometimes turn out not to be nearly enough.

Then, to avoid any danger of getting any exercise at all, you have to rent an electric cart. That, by the way, costs as much as the game itself. It's amazing just how much fun you can have playing golf, when you think the high score wins, or you don't keep a score at all. My golf and bowling scores are about the same.

When playing golf, the safest place to stand is on the green. You'll never get hit by a ball there. What else that's so great about the game is, you can smoke and drink while you're playing. As matter of fact, they encourage it. There's a so-called marshal that rides around in one of those electric carts and sells cigarettes and beer. Besides that, all golf courses are laid out in such a matter that half way through your game you're at the clubhouse where you can have another drink or two before you attempt the second half. This has always amazed me. All through the game, everybody is rushing you. If you're a little slow, the marshal will come around and tell you to hurry up (after he asks you if you would like to buy a beer). But, when you're half through with the game, they don't seem to care how long you spend in the ClubHouse, drinking. What a sport…!

*   *   *

I stop at a Tasty Freeze, in Wolf Point. Directly across the road is the Homestead Motel, which I check into at 4:53 p.m. It's only $24.00 and it's a nice motel. I would have liked to ride onto Popler, but I was told that there weren't any motels there, besides, 122 miles is O.K. for today.

I shower and change, then walk over to a Case International dealer right next door and inquire about the price of their 9150 Case International tractor. All right…! It's a mere seventy-five-thousand dollars.

Now, it's off to the local tavern.

The tavern is done up with wood paneling and stuffed deer heads. This is where I make my acquaintance of Janet, the girl that served me at the Tasty Freeze. Normally, I wouldn't go over and talk to a girl. I used to sit at a bar for hours trying to get up enough courage to ask a fat girl with a beehive hairdo to dance. Maybe I decide to talk to her because my hormones are racing, or maybe it's just because she looks so beautiful. I don't know.

Her features are so lovely, and her hair looks so soft. Her legs are long and graceful, her buttocks are small but well formed. Her breasts are small but well shaped. We talk about stories from my travels, and her last boyfriend who is in the service, far…far…away. Sometimes she wished it were even further. Then we go out into the star-riddled night. It's a warm, lovely night, and a cool and refreshing breeze is on the prairie. I feel like a teenager as we talk about silly things. Like, are the stars hot…? And the simple things in life like making love with your boots on. The dew is settling on the grass and with the darkness come thousands of fireflies. They're like tiny explosions of light rising from the wet grass. We sit and hold hands, then I put my cheek to hers (which is as cool as the other side of the pillow on a hot August evening). She's fascinated when I tell her that I'm riding all the way across the United States. Her reply is, "How would you like to go around the World with me?" We kiss as shooting stars fill the sky.

*   *   *

*Statistics for **DAY NINE** Tuesday, June 20, 1989.*
122 miles of riding today, 15.6 average miles per hour for today, 1,045 miles of riding in nine days, 116 average miles of riding per day.

Day Ten

From Wolf Point, Montana
To Williston, North Dakota

It's 5:05 a.m. A new day is dawning, or rather, it's crawling out, just like I am. It looks like the heavy clouds might just cover the sky all day. In any case, I've got to get up and pack my stuff. I noticed yesterday as I rode into town that one of the local restaurants opened at 6:00 a.m., which is right about now. I'm on the outskirts of Wolf Point, but I'll ride back into town and look for the restaurant.

I sniff the air and recognize the smell of hot, toasted bread, sausages, and strong coffee coming from this nice little country restaurant. I can't resist it.

It's raining just a few miles away and it looks like it's coming this way. I ask the waitress what would be the quickest breakfast I could get, so I can get on my way before it starts to rain. She suggested biscuits and gravy and that being one of my favorites, I say, "Sure, that's what I'll have". But after eating them, I'm not so sure it was the best choice. The biscuits were so hard the gravy didn't even soften them. I mean they were as hard as a rock and just about as heavy. I'm sure they are going to lie there and roll around like lead in my stomach for a long time.

It's 54 degrees as I leave the restaurant.

There is a little filling station that carries a limited amount of groceries just across the road. I'm going to see if they've got any granola bars and maybe some Tang. As I approach, a work-weathered man fills the doorway of the station. His skin hangs on him like an old secondhand suit. As I approach he shows me his yellow teeth and says, "Good morning." I walk in and find some granola bars. But I can't find any Tang so I ask the old gent if he has any. I don't think the guy even knows what Tang is. He looks puzzled. I tell him it is the kind of drink the astronauts take on all the space flights. He says, "What's a space flight?" He says he doesn't have any, and for some strange reason I believe him.

I'm going to get out of this town now. Nobody told me to get out of town, but I think it's a good idea. It's really overcast and it looks like I'm going to have a headwind.

I'm getting a lot of front-end wobble this morning. I just don't know what's wrong with this bike.

I watch as the clouds float in over the prairie and gather overhead to deposit their load just across the field from me.

It doesn't look as though I'll be making very good time on this road. I have a 12-mile stretch of road with loose gravel that takes up the entire road from ditch to ditch. It definitely deserves a "Detour" sign instead of a "Road Construction" one. It's like riding a bike in a giant earthquake (being from California, I know all about earthquakes). Ahead, I can see no end to the construction zone. Cars approaching from the rear especially worry me because they tend to throw up rocks without even knowing it. A rock flying at sixty miles an hour can hurt really badly. I'm slowly crunching along on the gravel, which acts like marbles trying to skid my wheels sideways and dump me.

At 7:04 a.m. I'm ten miles east of Wolf Point and the road has improved a little. There is not quite as much loose gravel on it. I also have about a 10 mph crosswind, from the north.

I'm finally out of the road construction.

*   *   *

Caution…! The following is NOT recommend for children.

I just laid my finger beside my nostril and blew a big wad of snot and it stuck on my left sleeve. GROSS…! But I guess it's a good learning experience. Now I know that with a 9 mph crosswind it's all right to blow a wad, it'll just miss my sleeve, but with a 10 mph crosswind it'll stick right on. Ugh…! I've talked to bicycle racers and they've told me that in races, if they're about to be passed, some racers, not all, but some, will deliberately blow a wad of snot right in the face of the guy that's about to pass them. Another nice sport, huh?

Hey…! I'm getting good at this I can stop and take a leak without even laying my bike down…I do have to stop though. That's one of the many advantages of riding alone. Of course, again, for this activity I have to watch my wind direction very closely. The old saying goes, "Don't spit into the wind." I would like to expand on that and say, it's not a good idea to piss or blow a wad of snot into it either.

It's just another beautiful day for riding. It's overcast, the sky has a shark gray color to it, but it looks nice and clear ahead of me. Somebody up there loves me. I think God gave me that 90 degree weather and a 20 mph headwind the other day just so I would appreciate days like today more, and believe me, I do.

I'm not going too fast today but I think Williston is as far as I can ride anyway. I have to stop where there is a motel or campground. There aren't any for a long way after Williston. The towns out here are 50 miles apart and I've found out that some of the little towns I see on my map, are actually about a mile or two off the main road, usually on a dirt road. I've even followed signs that lead to nothing.

I've actually gone out of my way and ridden to several of these so-called "Towns." I'm sure they had fewer then 20 residents. They almost appear to be deserted. There are no traffic lights, no banks, no movie houses and no shopping centers, or Seven-Elevens. I was told at one filling station that some of the residents still live without electricity and telephones, as they did fifty years ago, and they like it that way. Most of these "towns" have a grain elevator, three or four trailers, a small general store, and that is about it.

As I ride along, a lot of the cars coming from the other way wave to me. There seem to be a lot of friendly people out here. Actually all the way from Seattle most of the cars seem to be very courteous to me. They always yield the widest berth possible, going clear on the other side of the road when they pass, if possible. Nobody has crowded me yet.

As I ride into Poplar I can see doors hanging crooked on their rusty hinges and windows (some with and some without glass) are propped permanently open. Underneath one sagging front porch a seemingly lifeless dog sleeps. His skin is stretched tightly over his bony skeleton. Eastern Montana is the hottest and the poorest part of the country I've ridden through yet.

There are train tracks paralleling this road and all the trains that go by me blow their whistles. I wonder, maybe they ride bicycle too.

It looks like Popler is a good-sized town. It's got two, yes count them, two, water towers. I don't know. They told me in Wolf Point that there weren't any motels here. I guess I'll find out pretty soon. There is a motel, but I wouldn't stay in it. It looks like this is another poverty-stricken town.

I am about to stop in a small grocery store. But as I ride up I notice a "Closed" sign in the window. As I get even closer, I can see no less than six bullet holes in the window...! I can't help but to wonder, were they there before the store closed or after...? Anyway, I pedal on. I've decided not to stop in this town unless it's absolutely necessary, and it isn't. It seems to be another Indian town.

I have about a five-foot wide shoulder now and at 27 miles (six miles out of Poplar) I stop to put my radio on. I wonder why they have a right and a left ear plug on my headset. Will it, or I, self-destruct if I were to put the wrong speaker in the wrong ear?

Whoa...! I can get three FM stations now. Of course, they're all playing shit-kicking music, but that's just fine with me.

At 8:27 a.m. I'm six miles west of Brockton and it's 57 degrees.

Whenever I listen to the radio, 98% of the time I listen to country western music. (That's what I mean by "shit-kicking.")Granted, they're usually singing about lonesome cowboys, gunfights and broken hearts, but I like it anyway. I also enjoy classical music and reggae. As a matter of fact, I like all music except hard rock and rap (which I don't even consider to be music). I especially enjoy listening to the piano, which, some day, I intend to learn how to play. By the way, I'm a secret singer. That is, I sing in the shower and out in the country when I'm by myself. "Listen to the radio, Oh Listen to the radio, I heard it on the radio." Nobody said I could actually sing, but it's one of the things I enjoy doing by myself. "Let's spend the night together, I heard it on the radio, the radio."

Actually, down deep in my heart, I know I'm a good singer. After all, whenever I sing in church, everybody turns around to see just who's got that wonderful voice.

I stop in a little grocery store in Brockton for a Reese's Peanut Butter Cup and some Tang. I also have a cup of coffee.

I'm on the road and singing again "Oh, I'm doing it my way with you, as long as I'm doing it with you." I guess I'm filled with the gladness of being alive. This is truly a tour of a lifetime. So inspiring…!

It's turned into rolling terrain now. It sure would be nice if I could ride down these hills faster. But, unfortunately I can't go over 20 mph because of the front-end wobble. I've decided that if the wobble doesn't get any worse I'm just not going to worry about it anymore. After all, the earth is slightly pear-shaped and it has been spinning pretty well for quite some time.

As I ride along, the hills are softening into a series of gentle rolls. Every once in a while a 18-wheeler flies past me. These long-distance truckers are a much different breed from me. They cruise over the surface of this nation without even being a part of it. Trucks can be a greater hazard to me than cars, especially on older narrow highways (like this one) which are still used as shipping routes. Truckers often sail past me at seventy miles per hour, leaving only a foot or two of clearance between them and me. The heavy windblast they create makes it hard to keep my bike steady. Whenever I see one coming, I quickly brace myself and put my head down in the best aerodynamic position I can. Trimming my sails. My heart is pounding as the speeding bicycle-sucking beast storms past me...! Its excessive speed is followed by an aftershock of wind that shakes the Hell out of me. The truck couldn't give me much room because I'm riding on a two-lane blacktop highway and traffic was coming from the other direction. He has no choice but to stay on his side of the road. That forces me to do a bicycle tight rope act on the white line on the edge of the road. If I were to swerve a little to the left I would become a hood ornament. And if I was to swerve a little to the right I would drop off the shoulder into the gravel, which is just waiting to embed pebbles in my knees and elbows. After a few near misses I can understand why I'm turning into a religious man.

I have 45 miles on the odometer and I'm ten miles west of Culbertson.

The wind is blowing at about 10 mph. It is a little bit of a crosswind and a little bit of a tailwind. It sure would be nice if it would switch all the way around to my back.

* * *

I used to drive an 18-wheeler cross-country and here is an interesting fact that I learned: Trucks (unlike cars that get miles per gallon) get gallons per hour. A diesel rig burns, I'm not quite sure anymore, but let's say, 10 gallons per hour. Trucks differ from cars in the fact that if you drive a car at 35 mph you're going to get better gas mileage than if you were to drive at, let's say, 70 mph. Big rigs have to hold their rpm's between 1750 to 2100 all the time. If they go under that they don't have any power and if they go over that they blow their engine up. So, they burn the same amount of fuel no matter how fast or slow they are going. For example, if they were driving 35 mph in one hour they would have traveled 35 miles and used 10 gallons of fuel. If they were driving at 70 mph, in one hour they would have traveled 70 miles and still only use 10 gallons of fuel. So, you can see that's another reason why truckers drive as fast as they can get away with. They also get paid by the mile.

*   *   *

I feel a rumbling in my stomach, I think it's those biscuits rolling around.

I stop to have lunch at a cheerful-looking little fifty's cafe in Culbertson. It has red-checkered curtains and tablecloths. I order pancakes and, when they arrive I can't believe my eyes…they're the biggest pancakes I have ever seen! They are not quite as big as my bike wheel, but they hang over the edges of a very large plate. Not only are they large but they have just the right combination of fluffiness and crispness and a brown ring on the edges that make them done just right for me. They are a real work of art that encourages me to plop a big gob of butter down on them and get right to it. They are so big that I have to bore a hole in the middle, fill it with butter and syrup, and start eating from the inside out. With a mountain of hash browns and two eggs on the side, and, of course, my coffee, it's a real feast…! The coffee tastes a little like mud. The waitress tells me, "It should taste like mud, It was ground this morning."

I guess they have big eaters around these parts. I notice that all the omelets on the menu are made with five eggs. I slowly drag myself out of the restaurant, at about eleven thirty on a fine early spring morning. I still have my 10 mph cross-tail-wind from the northwest. It's really cloudy and overcast.

*   *   *

I see a couple of young touring cyclists that are stopped alongside the road. They are working on a broken spoke on one of their bikes. They are the only guys I've seen in the last ten days that look worse than I do. One of the fellow's hair is cut very close to his head and the other kid's head is sort of flat and very long. It looks like it had been run over by a Mac truck.

As matter of fact, I can't help but look for tire marks. I tell them that I'm from California and they start talking about the Hell's Angels. I assure them that not everybody in California is a Hell's Angel. One kid has a shirt on that says, "Hawaii 1989." Personally, I think that if you need a T-shirt to remind you of your vacation, it probably wasn't worth going on in the first place. But, seeing as how I've always wanted to go to Hawaii and haven't yet, I thought I'd ask him if he enjoyed it. So I say to him, "I see you went to Hawaii. How did you like it?" He smiles and answers, "I'd like to go myself. Hell, I barely had enough money to buy this damn tee-shirt, let alone a ticket to Hawaii." They tell me that they've been breaking a lot of spokes. I can identify with that. I tell them that I broke a few myself. I tell them that I also I have front end wobble at 20 mph. They say they did too. So, maybe it's just a common thing. Just as natural as a dog scratching fleas. They are from Racine, Wisconsin and they are riding to Portland, Oregon, using the *Bike Centennial Route*. I'm not sure if it's because of my age or the fact that I got the summer off, but most people I talk to, including these kids, ask me if I am a school teacher on a sabbatical. Maybe it's because I look so smart. They proceed with the usual questions like, "Where you from?" "Where you riding to?" "How many miles are you riding a day?" and so on. They tell me they've had good weather all the way, except for the one day when they had such a strong headwind that they had to push their bikes downhill (a slight exaggeration I'm sure, but I know exactly how they felt). I tell them to be prepared for some of the most difficult, but pleasant riding on the road up ahead. I'm sure they'll always remember me as the old fart that rode across America. They are probably saying to each other that if that overweight, pot-bellied, grandpa could do it, I'm sure we can.

At 12:08 p.m. I'm one mile west of Bainville and it's 68 degrees.

I'm out here riding along with very little traffic. All I can hear is the humming of my own tires, an occasional "Tweet" from a bird and the wind gently blowing through the grass. I'm totally relaxed. Then, without any warning at all, I scare up a flock of quail next to the road. It just scares the shit out of me. I have to stop and check my pants and heart rate before continuing on.

At 75 miles I'm going to stop and take a rest. I have filtered sunshine.

I'm at the North Dakota state line. Dakota is the Sioux word for "Friend." This is where the time changes again. I'm riding out of the *Mountain Time Zone* (it's good to be out of the mountains) and into the *Central Time Zone*. I'm not going to bother with changing the time on my camera and watch now. I'll do it after I stop for the night.

This is also the first day of Summer.

* * *

I'm going to tell you a little about my childhood days. Spring and summer in Indiana. This is when the storm windows came off and I could climb out my second story window and climb up the rain gutter to the roof. I'd go across the roof and get on one of the many huge maple tree limbs that hung over the roof. I would climb onto the limb, shinny along it until I got to the trunk, then climb down to the ground. I loved the spring and summer then, and I still do now.

I must say Washington, Idaho and Montana are all beautiful states. When I wrote to the *Department of Transportation* in the state of North Dakota, they replied and said, "We're so excited that you'll be riding through our state…!" This led me to believe that not too many people are interested in pedaling across North Dakota.

This may be North Dakota, but I've already determined that there is no such thing as flat land. It's either up or down hill. Some of these grades are really tough. I'm down in my second gear right now.

I'm nineteen miles west of Williston. There are lots of heavy clouds in the sky and there's a good possibility that I might get wet.

Let me tell you what I know about Jackalopes, which are in this area. Yes, they are real. Just like a shadow is real. They mate only during lightning flashes, which is one reason why they're so rare. There is a hunting season on them that requires a hunting license and the hunter must have an IQ of at least 50, but not more than 72 to purchase one.

I'm told that cumulus clouds, like the one floating above me, frequently give way to heavy afternoon thunderstorms. There is nothing in sight but clouds and the road and a vast open prairie. Everything looks good to me. As I get older, I seem to appreciate things more.

*   *   *

I see some road kill along here. You know in Missouri they have a restaurant named, The Road Kill Cafe. "Where eating food is more fun, when you know it was hit on the run." Their entrees include:

The Chicken . . . that didn't cross the road.

Flat Cat . . . served in a stack.

Then there is the Taste of the wild side (still in the hide):

Chunk of Skunk...Road Toad a la mode...Shake'n Bake Snake...Swirl of Squirrel...and Whippoorwill on a Grill.

Then there is the canine cuisine:

Slab of Lab, Pit Bull PotPie, Poodles N Noodles, and German Shepherd Pie.

Then there is the Late Night Delight:

Rack of Raccoon, and Awesome Possum.

*   *   *

It's 2:05 p.m. I have 99 miles in as I check into a motel in Williston. That's right, at 2:05 p.m. midday. My room in the Super 8 Motel is only $22.00 for the night and they've got a lounge, a restaurant, and a swimming pool, and I'm going swimming. Getting here this early and being able to go swimming and to the restaurant and the lounge later, is just like having a day off.

I just got back from swimming. I found out that they also have a Jacuzzi, so I relaxed in it for a while. Now I'm going to go outside and look around and take in the sights, all two of them. There are some kids playing hopscotch. That brings back memories. I walked over to the restaurant across the street and as I'm walking back to the motel, someone calls out "Harold." I look around to see who it could possibly be and I can't believe my eyes. It's the two couples on the tandems. I hadn't seen them in days. They tell me that they rode 140 miles today. I only rode 99. So they are beat and I'm quite refreshed. What a surprise it is to end up in the same town and the same motel. By the time they got here there was only an upstairs room left, so I help them up with their gear and bikes. They are beat...! We chat and they tell me that when their vacation is over, they have made up their minds to never go back to L.A.

I go back down in the swimming pool and Jacuzzi for about another hour. Then it's back to my room to get ready to go to the lounge for an undetermined amount of time. There I talk to a man who asks me if I took advantage of the Montana's speed laws. I say, "No, what law?" He says that you can drive as fast as you want in the daytime and if you get stopped your ticket will only be $5.00. They call it, "unuseful use of energy" not speeding. Now I understand why everybody was flying by me. When I told him that it took me six days to travel across Montana he says, "Yea...! I had a car like that once."

After I leave the bar, I step outside for some fresh air. I immediately notice that there are just enough clouds in the west to make the sunset interesting. So I go back in and get my camera and take a picture of the sunset. The sun is slowly setting in the direction I rode in from. It's nearing the horizon, casting a yellow light under the clouds. Then the sun disappears behind a pearl gray cloud and turns the sky to silver. It's beautiful, but the sunsets just don't seem as spectacular as they are as when I'm sharing them with my girlfriend. I think I'll give her a call tonight.

It's 11:00 p.m. and I'm going to bed now.

*   *   *

*Statistics for **DAY TEN** Wednesday, June 21, 1989.*
99 miles of riding today, 15 average miles per hour for today, 1,144 miles of riding in ten days, 114 average miles of riding per day.

Day Eleven

From Williston, North Dakota
To New Town, North Dakota

This is Thursday, I guess and I have to get up and pack now. It's 6:17 a.m. and I'm just now leaving the motel. I'm going to ride over to McDonalds to get something to eat.

A spectacular storm slipped through during the night without dropping a single drop of rain on Williston. The morning breaks with a pastel blue sky and the air is so clean and crisp it looks like you could possibly drink it.

As I leave Mickey D's I can see that there is no wind at all this morning.

On early summer mornings (like this) the prairie starts out as an endless purple. Then as soon as the sun creeps over the hills in the east, fuzzy dark shadows roll into every little hollow and ditch, and the plains turn into a gold color.

There are lots of birds around announcing the clear, crisp, cloudless dawn to me. The road for the most part is straight as an arrow but there is long…long…uphill…six or seven miles worth…starting just two miles out of Williston. I just accomplished that long gentle climb and I'm in second gear, climbing another hill.

I'm ten miles east of Williston. This morning I've been blessed with clear sunny skies and a light tailwind. But there is rolling terrain out here with a couple of pretty damn good hills. I work up quite a sweat climbing up these hills. Then, seeing as how it's only 52 degrees out, it's pretty damn chilly descending the other side, even though I have my windbreaker on.

There is a sign that says, "No Services for the Next 70 Miles." Now that sign would make people traveling at 70 mph in a car nervous. What it means to me is, I have about six hours of nothing to eat or drink except for what I carry with me-Granola Bars, Reese's Peanut Butter Cups and Tang.

There's a red fox right in the middle of the road. Since I don't have a noisy engine, it hasn't noticed me yet. I find it a little strange that it would be in the road, right out here in the open. There are no woods or any kind of cover around. But, I guess, when you're as fast as a fox you don't need much cover.

The landscape and I are both rolling along.

So far today it's been quite hard riding. Some of these hills are really steep.

The *Trans-America Bicycle Trek* for the *Lung Association* started out riding from Seattle a week before I did and they are riding to Atlantic City. I caught up with them, back there in Williston. They are doing the same route as I am today.

I'm ahead of them, but they've got a lot of busses and vans going by. There are big trucks loaded with toilets and all kinds of equipment going by. The bike riders don't carry any of their own gear. They put it all on a bus, which takes it to their next overnight stop. They are only riding to New Town today which is 70 miles away. That would be a very short day for me.

I didn't think I would take many pictures today, But Shit…! It's beautiful out here…! I've already taken seven pictures, and it's only 8:00 a.m. Traveling much slower than cars, I see so much more. I would imagine that if I were traveling through here in a speeding car, with glass between me and the sun and wind, I would be certain that North Dakota is a Godforsaken place. And I'll bet North Dakota natives kind of like that, it keeps the majority of people away.

I'm twenty miles east of Williston. with about a 10 mph tailwind.

*   *   *

I'm starting to get passed now by these young guys from the *Bike-Trek* who are riding in a pace line. Most of them have a mid-section about as flat as a knife blade. They are so skinny that it would take two of them to make a shadow. I have a membership in a health club that I never go to. I had them measure my body fat years ago and it was 84%. Well, it actually wasn't quite that high, but it was high.

Let me explain what a pace line is. Your body accounts for approximately 70% of your wind resistance and your bike only 30%. Riding at 20 mph within 12 inches of the bicycle wheel ahead of you, or in a pace line, you will reduce the energy expended by 30%. The disadvantage of this is that you have to keep your eye on the wheel ahead of you and that's about all you see. If your wheels were to touch, it would set off a chain reaction that would catch you, much like an ocean breaker slamming into an unsuspecting wader, and down you would go, and everyone in the pace line as well.

Nobody that's passed me yet has had a camera. Of course, they don't need one. They pretty much know what a wheel looks like by now. I'm usually last in a club ride. At least that way I know where everybody else is.

Here I am, riding two-and-a-half hours out of town on a lovely June morning. Traffic is very light on this secondary highway that seems to wind endlessly through open pastureland. The two cups of coffee I had for breakfast this morning seem to have multiplied by four. Every bump in the road increases the pain as my bladder calls for relief, but there is no place to go. How come all those stories about the joys of bike touring never told me about this? When seeking privacy, it's amazing just how many cars, houses and people there are around. Especially today, with the *Bike-Trek* being on the same route as I am. They have a lot of female riders, so I can't just stop and piss along side the road. I have to ride until I find a bush or some sort of cover. Then there are a lot of minor hazards to be found in these roadside stops, like thorn bushes and poison ivy, and, of course, my biggest fear, snakes.

The reason I say 40 miles out of Williston is because there hasn't been as much as a roadside stop since I left Williston. In the last 40 desolate miles car traffic has been nonexistent. Only a few trucks and bikes from the *Bike-Trek* have passed me. All I can see up ahead (or in any other direction) is the horizon. I'm going to stop here and eat a little snack. This would be a good place to order *Domino's Pizza* (if they don't deliver in thirty minutes, it's free). But, with no phone to order pizza with, I thank God for Reese's Peanut Butter Cups. Besides tasting wonderful, they help me keep my mind off sex. I think I'm addicted to peanut butter. There are centers for alcohol and drug addictions, but I've never heard of one for peanut butter. I can honestly say that beer and malts, granola bars and peanut butter cups on this tour, have primarily fueled me.

I'm twenty-five miles west of New Town. I still have about a 10 mph tailwind and it's 67 degrees.

I figure I'll just keep taking a lot of pictures, then if only half of them turn out, I'll still have enough good ones. There are quite a few unnamed dirt roads branching off this road. I've always assumed that the desert was flat, even boring. But exploring this desert on a bicycle, I'm soon to realize that its flatness is only an optical illusion. Actually, I find the desert to be fascinating. Its scale is almost too large to comprehend and there are lots of plants that are strange to my eyes.

Spring is a nice time of the year to be out here, with dandelions and all kinds of other small flowers in bloom. I'm not to sure if I would want to be out here in the middle of summer, though. I'm discovering that out here places to get water are like cops, in that you can never find one when you want one.

I have just about to run out of water when I spot a sign along side the road that reads: "Fresh Well Water." One thing's for sure, I'm going to stop because there's no telling how much farther it will be to the next watering hole.

As I ride a little farther up the road, I can see a couple of kids standing on the shoulder of the road. One has a well-worn cowboy hat on and the other is bare headed. They are yelling to me, "You need water…? Come on in…"

So, as they run ahead of me, I ride down their rather steep gravel driveway and over to a horse-tank. I hand one kid my water bottles. The other kid runs into the barn where he pumps the water by hand, while the first kid holds my bottles under an overhead galvanized pipe which comes out of the weather-beaten barn. After what seems to be five minutes the water shot out of the pipe like a watermelon seed. This kid has extremely dirty hands and my water bottles are all muddy now. But that's all right, at least, I have clean, cool water. You know, kids are funny. Even right after they take a bath, they are still sticky. As I leave, I think to myself, what would I do if I lived way out here in the middle of nowhere?

Traveling alone is beginning to grow on me. For the first time in my life, I have responsibilities to no one but myself. No arguments over petty decisions, no compromising over what I consider to be right. For what seems like the first time in my life, I am becoming my own best friend. I am learning that, choosing to like myself (just the way I am) is just that, a choice.

In the distance far ahead of me I can faintly make out the figure of a bike rider. This always encourages any bike rider, including myself, to ride a little faster to see if he can catch up and pass the rider ahead of them.

It's definitely not flat out here. I'm riding over long rolling terrain. Some of these hills are two miles up and one mile down. I don't know why, but they are never one mile up and two miles down.

I have to shift down into second or third gear going up them. It's not easy, but nobody said it was going to be easy. I thought today's ride might be a little boring. With all the peace and quiet I thought I might be in need of some company. That's why I brought my *Sony Walkman* radio along, and I even brought an extra battery for it. But it's interesting, beautiful, stimulating, and exciting out here. I find it never to be boring.

I seem to be gaining on the rider ahead of me, so I'll continue to pick up my pace.

At 11:07 a.m. I have 60 miles in and I'm fifteen miles west of New Town. I still have my 10 mph tailwind. Well, actually, I don't. It's turned into a crosswind from my right side and it's picked up to about 15 mph.

I can clearly see now that the rider ahead of me is a female. I quicken my pace even more. I've finally caught up with the young lady, but I'm a little hesitant to pass. I have a beautiful view from where I'm at, right behind her. She's wearing a pair of ultra-short riding shorts which offer me a view from behind that leaves little to the imagination, but leaves a lot to remember. Out of nowhere a woman's face just came to me. A face out of the past that I know well. But that's another story that I don't want to get into right now.

The prairie is stretched from horizon to horizon. Everything seems so big out here.

Being able to stay ahead of most of these young riders on the *Bike-Trek* makes me feel younger than I did yesterday.

Before my tour, I was telling a friend at work that I was going to stop and take a picture every 10 miles so I would have a record of the difference in the terrain. He laughed and said, "That won't be necessary when you're riding through North Dakota. You'll only have to take one picture because it's the same old flat nothing, all the way across the state." But, actually, it all depends on how you look at it. I suppose if you're driving through at 70 mph in a car, with your windows rolled up and the air conditioner and radio on full blast, it would appear to be very much all the same. But, riding along at a 15 mph pace on my bicycle is a lot different. Every day…no…every mile is totally different from the last one. When I'm out here riding along with the wind in my face, or better yet, on my back, I immediately get the sensation of being free. All my troubles and worries are left far behind me and only the uncertainty of the future is ahead of me. I think this, and the young girl riding right in front of me makes for an exciting tour.

I'm getting extremely horny.

I've found that, when I spend all day out here, my body adjusts to the weather. The only air conditioning I get is when the clouds occasionally block the sun's rays, and that's all I need. The birds singing and the wind blowing through the barbed wire fence and power lines, acts as my radio. It just feels good to be out here in nature and to know that I'm not polluting it in any way.

White puffy clouds drift over me, swelling up, rising, following each other as if they were having a pillow fight in slow motion.

Unlike an automobile trip, I'm sure that if I were to do the exact same tour again, everything would be different. My tailwind might have turned into a cross or, even worse, a headwind and my clear skies may have turned into overcast or maybe even thunderstorms. My beautiful 70-degree temperatures could easily turn into 100 plus degrees, God only knows. Even the traffic could be totally different from day to day. These and the young lady in front of me are some of the many things that make cycling exciting, and I wouldn't trade it for anything.

The few clouds mixed in with the blue sky out here are unbelievably beautiful. It's evident that summer is here. There are all kinds of wildflowers blooming right alongside the road.

I'm rested and my ego finally tells me that it's time to pass the young lady. As I slowly overtake her, I look over and see that she's a tall, ageless girl, with what seems to be a lot of blond hair tucked up under her helmet. I say, "Hi" and as she looks over at me, and her lips give a shy smile and her eyes shine with a light that could only come from her heart as she softly says, "Hi" back to me. This is when I notice her short-sleeved skintight jersey. Unlike most jerseys it has a plunging neckline which reveals an abundance of flesh from time to time as she reaches for her water bottle and douses her turquoise blue jersey, a manner I thoroughly approved of. But, being macho, instead of riding with her, I ride on. Now, I'm not recording all the times sex has crossed my mind on this tour. I've heard that the average person thinks about sex ten times a minute, and I'm sure as hell not average. I think sex is great, especially when you're with someone. I'm thinking about writing a book about sex, but I'll have to do a lot of research

It's been a long time since I've been with a girl. I think I'm getting withdrawal pains.

My stomach is sending urgent signals that I have missed lunch. I've been riding in, what you might call, desolate country. I've only seen one farmhouse in the last 72 miles. That's where the kids gave me the water. Otherwise, it's been quite barren, with no food stops anywhere. I'm just about starved. Granola bars are all right, once in a while, but I sure wouldn't want to live on them. Once, when I was in grade school, I had it all figured out how I could live forever, camping out and eating nothing but *Campbells* soup. The idea still crosses my mind once in a while.

It's 12:11 o'clock in the afternoon and I've ridden 75 miles. I'm in the town of New Town. I'm definitely going to get something to eat. I'm famished.

I go in the first restaurant I see.

I order a roast beef sandwich and a bowl of the soup of the day and a cup of coffee. When it arrives, I am surprised to find out that it's a cold roast beef sandwich and the soup is cauliflower (sort of the color of pee). The coffee looks and tastes like mud. It's terrible. Now, I drink a lot of coffee and let me tell you, I wouldn't even call this stuff coffee. Its taste doesn't differ from its appearance, roughly like dirty dishwater. The food is on the same level as the coffee. Even though I'm starved, I push the tasteless soup around with my spoon and do my best to eat it, but in the end it defeats me.

After leaving this fine establishment, I ride on down to a Tasty Freeze and have a bacon-cheeseburger, french fries and a butterscotch malt. Much better. I love good food.

I go over to the Post Office and mail some things back to my daughter, just to get rid of some unnecessary weight and I check around and ask people if there are any towns up the road that have motels.

I ride around try to find a motel but most of them are full because of the *Bike-Trek* that's spending the night here also.

I finally find a motel that has a cancellation, and it seems to be the only room available in town. It's only $26.00, so I take it.

Today was a short day. I would have liked to ride farther. I had a nice tail wind and it's beautiful out. But, there is no place to stay, not even a campground for the next 100 miles, so I have no choice but to stay in this town. I'll be glad when I get a little farther east where the towns are closer together, so I can ride as far as I want, then stop.

I start to go into this restaurant and I'm turned away by a sign. Just once I would love to see a sign that says, "No ties allowed." So, I go in this other restaurant two doors down. I eat enchiladas, tacos, chicken, and mushrooms. I love mushrooms. In Wisconsin we used to go mushroom hunting. Then we would clean them and get all the bugs out of them that we could. Next, we'd put them in salt water and hope the salt water killed the rest of the bugs. Then we'd fry them and whatever bugs were left we just chew up. Anyway, the salad and soup and dessert bar went down with ease and in great quantities in this restaurant. I'm in heaven. When you add to this great meal an afternoon with no headwinds to speak of, you have yourself a great day.

It's 6:40 p.m. I've cleaned up and watched a little television. I took a short nap and now I'm ready to go check the town out. As I walk downtown or uptown (I never did know which is right) I see an old man sitting on a bench outside a store, whittling, not carving anything, just whittling, making a pile of shavings. He's nearly seventy-five I'd guess, but he still appears strong. He's thin and leathery and looks as though he hasn't shaved for a day or two. He's smoking a pipe and looking out into the afternoon that I just rode through. He tells me that it's the view that keeps him getting up every morning. It's his payoff. He tells me that when he was a child there was only one tree in the park across the road. Now there are hundreds. He says he knows that there was only one because he counted it many times and he couldn't be mistaken.

I just talked to some really nice people riding on the *Bike-Trek*. I think this would be a very good group to travel with. If I were riding with my son, or daughter, or grandson, or granddaughter, it would surely develop a relationship that would benefit both of us, now, as well as later in life.

Winning a bike race, or getting a very good time on a time trial, is an exciting thing for me. But it's like getting a new car. The excitement wears off after a while. But having a close relationship with my daughter, or son, or granddaughter, or grandson, is something that would last a lifetime.

*   *   *

As I walk through the *Bike-Trek* camp, which is in the City Park, I can't help but notice this girl. She has a long neck and legs, and a cute little butt, light blue eyes and a full mouth. Her cheeks are flushed, tomato-red. Her loosely falling waves of golden hair are gleaming in the late afternoon sun. She's wearing a halter-top that shows the curve of her breasts and the upturn of her nipples. She's wearing short…short shorts. She's as pretty as a picture. She's so perfectly proportioned that, after seeing her, all the other girls look like they're made of plastic. I just took a mental picture of her in the nude, and, let me tell you, she looks good. I recall that my mother once told me that if a boy under the age of eighteen were to see a naked girl he would turn to stone. Although I didn't believe her then, I'm definitely more than eighteen now, and I think it just might be happening to me now, I'm getting hard. My head always tells me what to do, although it's not always the same head.

I notice that most everyone is in the chow line, but she isn't. I walk over and start to talk with her. I ask her why she isn't eating? She says that she's a little tired of the food they are serving (not that it wasn't good). I suggest that we go downtown and eat. She gracefully accepts. So we walk downtown making small talk. As we're seated in this dimly lit restaurant, I notice that the two couples riding the tandems are also having dinner here. I suggest that we go over and say "Hi" to them, and we do. Did you ever notice that when it comes to restaurants, the lower they have the lights the higher the prices are?

As we're waiting for our salad to arrive, Rose (not her real name, but she looks like a rose to me), asks me if I ski. I said, "Sure." Now, I never have, but how am I to know I couldn't, unless I tried...? Besides, it's all right to lie about unimportant things as long as it's entertaining, like adding a few points to your buck, or a few inches to your trout, or a few miles to a hiking trail.

As we finish our filet mignon I can't help but notice how the candle make Rose's eyes sparkle and her skin looks as smooth as I know it is. I ask her what made her decide to come on this tour? She tells me about her boyfriend of six years that she believes lives like a dog. She says his refrigerator usually has milk cartons in it that are three weeks old or more. And he has dirty laundry and unironed shirts just waiting for her to come over and take care of. As she goes on...and on...I can't help but think that this guy sounds an awful lot like me. So, she decided to go on this tour to work thinks out. She says that she believes that everyone has a deep-seated longing to escape their present routine, and to embark on some romantic undertaking...whether it is...to sail across the ocean...or to fly around the world...to see exotic countries...or to ride across America...to explore and discover.

I tell her about my girlfriend and how we had a major disagreement right before I left on my tour. We go to three different honky tonks. On one of the doors is a sign that reads, "No Dogs, Bare Feet, Bicycles." As we walk into another, the air is so heavy that the smoke doesn't even spiral upward. It just hangs there, so we don't stay long. After leaving the bars, there's a soft warmth in the air as we stroll across the street to the park. A half-dozen couples are leaning against a low wall, too wrapped around each other to even notice anyone else. I tell her that that was the third time I had eaten since I've been in this town. I say that I seem to be turning into a regular (or irregular) eating machine. I go on to tell her that I was eating anything and everything I could get my hands on. She says, "Give me your hand."

We stop on our way back to the motel and get a big package of cinnamon rolls. I plan on eating them for breakfast, but of course, I won't be able to resist trying one tonight, just to see if it's all right for breakfast. I did a lot of carbo loading this afternoon and evening.

Well, it's 9:30 p.m. Rose is in the bathroom and I'm feeling my oats as I dig through my panniers looking for the condoms. I know I brought an ample supply along, but I don't remember where the hell I put them. Now I wonder...is that long term or short term memory? There must be a thin line between the two. Ah...! Thank God, I found them and I'm glad I brought them along. Tonight would be sort of like getting a Christmas present, only to find out that there weren't any batteries included. She's coming out of the bathroom now, with only a towel wrapped around her. She gets to the side of the bed and lets the towel drop to the floor. And there she stands. Naked as a new born baby. She's lovely, stunning, and magnificent. I've never seen a more breathtakingly beautiful girl. As she gets in bed, she softly whispers to me that she hasn't made love in such a long time that she thinks she just might be a virgin again.

* * *

*Statistics for **DAY ELEVEN** Thursday, June 22, 1989.*
75 miles of riding today, 13.8 average miles per hour for today, 1,219 miles of riding in eleven days, 111 average miles of riding per day.

Day Twelve

From New Town, North Dakota
To Harvey, North Dakota

I waken early in the morning (very early) 3:45 a.m.

I knew I was going to wake up early because I went to bed early. It was a good night…a very good night. I slept well…very well. Awake bright and early (well, not really bright, but early), long before sunrise. Rose is asleep beside me with a lovely smile on her face. As I lie in bed I'm thinking that I want to get an early start this morning, so I can get ahead of the *Bike-Trek* riders, not that they are not nice people, because they are, but I prefer to ride alone. Rose slowly opens her robins egg blue eyes and she looks just as beautiful as she did last night. I tell her of my plans of riding on alone. I explain to her that I like to avoid people as much as possible, and that, especially this morning, I just want to be alone with God. She understands, she says that she has to get back to her group before she's missed anyway. She's a wonderful understanding person.

After a quickie, and a long satisfying piss, I pack my bike up. It's 4:20 a.m. as I get back from walking Rose back to the park, and I feel like a racehorse pawing at the starting gate, ready to break from the chute. I feel revived and ready to go. My water bottles are filled, the tires are pumped and my camera is loaded with film. All I have to do is wait for it to get light enough to ride.

At 5:00 a.m. I watch the stars as they disappear into the morning sky. They flicker then fade away. I'm growing increasingly anxious, so, with the moon and God overhead, I start out. It's amazing how still it is just before sunrise. I'm on the highway before it's light enough for safety but the shoulder is broad and the cars are few. I know it'll be all right.

It's not quite light enough to see my computer or thermometer yet. There is no wind at all this morning. I just saw a horse standing next to the road. It's all white or I would have missed it. I wouldn't say it's early or anything, but I just saw a rooster sleeping. That's the second police officer I've seen, going the other way. Legally, I'm supposed to have a light on. But I guess they've got better things to do than to harass me. They didn't even give me a second look. I can just make out a big lake off to my right. There is a soft mist on the ground, but the sky looks clear. I don't think it's quite light enough to take a picture but I'm going to try to get one of the sun coming up. It's a beautiful sunrise.

So far the terrain looks a lot like it did yesterday with a lot of rolling hills. I have to shift into second gear to get up some of them. If they keep up, it's going to be a rough day.

The birds are all up and singing away and there are a lot of clouds in the sky this morning. Up ahead the sky is turning the color of chimney soot. It looks like it's raining, way on up the road ahead of me. There are no cars or anybody around. It's nice and quiet. All I can hear is the wonderful sound of the birds singing. It's just beautiful out here this morning.

I'm ten miles east of New Town. There is no wind at all. The air is still and it's bitterly cold. The terrain has leveled off somewhat now. It looks very flat for as far as I can see. It's pretty damn cold though, especially for a Southern California boy. It's only 47 degrees.

I keep watching the sky in awe as I ride along. The sun is rising into the overcast clouds. It looks like a bright orange ball as it starts to fade behind the dark clouds, spurting out red streaks across the dark sky. The streaks grow longer, changing colors every second. Wherever You are…God…I thank you for this day. I like those words so much that I say them again, out loud. "Wherever You Are, God, I Thank You for this Day…!"

It's colder than winter out here. I pinch my fingers to check for frostbite. I count to nine, so I recount. I count to ten this time.

The sun has turned the sky a blood red now with beams of orange and purple, with a few with holes of remaining blue. Shades of orange and red are shining on everything.

The wind's blowing in my face. It's a sharp wind and the air is cold. I'm chilled to the bone. Thank God the sky is so beautiful, it helps me keep my mind off just how cold it is. You see, I didn't dress warmly this morning. I wanted to look macho when I left Rose.

Out of the darkness that surrounds me, I'm getting the fragrance of green grass and fresh flowers. There is light coming in over the prairies now, spreading ever so slowly, filling in a hollow here, and pushing out a shadow there. It's working gradually to bring on the colors and forms of this new day.

I stop and have myself a "pre-breakfast" (a cinnamon roll) to hold me over until I can get a more substantial meal. The sun's casting long morning shadows as I continue east into the rolling hills toward Ryder. I knew it was raining up here this morning. The road is all wet but it's nice and clear now. You see, sometimes it pays to ride slowly.

At least the countryside isn't completely abandoned like yesterday. There are a few farmhouses along here. They're quite a ways apart, though.

The sun's up quite a ways now. It's dried the road off and it's starting to warm up a little. My fingers are starting to thaw out. It really feels good.

The open pastureland is turning into farmland now. Everything is green, greener than an Irish bar on St. Patrick's Day. I'm surely glad I took the northern route instead of going through the southern desert where nothing is green.

There's no wind at all and it's 55 degrees now.

I stop and have another pre-breakfast (yes, another cinnamon roll) before I take off again. Besides tasting good, cinnamon rolls have a lot of carbohydrates and I need my carbohydrates. I sure could use a steaming cup of coffee.

At 7:25 a.m., I'm thirty miles east of New Town and I'm on my way again.

I sure hope Rose saw the beautiful sunrise.

The two couples riding the tandems that I talked to last night in the restaurant said they didn't start riding until 10:00 a.m. yesterday morning. By 10:00 a.m. today I should have 60 miles in if I don't get a strong headwind. Right now there isn't even enough of a breeze to turn a windmill that's out in the pasture.

I just turned off Route 23. Now I'm riding south on Route 28 toward the town of Ryder. There are a lot of prairie dogs out all along here. They're kind of cute as they stand on their hind legs and watch as I ride by. A big, fat jack rabbit just jumped across the road in front of me as if to say, "Good morning." There is a bright yellow butterfly hovering around me and some smaller ones skipping along from one weed to another. This doesn't mean I'm riding slowly, it just means that they are fast.

I'm two miles north of Ryder. There is very little traffic out this morning. I've only seen two cars and four pickup trucks in the last 40 miles. It's a wonderful feeling, riding alone on a strange road. This way I can feel, hear, and see things with more clarity. It seems to sharpen my senses. There is no wind at all and it's just another beautiful, sunny, clear, day.

* * *

My girlfriend is an artist, and she observes things differently than I guess most of us do. She looks at something and pictures certain characteristics in her mind. Then, when she's at home painting a picture, she knows what special touches she wants to add to enhance her painting. I recall this one time when we went to an art show and I saw this landscape that I particularly liked. I told her that I really liked it. As we looked at it she said, "Tell me what you like about it." After being around her, I've noticed that I'm starting to observe things differently myself.

For instance, instead of just seeing a tree now, I don't only see the tree, I look at it. I see the many different colors of the leaves as the sun shines through them. I notice the tree's trunk isn't just a solid brown, but it's made up of many different shades of brown and black. I notice that the tree limbs start out as a dark brown and as they get smaller they turn into a lighter brown with a new growth at the very end turning it into a light greenish color. I notice the knots on the upper portion of the tree trunk. I even notice the dead limbs. Barren of bark and leaves, they are usually roughly broken off at the ends. I notice the dead limbs where woodpeckers have bored holes and deposited acorns, which they use as their winter food supply.

I also notice the light to dark blue sky behind the tree with white and gray clouds in the background. Some clouds are round and fluffy, while others are just gray streaks in the sky.

I notice the shadow that the tree makes in the tall grass, moving ever so slightly back and forth as a gentle wind bends the grass from side to side. My girlfriend has taught me how to appreciate things more and I have a great admiration for her.

*   *   *

I'm going to stop here and take my wind-jacket off. Of course, this calls for another cinnamon roll. You might think I'd get sick of cinnamon rolls but I love, what some people would call, junk food. I call it down right good food.

At 8:55 a.m. I have 50 miles on the odometer and I'm on my way again. I just turned left on Route 53.

The air is filled with bugs. I just rode through about a two-mile stretch of road, infested with gnats or mosquitoes. I don't know which, but I think they were gnats. I ate a few and they tasted like gnats. I just swallowed a much bigger bug (I don't know what kind it was) but it wasn't as tasty as the gnats. I have to stop and put my glasses on now. There are swarms of bugs as big as a house crossing the road. I'm hitting them and they are all over me. There is a lot of stagnant water around. That's probably why there are so many bugs here.

I'm riding through Douglas now.

There's no wind at all now.

The sky and a small lake off to my right are both blue, but I'm not. I'm as happy as a pig wallowing in mud.

I turn south on Route 83. It's three more miles to Max. After sixty-six miles of riding I'm so hungry, I could eat almost anything. I'm sure that my stomach thinks that my throat is cut. So, I'm going to roll into a cheerful looking fifties cafe in Max. It's not a Mom and Pop's, it's "Grandma's Place."

A man with sunken cheeks and a short-sleeved shirt and an older church-dressed and white-haired woman greet me as I enter. He has beads of sweat trickling from the bald spot on top of his head. His forearms are dusted with flour, much like my dad's used to be when he was making donuts. She (Grandma) has to be more than sixty. She's wearing a sleeveless dress and blue sneakers. I eat country sausage, homemade biscuits and gravy, home fries, two eggs, and of course, coffee. They've got pies like mother would have made, that is if mother could have cooked. The food is absolutely delicious and it comes in a generous setting. I ask Granny how to get to highway 53, which is a mistake. She tells me to follow the road out front to its end and then turn right, turn left two times and right two times, and it is a quarter-mile on my right. She gives me a lot of useless information. I'll forget it before I mount my bike. At 10:46 a.m. I leave the restaurant.

I think excellent food is a good omen.

I have a 5 mph crosswind now, blowing out of the north. I know that doesn't sound like much, but it sure slows me down. I know I have a crosswind and it's a little uphill, but I didn't think I was crawling along at a turtle's pace until I look down in the grass alongside the road there he is, a turtle. Seeing as how we both have something in common, speed, I stop to take his picture. The underneath side of most turtles is very colorful, so I reach down to turn him over and he takes off like a shot into the tall grass. I guess he's a little shy and doesn't want his underneath exposed, so I'll just leave him alone. If I were to compare myself to the tortoise and the hare, I would probably be the tortoise, slow but steady. The terrain has flattened out a little bit. It's not nearly as rolling as it was yesterday. I really enjoy cycling undisturbed by hills, traffic or noise.

Something bit me on the ear three or four days ago and that sucker is still red and itching.

I smell pigs, I don't see them, but I sure can smell them.

Everybody told me I was going to hate riding across North Dakota. They said there is nothing to see. They are crazy…! It's beautiful out here. It's just like the sign I saw the other day just outside of Davenport, "Have any kind of day you want."

I'm going to take a couple of pictures here. I don't know how anyone can say this isn't beautiful. From now on, if anyone says that North Dakota is nothing but flat empty, naked plains and U.S. Route 2 is the most desolate of the east-west routes with it's two lanes of patched, broken, rutted, pavement running from horizon to horizon, I know they're talking bullshit.

In this part of North Dakota unpaved farm roads run at right angles to each other. This road is straight, and I mean straight. It looks like the Equator on my globe, so I know I can't go wrong. If I travel far enough in this direction, eventually I'll end up right back here, in Benedick, North Dakota.

Rose crosses my mind, about every second. Thank God I'm not Catholic or I would have to go to confession on Sunday.

I just love the smell of new-mown hay.

The Rocky Mountains lie behind me and, sweeping ahead of me, are the grasslands of this huge country of ours. The road goes on…and on…and on. Straight…and straight…and straight. Ahead and behind, it runs through me like an arrow. North Dakota is a curveless place.

I have 75 miles on the odometer now.

What a pleasant surprise to discover how unlonely being alone can be.

A motorcycle approached and gives me thumbs up. My brother said he would like to do the same tour as I'm doing, only he would do it on his motorcycle. I believe with the roar of the engine and the rushing of the wind, he would be missing out on half the fun. Besides he drives at 90 mph.

I've got to stop here for a minute and oil my front derailleur. It's been shifting kind of hard lately. I can't imagine just how many times I've shifted this bike already.

I have a 10 mph crosswind and it's 73 degrees as I ride out of Ruso. I really expect the tandems to catch me again, seeing as how it's so flat. Tandems can go a lot faster than I can on the flats, but not on hills.

As long as I'm stopped, I'm going to put my radio back on.

Every once in a while I ride into a strip of rough road that's about ten yards wide. I think they patched the road and packed it down by running over it with a tractor, instead of a roller. It's rougher than a cob.

It seems like the road is always better where they haven't fixed it.

As I ride into Butte I have 100 miles on the odometer.

All these towns out here are about one block long.

I took a lot of weight out of my handlebar bag and it seemed to help. I don't have quite as much front-end wobble as I had before. I think I'll take a little more out tonight and see if I can get rid of all the wobble.

I think I fell in love again last night. Rose gave me her phone number. I think I'll have it laminated.

*   *   *

Here I am, riding along minding my own business, three miles north of Kief. I can see that the road ahead of me has a dark spot, all the way across it, as if a cloud is blocking the sun and it's casting a shadow on the road. I look up, and there aren't any clouds in the vicinity of the sun. My next guess is maybe there is some water in the road, but this is in the middle of North Dakota and it hasn't rained here in years. Well, I'm thinking, maybe it's a mirage. Sometimes when it's really hot out the heat waves come up off the road and it sort of looks like water. The problem with that theory is that it isn't that hot out. By now I'm up to the spot and I don't have to guess anymore. It's Grasshoppers…! Going across the road…thousands of them…! Grasshoppers are everywhere…! They're supplying me with music as I ride on through huge masses of them. They are whirling past my ears, sticking to my clothes, banging against my bare arms and legs. They're completely covering the road. As they fly, they ping against the spokes of my bicycle wheels. It's like bicycling through a popcorn popper full of green popcorn. As I ride through, I can hear the rustle of the grass and I watch as the grasshoppers jump in the field and go through the grass. They are jumping about like sailors during a storm. They're hopping up and hanging onto my legs. I don't know if these suckers bite or not, and I didn't want to find out. I brush them off as soon as they land. There seems to be an endless river of them about a mile wide.

CLOUD OF GRASSHOPPERS

Well, I've had mosquitoes...gnats...and grasshoppers...what next?

I didn't realize it when I planned my route but it travels over a gravel road here for a way. So I'm going to alter my plans and go out of my way a little, because I really don't want to ride on the gravel. I'll have to ride about 10 miles out of my way, into a headwind, to get to Highway 52 but I think it'll be much better than the gravel road to ride on.

Well, here I am riding on the edge, the shoulder of Highway 52. I'm riding in litter, debris, and broken beer bottles and such, just to avoid being run down, but I guess that's a fact of life. I have a perfect right to ride on the main part of the road, but it won't do me any good if I'm run over asserting my right. Most of the motorists are not hostile to me. They'll pass giving me a wide margin provided they see me in time. That's why I always wear bright-colored, visible clothing. The highway has been torn up in preparation for repaving. It has no shoulder and it's rougher then hell. I have to ride on, or along side of, this road for the next 30 miles. I sure hope it isn't torn up all the way.

The road's so rough I have to stop and rest my ass. As long as I stopped, I might as well have another cinnamon roll. I just drank the last of my water.

This is an Interstate Highway with lots…and lots…of traffic, mostly big trucks. I cringe as I hear these huge trucks rapidly closing from behind, with jake brakes snapping as they roar down the hills. They spray me with dust and gravel, sometimes hitting my bike and me. It hurts…a lot…but what can I do…? I have to concentrate to remain upright, riding over this loose, uneven surface.

This is really hard on my ass. It's not too good on the bike either.

The other side of the road isn't all grooved up, now, and if there weren't so much traffic I would ride on that side.

Sharidan County has set a new standard for me to measure bad roads by. The pavement is nothing but a ragged strip of craters and ground-up asphalt. Semi-trucks and buses never consider slowing down from their seventy miles per hour as they fly pass me.

Tractor-trailers, with their noses into the wind and hammers to the floor, whiz by me without giving an inch. My bike and I shake like an old Ford without springs going down a huge washboard road.

It's 3:03 p.m. I have 122 miles in as I stop in a little cafe in Drake to get something to eat and drink and to stop my hands from shaking. I fill my water bottles and have a B.L.T., large fries and two cokes.

It's warmed up to 81 degrees as I leave the restaurant. It was a very good stop.

Things are looking a little better now, even the road is a little bit better. It's not all dug up. It's just an old concrete road with tar-filled cracks that have swollen into rather large humps. I can't make very good time on this road. It's just too hard on all the equipment. To put it bluntly, "It's a Pain in the Ass." I have to stop and rest my body parts, they are taking a real beating. I've got to check all my nuts and bolts out tonight.

Now, the shoulder of the road has soft tar on it, so I can't ride on it. So, instead of having my own lane, I have to ride out with the semis and cars. When they pass they never seem to pull over to the left, not even when there's no oncoming traffic. It's just no fun at all riding on this #x/z#! road.

I stop to rest and as I put my foot down, it sinks right into the tar.

I'll surely be glad when I get off this road. Being an Interstate Highway, I thought it would be a good road. I thought I could really fly on this sucker. But it's a bitch...! The only thing that could make this afternoon's ride any worse is if one of the farmers' half-starved timber wolves that they keep for watchdogs were to chase after me. This is undoubtedly the worst road I've ridden on yet. It's got potholes big enough to swallow my bicycle and there are rocks all over the road. The gravel road I had originally planned on riding on would have been much better than this lousy highway. It couldn't have been any worse.

I have a 5 mph side wind, crosswind, as I ride into Anamosse.

This is really a screwed-up road. I have to cling to a narrow line of asphalt while the trucks, pickups, and cars scrape past me. Besides rattling my brains and teeth, pounding my butt, the jolting vibrations of the road do something else...they're numb. I've got to stop again and rest my body. After standing beside my bike for a while I can feel a tingling sensation and offer thanks to the merciful heavens above. My genitals are back to normal. I guess this is a common syndrome to bicyclers who cover long distances over rough surfaces.

I stop again. This road is really awful. They overfilled the cracks across the road and it's just like I'm riding over a speed bump every 10 feet or so. I just saw a road sign that read there are nine more miles of this shit.

I have to take my camera out of my handlebar bag and put it in my jersey pocket. It's taking an awful beating. This is the worst sucking Interstate I've ever seen. I have to stop again in the town of Martin.

This road is really taking its toll on me. I have to stop again and see what condition my condition is in. I swear from this moment on I'll avoid Interstates at all costs. I'll zigzag miles out of my way to stay on little old country roads.

*   *   *

It's 5:40 p.m. I've ridden 146 miles today. I'm going to check on a motel here.

Well, the motel's booked full. The desk clerk was nice enough to call a couple of other motels for me. One was also booked full, the other one had one room left. The clerk warns me that it isn't a very nice motel. I'm thinking…so what…it's the only room in town and it's getting really dark out here and it's going to rain in a few minutes, and I sure don't want to camp-out. Anyway, how bad can a room be?

As I ride up to the office of the motel. The skies in the southwest are growing darker and darker by the minute.

There is this disfigured dog, with bloodlines so crossed it looks as if it might be the first dog on earth. It's taking up a crouched position at the door. It's giving me a long…low…ugly snarl as I approach. A woman, shrunken into off angles, comes out of the office and with one swing of her cane she sends the son-of-a-bitch a howling. She says, "She's the best dog anybody ever had, bar none." I go in and pay the $18.00 for my room, which I'm soon to find out was way over-priced. I ask the old woman if there are any restaurants around close. She says, "There's a grocery store right across the road and they have everything you would ever want."

Let me tell you a little about this room so if you're ever in Harvey, you'll know where not to stay. The wooden steps in front of the door are a little shaky, to say the least. As I open the screen door (minus the screen) and put the key in to unlock the door, I can't help but to notice that it has chisel marks all around the lock, as if someone had tried to break in. After

I open the sticking door, I wonder why anyone would want to break in…break out…. maybe but not in. As I walk in, I find out just how bad a motel room can be. The room is so incensed with deodorants and detergents that it's taking me a little time to get my sense of smell back.

Now deodorants are not correctly named. They should be called cover-ups because they substitute one smell for another, and the substitute must be much stronger then the odor it conquers.

A small, very small bathroom is to the immediate right of the entrance. There is no door on it. The floor smells strongly of disinfectant. By now all the cinnamon rolls I ate have turned to shit and as I sit on the throne it rocks from side to side. The bathroom consists of a toilet, a ceramic washbasin, and a rust-stained box used for a shower. A naked light bulb hanging at the end of a long black cord is strung across the room and hangs from the ceiling. It gives off very little light. You have to turn it on by plugging it into a wall outlet.

Hang on, it gets better…I mean worse…when I push my bike into a room containing two lamps, one of which has a burned out bulb. The whole room, including the so-called bathroom…is, at the most…a ten by ten-foot square.   As I squeeze past the bath, on my right is a double bed, against the wall on two sides. It's made of rusting iron curves, much like a brass bed, but a lot cheaper. I sit on the bed and my ass almost touches the floor. There is another light bulb hanging over the bed, this one equipped with a pull chain. Against the wall to my left is an oak dresser with a broken mirror. The mirror, I'm sure has certainly seen many cowboys, outlaws and saloon ladies in its day. There is no telling what things it's seen.

I have to take the panniers off my bike in order to get it between the dresser and the bed. At the foot of the bed is a small table, just large enough to accompany a nine-inch television set equipped with rabbit ears with tinfoil stretched between. I never turned that sucker on. There is a very small air-conditioner in a boarded up window at the foot of my bed.

The walls are so thin that I can hear an alarm clock ticking in the adjoining room. The wood floors are covered with a worn-out rug (and when I say worn-out, I mean worn-out). In spots I can actually see the ground through the cracks in the floor. The whole motel consists of three rooms…and that…in my opinion is three too many. The floor squeaks with my every step. I swear I can hear people walking around, two rooms down.

I don't see any visible cockroaches or bugs, and I stress the word visible. Any bug with any self-respect at all wouldn't live here.

Well, I thought, what the heck. I'll just make the best of it and get cleaned up. So I try to bolt the front door, but the bolt's been yanked apart. I jump into the shower anyway. The semi-warm water that squirts from the nozzle sends one stinging jet into my eye and another up my nose and two others over the shower curtain. Most of the water washes down the side of the metal box and stands, icy cold, in the plugged bottom.

Have you ever noticed that when you're finished with a shower or bath, there is always a little clump of hair covering the drain? Well I've come to the conclusion that my hair only falls out when I take a shower or bath. So, to keep from going bald, I'm not going to take anymore showers or baths. On second thought, I'd rather be baldheaded with friends, than someone with a full head of hair, and no friends.

I decide to brush my teeth, get dressed, and head on downtown for a little attitude adjustment. As I turn on the faucet in the washbowl, the water splashes all over my feet. I explore beneath the bowl and find that the trap is detached. Now, I'm ready to throw in the towel.

"It's Miller Time."

I walk downtown to explore the village of Harvey. There is a strong wind blowing, turning back the leaves on the trees and it's going to rain on me any minute now. So I really didn't have to take a shower and lose all that hair.

That motel I'm staying at is on the same highway as I rode into town on and it belongs there…they both suck. After playing road warrior all day, I'm looking for an *A.A.E. (Attitude Adjustment Emporium)*. In other words, a tavern.

It's starting to sprinkle. A mist from a neon beer sign is glowing orange. This, I figure, is my sign. Now you may be thinking that I sure drink a lot. This is not true I only drink on days that end with "y".

Why is it that sometimes you can't make up your mind about what you want to eat? Then…other times…you know exactly what you want. I know I wouldn't like liver today without even tasting it. What I want is pizza, and the neon sign in the window of a pizza joint says it serves beer too. Now that's about as good as it gets.

I go in and order a pizza and a pitcher of beer. The waiter brings me two beer mugs, apparently he's expecting someone is going to join me. I sit at a window table and watch as the clouds close in over the rooftops of the village. Then the rain comes down in buckets while I finish my large pizza, supplemented with three pitchers of beer. It was that kind of day. I'm thinking to myself, why can't roads be as smooth as this beer is going down?

*   *   *

Statistics for **DAY TWELVE** *Friday, June 23, 1989.*
147 miles of riding today, 13.9 average miles per hour for today, 1,366 miles of riding in twelve days, 114 average miles of riding per day.

Day Thirteen

From Harvey, North Dakota
To Cooperstown, North Dakota

Its 6:00 a.m.: I guess I have to get up and pack.

I finally get up and out the door one hour later.

Some mornings it's just hard to get moving, actually it was hard to get out of bed this morning. Dawn's revealing a glorious blue sky as I ride downtown and find a place to eat.

This town is only about four blocks long and it's got five…yes…folks…count them…five taverns…and one restaurant. Does that tell you anything about this town…? I know it has five because I checked them all out last night. That might be one reason why I'm getting off to a slow start this morning.

There's this weathered cowhand in the restaurant asking me all kinds of questions about my tour while I'm trying to eat. He's wearing the uniform of a cowboy: a blue denim shirt, Levi's, boots and a ten-gallon hat. He says that he has everlasting respect for what I'm doing. Everlasting nowadays means approximately two days. Anyway, I did have a great breakfast and conversation. I had the usual, two eggs and hash-browns, toast and jelly and, of course, my coffee. And the coffee was good this time.

I'm on my way down the road and it is a beautiful day. It's nice and warm. I don't know exactly what the temperature is but I'll check. Ah…! It's 62 degrees already this morning. I sure won't need my wind-jacket today.

The birds are all up and singing, "Good Morning" to me.

I'm getting a late start this morning (about three hours later than yesterday) but that's all right. The next town with a motel is only about 100 miles up the road, so there is no rush. Then the next motel after that is another 100 miles but I'm not about to ride 200 today. This isn't the *Race Across America*.

God, it smells good out here...! It smells like freshly cut hay.

I didn't sleep worth a shit last night. I was crammed into a room, roughly the size of a Super 8's bathroom. It was the smallest motel room I've ever seen. It was a very hot and humid night, so I turned the air-conditioner on before I went to bed. I was wakened in the middle of the night by this awful banging and rattling. It seems that the air-conditioner had frozen up and was making so much noise I had to shut it off. Then it got terribly hot in that small room, without any windows to open. I probably got a total of three or four hours sleep all night. I'm putting that motel on my mental list of things in America that I don't care to revisit.

Of course, to look at the bright side of things. It's one place I don't mind leaving.

When I ventured outside my motel this morning, I found the storm-washed morning to be fresh, cool, and clear. But the sun's behind a big cloud now, taking a nap, I guess, and it looks like it will be there for a couple of hours, at least that's usually the length on my naps.

I'm riding on County Road 3. It's a blacktop road. It's surely nice to get off that rough speed bump Interstate. I didn't oil my chain this morning, it looks like it has enough oil on it to start an oil slick if it rains.

The sun's coming out from behind the clouds. That was a very short two hours...!

It's 9:05 a.m. and I'm ten miles south of Harvey. There is no wind at all. Basically it's flat, farm land with crops as far as I can see in all directions.

Whenever I come to a clump of trees, I know it's a windbreak that's been planted around a farmhouse. Everything is so green out here, except the sky, which is a beautiful blue with streaks of white added in for texture.

You know everyone wants to go to Europe, New Zealand, Australia or Africa...I say, "See America first."

Like many people...I was reintroduced to bicycle riding to get into shape (not to mention a few traffic violations that prohibited me from driving). I ride for a totally different reason now...I ride for the fresh air, beautiful scenery and to see new and exciting places, and...of course...to have fun. After all, isn't having fun the most important point of bicycle riding?

Ever notice how often people say, "I wish I'd done something really exciting and challenging when I was younger, because now I'm too old and I don't have much to look back on?" They put things off until the last minute, or even longer. Or they say, "I've always wanted to do something like what you're doing, to travel across the United States. But I never did. I just got caught up in the routine of work and buying things, I guess, and now it's too late."

Society says, "Keep working, buy a house, start a family, save for your retirement, and along the way be sure to pick up a color television, microwave oven, stereo, new car, and an electric knife sharpener."

*   *   *

Let's talk about L.A. for a minute. All anyone there thinks about is acquiring things...a house, cars, hot tubs, stereo systems. Everybody talks about their jobs and how much they're making and what all they've bought lately, and that's about it. What really gets me is when they complain about things like the price of gas and, yet...everyone drives everywhere. Very few people would even consider biking or walking anywhere to save gas even when it's only a matter of one or two blocks. Have you ever noticed how people will drive around and around a parking lot, wasting gas, just so they can get a few feet closer to the shopping mall? They drive two blocks to the Health Club to work out.

After bicycling through an Indian reservation and seeing how little the people have there, it's hard for me to feel any sympathy for people in L.A. who complain because they can't seem to save enough to buy that super-deluxe television or microwave they saw in the store window a month or so back.

I'm stopping here to take a picture of a typical windbreak…three rows of tall trees surrounding the farmhouse. The farms out here seem to be between two to three miles apart. There is not a lot to see out here except large fields of green grass. So I have plenty of time to think and reflect on my life.

When I was planning my tour, a few people said that I was crazy to try it alone. They said I should at least have a sag wagon (a car or van) following me. I wonder if our pioneer ancestors would have ever made it west today, without having something to fall back on or if they were burdened by our twentieth century "necessities."

While touring, I've come to appreciate the world's vastness and I realize that there is a place in it for me. I feel just like the little blade of grass that cracks the highway pavement, pushing its way up to meet the light, to find its place, nothing can stop it. Living in the halogen lamp lit city, I rarely see the stars at night and I let the newspapers and television define the world for me. As a touring bicyclist, I have come to appreciate the great outdoors and the important things in life.

You know it's kind of nice to know that if, for some reason, there was a (real) gas shortage, I could ride my bike anywhere, given enough time…and the best part is that the road would be traffic free.

I don't seem to be making very good time today; it must be I drank the wrong kind of fuel last night.

Every once in a while I see a bunch of beehives out in the fields, then I know I have to watch for the honeybees. These guys fly about one to five feet off the ground, and they go across the road like bullets. They don't look where they're going, they just head in a straight line. If I happen to get in that line, they just run right into me. Most of the time they bounce off. If they don't, it's a sure thing that they will sting me, my punishment for being in their way, I guess. So far I've been lucky. They've all bounced off, or I've been able to brush them off, before I got stung. When I see one, I can expect hundreds to follow. They all seem to be going in the same direction, probably back to their hive to make honey.

There are a lot of flowers all along here, the same kind as I saw yesterday and the day before...and the day before that. But they're just as beautiful today as they were three days ago.

Well, I guess, by now, I'm at least one day ahead of the tandem riders.

The prairie is flying past my feet and the sky is rolling overhead and, between the two...are miles after miles of small gophers (ground squirrels or woodchucks or groundhogs, I'm not sure what they're called). Prairie dogs...! Yea...! That's what they're called, because of their "bark" and they live in "towns" of several hundred burrows. They stand at attention alongside the highway and, as I approach...the little rodents make a madcap, hightailed dash for the other side of the road, only to stop a couple of feet from the shoulder before turning around and making a last-ditch dive for the side it had started from. Again...and again...this has happened. It looks like some sort of crazy Russian roulette game, in which many have met eternity on the blacktop. They often end up as mashed clots of fur on the road when they play this game with unforgiving motor vehicles.

If you are wondering why I decided to ride from the West Coast to the East Coast, instead of the other way around, well...there are several reasons. One, is that I wanted to start my vacation by taking the train to Seattle. Secondly, I wanted to be in Wisconsin somewhere around the Fourth of July. Thirdly, because there is supposed to be, and I stress the phrase...supposed to be...2,000 miles of prevailing tailwinds, going from the west to the east, versus 1,000 from the east to the west.

Now, just wait until you hear this scientific reason of mine...! The earth is rotating from the west to the east (I think) at approximately 1,000 mph...and who in their right mind would want to ride against a force like that on a bike?

Just another thought here. (It must be a good day for thinking). Man was put on this earth to live, not just to exist. And I refuse to waste my time trying to prolong my days. I'm going to live them to the fullest, every day.

My philosophy is don't wait until you retire, or until you graduate, or until you can afford to take a tour of a lifetime. Make the time, borrow the money (if you have to) because the longer you wait, the greater your chances are of never going.

As I ride past this typical farm with rows and rows of vegetables in the garden, it looks like a *Norman Rockwell* painting that has come alive. I can't help but recall that, back when I was a kid, we always had a big lush vegetable garden. It was a source of pride during the growing season and throughout the winter as well. My mother canned dozens of jars of produce each summer, which she lined up in colorful rows in the fruit cellar for the long cold winter.

It's a little overcast and I have about a 5 mph crosswind now, from the east, which is not good, because I'm riding straight south now and in a very short time I'll be turning east.

The terrain ranges from rolling to table flat (of course that would depend a lot on just how flat your table is). I'm not going very fast this morning, then again, if I wanted to go fast I would have taken an airplane. I say if you can't ride fast, ride far.

At 10:25 a.m. I have 26 miles on the odometer and I'm two miles west of Chaseley, riding straight south on Highway 3. The sky's getting darker and darker by the minute, and there is no doubt in my mind that it's going to rain.

I just made a left turn onto route 200, and now I'm riding straight east. The wind has shifted so I still have a 5 mph crosswind, which seems to be blowing the rain clouds away. It looks clear ahead of me.

Somebody up there loves me.

There is still a dark cloud cover, off to my right...covering the entire sky. So, I pick up my pace a little, trying to get out of here before that storm front hits. The weather report says thunderstorms can be expected this afternoon. I don't have to listen to this, I already know what the weather is, and I'm out here in it...! Anyway, if I'm ever going to see a rainbow, I'll have to withstand a little rain. The radio is playing some good old shit kickin' country music as I ride into Bowdon.

At 49 miles, I stop at a roadside rest area to see if there is any water here. All Right...! There is...! I pump the rusty handle up and down a dozen times until rusty water comes out, but with a few more pumps it clears up and I fill my bottles with clear, cold water. It's 70 degrees when I leave the rest area.

As I ride and look east at the long...straight...pavement that cuts through the flat plains...I can imagine that...if I were to fire a rifle down the highway...a mile or so east of here...I'd find the lead in the middle of the road.

The sun is dimming in the western sky as I ride into Sykeston.

I still have my 5 mph crosswind and the ragged clouds that are washing across the sky keep it overcast. I just rode through this little shut-up town whose name escapes me because I never learnt it. Everything was closed-everything...but one small general merchandise store which had two gas pumps and a mongrel (with a baseball bat clenched in it's teeth) on the porch. I didn't need any gas so I rode right on by.

I can see the massive thunderclouds forming in a sky that's growing almost black. I have a constant 10 mph crosswind, which keeps me in my middle chain ring all the time. It's really hard pedaling.

At 1:22 p.m. I stop in a restaurant in Carrington. I'm famished. I have a baked potato with ham and cheese on it, coffee, and an apple pie a la mode with cinnamon ice cream for dessert. It's very good. I discover in the restaurant that the Post Office and Telephone Company don't even recognize this little town as an official town.

Here's a sign. Oh Goody...! Road Construction for the next 26 miles...!

It's raining just off to my right and the clouds are coming my way. I'm going to try to outride the rain. But the rain clouds are catching up with me. It's sprinkling lightly now and I still have that 10 mph crosswind. It looks clear up ahead so I go down on my drops and try to get out of here before the weather really turns foul. All the cars have their windshield wipers on now, so I guess it's official…it's raining. I'm going to have to stop and put my camera and tape-recorder in plastic bags. I think I'll put my rain jacket on, too.

I'm pedaling along to the rhythm of the rain. It's not coming down quite hard enough to keep the road wet although most of the cars have their windshield wipers on, pushing the rain aside.

What a difference ten minutes can make. The temperature has dropped and it's starting to rain fairly heavy now. My rear wheel is sending out arcs of spray. Actually, the rain feels quite good. The only thing I don't care for is the crosswind. It has picked up to about 20 mph and, with the road all wet…it sort of reduces my grip on this planet. It also reduces the slowing effect of my brake pads against the wheel rims.

I have 80 miles in and I'm eight miles west of Glenfield.

I don't believe it…! It's still raining and I just rode through a mile and half wide strip of bees going across the road. At first I try to dodge the bees, but it is no use. They just keep running into my bike and me. They are running into me. I'm not running into them. I know this because they're traveling much faster than I am and they just put it into autopilot. They are just lucky they ran into me and not a car or truck. As I look off to my left, I can see this field full of flowers…yellow mustard…I imagine.

Remembering my boyhood, I recall a little tool shed we had beside the garage on our farm. It was always dark inside because there were no windows or lights in it. I watched as bumblebees flew in and out from under the rafters of the shed. Being a curious youngster, I wanted to find out where their nest was. So, I stood in the doorway of the tool shed for quite some time…just watching to see where they were going. I could see that they were going under a pile of boards and gunnysacks that were piled on the floor. Leaving the door open for light and an easy escape route, I started removing the gunny sacks…very slowly…one at a time…but I still didn't find their nest. So, I stood back and waited for another bee to come in…or out. It flew right to where I had removed the pile of bags and went down in to a hole in the ground. As I stood in the doorway and watched, I could see that they were going in and out of the hole at about one minute intervals. I immediately thought of a fun game to play. I picked up a board, about three feet long and maybe three inches wide, stood by the hole and waited. As soon as the first bee came out…I swung…and Splat…! A perfect shot. I waited for the next one, Splat…! Another home run. This was fun…! Splat…! Another one bites the dust. Another one, two swings this time, but it was still a home run. It was the bottom of the ninth, no outs, and the score was 18 me…zero them. Not a single one got by my makeshift bat. Well, being an anxious kid, I wanted to speed the game up a little. After all, they were pitching pretty slowly. So…I decided to pound on the ground around the pitcher's mound. Well, it worked all right! They started coming out of there like bullets out of a gattling gun. I was swinging as fast as I could. Splat…! Splat…! Swish, a miss, Splat…! Swish…Swish…This would have been all right if the ones I missed would have flown out of the hole in the rafters…but…they were pissed…! They started swarming around me. I threw down my bat and ran for the door…tripped over the threshold and was "Out." I scrambled to my feet and ran as fast as I could toward the house. The score was now…me 26…them three. One stung me on the lip, which puffed up to an enormous size, and stayed that way for days. Kids that age are mean to kids their own age. In school they called me "Nigger Lips" for a long time afterwards.

*   *   *

It's quit raining now it looks like it's going to rain again on up the road though.

There is a church about a mile ahead of me sitting on top of a small hill. It's a pretty sight. It gets me to thinking about how much I hate it when people say, Jesus Christ this, or Jesus Christ that. It states right in the Bible, don't use the Lord's name in vain. So…I guess…I really shouldn't get too upset over it. That's something that will take care of itself.

I'm on one of those roads that's all chewed up. I'm bouncing along a stretch of rough pavement with huge potholes. It's not raining anymore. All over in North Dakota, so far…they have rubber pads at all the railroad crossings. It makes crossing them nice and smooth.

As I look down the road and across the broad prairie, I can see thunderheads a-brewing in the sky. If they continue to develop, it'll cause the clouds to dump their load of moisture, possibly…right on me…seeing as how I'm riding straight east toward them and the town of Glenfield.

I have a 20 mph crosswind now. The wind always increases as a storm approaches. A gust of wind just blew up in the fencerow and tested the tree's ability to bend. The rain and wind are flattening the long grass alongside the road and in the prairie.

I have 100 miles on the odometer and I'm eleven miles west of Cooperstown.

I'm riding in a light sprinkle now. It's warmed up to 79 degrees. With this strong of a cross-tail-wind, it's hard to hold my bike up on this wet pavement, but I'm determined to push on. I'd rather run the risk of wearing out…than stop and running the risk of rusting out.

Out here the barns don't need wind vanes on them because, what I normally see in winds like this…is the barn itself leaning…and that pretty much tells me which way the prevailing wind's blow.

I can see Coopersville just up the road. It's drizzling real light now.

Coopersville, Cooperstown, what's the difference?

It's 5:30 p.m. I have 112 miles in so I stop and check on a motel. They tell me that all the motels in town are full. Seeing as how it's drizzling…I ask them to call around and see if they could possibly find me a cancellation somewhere. Luckily, they found me one.

Maybe I'm lucky it's raining, the room I got was a cancellation from a construction worker who couldn't work today because it was too wet. It's $18.00 for the night. It's another no-star motel, but it's a lot better than the one I had last night and the showers hot.

I'm all cleaned up, and I'm going to go downtown and check it out. There is this sign outside *The Sirloin Stockade*, which reads, "All You Can Eat…$5.79." "WOW…!" I decide right then and there that that's just what I'm looking for…!

As I go in, the hostess comes over and asks me, "How many?" I reply, "A party of one." The salad bar and entrees include everything you could imagine. There are several kinds of potato and macaroni salads, lots of fruits, and every kind of vegetable that is eaten raw or pickled, as well as a number that aren't. By the way, have you ever noticed that at a salad bar they always put the best foods in the top center row…where…if you don't have six foot long arms, it's almost impossible to reach? The waitress is a bubbling girl of about nineteen…I'd guess. She's about as flat as a deboned chicken breast. She tells me that she is home from her first year of college. She wants to hear all about my tour, and, of course…I can't refuse her. I have three plates of salad and seven cups of coffee and am about to begin the eighth when my 16-ounce steak arrives. Someone once told me that if I were to take little bites, I would burn up a lot of calories eating. I'm not sure if that's true or not but I'm going to take my time eating anyway.

I usually seem to have a bottomless pit, but I don't think I can hold anymore. I put away an unbelievable amount of food. I ate six dinner rolls, smothered in butter, with my meal. I had apple pie a la mode, with whipped-cream for dessert. And…after dinner…I drank a pitcher of ice-tea.

God…! I hate that: seeing a pretty girl when I'm walking out of an all-you-can-eat restaurant. It's hard to suck my stomach in right after I've just pigged out. I need to walk around town to help pack my food down.

Back to the motel now, I'm feeling a little sick. I mean, I'm really stuffed…!

*   *   *

*Statistics for **DAY THIRTEEN** Saturday, June 24, 1989.*
112 miles of riding today, 13.6 average miles per hour for today, 1,478 miles of riding in thirteen days, 114 average miles of riding per day.

Day Fourteen

From Cooperstown, North Dakota
To Barnesville, Minnesota

At 6:00 a.m. I get up and pack and an hour later I leave the motel. I've decided to eat at the same restaurant as I did for dinner last night. They have an all-you-can-eat breakfast, as well. I'm a little leery about going in again. I'll probably gorge myself. I'm sure last night I set a new personal record for food consumption. I sure hope they don't ask me to leave. It would embarrass everyone. But, what the heck, that's another good thing about bicycle touring. You can eat…and eat…and eat…without gaining any weight. Being too full, last night…after dinner to drink beer…I drank seven-sevens. They filled my glass almost full of booze, then topped it off with a shot of seven-up. I went to three different bars, mind you…just for comparison…and they all did the same thing.

I'm just now leaving the restaurant. I had a breakfast big enough for three normal people which included a plate full of hash browns, covered with gravy…a plate of pancakes smothered with syrup…sausage… eggs…toast and…of course…my usual pot of coffee. I had to close my eyes and take a series of long…deep breaths to help force the food farther down into my stomach. I'm full, but I feel very good this morning.

It rained last night and the roads are all wet but it's a nice, warm, overcast day.

As I ride out of town, I spot this elderly gentleman. He looks to be as fit as a fiddle. I can't help but notice that he has oversize hands and feet, as he stands there looking at his flowers in his front yard. I don't know what kind of flowers they are, but they're the same kind as my mother use to grow in Indiana. I'm impressed, to say the least, by the huge beautiful flowers. So, I stop and talk to him for a while. He is more than anxious to show me his back yard, where he has a whole garden of beautiful flowers. He tells me that he retired two years ago and the trouble with doing nothing, is that it's too difficult to tell when you're finished. And that's why he plants and takes care of so many flowers. This man…this garden…these flowers…might have been anywhere in the nation, but actually they're in Cooperstown. And I'm glad they are, and I'm sure that the people of Cooperstown are glad, too.

I must be living right. As I ride along and look behind me, the sky is dark and cloudy. It almost looks like night. And as I look ahead, it's a nice clear light blue. It's been that way almost every day.

Oh…! Lucky Me…! Road construction for the next 13 miles…! There were very few cars on the road all day yesterday and I haven't seen any, yet, today.

God…! It's a beautiful day…! After the rain last night, everything is so fresh and clean. It's so nice to be out here. I can't think of anything in the world I would rather be doing.

The first 25 miles yesterday were rolling terrain. After that it was pretty much flat. And it looks like it's going to be quite flat today. So, that means that the wind direction pretty much determines how fast I can ride.

There is some beef out here, just the way I like to see it…on four hoofs and walking around. I may very well see some real cowboys out here, and I don't mean urban cowboys.

There is a 50% chance of rain for today, so I packed everything up in plastic bags. I double-bagged my film and tape cassettes which is why it took a little longer to pack this morning. Everything I had packed in plastic bags yesterday stayed dry in the rain.

A sign back there said Road Construction, but it's not bad, yet.

Oh…! Wow…! A 6% downhill. The only problem with that is that I can see the 7% uphill…! So, the landscape isn't flat, like I thought it would be. It's turning into a series of rolling hills now…the kind I have to attack and descend. I really didn't need all these hills right away this morning on a full stomach.

It's 8:40 a.m. and I'm ten miles east of Cooperstown. There is no wind at all and the sky is filled with purple-gray clouds. It's 60 degrees. The light is a little dull because the sun is behind a large cloudbank hanging in the west.

According to all the maps I have, and the mileage markers, and the signs that tell me how far it is to the next town…my odometer seems to be right on.

This road has cracks all the way across it. They are not nearly as bad as they were the other day, but they are still rough.

My bike seems to be a little hard pedaling I wonder if my brake calipers are out of calibration and the brakes are dragging…Sure enough, they are. Actually, the problem is with the brake cable. It's sticking…so I oiled it. You know, there is a simple solution to just about everything. My bike sure pedals a lot easier without the brakes dragging. It feels like I'm riding downhill with a new pair of legs now.

I have gray-blue skies with, of course, the possibility of light showers. I now have a 5 mph crosswind, from my right, out of the west. After about 15 miles, I'm going to make a turn, then I should have a tailwind…unless the wind stops or changes directions, which isn't unusual.

I have 30 miles on the odometer and I'm four miles north of Pillsbury and…sure enough…I have a 5 mph tailwind. It's starting to clear up in the west. Too bad I'm riding east.

I don't know exactly what's up ahead here, but I just rode past a sign that says, "Pavement Ends." There is road construction and the road is all mud. I can see cars up ahead turning around and coming back. I don't know if there's any way around this mess.

I can see this pickup truck, pulling a boat, about a quarter of the way up this muddy overpass. He just stopped and turned around, and he's coming back. Oh…! Shit…! If he can't make it, what am I going to do? When I get up to him, he waves me over. He says he knew that I couldn't ride through all the mud and he felt sorry for me if I had to push my bike through it. So, he tells me to throw my bike in the back of his pickup and he'll take me through. I thank him, as he helps me lift my bike into his truck.

This road construction is only about a mile long, but it probably would have taken me an hour to push my bike through all the mud. There is no way I could have ridden through it. It's a mile long stretch of mud about six inches deep. The pickup is spinning his tires all the way through. I don't know if the *Bike-Trek* rides through here or not.

I'm riding east now and the wind has switched around. I have a 10 mph crosswind from my left, now, out of the north. I don't even know what road this is...it doesn't tell me on my map...and there are no road signs anywhere.

The red-winged blackbirds seem to be out in force today. One flew straight toward me at eye level. I could see its red shoulder pads glittering in the sunlight as its black wings pump it forward, just over my helmet.

As I ride toward Pillsbury, I enter into a different county. It seems that this is Highway 26. Roads always get a lot better...or worse...at county lines. This one got better. It's really nice riding now. Seven miles west of Page, the weather is turning ugly. Clouds hang in the treetops. There's definitely a threat of rain.

I'm pleasantly surprised with North Dakota so far. I expected flat...wind-blown...boring terrain. Instead, the houses are trim and neat, and the lawns are carefully tended...and the flowers are brilliant. Although, not all the railroad crossings in North Dakota are equipped with the rubber pads. I just went over one that was really rough.

I'm riding south now. The road's a little wet. There are some heavy clouds still hanging overhead. This road has a crack every ten feet or so. It's rough, but it's not too bad.

So far, I've only had one dog come out in the road after me and he was too lazy to chase me very far. I don't mean today...I mean on my whole tour. I don't like dogs…let me rephrase that…I don't like dogs that chase or try to bite me. I like big, lazy dogs.

Anyway, here I am riding along at a nice and easy pace and I hear this dog bark. It really gets my adrenaline flowing and I immediately pick my pace up. I don't know what kind of dog it is…but whatever it is…there's entirely too much of it. Nothing arouses a dog's warfare instincts more than moving bicycle wheels. I normally ride at a moderate pace. The guys I usually ride with at home say, that if they would turn a dog loose every mile or so, I would be unbelievably fast.

Let me tell you what I've learned about how to react to dog attacks.

1) Don't get mad at the dog. Instead, concentrate on your own reactions.

2) Check the road out ahead of you and the size of the dog. If it's a friendly Chihuahua and your path is downhill, there's no reason to panic. However, if you're laboring uphill and the animal is a stray version of Cujo, with red-rimmed eyes and frothy jowls, you may be in deep trouble.

3) Don't show fear. Dogs sense it. They sense aggression too, so don't try that either.

4) Keep any parts of your body you treasure out of snipping radius while cooing sweet nothings in the canine's ear.

Exception: If you're riding by a house and the owner yells out something like, "Watch Out…! He's a Trained Killer…!" Your best response would be to shift into a lower rear sprocket and try setting a new land speed record.

5) Never kick at a dog. You might miss and end up being pulled out of your saddle by a set of teeth.

6) Decide whether dismounting and keeping your bike between you and the "Beast" is the best thing to do.

7) If the dog attacks, try a loud air horn, if you happen to have one, I don't. This will scare away every animal but a Cujo, who will probably take your leg off anyway.

*   *   *

I don't know what happened to Page, I never saw it

I've got to buy some more film when I get to Wisconsin. I've already taken more than 450 pictures.

You know, thanks to the *Interstate Highway System*, it is now possible to travel across the country from Seattle to New York City without seeing a single thing. From the Interstate, America is all steel guardrails and plastic signs, and every place looks and feels and sounds and smells like every other place. What a shame…! I'll stick to the back roads where Washington and Montana still look like Washington and Montana. Where there are roadside stands selling apples and strawberries…Mom and Pop Cafe's…pick your own farm products and limeade stands.

This road's pretty good now.

I've always loved the spring of the year. This was when I could get out and plow the fields and smell the freshly turned soil. That's a satisfying thing to a farmer. After the plowing was finished, it was time to disc the fields. After that was completed, it was time to plant. My favorite crop was corn because that's a two-man job, and my dad would always have me excused from school to help him.

I hated my school daze. My brain was an organ that started working the minute I got up in the morning and didn't stop until I got to school. Besides, I believe the same way Mark Twain did, he once said, "I have never let my schooling interfere with my education."

I just turned onto an unknown county road and I'm riding toward the village of Ayr.

I recall back on the farm we had milking machines but we also had a few cows that refused to let us put a machine on them. They preferred the gentle squeeze of a warm hand to the cold…rapid…pulsating of these newfangled machines, and I for one, can't say that I blame them. When I started milking these contented cows (by hand) our cats started to gather around, taking their places about eight to 10 feet away, just waiting for me to spurt them with some warm milk…which I did.

I didn't care much for milking though, I would rather be cleaning the barn. This way I could drive the tractor and be outside. In the summer, I could just drive the tractor and manure spreader through the barn, filling it as I went. But, in the winter it was a whole new ball game. When the snow was too deep and I couldn't get into the fields, I would have to load the manure in a wheelbarrow and wheel it out onto a pile behind the barn. As the pile got higher…and higher…this became quite a challenge. I would have to lay 2 by 6's down and push the loaded wheelbarrow up the slippery plank without spilling it. After I had the barn cleaned out, I would sprinkle lime on the center aisles and sweep it back and forth, until the floor was as white and smooth as an eggshell. I remember this one time I'd just finished the floor, and one of our cats walked across it, leaving its tracks on my picture perfect floor. They say that cats have nine lives. Well…if I could have caught that cat it would have only had eight left.

I just turned east again. I have a 10 mph crosswind from my left, out of the north. The farmers plant wind breaks out here to stop the wind from blowing down their crops and soil. It doesn't stop the wind from blowing down the road, though.

A little dog chases me but it has such short legs and it can't keep up with me. Even though this is a little dog, it has a system whereby it can quickly establish an entire neighborhood network of barking. So, I have to watch for them at the next farmhouse I come to as well.

*   *   *

The sky is starting to clear up. I see this spiked buck standing alongside the road, so I stop to take a picture of it. You know, Mother Nature has always created the male of the species to be the better looking.

It seems a shame that so many deer are killed every year, just for the sport of it. It isn't hunger or a winter supply of meat that drives millions of armed men and women to the forests and hills every autumn. I know there are a few good and efficient hunters who know what they are doing...but many more are overweight city slickers who have never missed a meal, primed with whiskey and armed with high-powered rifles, not knowing a turnip from a carrot. They shoot at anything that moves or looks as though it might, and their success in killing one another may well prevent a population explosion. If the casualties were limited to their own kind, I would have no problem with that. But they slaughter cows...pigs...farmers...dogs...and highway signs...which makes autumn a dangerous season in which to travel. In Winnebago County last year, four automobiles were hit by rifle fire on opening day alone. Radios warned you against carrying a white handkerchief. Too many hunters, seeing a flash of white, have taken it for the tail of a running deer and cured a head cold with a single shot.

* * *

I've ridden 60 miles today and there hasn't been any place to stop and eat along this road yet. Of course, I've been eating my granola bars. This must be my lucky day. I just opened a twin pack of Reese's Peanut Butter Cups and...lo and behold...! There are three cups in it...!

It seems that I can ride for sixty plus miles and never see a single car, until I have to take a leak, then there is no end to the traffic.

I liked my dad. He was a wonderful person. I learned a lot from him. Once, he told me that you get a lot closer to nature if you piss outside...and I believe he was right. He also told me that I should whistle at all the girls. He said that if they were good looking, it would make you feel good, and if they weren't, it would make them feel good.

As I ride along, this full-grown Doberman with a studded collar comes chasing after me. I'm thinking, "Oh Shit...!" This is the kind of dog that claws at chain link fences...the kind that's trained to go for the necks of burglars...! And he's gaining on me. As I look back, I can see his lowered jaw with drool rolling off his monstrous tongue as his ivory fangs gleam.

This is not good. Man's best friend has turned out to be this biker's worst enemy. And, unfortunately, no one has figured out the mystery of why most dogs become enraged at passing bikers. There are a lot of theories though.

One is that the spinning spokes of a bicycle create a sound above the human hearing level but within the irritation zone of dogs. Much like a dog whistle that is silent to humans. The dogs seem to respond to the high-frequency sound-waves coming from the wheels.

Another theory is that the bicycle is intruding upon a dog's territory and, unlike the massive bulk of an automobile…its slow-moving…light-weight body can easily be attacked. Besides that, the biker himself is in a vulnerable position on his flimsy machine and can be harassed easily.

One more theory is that the simple movement of a bicycle on the road is a challenge to a dog to run it down, to compete with the rolling wheels, and to scare the shit out of the rider. And this Doberman is succeeding in doing just that.

Whatever the case may be, the dogs outnumber the theories. Some dogs just stare and yawn as I ride pass. Others stare and wait to attack until I have passed the mid-way point. Still others leap to a frontal charge at the first sound of my rolling wheels. No two dogs are alike. As far as that goes, neither are two bikers. I've known some bikers to carry a can of *Halt* in their handlebar bag. Then, when a dog growls…barks…and tries to run down his bike…he takes the aerosol can and sprays the dog in the face. The disadvantage of this is that, by the time he reaches into his front bag to retrieve the can, aim…and fire the spray accurately…the dog has either already done his damage or is intimidating you so much you can't control your bike…much less the spray can.

Kicking at a dog only induces more anger and challenge in the dog's attack. So avoid kicking. Besides, it takes your feet off the pedals and reduces your control and your speed.

You also run several risks by slowing down and taking your air pump to bop the monster on the head. Such as missing and putting the pump through your spokes, sending you over the handlebars…breaking some spokes as well as your neck.

I've found that the best way to get away from them is to sprint as fast as I can (like I'm doing with this Doberman). They usually won't follow me much further than their property line.

I take a picture of the first cornfield I've seen on my tour. The corn is about eight to 9 inches tall. This might sound corny, but I remember the old saying the farmers used to use, and probably still do: Corn should be knee high, by the Fourth-of-July.

This road's still got cracks all the way across it and it's rougher than a corncob.

Just because I'm stopping here and taking a picture of these beautiful sheep, it doesn't mean a thing. I think I better give my girlfriend a call tonight. My dad used to raise sheep. And, let me tell you…what they say about sheep is true. NO…! I mean about how dumb they are. Your quick mind has already supplied you with what I omitted. He would let them graze in the woods behind the barn, and, every once in a while, we would find one with its head stuck in an Y of a tree. They would stick their heads through the Y and try to back out. They would keep pulling backwards until they strangled themselves…when all they had to do was to stop pulling backwards and lift their heads up then back out. I'm sure you've heard someone say that they followed her around like a flock of sheep. I swear to God…if the lead sheep would walk off a cliff and kill itself, all the other sheep in the flock would do the same.

This sure would be a good place for a hundred-mile time trial. It's straight and flat.

Can you imagine, that a guy in a passing car just flagged me down? As I ride over to his window and stop, he exposes a mouthful of rabbit teeth as he asks me for directions. He's completely dressed in earth tones. He looks like a down-to-earth person. The seats in his car are covered with plastic. I can't think of anything more useless than plastic seat covers. Why would anyone want their car seats to last longer than their car? He's sure was surprised when I tell him that I'm from L.A. Anyway, we look at my maps and find where he wants to go. He has written directions from someone on how to get there. They are detailed and accurate directions, but he still got lost. He says he also got lost in Cooperstown. Now Cooperstown is a very small town and, I think, it would be impossible to get lost there. I believe he has a little less than the average intelligence. You know, the kind of guy that buys a new wristwatch every year because he doesn't know how to reset it for daylight-saving time.

I'm ready for a food stop, anytime now. I'm ten miles west of Argusville and I have about a five to 10 mph crosswind. It's clearing up a little. It's 75 degrees.

This is the second time today this has happened. Quail hiding in the tall grass right alongside the road, and...as I ride past them...they fly up and scare the shit out of me.

These fields out here are unbelievably huge. There has to be at least a hundred acres in each one. They are vast rolling oceans of grass, rippling with the wind. They look much like a lake. If you were to toss a stone into the lake and watch the ripples they would seem to go on forever.

As I ride along, I'm thinking I might change my route and go to Boston instead of New York City. I don't know...I'll have to look at my maps tonight and see. I think there might be a mountain range I would have to ride over though.

What the Hell is that...? Oh Shit...! I heard the flapping of wings as this huge black crow sailed over me. And, as the beef cows watch from a nearby field, the dirty bird just dropped a load on my hand...! There's a BIG...juicy...green...yellow...brown...and white glob of shit running down the back of my hand and dripping off my finger tips.

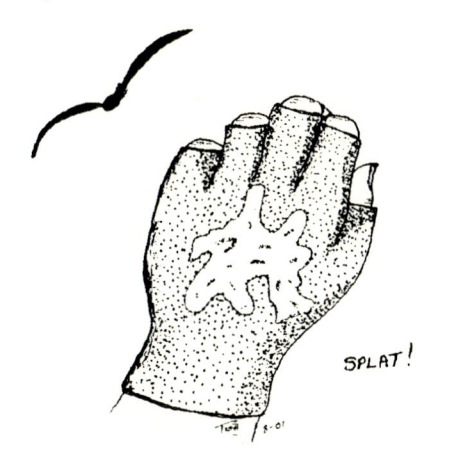

It's sure a good thing cows can't fly. I stop and before I can get my water bottle out and rinse my hand off, it gets quite sticky. Oh, well. As long as I'm stopped, I think I'll put my radio on.

I ride through Argusville and I see a line of clouds in the west, which has been advancing for quite some time. It gives me evidence that a storm of no ordinary character is forming.

I've been riding for 90 miles today and there hasn't been any place to stop and eat yet. At the outskirts of Moorhead I find myself riding alongside a train. It's going about the same speed as I am.

Thank God…! There's a Burger King…! I'm as hungry as a bear. It's 2:44 p.m. and I'm stopping. I was a little afraid my stomach might collapse.

I had a burger, fries, and a coke. The coke tasted awful. I couldn't even drink it. It must be the water. The water was probably fit for instant coffee or iced tea, but not for me. I filled my water bottles anyway…they were empty.

I'm finally out of North Dakota and in Minnesota. You have to be careful crossing state lines-you have to ride between the dotted lines…! They don't bother cars much but they'll send me head over heels if you were to hit one squarely with your bike wheel…! Hey…! Lighten up…! I'm having fun.

Well, what do you know, the sun's finally coming out from behind the clouds to show me the way. The sky's a dark blue with a few white clouds.

I have a five to 10 mph tail wind and I'm in Moorhead, Minnesota. It's warmed up to 80 degrees.

A Highway Patrol car, with two officers in it…goes by me…really slow. They go about a half-mile up the road then pull over and stop in the grass along the shoulder of the road. I quickly take my radio off (without stopping). I don't know if it's illegal to ride with it on here or not. It's legal in California if you only have one speaker in one ear. As I'm about to pass them, they take off again. They go up the road about another mile, slam on their brakes and stop right in the middle of the road…! They turn on their red lights and get out and open up the trunk. As I ride passed them, I say, "Hi…!" And they say "Hi…!" Back to me. To this day I don't know what the hell they were doing.

*   *   *

I'm just riding along soaking up the sun and atmosphere, and I come across these huge trees in the fencerow. They seem to be standing all alone, just like me. I'm thinking, this is truly a gentleman's countryside. There are lots of big beautiful clouds in the sky so I'm going to stop and take a picture and rest a bit under the trees. There's nothing to lean my bike up against without pushing it through the tall grass in the ditch and over to the trees, so I just lay it down in the grass along side the road. By the way, do you know why a bicycle can't stand up by itself? "Because it's two-tired." Anyway, I lay my tired bike (and myself) down in the grass and watch as the cloud formations float overhead. Sometimes it's nice just to do nothing. As I lie here appreciating the day and admiring the majestic trees, a thought crosses my mind. You know, if you were to plant a tree, you would have to wait about a hundred years for it to grow as large as these. I've come to the conclusion that trees that grow alone have room to go their own way and have all sorts of crooks and curves in their branches. Like men, some grow best in company, striving to outdo the rest. But others need to grow their own way, even though it may be lonely. They both have their own value. Sometimes I find two trees growing together, like these, bending and giving only for each other. I believe if one was to be cut down, the other one would die, also. "Poems are made by fools like me, but only God can make a tree." As I'm lying here…totally enjoying myself…along comes this car. He goes by me a little way, and then he slams on his breaks…backs up…and jumps out. He runs over to me, and says, "Are you all right?" I guess with my bike and me lying in the ditch, it does look like I might have been in an accident. I thank him for being concerned and lie back down as soon as he's out of sight. I hear another car approaching and I think, instead of putting him in question, I'd better get up and leave.

The sun's out and I have a five to 10 mph tailwind.

There are big, and I do mean, "BIG" potato fields, all through this area. As a green diesel tractor works its way up and down the potato rows cultivating the field, a slight breeze brings me the smell of freshly tilled earth.

Shit…! I just wiped my nose off with the back of my right glove. I had totally forgotten about the bird shit…! It's amazing how your sense of smell brings back memories. One thing's for sure, I'm going to have to wash my gloves out in the sink tonight.

I understand they have machines to harvest potatoes with now. They dig and bag them all in one operation. I sure hope…as a nation…we never come to the point where our people become too proud…or too lazy…or too soft…to bend to the earth and pick the things we eat.

Pretty clouds are everywhere as a rule rather than the exception.

It's 5:08 p.m. I've ridden 122 miles today as I stop at a Tasty Freeze in Barnesville. Another of my personal rules is never to ride by a Tasty Freeze or Dairy Queen without stopping. I talk to this guy, whom I take to be the owner, he tells me that he's 76. He's short and round with skin the color of clay. He's mostly baldheaded with only a fringe of sandy hair. He tells me that there is a nice motel right across the road. He says that's where he always puts up his mother-in-law when she comes to visit.

I go to check the motel out and see if he likes his mother-in-law or not. It's a nice motel and it's only $20.00 for the night. The gentleman behind the desk looks at me, then out the window at my bike. He says, "You can lock your bike to a post in front of the window if you want to." Well, another rule I have is I never ask permission from managers if I can put my bike inside my room. I always assume it's all right.

So, I push my bike around to the side door and into my room. I lie down on the bed and watch television and wait to see if the manager is going to say anything. He doesn't. So, I wash my gloves and clothes out and drape them over the warm coils of a radiator.

I guess I could say that I lead a very simple life. All I need at the end of a day is a lot of food…a hot shower…a drink and a warm bed.

I'm going to walk downtown to see what's going on, if anything. It's cleared up nicely. This looks like a pleasant enough little town. As I walk past a church its bells are ringing. I just love the sound of church bells.

*   *   *

I walk along Main Street, and hear loud music coming from a tavern where pickup trucks (most of which have gun racks in the rear windows) are parked out front. As I walk in, I'm quite surprised. There's actually quite a lot going on. There are men and women on the dance floor and others sitting at their tables smoking Camels, nursing their beers and, of course…watching all the action. The jukebox is playing country-western music. I think its *Willie Nelson and Waylon Jennings* singing to each other. This place makes this little town almost seem like a big city. I manage to find an empty stool and sit down at the bar. There is a Hamm's clock above the cash register and Budweiser lampshades hang above the pool tables that are in constant use. Other beer signs are glowing here and there for general decor. Trash barrels are overflowing with empty Budweiser cans. I talk to the bartender a little. He's a stocky man, and his belly is hanging over his belt. He has a rust-colored beard and his face is red from sunburn, as well as from the soft light of the setting sun coming in from the open door. He tells me that it had rained an inch here this morning.

As I sit here having a few cool ones, an old, tired-looking dog wanders into the bar and lies down. Then, this old rusted out pickup truck pulls up out front. A guy wearing Levi's and worn cowboy boots…dusted with cow dung…and a long-sleeved plaid shirt with the sleeves rolled up…a black cowboy hat…and carrying a large knife on his belt…walks in and sits down right next to me. He's got a roll-your-own cigarette poking through his shaggy mustache. He has big, bushy eyebrows. He doesn't have a beard, he's just plain unshaven. I'm sure that if he brushes his teeth at all he'd use a wire brush. There is no doubt in my mind about his occupation. He has to be a cattle rustler. As he picks up his mug of draft beer I can't help but notice an open sore on his hand. I just sit there and ignore him. As I tell the barkeep about my tour, I happen to mention that I think that Western Washington is truly God's country. This rough looking guy that's sitting beside me says,

"Do you really believe in God…?"

I say, "Absolutely…!"

He speaks up and says,

"I only believe in scientific facts, not inspirational images, like God."

I think, Wow...! This guy is using some really big words there. Maybe...just maybe...he's not as dumb as he looks. Being the passive person I am...I normally would have said nothing...or if I had enough to drink I might have said something like..."that's all right you can believe in whatever you want and I'll believe in what I want," and that would be the end of it. After all, people have to move to a different drum or this would be a very boring world.

Next he says, "You're not one of those born-again-Christians, are you?"

Now, I don't exactly know why, but most Christians don't come right out and tell you that they are born-again. It's as if they have six toes and would rather leave their shoes on. Well, for some reason...I'm not exactly sure why...maybe because it's Sunday...maybe because I was inspired by all the natural beauty I'd been riding through for the last two weeks, or maybe I was inspired by God Himself. In any case, it was irresistible, I instantly recalled something I had heard a long...long...time ago...and seeing as how this guy only believed in facts, I felt like it was my obligation to relate some facts to him. So I begin by saying, "You know that with all the modern technology we have today, scientists can take a seed from any plant apart and analyze it, and find out exactly what it is made of. Do you agree with me?"

He says, "Absolutely."

So I continue, "Then the scientists can make all the different components and put them together, with exactly the same percent of everything. I mean that he can even make it look exactly like the original seed, right?"

He says, "Yea, so what's your point?"

I say, "My point is...if you were to plant that man-made seed, I can guarantee you it wouldn't grow. Only God can create life...!"

I may not have stated it quite right, but I think I got my point across. With that, I granted him a good evening, and drifted out the door like a shadow, feeling grateful to be alive myself.

A lot of things went through my mind on my way back to the motel. I thought, what if he had asked me if I believed in the Trinity. Of course...I do…but if he wanted facts how could I explain my views to him…? So I rehearsed this in my mind and came up with this: I would start by saying,

Water is water, just like God is God.

If you freeze water, it becomes ice, just like God can become Jesus Christ.

Then if you were to heat water to the max, it would become steam, just like God can become the Holy Ghost.

So you see water can be water, ice, and steam, but it's still water.

Just like God can be, God, Jesus Christ, and the Holy Ghost, but he's still God.

As I walk back to the motel, the late afternoon sun still hangs in the sky like a giant fried egg in a blue-steel griddle. There is hardly a cloud in the brilliant blue sky except along the horizon where a few flat ribbons hang above the fields. I feel both relaxed and energized. I stop at *The Wagon Wheel Restaurant*. I'm hungry again, and I'm ready for their salad bar and roast beef dinner, and a piece of peanut-butter pie for dessert.

God, it's good. As I eat, I watch the sun lower itself into a sea of grass.

This gentleman is telling me that, at this time of year, on the road I ride out of town on…in the morning…there are usually huge herds of deer, standing right next to the road.

I can tell you right now that I rode east in North Dakota, roughly paralleling U.S. Highway 94 through Hope and Ayr, turned southward, still on Route 32, past Pillsbury and Page, then I went due east on Route 26 past Argusville, Harwood and West Fargo. I can report this because I have a map in front of me, but what I remember has no reference to the numbers or colored lines squiggled on the map.

What I remember are the long stretches of road through the forest, the farms and houses, the crossroads stores where I stopped to get water and where many deer crossed the road right in front of me. I also remember the land and the forest…the animals…the hot and the cold…and the wind…the hills and the flat prairies. I've noticed that the big towns are getting bigger and the villages smaller. The Mom and

Pop's...the grocery...general...hardware and the clothing stores, cannot compete with the supermarket and the chain organization. Our treasured and nostalgic picture of the village general store...the cracker-barrel store...is very rapidly disappearing.

It's 11:00 p.m. I'm going to call my daughter before I go back to the motel. Oh, well...she isn't home.

I'm going to go to bed now. A good hot meal and a comfortable bed do wonders to rejuvenate my body and spirit for another hundred miles the next day. Hopefully, I'll get up early enough to see some deer. I don't know, but I don't intend to set any alarms on this tour. I'll just get up when I wake up.

As I lie here and think back over the day, I've decided that it's been a very good one.

     *   *   *

*Statistic for **DAY FOURTEEN** Sunday, June 25, 1989.*
122 miles of riding today, 14.9 average miles per hour for today, 1,600 miles of riding in fourteen days, 114 average miles of riding per day.

Day Fifteen

From Barnesville, Minnesota
To St. Cloud, Minnesota

It's 6:30 a.m. I guess I'll have to get up and pack. As I look out the window, it reveals to me a cloudy but dry morning. A little after seven I pedal out of the motel parking lot. It's overcast and looks like rain. I ride over to a restaurant and have a great breakfast of two eggs…sausage…homemade biscuits…gravy…home fries…and coffee.

I get on my way and am forced down on my drops, in my little chainring, already this morning because of a 15 mph headwind. I ride this way through Lawndale. If the wind doesn't let up or stop, it'll be a short riding day for me. I'm tired already.

I finished some notes last night, they read: "June 25 (yesterday) is a Sunday that saw me fourteen days on the road and 1,600 miles away from Seattle." Riding along out here, all alone, I get a lot of time to think, and I was just thinking about this tour I'm doing. For me, cycling across the United States is more than a vacation or a means of getting from one coast to the other, or a mere physical challenge. It allows me to see our country under my own power, pollution free. You know, to talk about the winds that blow across our Plains is one thing, but to bicycle headlong into them…days at a time…gives me a whole new realm of understanding.

At 8:24 a.m. I have 20 miles on the odometer and I'm two miles south of Lawndale. It sure looks like it might rain. It's 65 degrees. Heavy clouds have pulled over the sky like a giant down comforter. But there are still slivers of lighter, almost blue spots where the sky is open.

I may say that these heavy headwinds have been "Blowing" in my face, but let me tell you…they "Suck…!" I have a 15 mph headwind. Well, it's not quite a straight headwind. It's a little bit from the right, but for the most part, it's a headwind.

I ride along and watch the clouds change formation and I listen to the wind whistle through the trees as windblown branches rub together. It's looking more like rain all the time.

I'm going to stop here in Carlisle and change my shoes. It's awful hard riding into this headwind. I'm not talking into this tape-recorder much today. Some things are just better not said. This headwind I've been riding into the last 25 miles is no fun, and I've been taught, that if you don't have something nice to say, don't say anything at all.

I ignore the thunder and the wind of a threatening storm as I savor the spectacular sounds of a flowing stream.

* * *

Just a little food for thought here. I hate dating, for a lot of reasons:

1) I usually dress the wrong way. I recall this one particular time when I was taking this girl to a Polo game. I wanted to impress her so I went out and bought a complete cowboy outfit (WRONG…!). When I paid for the shirt, the girl at the register asks me if I had the right change. I said, "NO…!" Anyone that pays more than $85.00 for a shirt doesn't have any cents.

2) I'm not a good conversationalist, I tend to say a lot of wrong things. Like the time when I spent a weekend at *Yosemite National Park* with this girl. A bear chased us and afterwards I mentioned that that was the most exciting thing that happened on the whole trip…! (True, but definitely the wrong thing to say).

3) I hate making plans. For most concerts or any other event you have to purchase your tickets a long time in advance. And, when the event finally arrives, you may want to go somewhere else…with someone else…(Oops).

4) A lot of girls seem to think that there is something wrong with you if you don't try to get into their pants at least by the third date. I guess for

some men sex is the one and only important thing in life, but not me. I don't like to rush into anything, I'm as patient as a spider that's been living in the rafters for years. It takes me at least until the third date before I start holding hands. I honestly believe that you should have a good friendship before you even think about a relationship...thank you very much.

The force of this 15 mph headwind I've had for the last 40 miles is like a flexible but impenetrable wall. My pedals seem to be pushing harder and harder against my feet and, to make it even worse...I'm riding in rolling terrain again.

I feel pity for the motorist who zips by me unaware of the Canada Geese with six goslings standing in the field right next to the road. I can hear the sounds of far off birds and the voices of the frogs, and I can feel the wind on my face. Granted more wind than I would like.

I stop to take my camera out and take a picture of the geese waddling along nonchalantly through the tall grass. Unfortunately, they got quite a-ways away before I get the photo.

I remember reading somewhere that you can stand anywhere in Minnesota and be within six miles of water and I believe it. I've seldom been out of the sight of a pond or lake since I rode into Minnesota. Every couple of miles or so I come to a small pond full of wildlife.

I sure have to do a lot of shifting gears in this rolling terrain around Dalton.

There are a lot of chipmunks along the side of the road.

Minnesota seems to have a lot of unspoiled land and sky-tinted water. The waterfowl are plentiful as I ride on this road along farm fields, dotted with small lakes. I love to see wild animals much more than tame ones. If you were to take the time and watch the busy ducks in a park pond, there would appear to be no direction to their activity. Then, as I gaze up at wild ducks crossing the skies, they seem to have a goal.

These back roads are lightly traveled and are great for cycling. The sky is a light blue, filled with big fluffy white clouds floating overhead. As I ride by another small lake, I startle a turtle that plunges into the water making ripples that break the mirror image of maple trees on the far bank. There are some ducks swimming around. These lakes are just beautiful. I can't help but think that, if there were a lake like this one in California, it would have houses every four feet, all the way around it. It's nice to see nature the way it was intended to be.

I just took a picture of a pretty pink flower. I wonder what the color of the next flower will be. I say color because I don't know their names of most plants, but I don't believe you have to know there names to enjoy them.

I'm riding into Ashby. If there's a place to eat in this town, that's exactly what I will do. I always say, don't wait until you're hungry before you eat. By then, it's too late. The average biker burns 660 calories an hour, traveling at a thirteen miles per hour pace. My body also demands great quantities of water. So, I drink small quantities of Tang, but I drink frequently at regular intervals. I must admit, though, I do most of my heavy drinking at night.

I ride by a kid sitting on some concrete steps in Ashby. He's frying ants with a magnifying glass…!

It's "High Noon" as I find a restaurant. I have a bowl of soup, a sandwich, fries and coffee. It's not bad.

I don't see any pelicans on Pelican Lake. But, I do see some big blue cranes. I don't know, maybe they are pelicans. They are really close to the road but they fly off as soon as I ride by. I don't have time to take my camera out and get a picture. So, I just take a picture with my eyes. That's just one of the many things you miss by not being here. After all, I can't take a picture of everything.

You know, now when I think of the grasslands of North America, I think of the way the wind pushes the grass in waves. The wind is the breath of Mother Earth…Father Sky. There is water everywhere and the grass or wheat or rye is knee to waist high. I guess that would depend on how tall you are. Whenever I see these fields with a lot of yellow in them (probably mustard) I watch out for hundreds of unidentified flying objects going across the road. Well, actually they're not unidentified, they are bees.

Just south of Evansville I have 60 miles on the odometer as an elderly lady and, I'm soon to find out, her granddaughter (a scaled-down model of her grandmother) see me stopped here taking a picture, so they pull over and stop. The driver gets out and yells over to me, "Hay, young fella. Would you like a Pepsi?"

I almost yelled back and say, "Hay, little girl would you like a piece of candy?" But I don't, because old ladies can get away with a lot. Instead I politely say, "Sure...!"

As she comes closer, I can see that she is almost completely round, and she has a brilliant smile. She tells me that she doesn't mind being fat because balloons don't have wrinkles...! Gret, her granddaughter, (she told me her name was Gret) comes out of the car with some chocolate chip cookies. It's surely nice to know that there are nice people around.

"Thank God for all the friendly old ladies and Grets in this world."

I know Minnesota is the state with 10,000 lakes, but I didn't expect to see so many of them. Every few miles I ride past a small lake that's a deep blue out in the middle and closer to shore it turns into a greenish color. Most of these small lakes or ponds have tall, lush...green grass and cattails growing around them. There is an absence of houses and other construction around to take the beauty away. I watch as a family of ducks swim beside their reflections and into the shadows of some big beautiful trees. Have I mentioned that I love trees?

At our farm in Indiana we had a grove of sugar maples surrounding the house. In the fall of the year, my dad would tap the trees and collect the sap, which he boiled down to make maple syrup.

We didn't have indoor plumbing. I remember, as a kid...getting up in the cold winter months and having to go out to the outhouse. It would wake me up really quick. It was a lot nicer in the summer though, when there weren't any storm windows on. My bedroom was upstairs and instead of getting dressed and going all the way downstairs and out to the outhouse, I would simply pee right out of my window. I loved the summer...! I could just get up and put my shorts on, and go. No need for underwear, or socks and shoes or a shirt. It was great...!

It's 1:37 p.m. and 70 degrees, and I'm on the outskirts of Garfield. I can see a green water tower...a tower for radio or television...at least two-grain elevators...and a church steeple.

All these small towns have a few common landmarks. The first thing I see riding into these small towns, are tall grain elevators surrounded by round metal bins. And each town has its feed and grain store, just like each farm has its grain bin and corncrib. I can usually spot the grain elevators four miles away. The next thing I notice is the water tower with the town name painted on it. And then, of course the church steeple. Every town, no matter how small it is, has at least one church.

The clouds blowing in from the west have darkened the whole sky. Prevailing winds through here are out of the west and luckily I have a 15 mph tailwind now. That's Right...! A Tail Wind...! Let the Good Times Roll...!

     *   *   *

I just took my five-hundredth picture at a snowmobile crossing four miles north of Alexandria. Yes, at a snowmobile crossing. It reminds me of my winters in Wisconsin. I wouldn't want to live there now, but I guess it was a good place to be from. As I grew older, I learned to hate the winters and I think now I understand the reason why. In civilization we try to combat things...like winter. We try to modify it so that we can continue to live the same sort of life that we lived in the summer. We plow the sidewalks so we can wear low top shoes...and the roads...so we can drive our cars. We heat every enclosed space and then...dash quickly from one little pocket of warm air, through a bitter no-man's land of cold, to another. We fool around with sun lamps, trying to convince our skin that it's really August...and we eat travel-worn spinach in an attempt to sell the same idea to our stomachs. Naturally, it doesn't work very well. You can neither remodel nor ignore a thing as BIG as Winter. One thing I particularly remember about the winters on our dairy farm in Wisconsin, was that the windows in the barn would have about an inch of frost on the inside, and I would draw pictures on them with my fingers.

I'm riding past mile…after mile…after mile…of tall grass waving in the 15 mph wind. These green grasses are just made for lying on and that's exactly what I'm going to do.

I lie in the ditch, eating a peanut butter cup, with a dirt bank that's about two feet above me blocking the wind that's blowing and bending the tall grasses at the top. Well, actually, about one foot above my stomach. It's so nice out here, listening to the wind blowing through the grass and not hitting me. It's almost like being in a shelter only I'm outside. I lie here for a while, getting up only when a car goes by, just watching the clouds drift by and change shapes. There are no hawks playing in the thermals, but, what the heck, I don't need everything. It's great just to lie here and watch the ever-changing world around me. I'm lying here trying to teach a beetle to dive off a blade of grass and some thoughts come to mind: I've made several mistakes in my life. One was not learning how to dance. I feel that I've missed out on a lot because of this. I also wish I had learned how to play a musical instrument. I enjoy music a lot, and the piano is my favorite.

Well, the ants are crawling over my legs motivating me to move on. You know, it's amazing how much good a 20-minute lay in the hay will do for you.

It's 2:27 p.m. I have 81 miles on the odometer as I ride into Alexandria, there is a sign that says, "Goose Crossing." I don't see any geese but I do see a girl with big hooters. As I ride on, I know I have to take Highway 27 out of Alexandria to Osakis. But the road just made a split, and I'm not quite sure which way to go. So I stop at this filling station to ask the garage mechanic, "Which way to Osakis?"

Yes, I know…real men don't ask directions…drink beer out of a glass…cry…or use hankies. (It's much easier, faster, and it makes more sense to simply put your index finger alongside your nostril and blow. I don't know why anyone would use a hanky and put something as disgusting as mucus, a waste product of your body into your pocket. I mean, would this same person put used toilet paper in his pocket, also?) Real men also don't use fingernail clippers, they just chew their nails off. And they don't wear rings (especially wedding rings) or any kind of jewelry. Jewelry is for women to wear and real men don't use hair dryers. It's a well-known fact…to men anyway…that if you leave your hair alone it will dry all by itself. Real men don't shave every day, they only shave on rare occasions like when they have a date, or when they have to appear in court. And they don't drive cars…especially those little Japanese ones…they drive trucks. Four wheel drives are the best, even if they never go off road or use the four-wheel drive. I believe this is true. Just like women don't fart…pick their noises…eat onions or garlic…drink beer…spit…or go to drag races or prize fights.

Anyway, let's get back to this man at the garage. He looks like he belongs somewhere in the future or the past, but not in the present. He's a heavyset gentleman, kind of thick around the middle…kind of thin on the top…and he's got little puffs of hair sticking out of his ears. He's wearing grease-covered brown overalls and thick glasses and has a large rubber band wrapped around the back of his head, holding his glasses on. He's apparently been using this technique to hold his glasses on for many, many years, because the bridge of his noise has a groove in it where the nose piece goes across, as deep as the nose piece itself. His chins are unshaven and he's wearing a cap advertising fertilizer or chewing tobacco, I'm not sure which. His hands look as though they have never touched water.

I ask him, "Which way is it to Osakis?"

He says, "Osakis Street?"

I say, "No the town of Osakis."

He says, "Are you kidding me, that's BIG miles, that's nine miles down that there road."

I have a 15 mph tailwind and it's 79 degrees at 3:11 p.m. I stop at a Dairy Bar, in Osakis. I have my usual...a butterscotch malt...just for the health of it. God, it's good.

Oh...! Goody...! A sign says, "Rough road for the next six miles." I mean, it's rough enough when they don't tell me, I can't imagine how rough it's going to be when they tell me.

Well, Minnesota is in the Midwest so I guess I'm about halfway across America. A crop-dusting plane just flew right over me. It seemed to have come out of nowhere. It's pulling up just high enough to clear the wires over my head. Now, how can anyone say it's boring out here? Many of the fields out here contain haystacks, which resemble freshly baked loaves of bread two stories high.

It's 4:33 p.m. I have 110 miles on the odometer and I'm six miles east of Saul Center. A sign says, "Limited Visibility for the next 4.3 miles." I wonder just what that means? The road I'm riding on parallels pastures of green with ponds filled with wildlife.

It's rolling terrain out here. Whoa...! What's that? Even the crows playing in the corn stalks stop and the fields become silent except for a distant sound. Clip-clop...clip-clop...clip-clop...This guy (probably Amish) No, he's not dressed like the Amish. Anyway, he's mowing the grass along side the road with a horse drawn mower and two huge workhorses. It's a scene from yesteryear. I guess I would say he's making hay while the sun shines. By the way, did you know that horses have gas problems. Speaking of the Amish (which he's not), their lives seem simple…they never seem to be in a hurry…they rise when it's light, and go to bed when they are tired. They eat when they are hungry and they seldom look at a clock. But that doesn't mean they have an easy life.

Getting back to this guy. As I ride by slowly he looks at my wheels, spoked with shiny steel and I studied his, spoked with rusting iron.

My dad told me that I'm Pennsylvania Dutch, but once in a while…like when I'm in a bar, I tend to disbelieve him. I feel more like an Italian…the Latin lover kind.

It's 5:21 p.m. as I approach the town of St. Rosa…I have a 10 mph tailwind. I would like to make a note to map makers: Without a gas station…cafe…water tower…or stop signs you don't have a town. All that's in St. Rosa is a church.

Anyway, as soon as the sound of my spinning wheels reached the Church, a deep, snarling growl comes from under the steps. At the sound, my heart immediately pumps adrenaline to the far reaches of my body. My hair…fingernails…and toenails must have grown half an inch within seconds. The expression on my face is frozen with fear. I instantly accelerate my bike and in one second, my brain has scanned the yard for giant dog dishes and piles of human bones. In less than a second the monster is right by my back wheel. As I look around, I can see my reflection in its eyes. The dog growls a low throaty growl and shows me a mouthful of teeth. It's so close now that I can smell its bad breath. I'm standing up on my pedals and riding as hard as I can as the monster chases me all the way out of town. Phew…! That was close.

I have a 10 mph tailwind and rolling terrain out here. There's a little town called St. Francis where I get some snacks. It looks like it's going to be a long ride for me yet, today. I don't think there are any motels in between here and St. Joseph, and I already have 130 miles on my odometer.

Why is it that at the end of every day, I get these rough #&@#! roads? I'm on another speed bump road here.

I turn south on Highway 3, and I have about a 15 mph crosswind now.

I'm in my middle chain-ring...on my drops. I was hoping that the wind would have died down by the time I got to this road, being this late in the afternoon...but it hasn't. I'm tired as a dog but I'm off to my evening dog races again as a vicious pair of mixed-breed German shepherds come racing along after me. NOT AGAIN...! They are trying to eat my tires. They are well-trained, they don't even have to think about it...they do it well. With their teeth bared and thunder coming out of their throats they continue to chase after me. One is bad enough but now they're ganging up on me. I'm standing up picking up my pace as fast as I can as they nip at my back tire. I finally leave them behind.

I'm so tired I feel as though I just might crumble like a stale cake. I stop at this little "town" of St. Wendel, which, I believe only got on the map because some cartographer had a blank space to fill. I eat a Reese's peanut butter cup. God, I love peanut butter.

At 6:54 p.m. and I'm on my way again.

A couple more barking dogs are chasing after me. They seem more interested in making lunch out of me than making new friends. I can actually feel their hot breath on the back of my legs. By now I don't have to look back at the dogs, I can tell by the claws scratching on the road just how big and how many there are. I'm also riding on a really rough speed bump road here.

The road may be rough, but it's still a beautiful day and I'm making very good time, thanks to all the dogs.

I just spotted this young lad wearing overalls and no shirt. He's immensely tall and thin. He's got big ears and short hair the color of Kellogg's corn flakes. He's drifting slightly sideways as he carries a bucket of feed to some pigs.

Seeing him makes me think about my own farm days. After my dad gave up farming, I ran his 115-acre dairy farm for two years in which time I discovered that it was a good life…but not a profitable one.

As I pull to a stop, this lad is looking at me as if he's never seen tight spandex shorts, a bicycling helmet or gloves with no fingers and a jersey with a game pocket in the rear big enough to smuggle an Indian princess into. Then, when I think about where I am, I realize he probably hasn't. So he probably does think an alien has just rolled to a stop.

I talk to him and…as with other people on my tour…I see over and over again, in every part of the nation-a burning desire to go…to move…to get under way…anyplace…away from any "Here."

When I was a young lad, back on the farm, I use to ride pigs. They were really exciting…! They were fast…hard to hang onto…and they made unexpected turns. I also rode the cows. They were pretty boring though, and easy to hang onto. For the most part, they just stuck to their paths and walked along not caring if you rode them or not. I do, however, consider myself to be a real cowboy, because I used to ride cows when I was a boy.

I guess my dad realized he had better do something before I started riding the sheep. So, this one Christmas morning, my brothers and I got up extra early and opened our presents. Then our dad told us to put our coats on and come on outside with him. We went out and in the front yard, and tied to a tree, was a Shetland Pony. We all took turns riding it. It was fun for a while. Then after about a month or two, I was the only one left riding it. And, to tell you the truth, I was losing interest too. That little sucker was one mean pony. It would always try its hardest to brush or throw you off. It would get as close as it could to buildings and fences, rubbing the skin off your legs. But the meanest trick it did…was to get into a full gallop and come to a screeching halt…putting its head down to the ground. It was impossible not to fly head over heels and land on your back, right in front of the mean beast. I can remember lying there…looking up…and, I'll swear to God, it was laughing at me.

As I approach St. Joseph, a S.B.B. (a small brown bird) flies about two feet in front of my nose.

I have a 10 mph tailwind and it's 72 degrees.

There's an old, rusty Ford pick-up of unknown color parked in a field, like some nostalgic piece of sculpture.

It's 8:00 p.m. and I've ridden 157 miles today.

A sign at the roadside bears the welcome words "Open" and "Vacancy."

I check into a motel in St. Cloud. (There sure seem to be a lot of Saints around here). I just got things organized a little. Now I call my son in Wisconsin, to let him know about when I expect to be there.

I find the slight soreness I'm experiencing, not unpleasant. It just means I've accomplished something today. The sun is flattening down behind St. Cloud's water tower for the night.

I'm going to go out and get something to eat. Lucky for me the Motel is more than that: It's a Bus Depot...Coffee Shop...Supper Club...Bar and Lounge. I go into the Supper Club and come out stuffed with soup, salad, fondue and bread sticks...steak...baked potato...two or three vegetables, and cheese cake-when this place said Supper Club it meant it...!

*   *   *

Statistics for ***DAY FIFTEEN*** *Monday, June 26, 1989.*
157 miles of riding today, 14.9 average miles per hour for today, 1,757 miles of riding in fifteen days, 117 average miles of riding per day.

Day Sixteen

From St. Cloud, Minnesota
To Hudson, Wisconsin

It's 6:30 a.m. I can see out of my window that the sunlight has just pierced the darkness. I guess I'd better get up.

I walk over to get a breakfast of potato skins, hash browns and eggs and some real coffee, not that instant excuse some restaurants use for coffee. I leave the motel and start to ride at 8:00 a.m. There is a sign at a bank that says it's 66 degrees out and that's exactly what my thermometer reads.

I'm in St. Cloud and there's not a Cloud in the sky. (I don't see any Saints either). As I ride along it looks like I'm going to be blessed with a full day of sunshine. It's a beautiful day, but I'm afraid it might get really hot today if the sun stays out in full force.

Five miles north of Clearwater, I have 10 miles on the odometer.

A thought just went through my mind…with all my planning and everything I did, it still probably won't come out right. But, what the Hell, when I was born I didn't come out right either.

I only have three rolls of film left. I'll have to stop in Clearwater or somewhere and buy 10 or 20 rolls. I certainly don't want to run out. It's nice gliding silently along through Hasty and all the other small sleeping villages. I have a new road before my front wheel and sunshine on my shoulder a 10 mph tailwind and a clear blue sky.

It's 75 degrees and perfect weather for freewheeling. The bright young colors of the season sparkle with new fresh-washed brilliance in the sun. The roads in Monticello County are just perfect, completely free of rocks, potholes and rough surfaces. It's really nice, I can spend my time looking at the scenery rather than watching the road.

Oh Shit...! The road just bent southward and I have a bothersome wind blowing against me now. I have to go in my little chain-ring and it's pretty hard pedaling. It seems like when something turns bad (the wind) everything else follows suit. The traffic just struck me like a tidal wave...it's horrendous! It's the worst I've had so far on my tour and there's no shoulder to ride on.

It's warming up nicely as I thought it might. It's 11:30 a.m. I have 50 miles on the odometer and it's 80 degrees already. I stop at an empty filling station in Rogers...which is a two-building town. I eat a couple of *Ding-Dongs* I had in my handlebar bag.

Have you ever walked through a drive-through...at a fast food restaurant? I have. There's a Jack-in-the-Box about a block from where I live. They close their doors at 11:00 p.m. Only the drive-through window is open until 2:00 a.m. I mean, it would be silly for me to drive my car one block now, wouldn't it? Of course, it's a little embarrassing standing in front of a line of cars talking to a sign but when you're hungry at 1:00 a.m. what's a fellow to do?

I still have a 10 mph tailwind as I cruise in the outskirts of Minneapolis...a BIG city. I wonder if they do things here like they do in L.A.? In L.A., they come out with the Sunday paper on Saturday. It's a mystery to me how they get the news a day early. It kind of makes you wonder, are the news people living a day in advance, or are we living a day in the past? What would really be bad about this is if you were to open the paper to the obituary section for the next day and you were in it...! As matter in fact, it always baffles me how everybody seems to die in alphabetical order. And another thing, why do they always say nice things about bad people at their funerals? I mean you could be a no-good murdering rapist and they would still say nice things about you at your funeral.

I ride into Minneapolis on what I'm sure used to be a nice little old country road lined with trees and bushes. But now they've stretched an eight-foot high chain-link fence topped with razor wire…enclosing a mile-long factory. I wonder why progress looks so much like destruction.

One of my main dangers in big cites, like this one, is car (as well as truck) drivers. They generally think of bicycles as being stationary…if they see them at all. The operator of a motor vehicle is often quite unaware that, when he passes me, I'm traveling at a fifteen miles per hour pace. So, a driver making a right-hand turn will pass me, then immediately, cut into a right turn, pushing me off the road and almost running me over. There is a positive side though…I have very few problems with parking spaces and no problem at all with gas stations.

I have 67 miles on the odometer so far today. It's 1:15 p.m. and I'm just riding over the Mississippi River. So, I guess I'm in Wisconsin now.

Well…! I guess I'm not in Wisconsin. I thought the Mississippi River was the borderline between Minnesota and Wisconsin, but it's not. The St. Croix River is.

I see an A&W and I'm going to get off the hot asphalt to get a little relief from the sticky heat. I order two big, frosted mugs of Root Beer.

There is this very interesting fellow sitting at a booth just across from me, who keeps rolling his lower lip up. His dark, curly hair is sticking out from under his obviously brand-new, wide-brimmed cowboy hat. He's wearing a western-cut shirt…you know the kind with pointed pockets and snaps, and he's carrying a new denim jacket that matches his jeans. His jeans are tucked into the tops of his new, black and shiny boots with silver pointed toes, not quite like the ones I saw in Montana. His glasses are thick with wide black rims. He pushes them back up his nose with his middle finger several times while he sits around telling lies to a woman sitting across from him. Now, brain researchers estimate that we use, at our best, only 15% of our brain capacity. This guy and the woman, whom I take to be his wife, are living proof that animals can survive with no intelligence at all. They appear to be only slightly smarter than a grapefruit. He's looking at the newspaper and apparently comes across this article dealing with automobile accident statistics. I overhear him comment to his wife, "Listen dear, it says here that the majority of all automobile accidents happen within a five-mile radius of your home." After a thoughtful silence, she says, "Do you think we should move?" Now get this, he answers back and says, "Maybe we should."

I'm on the road again. There is a lot of traffic out. I have to watch out for parked cars as well as the moving ones. They may suddenly open their doors right in front of me or pull out into my path unexpectedly. I also have to keep in mind that it takes a little extra space for me with my panniers on.

Actually in big cities, cyclists' brave enough to risk the traffic, can often chuckle to themselves over the fact that they can travel much faster than a car through the modern urban centers. However, cities do provide a hostile environment with their storm grates, trolley or railroad tracks, and expansion joints in bridges that frequently present traps for bicycle wheels and they're slippery in wet weather.

With frustrated motorists packed bumper to bumper, I can usually make it through town as fast, if not faster than the rest of the traffic. I ride past their gas fumes and through the heat waves. When a light turns green, I get a little jump on the motorist and I'm usually across the intersection before anyone else. Then a long line of traffic slowly passes by me, until the next light turns red and they have to stop and I slowly pass them and get to the front of the line again. So, we sort of seesaw back and forth through town.

This may seem hard to believe but I've been told that a large percent of the male population picks their nose on their way home from work. Of course, I would never do such a disgusting thing.

Anyway, as I was seesawing past traffic here, I observed this "lady," passenger, let me rephrase that, this "female" passenger picking her nose. She rolled down her window and let her arm and hand dangle outside. She slowly rolled the substance back and forth between her index finger and thumb until it thickened just enough for her to flip it off. Disgusting, absolutely disgusting. I wonder, is this instinct or do their mothers teach them this?

I have a 10 mph crosswind as I ride along catching sight of my own image in the store windows of this bustling metropolis. I would sure as hell like to get out of this town before rush hour. Rush hours, especially happy hours, always last longer than 60 minutes. It'll be a rat race out here and…in a rat race…even if you win, you're still a rat.

After riding 1,800 miles through little bitty towns and villages, not to mention, miles and miles of roads with no habitation at all…this is really a BIG City. Cars sway around me like stream water rounding rocks. There is a young fell wearing a *Sony Walkman* with earphones. You very seldom see this in L.A. The teenagers there carry huge (and I mean huge) Ghetto Blasters on their shoulders with the volume cranked up to the max.

It's 2:43 p.m. 88 degrees and I'm in St. Paul. It's just one traffic light after another whose favorite color is red, just like mine…that is…on everything except traffic lights.

As I ride behind this old bus, the smell of half-burnt fuel surrounds me like bad perfume.

I stop at a McDonalds and chow down some food.

I'm on the road again. I know I've mentioned it before but this is a BIG town. I don't think I'll ever get out of it. I'm really anxious to escape this city. After living in the out-of-doors for the last two weeks, breathing nothing but fresh air and getting my exercise, riding in this crowded city is suffocating. There is too much congestion, pollution and noise in Minneapolis/St. Paul to suit me. I started out on this tour to see the country, not the cities. As the old saying goes, if you don't like the heat, get out of the kitchen. It's hot in this kitchen and nothing would suit me better than to get out. This road I'm on seems to span the most congested area of this city.

Back in L.A., where I work, I spend eight to ten hours a day standing on a concrete floor in a building without any windows or open doors. On all the doors there are signs that read, Warning This Area Contains a

Chemicals Known to the State of California to Cause Cancer. I was told the reason we can't leave any of the doors or windows open is because they are afraid it might contaminate the air outside. I have to get out of L.A. Hardly anyone speaks my language there anymore.

Oh Great…! There's a sign that says, "Your Highway Taxes at Work." And there is a heart-sinking…orange…"Detour" sign.

After riding on the detour for a while I've decided the detour sign should read, "Abandon All Hope, Ye Who Enter Here." Just once, I would like to see a sign that read, "Main Highway Now Open for Traffic While the Detour is being Repaired."

There is no doubt about it, Summer is here. It's hot, unbearably HOT. I'm stirring the still air as I ride through it on melting asphalt.

MELT DOWN

Some of these cities just make me sick. They cut down all the beautiful trees to make the roads wider, then they have the nerve to name the streets after the trees they just cut down. Oak Street…Hemlock Street…Birch Street…Pine Street. It's sad really sad.

Near Lake Elmo I have 90 miles on the odometer and its 4:14 p.m.

I just rode up a street and finally reached the summit of a long grade and now it's starting to drop fast. I can see a blessed, "End of Construction," sign just up ahead and the pavement has suddenly reappeared. I think this detour has taken me quite a way out of my way. I've ridden for 36 miles through the giant hive of Minneapolis/Saint Paul and it's as hot as an oven. I'm sure if you were to look down from an airplane on the bustling metropolis of Minneapolis, it would look like a giant anthill with no method or direction or purpose in its darting, hurrying, inhabitants.

But, I thank God, I'm finally out of it and I'm once again riding in the wonderful quiet country…on a road that's bordered with trees and fenced fields full of cows. There is a lake of clear, clean water where I can see the reflection of ducks and geese flying high overhead in an arrow formation.

A farmhouse along the road proudly displays Old Glory. I don't believe that there is anything more beautiful than an American flag blowing in the wind (especially when it's blowing the same way I'm riding).

Beads of perspiration are forming on my forehead and my jersey is beginning to discolor with sweat as I ride up to a lemonade stand in Stillwather. I rarely ride by a lemonade stand without stopping. I believe it's a great way for kids to learn about the real world, and I just love to see the smile that always comes across their little faces when I drink four or five glasses.

I know that there are college grads out there that believe the only place to learn things is in a classroom with four walls and a chalkboard and a teacher at the head of the class. They believe that if it isn't in a book, forget about it, and if it is…learn it for the exam and then forget about it. They think that grades, grade point averages and levels are more important than real people…real places and real experience. If this were true, I would be considered to be as dumb as an unplugged computer.

Anyway, back to this kid. He can't get the lemonade to flow from the small hole in the lid, because the ice cubes keep blocking it. So, he simply removes the lid, and I think that he is going to pour the lemonade into my paper cup. But, he doesn't. He takes the cup in hand and submerges it into the pitcher. I guess this served two purposes, it fills my cup with lemonade and ice and cleans his hand as well…! Aren't kids great?

Hey…! I'm finally in Wisconsin…! As I look down the river from a bridge, crossing the St. Croix River, I can see a fisherman standing waist deep in the water. I've never fished this way. I prefer cherry bomb fishing.

A group of cyclists on racing bikes zoom past me. A racing bike is the sports car of the cycling world and my heavily laden touring bike is the tractor-trailer. They are about as different as day and night. Driving a MG Midget hardly qualifies one to get behind the wheel of a hulking 18-wheeler and expect to climb hills, drive around corners, and dodge or jump potholes as effortlessly as I can on my 21-pound racing bike.

Riding through Houlton, I see something I've never seen before. You really aren't going to believe it, but I swear to God, it's the truth. I'm stopped at this red light, next to a new shiny black car, with tinted windows. Now, I think people with tinted windows are trying to hide something, so I look even harder to see what they are trying to hide. Well, this time I'm right. This guy is sitting there and a girl is lying on the seat beside him with her head in his lap. Now I know she isn't sleeping because nobody could sleep with his or her head bobbing up and down like hers is.

When I'm out here on the road for two or three weeks, I lose all track of time. I told my son I'd be in Eureka somewhere around the Fourth of July, give or take a few days. Time doesn't really mean a whole lot to me when I'm on vacation.

Now, as I recall, motels are usually on the outskirts of towns and, seeing as how there aren't any on this end of town, I'll continue to ride through town (which I would have done anyway, because I always try to get a motel after I've ridden through town, so I won't have to ride through at rush hour in the morning).

I've ridden all the way through Houlton to the town of Hudson and I still don't see any motels. All I can see is a very busy highway. So, I'll just ride back into town. OH WHALL...! Now there is a fine-looking girl...! She's got long black hair that's thrown loosely over her shoulders and she's straddling a bicycle. She brings me to a halt, like a squirrel eyeing nuts. Needing to find a motel, I'm thinking it's my duty to take up a conversation with her. She's wearing cutoffs jeans (cut off so high that I can see her cheeks) and a low-cut cotton blouse that displays a beautiful suntan on her breast tops. She's about twenty-five, I'd guess, and very pretty. She tells me that all the motels are at the east edge of town on Highway 35, (a major Highway that I'm not allowed to, and definitely don't want to, ride on).

I ask her if there's a frontage road I could ride on to get to the motels. She says, "You have to go another five blocks up this road then make a right, then it's four more blocks, then you turn right again, then I believe its the first road to your left. It's kind of hard to explain just how to get there." So she says, "If you want to follow me, I'll show you the way." Now this sounds like a message from God to me and I'd follow her anywhere...anytime...anyway.

We zigzagged our way through town and started to ride out of town on a small country road. I'm keeping up pretty well until we come to this steep grade. Now, she's twenty years younger and probably 70 pounds lighter then me. She crests the summit and I'm only about halfway up when I hear this hissing...that sounds like a cornered cat. I look at my back tire, and, sure enough, it's beginning to go soft. But, I'm going to continue to pump on up the hill in the pounding sun and motionless air. I'm thinking that, if the tire were to go completely flat I would be up a creek without a paddle. In other words...I may never see this girl again. So I'll keep riding on, hoping to get to the top of the grade before the rim meets the pavement. One thing's for sure, I don't want to lose sight of this girl. It's not too often I get such a beautiful young thing to lead me to a motel. It's not working out that way, though. I have to stop and pump the damn tire up, which I do as quickly as I can.

I jump back on and start riding as fast as I can when the girl with the big country smile comes riding over the crest. She stops on the other side of the road and tells me to keep riding on up the road about a half mile then to make the first right, from there I'll be able to see the motels. By now, I'm dripping with sweat and I probably look like an old bear, out looking for some fresh honey. I once had a friend who claimed that cycling was better than sex and I've been trying to prove him wrong for years. You know, I wonder why they call one night stands, one night stands, when nobody is standing. I really think I would have looked good on top of her. Anyway, I thank her as she rides away. I sigh and wish the world had more Daisies (her name was Daisy, and she looked as fresh as a Daisy). I know I'll never see her again and I never really had the chance to thank her properly for all she had done for me. She did more than she'll ever know.

I'm riding slowly now, no sense to hurry anymore. I finally get up the hill and to the corner where I can see the motels, just like she said. I stop to pump my tire up again. I ride as fast as I can toward the motel so I won't have to pump the tire up again. I'm tired and I don't feel much like fixing it right now. But I have to pump it up one more time before I get to the motel.

It's 6:45 p.m. I have 113 miles on the odometer as I arrive at a Super 8 Motel. Some mahogany blades on a polished brass ceiling fan are circulating the cigar smoke the guy behind the counter blows out of the corner of his mouth. As I walk up to the counter, dripping with sweat, he picks up a yellow pencil from his desk and starts to doodle on a pad. As I check in, I notice that the rooms are getting more expensive. They are $38.00 for one, and that's what I am. One.

I clean up, take a short nap, fix my tire, then go out to eat. After getting back from dinner I soak in the whirlpool for a while. Then it's off to the bar to replenish my liquids.

I get back and go to sleep at 12 midnight.

* * *

*Statistics for **DAY SIXTEEN** Tuesday, June 27, 1989.*
113 miles of riding today, 13.5 average miles per hour for today, 1,870 miles of riding in sixteen days, 116 average miles of riding per day.

Day Seventeen

From Hudson, Wisconsin
To Eau Claire, Wisconsin

It's 7:00 a.m. and I've got to get up and pack now, I guess.

It's 7:30 a.m. and I've got to get up now.

Well…I'm finally up. I'm in slow motion this morning. I feel sort of like a bear, awakening from a long winter's hibernation. I slept in keeping to my own schedule, which is no schedule.

I have a Burger King breakfast before I even start to pack my stuff. And, when I return to the motel, I discover that they have a free continental breakfast here so I get a doughnut and some more coffee, and sit down to eat it before I attempt to pack my gear.

Well, it's 8:45 a.m. and I'm finally leaving the motel. The sun is well up by now. It's another perfect day except for the 15 mph headwind I have…Yes it's a bitch. I guess the Wind Gods know when I start late and they punish me for it. I have to go down on my drops, in my middle chain ring, right away.

Good old Wisconsin.

My brakes are dragging a little again. I stop to loosen them. I get back in the saddle only to find that the wind's picked up some more. I have a 20 mph headwind, so I'm down in my little chain-ring.

Welcome to Wisconsin.

I'm riding into this damn 20 mph headwind and, with the rolling terrain, it keeps me down in second gear most of the time. I've discovered that, when I'm riding into a headwind or up a hard hill, I'm not very creative. I guess it takes too much energy to just ride.

Well, things are looking even worse now. There's a Road Construction sign just up ahead.

No doubt about it, this is dairy country. There are herds of cattle grazing in all the meadows. In addition to the peaceful rural scenery, brilliant green fields and hundreds of dairy cows…charming little towns and villages…rolling roads…and 20 mph winds…(blowing in the wrong direction) each and every day of my tour offers me a memorable and unique new experience.

At the edge of Roberts there is a sign warning hunters about trespassing.

Chewing Holsteins and Guernseys switch their tails and flicker their skins as the sun rises higher and higher, and the winds blow harder and harder. This is unmistakably the "Dairy Capital" of the world. There are miles and miles of cow piles, some of which have beautiful little flowers growing out of them.

I stop at a sheep farm to get some "Sheep Thrills". (I think I'd better call my girlfriend tonight).

This reminds me of the story about the retired ventriloquist who decided to try the rural life. As a farmer was taking him around, the ventriloquist couldn't resist playing a prank on him. As they walked through the barnyard, a cow standing by the fence suddenly spoke, or seemed to.

"Your hands are awfully cold when you milk me in the mornings," the cow said.

The farmer gave the cow a startled look.

Then a passing chicken complained, "I wish you'd collect the eggs sooner," the farmer looked shocked.

The ventriloquist didn't say a word, and they continued walking on.

As they approached some sheep, the farmer said, "Don't believe anything these sheep say, they're terrible liars."

Fighting these unfavorable winds is a job as thankless and never-ending as washing dishes. I have a 15…No…! It's at least a 20 mph headwind and it's 76 degrees.

At 11:00 a.m. I have 20 miles on the odometer as I stop to quench my desert-like thirst at a Dairy Queen in Baldwin. I chat with a gentleman in Dairy Queen about the weather. He's got a copper-colored face and his skin has a leathery texture…probably from endless days of being under the hot sun. He says that in the summertime, the west-wind blows so damn hard that it causes the sun to set three hours later than it does in the wintertime.

I leave the Dairy Queen, and am greeted by a good (well, not so good) 25 mph headwind, now. It is forcing me to be in my little chain-ring, down on my drops, and pedaling as hard as I can. I'm barely moving but I have as much stubbornness and persistence as the wind itself.

Near Woodville this Wednesday morning, there isn't much traffic, but with this 20 mph headwind, I'm getting nowhere, real fast.

I'm using my recorder so I can keep an accurate record of the events that happen on my tour, as they happen. There is so much to see, and my morning eyes describe a different world than my afternoon eyes would…and surely my wearied evening eyes would report only a weary evening world.

I'm close, very close to Hersey. I tend to stop and take more pictures when I have unforgiving headwinds, like these. As I ride out of the shaded forest and look over the grassy knolls, I can see the thick brown bark of the oak intermixed with the thin white bark of the birch trees.

There's a sweet smell riding along on this strong wind that I can't readily identify. The delicate soft pink and white petals of the many wild flowers are showing me their undersides as the strong wind whips them from side to side.

As I ride into a rest stop there's a rancher coming out of the john. The wind blows his cap off and his hair is erect. I chase down his cap and, as he walks toward me, I notice that he has a golf-ball-size lump of something is his mouth. He really didn't have to tell me that the wind usually blows from the opposite direction. I can see that the treetops are bent toward the Atlantic, but their thinner branches are now pointing the other way, like a runner bent over and moving ahead with both arms streaming out behind him.

I just rode through Wilson and Knapp. The towns are getting closer and closer together, now.

This is the damnedest wind I've ever seen. It's at least a 25 mph headwind now. I'm down on my drops. If I were to sit up straight I would probably be blown back to Seattle. I have 45 miles on the odometer as I stop at another Dairy Queen, this one in Menomonie.

I stop to take this particular picture of the natural beauty that surrounds this house. There are so many different kinds of trees in the front yard. I have a rain-washed…crystal blue sky and outrageous views.

I just saw a sign on a wooden gate that read, "Never Mind the Dog, Beware of the Owner."

I take to the back roads on this tour so I can visit small villages and farms and avoid the heavy traffic, on busy super highways, that hurries one through and past life, at speeds out of proportion to life's value. I have a beautiful two-lane road to ride on now. It's lined with trees, and there is no traffic. This is what cyclist's dream about. This…and…of course… girls.

At 3:34 p.m. it's 83 degrees. I'm in second gear most of the time due to this rolling terrain and a 15 to 20 mph headwind.

I just propped my bike up against a "Tractor Crossing" sign, just outside of Fall City. I'm waiting for a tractor to come along and give me a pull.

Eventually, I know I'll have to ride out of these beautiful tree-lined roads. But I'll do my best to bypass all the big cities.

You might be thinking that, if I like the wilderness so much, then just why do I live in L.A.? Now that's a good question, I wish I had thought of it myself. Enough Harold, enough. The main reason is that's where the work is. I lived in Wisconsin for 15 years and today I can't for the life of me figure out why anyone would want to live there. It's colder than hell in the Winter, which drags on way into June. When you live in Wisconsin though, you don't complain about the cold, or the fact that it's flat. You expect and accept it. But I couldn't help but to get a little mad at my big brother, when he would call me from California, in December, and tell me all about the great motorcycle ride he just did. It seems that he went up *Angeles Crest Highway* into the mountains, with all its spectacular views, then on down to the Coast past the sunbathers. I had a Harley Davidson at the time and he would ask me if I'd been down in the basement (where I kept my bike in the winter) lately to sit on it or maybe even start it up. I remember once I got so mad at him that I hung up on him. I recall having to get up extra early in the freezing cold winter months and go out and shovel the driveway, then try to get my old car started. It would barely turn over. Then I'd drive 12 miles on ice-covered, slippery roads, just to get to work. I won't do that again for anything.

Now we come to the summer months in wonderful Wisconsin. They are hot and humid. I mean really humid. Sometimes it's so humid that it, made the bed sheets wet. And as soon as the sun goes down, you had better head for the house, because the flying hypodermic needles (mosquitoes) will eat you alive...! They are always hunting for a warm meal, and...if left to do so...they could suck a man dry in four hours.

I may live in the BIG City now, but as soon as I hit the lottery and retire, I'm moving out in the country. I made a list of all the things that I was going to buy with my lottery money. Like a new car...a mountain bike...a computer...a good pair of binoculars...another camera...and the list went on and on. Then I asked myself this hypothetical question, "What if I don't win the Lottery?"

As soon as I ride into town I see some utility workers, who, I think, should know about their town.

I stop and ask them, "Does this road go to Route Q?"

"Hmmm…" One man says, "I've been here nigh on 57 years and the road ain't gone anywhere but right here."

"So," I say, "You've lived here all your life, huh…?"

He says, "Not yet."

"Well," I say, "Can you tell me how to get to Route Q?"

"Nope…!" He says, "You can't get there from here. You got to go to Altoona first. You can get there from Altoona."

"Well," I say, "Does it matter which road I take to get to Altoona?"

"Not to me, it don't," he answers.

Well, welcome to country humor. I didn't have to ask about entertainment around here. I'm it. Anyway, they directed me around town on a bypass, which has lots of heavy traffic. Then, when I get off where they tell me, it isn't even close to where I want to be. I make several more wrong turns and learn the town better than I intend to. Then I ask someone else, and they tell me to take this business street through town, and it will run right into Q. So that's what I do, only it doesn't run into Q. So I ask this guy standing on a corner, who's as bald as a billiard ball and he tells me to stay on this road until I come to highway 53, then take 53 south, and I can't miss it. When I hear that, I know I'd soon be hopelessly lost again. So, I continue on the road until I find 53, go south on 53 about four miles, down a big hill, with a tailwind.

Then I get off and ask another guy, wearing a pair of reflector sunglasses, where this road went? He says, "This road? It doesn't go anywhere." Oh, No…! Not this again. So I ask him if he knows how to get to Route Q and he tells me that I have to go back up the hill I just came down and, turn right in Birch Street. Well, by this time I'm just about at the end of my tolerance. To put it mildly, I'm completely fed up. Another thing that I discover about Wisconsin Rapids that I don't like is that you are not allowed to ride bicycles on any of the main streets and trying to get through a strange town on side streets isn't much fun.

In the mornings, I'm in good spirits because I'm rested and I've just eaten a nice breakfast...so I can handle everybody crowding me and staring at me and blowing their horns at me...but by evening time I'm tired and hungry and irritable, and I'm in real need of some privacy. So, I start to look for a motel.

In Eau Clair I have a 10 mph headwind. I can't believe there are roads this sucken rough. It seems like at the end of every day I get these rough sucken roads!

I never got such a run-around as I did trying to get through town. I was directed to a motel, which had been closed for a year, and, Route Q, the road I'm going to ride out of town on, just doesn't seem to exist.

I finally find this motel and it's only $26.00 for the night. I would have given them $60.00 for it. It's a nice warm comfortable room. The walls are covered with knotty pine and the smells of hot coffee fill the room as I use the in-room coffee maker.

I'll just start over in the morning, trying to find highway Q out of town.

A gentleman, with very heavy eyebrows which nearly meet over his large nose, and no more hair on his head (which by the way is a large one and very shiny) than there is upon an egg, seems to be as proud as a peacock, wearing his big gold rings on more then one finger and two or three gold chains around his neck. He has a Rolex watch with a wide gold band and a huge gold bracelet on his other wrist. I'm sure that the only exercise this guy gets is running from the sofa to the refrigerator every half-hour. Anyway, he shows me, on a map, how to find Route Q. I should be able to find it all right, now.

I checked into the motel at 6:15 p.m. I've ridden 80 very hard miles today, into a 20 mph headwind, most of the day. My feet are sore from pushing so hard on the pedals. I'm going to get cleaned up and see what's happening around here.

Now I'm ready to go for a walk downtown. As I walk by a Laundromat, I notice a beautiful girl inside doing her laundry. So, I rush back to the motel and grab some clean clothes out of my panniers and rush back to the Laundromat. But, by this time she's gone. So, I walk back to the motel and gather up all my dirty laundry and go back and do my laundry anyway. While my clothes are drying, I walk over and have myself a ham dinner.

On my way back to the motel, I go in a store, with my hands in my pockets, like I usually walk, and I'm greeted by this gentleman who asks me what part of the Midwest I'm from? I bought five rolls of film and some chocolate-covered raisins for dessert so I'm all set for the night.

*   *   *

*Statistics for **DAY SEVENTEEN** Wednesday, June 28, 1989.*
80 miles of riding today, 10.6 average miles per hour for today, 1,950 miles of riding in seventeen days, 115 average miles of riding per day.

Day Eighteen

From Eau Claire, Wisconsin
To Wisconsin Rapids, Wisconsin

It's 7:40 a.m. I guess it's time to get up. I've reached the point where, upon getting up in the morning, the first thing I do is to look out the door at the trees, or bushes or clumps of grass, to see which direction the wind is blowing and…how hard. It looks like it's going to be a nice day. The sun's out but it looks like I'm going to have swift headwinds again today.

Forty minutes later I leave the motel and go over to McDonalds to get something to eat.

Two miles out of town I have about a 15 mph crosswind, from the right. It's a strong wind but it's much better than a straight headwind and it's 63 degrees.

There is a deer just up ahead standing right in the middle of the road. As I ride along, I listen to the sounds of cattle bawling and birds calling. There is another deer. There seem to be plenty of deer, skunks, and birds to keep me company this morning. There's even some road kill, all laid out for me.

So far there have been a lot of woods right along side the road. It helps to block the wind, so it doesn't affect me, too much.

Boy…! I slept pretty late this morning. I don't set an alarm. I get up when I wake up, that way I'm sure I'll get as much sleep as my body requires. And, I guess it required a little extra this morning. I worked very hard yesterday, riding into a strong headwind all day. Right now I'm rolling along through rolling terrain this morning.

Just when I kick back and start to take it a little easy, I hear a dog bark and I immediately pick my pace up. The barks are getting louder and louder as I get closer to the next farmhouse. Now I have it in sight. It's a huge Doberman. Luckily, it's tied up with an oversized chain. The farthest it can reach is clearly marked out by a worn dirt semicircle in the yard. As I ride by it lunges and slobbers and bares its teeth. And, with an ugly snarl, it makes a dive for me. I just thank God he's chained up. Most of the farmers out here have watchdogs. I can only escape the less gifted ones, the short-legged ones, the ones that are too tired to chase me and the ones that are tied up. I guess, to a dog, I'm a strange looking creature, with pumping legs that never quite touch the ground.

There are a couple of horses out in the pasture. You know that horses mostly eat alfalfa and oats. Now, eating alfalfa and oats is supposed to bring you a vibrant healthy life. Then, tell me how come horses are considered old at twenty.

I have 10 miles on the odometer and I have a 10 to 15 mph headwind, which is blocked most of the time by big beautiful trees. That's another reason I like trees.

There is a barn, with a faded red roof. It is weathered and leaning a little. In the spring and summer time, the Heartland of Wisconsin is ablaze with wildflowers, and wildlife.

I wanted to travel across the United States, to see it…to smell it…to breathe it…to taste it. So, I stop occasionally…to listen to the songbirds and to smell the sweet wildflowers, and to chew on a blade of grass.

The magic words for today are, "Cows and Crops". I stop to take a picture of some cows. If you're wondering how I get the cows to pose for me, it's easy. I just tell them to say, "Cheese".

I'm riding by a very large cornfield and it's a fine-looking crop, too. I think my bike would look good propped up against the corn that's about five feet tall. So, I lean it up against the stalks. It falls over several times before I actually take the picture, but I believe it's worth it. I think that if

I were to live to be a hundred and fifty years old, I wouldn't take a better picture than this one.

I've heard and read that the best way to improve your riding speed is to buy the lightest rims and tires you can find. All right then, why do cars and all motors have flywheels? I think you should get the heaviest rims and wheels possible, maybe ones that weighed about 100 pounds each, would be good. Once you got those suckers a-rolling, there would be no stopping you.

The road just crested a small hill and the sun's shining through the trees in patches. The only sound I hear is that of the south wind blowing through the trees, and the hollow knocking of a redheaded woodpecker in the distance. I'm trying to keep time with it, but it doesn't seem to have any rhythm.

*   *   *

I'm riding along out in the middle of nowhere. There is no one around, so I stop to take a leak, right off my bike, of course. As long as I'm stopped, I think I might as well grab a granola bar out of my handlebar bag. So, here I am standing here straddling my bike, eating a granola bar and…much to my surprise…along comes this lady in her car. She pulls over and stops…gets out and starts to walk over to me. Now, here I am with this big puddle in the middle of the road. Needless to say, I'm embarrassed. I feel like a puppy that's just missed the paper. God, I hope she's not a schoolteacher. I can just see myself being punished like a 4th grader having to write, "I will not pee in the middle of the road," 2,000 times. As she gets closer, I can see a smile on her slightly wrinkled face that seems to be alive with joy. Her hair is the color of hothouse roses. You know that redheads taste better. Oops…! I mean redheads have better taste. She's not tall, but her body is ample and full-breasted. I've never seen a woman with a more beautifully sculptured body, and as she starts to talk to me I can see that there is much more to her then her body. It seems that she used to do a lot of bicycle touring in Europe. She tells me that she'd love to do what I'm doing but she's married now and she's pretty much settled in with the humble, private things. Like soft slippers…old clothes…old jokes and the thump of a sleepy dog's tail on the kitchen floor. As she's about to leave, she says something to me that I'll always remember. She says, "May the wind always be at your back and may your horizons always be blue." She's a very nice lady. That's the difference between girls and women, women are like vintage wine, they get better with age.

    *   *   *

 I'm riding out of Ludington. I don't know if I'm on the right road or not, but I know that I'm going the right direction because the wind is still in my face.
 You know, granola bars are cheap. Well, maybe not so cheap…but they are an imitation of food. Have you ever taken the piece of cardboard that's underneath a candy bar, and licked it? Well, if you were to eat that piece of cardboard, it would be a good example of what granola bars taste like. They are supposed to be good for you, but…so is cod liver oil.
 It's 70 degrees as I ride into the town of Wilson. If it weren't for this 15 mph headwind, it would be another perfect day. The wind doesn't seem to bother the cars. It's not all bad though. The road is good, and I only have slightly rolling terrain.
 There are buds on all the trees and bushes, that, are slowly growing into leaves. The soft, light green, end extensions of the branches and twigs indicate to me that it's definitely spring.
 I have to admit, sometimes it's hard riding, but I still love touring. I like to ride for the experience of it…for what I may or may not see…hear…smell…feel or touch. I ride because I like to move, but not too fast, and because I like to stop. I ride to absorb things…to shut off my mind or to turn it on. I ride and think about things. Sometimes, I purposely try to avoid people.

I stop to watch a pair of hawks watch me as the clouds slowly float overhead.

As I ride along, the smell of flowers fill my nostrils. It's just like riding through a huge flower garden with all these little yellow wild flowers growing right next to the road for mile after mile.

I peer into the woods and I can see it pierced with long, green-gold lances of light, and...all of a sudden...a thousand birds began to sing. The rich green of the broad-leafed trees and the lighter greens of the small-leafed varieties are beautiful. Mosses and grass add to the many shades of the lush growth and small plants. Wildflowers are scattered throughout the woods. Little white ones...yellow ones...and rose-colored ones...while yellow dominates the roadside.

My ride today is a delightful one, and I relish it. When I ride along this slowly (just because I want to) I can see so much more. It's a green wonderland of trees with an overwhelming abundance of small yellow flowers. And the sky is blue, and the sun is warm.

* * *

Ah...! The power of memories. I remember the time...I think I was a freshman in High School. When my older brother, and Jerry, a neighbor of ours, and I were going to do the "Ultimate Bike Ride." We were going to ride from Poy Sippi, where we lived, to Berlin, where we went to High School (a distance of 12 miles, each way, mind you). Jerry had an old...beat-up...single speed bike. My brother had a three speed, and I had the best bike of all, a new Sears five-speed. We started out early in the morning and it took, what seemed like forever, to get there. Right at the edge of Berlin there is, what we considered, a huge hill. Today, I would call it a small roller. Anyway, at the top of the hill (which we walked part of) was the City Limits sign. For some reason, I don't recall just why, maybe because we thought it wouldn't be hip, or something. Anyway, we stashed our bikes in the tall grass in a field, and walked into town. We walked around, smoking cigarettes, looking for chicks. Then we headed back to our bikes. Jerry and my brother were both one grade ahead of me in school, and they were best friends. They were whispering on the way back…then…about two blocks before we got to our bikes they took off a running. By the time I got to where the bikes were, only Jerry's old single speed was there. I was pissed, and the farther I pedaled that heavy beast, the more pissed I got. I kept looking ahead, hoping they would stop and give me back my bike, but they didn't. It was almost dark by the time I got home. They had arrived several hours earlier. I didn't talk to either of them for a few days after that. They were both too big to beat up.

* * *

For days now I've pedaled past rivers and streams, lakes and ponds of the Mid-West…through its rolling, green hills and tiny, well-kept towns and picturesque villages. The creeks aren't as clear as the ones were up in the mountains. I believe the ducks could walk on them more easily than swim…but they are beautiful…in their own way, just the same. I have a 15 mph headwind through this rolling terrain.

As far as this highway goes, it isn't much of one. It's got a speed bump every 50 feet or so.

It's 12:24 p.m. I have 40 miles on the odometer as I ride into Mead and it's 75 degrees. There is a pile of logs off to my right, probably going to be used for paper or lumber…or post…or firewood. How the hell am I supposed to know? I recall reading somewhere that it takes an entire forest…more than 500,000 trees…to supply Americans with their Sunday newspapers every week.

I, for one…don't buy the Sunday paper. I believe that the average person trashes the Sunday paper without even looking at half of it. That's 250,000 trees every week being destroyed for absolutely no reason at all.

At long intervals I often see a lonely hawk or other bird of prey circling, cutting through the sky that always seems to be blue and warm. Then it sinks out of sight. It moves without sound, much like me. I've read that the American eagle's talons hit its prey at fifty-five to seventy-five miles per hour. Its claws act like a latch lock and the bird can fly carrying three times its own weight. An average American eagle weighs between seven and eight pounds. So, prey less than twenty-five pounds is fair game for it. The bird has three-stage vision…panoramic vision like ours…telescopic vision, which enables it to see a bird in flight at five miles…and micro-vision…which can lock in on a running mouse.

Several deer just crossed the road, interrupting my thoughts but not my pedaling. This is an up and down roller coaster road, with short steep downhills and even shorter, steeper uphills. Forget about the 100-pound rims and tires.

This road doesn't have much traffic, but I've had nothing but strong headwinds ever since I rode into Wisconsin. I know they are strong, because I'm riding so slowly that I'm not a challenge for the dogs. They don't even bother chasing me anymore.

Boy…! This wind sucks…! I have a good, I mean bad, 20 mph headwind, now.

Everything is such a lush green…the trees…the ferns…and the grass. On my tour, I've realized that the journey is the best part, not my destination.

As the air warms, more human life emerges out of the buildings and the animal life seems to disappear into the woods. So which do you think is the smartest?

I'm hungry as a lion. The only thing standing between starvation and me is my stored fat (which I have an ample supply of). My water bottles are running dangerously low, also.

Last year I painted my racing bike white, and I call it "White Lightening." It's a slender, beautiful machine. I use my racing bike for fast, physical rides. It's a form of exercise as well as relaxation for me. It's a method of burning off aggressions and blue moods. As I ride on my racing bike, the world passes by me in a blur of colors and a rush of the wind. I never stop to rest when I'm on my racing bike.

Now, my touring bike is quite different. Touring is what I enjoy the most about cycling. Taking off for several days, and occasionally for several weeks, at a time, with the goal of exploring a particular place, to focus on a destination and see if I can ride that distance. My best tours move slowly, to allow for maximum absorption, though even the most laid-back cyclist has compulsive moments and wants to make good time.

* * *

There a sign, on a side-road, that says "Christie One Mile." The only problem is that there is a blockade across the road with a "Road Closed" sign on it. With a town only a mile away that might have food, I'm going through anyway. I ride south for a mile or so until I come to the town of Christie. A sign says it has the population of one hundred and forty-five (forty-five would be more believable). I ride up to a giant concrete grain elevator that's a step back in time. At 2:26 p.m., I stop in a country store, hopefully to get something to eat. It's the first place there has been to eat in the last 60 miles. In front of the store are three pickups with gun racks in their rear windows. But, instead of having guns…they have fishing rods in them.

I just realized that I haven't eaten anything since breakfast and I'm at my state of "acute starvation," which commonly sets in whenever I go longer than three or four hours without food.

I lean my bike up against some horse-tanks out front of the broken-down general store. As I walk in, I notice sacks of flour leaning against the wall by the door. A heavyset old lady, with a face like a full moon, appears from behind the counter. She's definitely not a Jane Fonda, age is unkind to her. I guess that's one of the troubles with having an hourglass figure. The sands of time always end up in the bottom half. Anyway, I ask her if she has any sandwiches? She says, "Oh yes we do…! We have a large variety of sandwiches. We have peanut-butter and jelly on white…peanut-butter on white…jelly on white…peanut-butter and jelly on wheat…peanut-butter on wheat…jelly on wheat…etc." In the meat cooler, right in front of me, there are a few ready-made sandwiches. I ask for the ham and cheese, some potato chips, and a quart of milk (I look for my ex-wife's picture on the milk carton, but, no such luck). I take my sandwich and go out onto the wooden sidewalk out front of the old general store, where they've got two benches on the porch. One bench is labeled "Democrat" the other "Republican." Unaware of the political leanings of the area, and not being a Democrat or Republican myself (I believe in voting for the best person for the job no matter what his party is) I sit down on the Democrat bench.

The sandwich I'm eating doesn't taste very fresh and, as I look for the expiration date, I discover that it has already past by a week. A farmer, wearing a baseball cap advertising fertilizer, and well-worn overalls comes out the doorway and glances briefly at me before continuing on down the steps to his truck. He looks over his shoulder and blows out his cheeks and says, "Don't let folks catch you sittin' there during tomato season…!" After wolfin' down my sandwich, I take my water bottles into the store, buy some rocket fuel (Tang) and ask the lady behind the counter where I can fill my water bottles. She yells out for Jan, her daughter, to come out of the back and show me. Now, Jan's a pretty twenty, twenty-five year old. She has apple-red cheeks, gorgeous eyes, and a nice smile. Oh Yea…! Her breasts stick out straight and true. She's leading me through her house (they lived in the back of the store) and out back to a pump house. There are birds taking a bath in a birdbath as a hummingbird darts between Jan and me. As I follow her, I can't help but to notice her long, lustrous black hair, and her little flanks look delicious. After refilling my water bottles with ice-cold well water, it's back to the road for me.

*   *   *

I'm on my way again.

Now, there is an interesting bumper sticker. It has a Chevy emblem with, "This is your Brain" written under it. Then under that, there's a Ford emblem, and written under it is, "This is your Brain on Drugs. Any questions?"

I'm on another speed bump road, and it sure makes it hard on the ass. God...! I hate these rough speed-bump roads. I have my old friend, a 15 mph headwind...a little bit off to my right side. The wind has been a bitch all day long. Actually it's been a bitch ever since I rode into Wisconsin.

As I ride past this farmhouse there is was a sign on the gate that reads, "Protected by a Pit-Bull, with AIDS." Just once, I would like to see a sign that says, "Beware of Cat."

I'm crossing over to the other side of the road to keep as far away from the two, yes...two...dogs, as I can. I'm yelling at them to go home. They are right beside me and I'm not going to take my eyes off the mongrels as they growl at me. The lead dog, (a cross between a Doberman and something else) seems to be laughing as he shows me his dental work. His front teeth are crooked, which'll keep him out of dog shows, and hopefully my leg. As I've mentioned before, one dog's barking alerts every dog in the country and...at the next farmhouse...another dog comes chasing after me. His lip curled up over glistening fangs...the bristle-like hairs on his neck and back are raised...and growls are rumbling up from his belly.

I've really had it with this rough #&@#! road and strong headwind. I don't usually talk like this, but my attitude seems to be closely related to my fatigue level. Pedaling mile after mile in Wisconsin, over roads that are either unpaved or have speed bumps and chuckholes...and always into a strong headwind...and being chased by dogs, just doesn't make me a happy camper.

At 4:38 p.m. I ride into Marshfield. The road is much better now. I wait at a railroad crossing for about 10 minutes, as the longest train I've ever seen makes its way by.

There is a beautiful maple tree in a pasture full of Holsteins.

I'm riding straight south now. Of course, straight into a 15 mph headwind.

Way out here they have a name for the wind. They call the wind Maria. I think they could, more sensibly, call it Son-of-a-Bitch.

* * *

I've ridden 94 miles today and I'm hungry and tired...and I don't see any restaurant in Bethel...so, I'm going to stop and go into a saloon where I know they'll at least have some snacks.

To look at this town, you would think it's 1889 not 1989. Main street looks like a western movie set, with stores having flat roofs with false fronts to make them look higher and fancier. To me, it looks like a bustling community with its grocery...hardware...and antique store and of course...this saloon. There are a couple of old, lazy dogs lying in the middle of the street. This is the kind of town where they could lie there for hours and not bother anyone. The saloon seems to be a watering hole for pickups and tractors. As I lift my bike up onto the wooden walkway and roll it past the door of the saloon, I take a quick look in at the clientele, and it looks inviting. I lean my bike up against a bench, in front of one of the windows by the entrance, so I can keep an eye on it. I push the swinging doors open and step in, with my bright colored jersey and my tight spandex riding shorts, and my cleats that make me look and sound and walk like a duck. I've got my helmet in hand, and my hair is all wet and messed up from hours and hours of sweating. I guess I do look a little different than the local folks sitting at the bar.

Standing in the doorway, I first notice two light bulbs dangling from the ceiling and old farm calendars hanging on all the walls. A ceiling fan above is old but it's still stirring the hot air around. As I step in farther, I notice two guys sitting on the left side of this U-shaped bar. One has a John Deere baseball cap on and the other a Ducks Unlimited cap. They are both wearing Levi's, tee shirts and…of course…cowboy boots. As best as I can make out, they're in their early 30s. They're slouching over the bar with their elbows resting on the brass railing that surrounds the bar. One has his hand firmly, and permanently, wrapped around his beer, as if he doesn't want anybody to steal it. In his other hand between his yellowed fingers he holds a short cigarette. It looks as though they've been in here drinking since early sunrise. Actually, it looks as though they were born here, and never left.

Then, at the far end of the bar, in the dim light, sits another farmer. He's sort of coffee-colored and it's obvious that he hasn't shaved for several days. He's also wearing a baseball cap, it's covered with dust…fertilizer…or maybe it's dust from the grain elevator…ground cattle feed…maybe.

Then, over on the right side of the bar, sits this gentleman (guy) next to a lady. Now, I consider all females ladies, until proven otherwise. This guy's uncombed hair is sticking out from under his dirty baseball cap. He's got on a torn, blue, checkered shirt and filthy blue jeans. Neatness definitely is the last thing on his list. He's very tanned. Actually his face is a bronze-red.

Anyway, everybody stops talking, as I walk in. It's as quiet as it is at one of my bicycle club meetings when they ask for volunteers. As I stand there, all heads rotate on their necks like owls, with all eyes focused on me. I guess I'm the strangest sight these people have ever seen. I imagine that today will be remembered (in this saloon anyway) as the day the fair-skinned alien appeared riding his bizarre looking bicycle into town. I froze for a minute or two, not knowing exactly what to say or do. But, I know they expect me to say or do something. So, I simply say, "Gee, you guys are dressed funny." At that they all cracked up. I can see the broken yellow teeth of the farmer who sits at the far end of the bar, as he spoke up and says, "Yea, you look like one of those divers I've seen on Jacques Cousteau."

I go over and belly up to the bar. Directly across the horseshoe shaped bar from me is a fetching babe. She has absolutely gorgeous young, firm, full breasts and long honey-colored hair. She's pleasant to look at, to say the least. She seems to know the bar tremendously well. She glances over at me several times. Of course, I had my eyes glued on her. When she receives her second long-necked Bud, since I sat down, it is foaming over. She looks right at me, leans over (exposing her firm chest even more) and commences to put her wet lips over the opening in the bottle, never taking her eyes off me. I guess I smile a little, which must please her because next she licks the foam from the sides of the bottle. I'm waiting and watching for her to deep throat it next, but she doesn't. I get up and go to the restroom to take a leak. I adjust things in my tight, revealing spandex shorts and proudly walk back to my stool. A short time later she gets up and walks over to the cigarette machine, just behind me. Now I can see what she was wearing from the breast down. She's got short cutoffs and a sleeveless shirt, tied in a knot around her small waist…it's unbuttoned half way. I would be lying if I were to tell you that she doesn't look good. She looks good enough to eat. She drops a quarter on the floor…bends over and picks it up…revealing things I've been dreaming about but hadn't seen for a long time.

I'd better call my girlfriend tonight.

I overhear a conversation between the two guys that are sitting next to each other. One of them say's that he's only got 22,000 miles on his 1970 Ford Fairlane. It seems a little funny to me that he would be so proud of having not gone anywhere.

The other guy raises his voice, and says to me, "Do you think you ride so fast that you really need that helmet?"

I replied, "Yea…! I'll put it on if I have to much to drink and am in danger of falling of the bar stool."

A short time later the guy next to the lady gets up and leaves. I hear a tractor snort and he is gone.

The lady, being a little curious (like all women are) comes around the bar and starts to talk to me. She tells me that the guy that was sitting next to her is so lazy that he married a pregnant woman. She asks me all about my tour. Anything and everything I say seems to be interesting to her. I could sit here and go on telling her lies till the cows come home and she would love it. She says that she'd like to go to the big city sometime and go to the Opera. I tell her that I wouldn't go anyplace I couldn't eat Cheetos. She laughs…God, I love a girl with a sense of humor.

She asks me, "How far are you going to ride today?"

I say, "I'm planning on spending the night in Wisconsin Rapids."

She then asks, "Which road are you going to take there?"

So I tell her what my plans are. She suggests that I go a different way because there aren't any motels on the route I have planned. I take her advice. She looks and talks like she knows where all the motels are.

I had three Pepsi's (that's right Pepsi, I still remember Dodson) and a couple of microwave hamburgers, well, actually…cheeseburgers.

As I stand outside putting my helmet on, the guy that made the comment about my helmet comes out of the saloon. He says, "Don't break any speed limits," and gets on his big red and black Massey Ferguson tractor and drives on down the road.

Well, it's time to hit the old trail again. I've got my feet in the stirrups of my iron horse.

Here I am riding along about two miles out of town, and along comes this old rusted-out reddish-brown pick-up truck, just a blowing on the horn. I get over to the right as far as possible. It goes around me, pulls over and stops. As I ride up to the open window, I can see that it's the lady from the saloon. She says, "Throw your bike in the back and I'll take you to the motel. It's right on my way." I (like a fool) say, "That's all right, I'll find it all right."

It's a good thing my feet are locked into these pedals, because I feel like kicking myself right in the ass for not taking her up on her offer. As she drives off she has an appropriate bumper sticker on her truck, it reads: "Save the horse, ride the cowboy."

It's 7:01 p.m. and I have between a 10 to 15 mph headwind as I ride toward Vesper.

I don't know, maybe it's because I just eaten, but I feel fat. Actually I'm about 20 lbs. overweight. When I was married, I was about 40 lbs. overweight. I told my wife that I would go on a diet and lose 5 lbs. a week, if she would too. Seeing as how she only weighed 125 lbs. I figured all my troubles would be over in 25 weeks. Think about it.

I'm chasing my own shadow, but I can't catch it. This wind just doesn't give up, and neither do I. I've been fighting it for two days, now.

When I called my son a couple of days ago to let him, know my E.T.A. (estimated time of arrival), I told him that I would probably get there on Friday afternoon, unless the wind blows me back to Washington, and it's been trying to do just that.

Anyway, he informed me that my daughter was really worried about me, seeing as how I told her that I would call her every couple of days and I haven't been able to get hold of her for over a week, now. My son said that she had the Montana and North Dakota State Police out looking for me. So, I guess I'd better give her a call and let her know that I am all right.

Boy, she's pissed…! She informed me that I was on my own, from now on…she wasn't going to worry about me anymore. Actually, I thought I was on my own all along.

As I stop to take a picture of a deer it smells of green hills and wild flowers.

You know, I guess I'm very fortunate to live in Southern California where there are a lot of good places to ride. And there are a lot of good bicycle clubs to ride with. I belong to four myself. They have all different kinds of rides, some for beginners, some for me, and some for racers.

We have recreational rides, which I prefer. They call them, "Rides for the Masses," which consist of anywhere from 500 to 15,000 riders. They are really fun, and you can see and ride with all kinds of riders.

Then there are the so-called training rides. These are usually for the young riders who want to become racers. I go on these rides once in a while, whenever I'm feeling especially fast. It's not long before they put me in my place.

What I get a kick out of, is that some of these guys never miss a training ride. They go out there and kill themselves, three or four times a week, and they never intend to race. I mean, if you're in training, you should be training for something.

Next, we have tours, which I enjoy the most. These are anywhere from a weekend, to one or two weeks long. On these tours I get to see a lot of virgin territory with usually 5 to 10 other cyclists.

I really notice a big difference in the attitude of people on this side of the Mississippi. West of the Mississippi they're great. They're friendly and they would wave to me. They were always courteous. They always give me the widest berth when ever possible. I mean, they would drive clear on the other side of the road when they went around me (that is, if there wasn't any traffic coming). And now, on this side of the Mississippi, they don't go on the other side of the road, no matter how much room they have, and nobody has waved to me in Wisconsin, yet.

As I ride through the lush pasturelands of Wisconsin, I marvel at the setting sun as it plays kaleidoscope with the rolling countryside, which is full of grazing cattle. The landscape has turned from a verdant green to a dozen different shades of purple as the sun turns from a wheel of cheese to an orange.

It's warm and this road has freshly filled cracks all the way across it. When I stop for a traffic light, I sometimes accidentally put my foot down in the tar. Of course, I don't think anything of it, until I start to get out of my pedals the next time and I can't get out because they are tarred in.

It's 8:45 p.m. as I check into a Best Western motel in Wisconsin Rapids. The room is $30.00 but I don't care. I've ridden 120 miles today, most of it with a 15 mph headwind, and I'm tired. Yes, I'm tired…! For several years I've been blaming it on middle age…high blood pressure…lack of vitamins…air pollution…water pollution…saccharin…dieting…and a dozen other things that make me wonder if life is really worth living. But now I've find out, it isn't that at all. The population of this country is 200 million and eighty-four million are retired. That leaves 116 million to do all the work. There are 75 million in school, which leaves 41 million to do all the work. Of this total, there are 22 million employed by the government. That leaves 19 million to do all the work. Four million are in the Armed Forces, which leaves 15 million to do all the work. Take from that total the 14,800,000 people whom work for State and City Government, and that leaves 200,000 to do all the work. There are 188,000 in hospitals, so that leaves 12,000 to do all the work. Now, there are 11,998 people in prisons, that leaves just two people to do all the work. You and me. And you're just sitting there reading this. No Wonder I'm Tired…!

Speaking of retiring, where I work, they have a point system to let you know just when you're eligible for retirement. Under their present system, if I don't get laid off…or get sick…or miss any work…I'll be eligible for retirement in 22 years. I'm really not looking forward to it, though, because I know by that time they'll change the rules and I'll have to work until I'm at least 75 years old.

"Come on Lottery…!"

I don't know why I'm even talking about retirement, I'm a young man of 23 (twice, almost).

Actually, I'm in better shape now than I was when I was 23 (once).

It's 11:00 p.m. and I'm ready to retire. I'm exhausted from battling the headwinds all day, and I know I'll fall right asleep.

*   *   *

*Statistics for **DAY EIGHTEEN** Thursday, June 29, 1989.*
120 miles of riding today, 11.6 average miles per hour for today, 2,070 miles of riding in eighteen days, 115 average miles of riding per day.

Day Nineteen

From Wisconsin Rapids, Wisconsin
To Eureka, Wisconsin

It's 6:05 a.m. I guess I'd better get up and get ready to ride. I slept like a log last night. With all systems on go I head across the street to get something to eat. What I would really like for breakfast is some cinnamon toast. I recall, as a kid, I would get a custard cup out of the cupboard and fill it 3/4 full of sugar then stir in cinnamon until it turned a dark brown. Put that on four or five pieces of hot buttered toast and you've got yourself a great breakfast.

It's 7:52 a.m. and I'm finally off down the road. It's taken me almost two hours from bed to bike this morning. It's another beautiful day out. I really don't like the fact that in this town bicyclists have to ride on the sidewalks on all the main drags. I sure can't make very good time riding on the sidewalks. Once, I'm off the main drag, I can get back on the road where I belong.

It's Friday morning, 65 degrees, and the spring countryside is bright and fresh, and brimming with life. The trees and flowers are all in bloom and the fragrance of the blossoms fills the air. Wisconsin Rapids and beyond is all a beautiful green vegetation.

I'm riding on a nice, brand-new road. It's as smooth as a porch swing. Why can't all roads be like this? I don't think too much of these new tires I put on right before I started this tour. I'm riding on a smooth road and they both feel like they have a bulge in them. When I get to my son's, I'm going to put some new ones on, a different kind, of course.

Oops…! I spoke too soon. That's the end of the new road. It was nice while it lasted, the whole six and a half miles of it. There is a magnificent church appearing in the east. There is a thick green canopy of trees separating me from the surrounding cornfields. The only signs of civilization I've seen for miles now are a few lazy old dogs that tilt their heads as I ride by.

I have 10 miles on the odometer and a 5 mph crosswind, and it's been quite flat.

I'm surrounded by a meadowland of purple flowers. I guess today's is similar to a lot of other mornings, but to me…it's always a little different. There is always that feeling of surprise. When I'm riding out here in the early morning sunshine, with the sweet scent of wildflowers…it's almost as if I'm doing it for the very first time in my life. After being buried in the big city for so many years, it's just gratifying to take in a big breath of clean, clear, fresh air and savor it

Butterflies are flying across the road right in front of me and lawnmowers fill the air with the sweet scent of freshly cut grass. I'm riding behind an old-timer in blue overalls bouncing down the road on his green John Deere tractor.

Seeing as how I'll be getting to my son's on the Fourth of July weekend, my son and his wife, both have Saturday, Sunday, and Monday off work. So, I don't know…I might spend three days with them. Maybe…I'll see. I might be too antsy to stay off my bike that long. I'm really enjoying this tour.

It's 70 degrees as I ride out of Bancroft, and everything is quite green. There are lots of birds around, mostly crows.

I just saw a sign that reads, "No Hunting, All Survivors will be Prosecuted." My son, goes duck hunting. He calls ducks "Fast Food." I just spotted two boys with .22 rifles, riding their bicycles toward the country. Their hair is close-cropped and their faces are tanned from the summer wind and the hot June sun.

There are a lot of potato fields all through this area. Some people say I have the shape of a potato. Well, that just goes to prove the old saying is true, "You are what you eat." I love potatoes. I remember growing up on a farm in this state. One room of our basement was full of 100 lb. sacks of potatoes…another room was lined with shelves of freshly canned vegetables…and yet another room was stacked to the ceiling with wood…which we burned in our furnace.

I smell that unmistakable odor of pigs. I don't see them, but I sure can smell them. I ride past a field of freshly bailed hay which sure smells a lot better than the pigs did. I remember as a youth, the planting and harvesting seasons. I recall mowing the hay, raking it…and bailing it…then putting it up in the barn.

I have a 10 mph crosswind. As I ride through Almond, I can't help but notice a man standing in his yard, watching me. He's a big fellow (at least in the stomach area). He has gray hair (a bit thin), reddish cheeks, and a big friendly smile. I decide to stop and chat with him awhile. I come to find out that he used to live in Glendale, California. Glendale is about twenty-mile from where I live now. Boy, it's a small world. You know, it's fun to stop and talk to people. You never know what they'll tell you. This fellow told me that he used to get headaches all the time, but he had to give them up because he couldn't figure out how to get the tops off the new childproof aspirin bottles.

I'm riding past vast green forests of pine trees stretching out in all directions. When I was in High School, I had a part-time job trimming Christmas trees, just like these. We would shape them so they would make good Christmas trees. That brings to mind other things. I absolutely hate it when people write X-mas. What they are doing is leaving Christ out of Christmas, and what we're doing at Christmas time is celebrating Christ's birth.

I'm riding on a tree-lined county road that's winding its way through an evergreen forest. The undergrowth in the forest is thick and lush. I'm pedaling along at a 10 mph pace…by choice. Some things just shouldn't be rushed. I'm admiring the lush green pastures, board fences and huge old shade trees. As I ride along slowly, I catch glimpses of many different kinds of animals on the wooded hillsides. This is what I consider to be some of the most spectacular scenery I've seen yet.

At 11:03 a.m. with 39 miles in, I'm seven miles east of Almond and it's 75 degrees. With all these trees right alongside the road, the winds don't bother me much.

Before I got into cycling, I would notice bicyclists wearing helmets. I would say to myself, "Boy, those guys must think they're fast…!" Well, later I found out that you don't have to be fast to hit a patch of gravel on a downhill corner or to drop your front wheel into a water drain or to run into a car door that's unexpectedly flung open right in front of you. Let me give you a little background about Styrofoam helmets first. They are made out of Styrofoam for several reasons.

1) Because Styrofoam is lightweight.

2) So they will break into pieces during a crash. This takes up a lot of the impact. They also have a thin cloth cover which holds the pieces together, in case there is more than one impact in an accident, which there usually is. Let me tell you about this guy in my bike club. He was riding around in a parking lot, at a very slow speed, paying more attention to the girls than anything, (quite understandable) and he went over a speed bump…fell over and landed on his head (like most cyclists do, because

their shoes are clipped into their pedals). Anyway, he broke his $65.00 helmet in half, still a small price to pay. If he wouldn't have had the helmet on he surely would have cracked his head open.

When I was training for this tour, I rode a lot of miles, day after day. I had a *Bell V1 Pro* helmet, which is twice as heavy as the *Gyro* helmet I have now. After riding so many miles with my old helmet, my neck would get a little tired. Now, with my new helmet, I don't even realize I have it on.

Everything I've read and was told when I bought my first pair of so-called racing shoes (the kind that lock into the pedals) said the shoes should fit pretty snug. So that's what I bought. I used them for a couple of years and my feet always got sore at exactly 70 miles into my ride…every time. I finally went out and bought some new shoes, two sizes larger and my feet never get sore…anymore. So, don't believe everything you're told or read.

So far on this tour, I feel great. The only thing that got the least bit sore was my ass, and, since I quit wearing underwear, it's fine.

I have a 5 mph crosswind, but it's blocked most of the time by all these big beautiful trees. As I ride along in the great outdoors through rolling pastureland and green hills…just minding my own business…I hear a low growl…like that of a mean dog. I look to both sides then behind, but there is no dog in sight. I hear the growl again and this time I can identify it. It's my stomach…! I guess it's time for a second breakfast.

I stop in a tiny cafe in Wild Rose. I sit at a booth by a window with red-checked curtains where I can overhear the conversation that four farmers are having as they sit around the biggest table in the cafe. They're talking about potatoes…pulpwood…dairy products…and somebody's broken fishing rod. I watch as they get up and leave. One of them, the big fellow…stops to pay the bill. He's got a pronounced belly…white hair…a gray-and-white peppered beard and bright blue eyes. He's walking with a limp. His belly, and pants, are held in place by a wide leather belt. The belt doesn't pass through all the loops, nor are his soiled pants zipped all the way up. This is definitely farm country.

No sooner have I remounted my bike than I'm riding in rolling terrain, with a lot of little wild flowers and butterflies right next to the road. When I was a little kid, and didn't know any better, I would go to the back of our farm where there was a cemetery. I would go around and get beautiful bouquets of flowers for my mother. Speaking of flowers, I'm riding out of Wild Rose right now. I still can't get the memory of Rose out of my mind, and I'm not too sure that I want to.

After miles and miles of riding on beautiful, unfenced country roads I roll my bike onto the shoulder…stop…get off…and lie my bike down gently in the delicate flowers. I struggle to take off my sweat-soaked jersey. It's stuck fast to my body. I finally get it off and spread it out over the tall grass to dry (wishful thinking). I lie on a cushion of lush green vegetation, letting a soft breeze blow over me. With the sun in my face, I look up…through half-closed eyes, at the light-blue sky. I watch a hawk soar on the thermals as jets autograph the sky with disappearing ink. It sort of reminds me of the way it used to be, and the way it is now. It's so peaceful and relaxing out here. As I lie here, with closed eyes now…I think of how different things would be if I were back in L.A. At this time of day, I would be at work in a building without any windows, where the doors are keep shut to keep out the petroleum fumes and traffic noise. In a building that has artificial lights and climate control. Sometimes, I think everything about L.A. is artificial.

Lazily, I open my eyes, and watch as the hawk still soars overhead. I can't help but say to myself, "Ain't Life Grand?"

* * *

A school bus just passed me on its way to Mt. Morris. Have I mentioned before that I hated school? But I rather enjoyed riding the bus to and from. It was 12 miles from our house to High School, so we had plenty of time for a little fun. The fun group, which I was a part of, always sat in the last two rows of seats in the bus. The mornings were usually uneventful. Oh…! One morning we passed around some rum and another morning we shared some blackberry brandy. But the morning I remember the most was the morning Larry brought some homemade dandelion wine. It was some awful tasting shit. It had long strings in it, which went down quite hard. But, being macho and cool, as we all were, we drank it anyway. The rides home were always the most fun. There always seemed to be a couple of fun-loving girls that joined us in the back of the bus. I learned more on those rides home then I ever did in school. On special occasions on the weekends we would have some wonderful keg parties. You know, the kind where beautiful girls would go out in the woods and throw up. My mother always thought we were a good…generous…sharing…group of kids. I think she thought this because, even though she was against smoking…she once saw a boy from our group light up a cigarette and pass it around. Although, at the time I didn't know what it was either, I remember one kid say that they were smoking grass. But I knew better, because I cut some grass and dried it and smoked it and it didn't smell anything like what they were smoking.

It's 1:00 p.m. and I have 50 miles on the odometer. I'm three miles east of Mt. Morris and it's 81 degrees. Being within a 30-mile radius of where I used to live some 20 years ago, I don't see any need to look at my map. Well…I should have looked at it. I didn't go much out of my way, but I'm riding on roads I've never heard of before. Maybe it isn't a mistake, though. This is a beautiful little…traffic-free…country road. The tree limbs stretch out over the road forming a stunning natural canopy that furnishes me with shade as well as a windbreak. There is no sound but the whistling of the wind and the birds, which are singing from the overhanging branches. I feel all alone out here in the backwoods. I'm a long way from the big buildings of the big cities of this big country. Here and there the sun's penetrating…changing my tree tunnel into a brilliant gold.

WISCONSIN

    I'm reminded of when, as a kid, I used to love to walk in the forest, especially on rainy days. My dad used to tell me that it was all right to go into the woods in a storm, but not to go under a single tree, because of the lightning. The woods never seemed to be so fresh and alive as they are in wet weather. Every leaf would have an edging of crystal drops. It's so peaceful. Only in the woods can you find solitude without loneliness.

    It's 1:33 p.m. and I have about a 10 mph crosswind, and I'm in Redgranite. Now, I'm getting into familiar territory. I ride past the best damn pizza joint in a fifty-mile radius of here. I used to have a bread route and I delivered in this town. I had 60 stops on that route. The store owners would like to talk to me, and, if each one only spent one minute talking (and I don't believe there is a store owner out there that can only talk for one minute) I would be one hour late at the end of the day. If they talked for five minutes, I would be five hours late getting home.

    There is the pickle factory I used to work at when I was on summer vacation from High School. It's been there since God was a boy.

    I have that good (bad) old Wisconsin 15 mph headwind, again.

    I just can't believe this wind. It's at least a 20 mph headwind now.

I'm heading straight east now, so it's turned into a 20 mph crosswind instead of a headwind. It may seem like all I talk about are the headwinds. Well, that's about all I've had since I rode into Wisconsin.

I have 70 miles in as I ride into Berlin. I just rode by a sign on a print shop that read, "We Print Anything, Except Money." I'm riding past the old granite quarry now. My mind wanders back to memories of the first time I went to the granite quarry at the edge of this town. We called this a "Swimsuits Prohibited" swimming area. In other words, this is where we went skinny-dipping. I remember it was cold and deep, but the girls were warm and shallow.

*   *   *

And there's the High School I went to, good old Berlin High.

My mother always told me that my high school days would be the best days of my life. Well, they might have been the best days of her life (and, with a nickname like Cindy Britches, they probably were) but they sure weren't the best days of my life. I hated High School…! I spent more time in the principal's office than I did in the classrooms (to this day I hate offices) for various uncalled-for reasons…like smoking or coming back from lunch one or two hours late. It was so stupid. They would make me sit in the office and write a full page on why I was smoking or why I was late getting back to school. Well, I didn't think it would take anyone a full page to explain that. So, I got in just as much trouble for what I wrote, as I did for what I did.

It seems like if they couldn't find anyone to pin something on, they always hauled me into the office. Case in point. Some clever guy was throwing marbles into the heating vents at the ceiling in my homeroom. They would rumble and make a really neat noise as they rolled down the vent, all the way into the basement. They hauled me into the office, and…just because I had a pocket half full of marbles…they thought I had something to do with it.

Then there was the time someone put rubbers over all the drinking fountains. They thought I might have something to do with that too. Just because some girl who knew I had rubbers, turned me in. The fact is, most of us boys walked around with rubbers in our wallets. I was a Boy Scout and, if you didn't have one, you were ignoring completely all the advantages of preparedness. The unfortunate truth was that most of us still had the same condoms we bought two years earlier. And, not knowing if they were still safe to use, we thought we might as well use them, some way.

Then there was the time when the smoke bomb went off on the school bus. I was the prime suspect, but it couldn't be proven without a doubt. But, when the cherry bomb exploded on the bus that's when I got hauled into the office and got kicked off the bus for the rest of the year. That's also when I quit school. Graduation didn't really matter to me because I was a below-average student, getting straight E's. I definitely had a learning disability…my attitude. Besides, by this time I figured I already knew more than I would ever use anyway. I could read and write and I knew the multiplication table up to six times seven and I don't reckon I could ever get any further than that if I was to stay in school until I was an old man. I may not have finished school, but let me tell you not everything can be learned is a classroom. I know a lot of idiot college graduates. In a recent multiple-choice high school test, 78% of the students identified Abraham Lincoln as a car builder. That's right. More than 3/4 of our nation's youths could not identify the man who invented the telephone.

Don't misunderstand me. I'm not saying that school's bad. Schooling is important. It's the best of all things. Money can be lost or stolen…health and strength may fail…but what you have committed to your mind is yours forever. I'm just saying that I hated school and I learned very little when I was there. It wasn't until I quit High School that I got my real education. That's when I started working in a punch press shop, only to discover that the employees were getting their fingers cut off in the presses regularly. That's when I decided to get out of that profession. I went to a trade school and took a course in blueprint reading and one on advanced math. This helped me considerably in landing a good job in a machine shop. Lately, I've taken class in typing, dancing, and computers. I'm a strong believer in trade schools. You go to these schools because you want to learn, not because you have to. An education is a wonderful thing. It's something that nobody can ever take away from you. Not even an ex-wife. What I don't understand about High School and College is why some people learn four or five different languages when they never intend to use them. "It's a known fact that college isn't a cure for stupidity . . . They're not sure, yet, whether or not it's a cause." And, another thing I have to say is, that I believe that students should stand firm in their refusal to do algebra. Let me tell you that there is no such thing as algebra in real life.

I wouldn't say that I was a bad student but, under my class picture, it didn't say "The person most likely to succeed." It said, "If there's trouble to be found, Harold's nowhere around…but you can bet he's been there."

* * *

Every time I played sick, my mother, who was a RN, always knew if I was really sick or just faking to get out of going to school. And, for some unexplainable reason, she would rat on me. My dad would come up to my room and say to me, "Get out of bed, get dressed and put on your coat and gloves. We're going to cut fire wood." We would hitch the wagon to the tractor and head out for the woods. We would cut down a couple of trees that weren't good for anything but firewood. My dad would build a fire and it was my job to cut the small limbs off the tree with an ax and drag them to the fire and throw them in. He would saw the trees into chunks and we would load them onto the wagon and haul them back to the house. I would get the wagon unloaded about the time my brothers were getting home from school. Then, while they played…my dad milked the cows…while I went up in the silo and threw the frozen silage down and carried it out to the cows. I fed them their ground feed and when they were done eating that, I would go up in the haymow and throw down their hay and distribute it. After the milking and feeding was done, my dad and I would clean out the barn.

Anyway, after the barn was cleaned, it was time to go in and eat supper. After supper it was down to the basement to stack the wood. Then, a little homework or television, then off to bed. My dad thought he was punishing me by making me do all that work, but…actually…I enjoyed it. It was a lot better then sitting in school.

The only joke I ever heard my mother tell (mind you she was a registered nurse) was about this patient of hers who had written on his penis, "Little" which the nurses thought was funny. Anyway, he asked each and every nurse to go out with him when he was released. Of coarse, they all said "No…!" All except one. After her date with him all the other nurses were anxious to hear how her date went. She said it was wonderful. They teased her and called her "Miss Little" She laughed and said that when that thing got BIG it read, "LITTLE ROCK, ARKANSAS."

I'm riding past the cheese factory where I used to be a cheese maker. I only lived about a quarter of a mile up the road, so it was very convenient. I worked the graveyard shift (from midnight to eight a.m.). This was also very convenient for my ex-wife. Her lover closed his tavern at two a.m. I may not be perfect, but I can honestly tell you that I never cheated on my wives.

There is my old house. It's a big old house and it took a lot of hard work to keep it up. It's got hardwood floors, which I sanded and varnished before moving in. It has about a two-acre yard, which took me all day every Saturday to mow. I had a three-hole outhouse on the farm, which I wanted to get rid of because it wasn't used anymore. I didn't want to tear it down because it was full of hornets. So, I decided to burn it down. It was fairly close to a tree and fence, so I hooked up the garden hose and sprayed it to hold the flames down a little. While I was doing this, cars going by would honk and laugh…some even stopped. Let me tell you what I know about outhouses. They shouldn't be next to a tree. There isn't any sound in nature more disturbing then an apple or acorn dropping on the roof while you are in there. And it should be in a straight line with the house. If the path were crooked, nobody would use it. And the door should always open inward. This is why. Imagine yourself in there with the door open about half way. This gives you air and lets the sunshine in. Then, if you hear anybody coming, you can give it a quick shove with your foot and it's shut. But if it swings outward you can't have it open for air or sunlight, because…if anyone comes…you can't get up off the seat…reach all the way round and grab it without being seen.

I remember remodeling the upstairs of the old house. I painted the ceilings and put in all new lights and switches. I paneled and carpeted the three bedrooms and stairs. I also remodeled the upstairs bathroom and took out three walls and a staircase and made a 20 by 50-foot recreation room.

The floors in this room were very uneven, so I tore the boards off all the floors. Then I put in new two-by-twelve joists to level everything up. Next, I put twelve inches of insulation between the joists, mainly so it would be quieter downstairs when we walked around upstairs. Next, I put down 3/4-inch plywood, for a sub-floor.

My next step was to rip all the plaster and lath off the walls. Then I put in all new electrical wiring, in conduit. I put in a huge picture window at the far end of the room. Next, I insulated the walls and ceiling and plywooded them up. Let me tell you, this was one big project.

*   *   *

I was raising four Polled Herefords, which I kept fenced in with a single hot wire, which didn't work properly all the time. I also had about ten Giant Flemish rabbits running around loose in my yard. These are huge rabbits. I had one that weighed 12 pounds. Anyway, they started to disappear because people would see them along the road at night and steal them. I decided to build a fence around my barnyard, which was about an acre. I bought a lot…and I mean a lot…of 6" X 6" square solid oak post…10 feet long. I sawed each one and made a point on the top, just for looks. Then I creosoted the other end. Then, I dug the holes, with a hand auger, three feet deep…running into many rocks. I put the posts in, making sure that they were all exactly the same height and straight. Next, I dug a trench one-foot deep from one post to the next. This was so that I could put the bottom of my fence one-foot under the ground so the rabbits couldn't dig under the fence and get out. I then put two coats of white paint on the post and I nailed the closely woven wire to the post. It was a lot of work, but it was a beautiful fence that would last a lifetime.

I had a horse tank out in the pasture and I used a garden hose to fill it. Well, I got the bright idea to run an underground water line to it. With the harsh Wisconsin winters I needed to bury the water line at least six feet deep to keep it from freezing. It was about 100 feet from the house to the horse tank. I dug a trench about two feet wide and six feet deep, with a pick and shovel. I had to dig through the driveway and work around large roots. Then, I had to chisel a hole through the three-foot thick rock foundation of the house. Next, I laid the water line and I thought, as long as I was at it I might as well run an electrical line out there too, so I could put up a yard light. Just for the heck of it, I also ran some speaker wires out there, too. I filled the trench in, and everything worked beautifully.

*   *   *

As a kid in Wisconsin, I remember breaking the icicles off the eves and sucking on them. Of course, I also put my tongue on the freezing pump handle, and…yes…it does stick to it.

In July in Wisconsin, it can hit a hundred and fifteen, and forty-five below in January. One hundred and sixty degrees of temperature change is how they keep the riffraff out. And, if that doesn't do it, then they turn the mosquitoes loose. If it weren't for them, and another thing or two, this piece of God's country would be overrun with people.

All these memories make me think of my kids…which make me think of my first marriage…which reminds me of my first divorce…which reminds me of child support.

Yes…! I believe in child support, but alimony, No Way…! I, for one, would never pay alimony. Luckily the courts saw it my way and I didn't have to pay any. Child support is a different story. You were part of bringing these children into the world and I believe it's up to you to do your part in supporting them. Which I did, believe me…I did…even though my kids were told whenever they were short of money, that it was my fault.

Child support is what I call a constant. It doesn't matter if you're on vacation…sick…or out of a job…you still have to pay…and rightfully so. Sometimes my second wife had a hard time dealing with me sending money to my first wife, no matter what it was for. Especially when she wasn't getting any child-support from her ex., and we didn't have enough money to pay our bills. There were times when my support payment took 100% of my check. I had to get a second job to survive. At one especially bad time in my life, I was working two 10-hour jobs, just to make ends meet. It wasn't easy, and I'm sure it wasn't easy for my ex-wife to raise four children on her own.

Being divorced twice, I don't have many material things left. You see, in a divorce everything, including the house is divided up equally. That's right, she gets the inside of the house and I got the outside. But, I have to look at what I have left, not at what I've have lost. I still have my health and peace of mind, and plenty of time to enjoy it. And that's more important to me than all the material things in the world. I've learned that more is not necessarily better. I honestly believe that there are more important things in life than acquiring things.

You might think that I'm against marriage, but I'm not. They say that there is someone out there for everyone.

In Wisconsin, the winters are nine months long, and snowstorms are no surprise on any day of the year. You wait and look forward to spring all winter long, but it never comes. It goes right from winter to summer. There is no spring in Wisconsin. They didn't have *GoreTex* when I lived there. You had to go around all winter with three or four layers of heavy clothing on. If you fell down there wasn't a chance of you getting hurt.

And there's *Granny's Green House*. When I lived back here, her roof started to leak, so I volunteered to put on a new roof for her. This turned out to be quite a project. First, I had to rip all the wood shingles off, only to discover that the boards underneath were spaced about four inches apart…and most of them were rotten. So, I had to replace most of them. I also found out that when I ripped the shingles off, that her attic was full of hornets. This is a very high…steep roof. I would never attempt such a project today, but here it is twenty years later and it still looks fine and it doesn't leak.

I also put plumbing in her house. I had to dig a two-foot wide trench about 150 feet long, with the correct pitch. If you have too much or too little pitch, it won' t work properly. I also dug a hole big enough to bury the septic tank. This meant the hole had to be about eight feet deep and eight feet across. Well, I got about six feet deep and hit the water table. Water kept seeping in, so the last two feet I was digging in mud and water, no fun at all. I dug all this by hand. But I did get it finished, and it's still working well.

Grandma, she's one fine lady. She's worked as a cleaning lady in a hospital practically all her life. Somehow, because it was a hospital…they got away with paying her less than minimum wage. She lived six miles from the hospital and she didn't drive, so she would catch rides from neighbors going that way. I don't think she's ever missed a day's work in her life. Her husband (passed away now) was unable to work for as long as I knew him, but he wasn't unable to drink. She supplemented her income by running her own greenhouse. Then, so she would have enough money to buy Christmas presents, she worked part-time…nights…at a Christmas card factory every November and December. She always managed to put on a feast every Sunday and for all the Holidays, for all her kids and grand kids.

It's 3:42 p.m. and I have 80 miles on the odometer as I ride into Eureka. I'm thinking that it's amazing how far I have ridden in such a short time. Neither my son, or his wife, will be home from work for a couple of hours. So, I ride around town. Seeing as how the whole town is only one block long, this doesn't take me long.

In the spring of the year, as soon as the ice goes out of the river, the walleye start to run and this is a booming fishing town. This is the only sport that comes to my mind that even comes close to golf. I mean, what other sport allows you to sit under a tree all day and drink beer (although there is a fine line between fishing and standing on the shore like an idiot). When you're fishing, you must have the proper bait, whether you put it on or not…is optional. I think most bait is repulsive. I would think that if you were to put something pleasant…say like Reese's Peanut Butter cups…on the hook…the fish would come from miles around.

Eureka, the town itself pretty much reflects just what there is to do here, or the lack of what there is to do…during the long winter months. Bars are as natural to Wisconsin folks as caves are to bears. Twenty, and probably forty, years ago…Eureka had a population of 300…the same as it does today. It has three thriving taverns within a stone's throw of each other. No one goes thirsty in Wisconsin. I stop in one (a combination house…store…bar…and Post Office) just to kill some time until my son and his wife gets home from work.

This tavern has changed hands several times since the last time I was in it. I don't know anyone in here and nobody recognizes me, but I get the usual stares. I have several lukewarm beers and am running low on cash. So, I ask them to cash a $10.00 traveler check for me. They say, "Sorry, we don't take checks." No problem, I don't especially care for warm beer anyway. I grab my handlebar bag and depart.

I ride over to the *Starlight Inn*. A bar owned by my ex-brother-in-law, and his wife. Before I can get off my bike, they both come out of the tavern and greet me. I haven't seen them for almost 13 years. You know, it's funny how much they have changed…and I haven't. We go inside and the old bar looks about the same. Three of my old-drinking buddies are bellied up to the bar, sitting on the same stools they were in…13 years ago. As I recall, they're very talented drinkers. Sometimes I wonder if they ever left. I have two or four or twenty beers, who's counting? Then my daughter, comes in, and tells me that my son and his wife are home. So, I have a few more quick beers and leave.

As I walk out the door I spot Jack Langeberg ("Happy Jack," as everyone calls him) sitting on his porch across the road from the tavern…where I'm told he enjoys spending his afternoons…now that he is retired. I believe he's in his mid-80's now. He knew me as a teenager. I've never seen him dressed any differently than he is today…in a long-sleeved shirt…bibbed overalls…and…of course…his Harley Davidson cap. Back in 1930 he was driving from California on his way to Buffalo, New York where he was offered a job as an airline pilot. His car broke down in Eureka and he asked the owner of the local garage if it was all right if he fixed it himself in the garage. Jack gave the garage owner a silver dollar for the use of the garage and tools. The owner of the garage was so impressed with how Jack had fixed his car he asked him to stick around for a while and work on other cars for him…which he did. That was 59 years ago. Jack never left Eureka. The airline's loss, Eureka's gain. He eventually bought the garage…a house in town…three farms…some land along the river…which he made into a baseball diamond for the kids…and next to it a landing strip for his airplane. In his heyday he also owned the local bar/restaurant, which…to this day…is named, *"Happy Jacks."* He also had the fastest race car around (170 mph) which he drove on the local roads. He always had two or three Cadillacs in his driveway. He told me that, in 1937, he owned ten Caddies. He also loved his Harley Davidson motorcycles. He bought a new one every year. He never worked on the Harleys…he said he bought them to ride…not to work on. He's owned 43 new Harleys in his lifetime. I always thought he was…and still is…a great guy. He taught me how to ride. I guess he was a little crazy, but we all were. He was a lot of fun to ride with and a very good rider. As I recall, he enjoyed passing cars when there was another one coming from the other direction. Then, he would stand up on the seat of his bike and go between them. But, what I remember the most about Jack…was that…anytime he was in his garage or anywhere…no matter how many people were there or how much work he had to do…when the clock struck 12 noon, he would say, "I'll be back, I'm going home for my nooner," and he was gone.

*   *   *

Statistics for DAY NINETEEN Friday, June 30, 1989.
80 miles of riding today, 12.7 average miles per hour for today, 2,150 miles of riding in nineteen days, 113 average miles of riding per day.

Day Twenty

From Eureka, Wisconsin
To Ludington, Michigan

I can't believe my son. He's 28 years old now, and he's really catching up to me. If he's not careful, in a few more years…he'll be as old as I am. He's an excellent hunter and fisherman. He and his wife pretty much live on venison and fish.

I got to my son's Friday afternoon. We went out for dinner and I spent the night there. I was ready to go to bed by one a.m. but my son said, "It's too early to go to bed. It's still dark out." So, we stayed up until dawn. Saturday we went shopping and I also cleaned my bike up a little. Sunday we went down to my daughter's. Let's see. I saw my son and his wife…my daughter and her husband…my other son…my other daughter…my brother and his wife…Grandma…and my ex-brother-in-law and his wife. I saw everyone I wanted to see. And I successfully avoided seeing relatives and ex-relatives I didn't want to see. It was a good weekend. It was a hot weekend though. It was in the 90's both days, and really humid.

I am ready to continue my tour and I'm up rather early this morning. I imagine the new day before I ever see it, with the warm morning sun on my skin. I'm anxious and ready to unfold my dreams (my map). My Trek's ready to roll. I put some new tires on my bike and we're ready for the open road and small towns.

As my wheels roll toward Oshkosh, I can't help but think of how happy I am to be back on the road again. It is 6:13 a.m. and 65 degrees as I ride out of my son's driveway. I guess I'm just too anxious…impatient…and restless and ready to start riding to stay here another day. There is not a whisper of a breeze this morning and the sun's up. With this early of a start, and with a little luck…maybe…just maybe…I'll be able to beat the heat.

It was definitely time for me to get back on my bike. As the old saying goes, today is the first day of the rest of my life.

I'm riding past a huge old house and legend has it that Al Capone used to use it as a hideout. It's in a perfect location for a gangster hideout. It sits on top of a hill, and from the outlook on its roof, you can see for miles in all directions. Grandpa, who's been in the house, told me that the basement is large enough to drive a full team of horses, pulling a wagon, and turn them around and drive them back out the same door. There are tunnels leading from the basement, big enough to drive a car through. One goes south and the other north into a forest about half a mile away.

The sun is shining making the water droplets on the grass sparkle like diamonds. I'm getting my first real taste of the famous east coast climate, here in the Midwest. Not only can I feel the humidity, I can see it. A mist is hanging in all the valleys I ride through this morning.

Two baby rabbits munching on the freshly mowed grass along the side of the road flee into the high grass as I approach. My dad used to raise rabbits to sell and to eat and to take to the fair. Now, my dad never told me about the birds and the bees but he did explain to me what a whore was. This is how he explained it to me. First of all, when you want to breed a rabbit, you always take the female to the male's cage and put her in. If the female is in heat, she will let the male mount her and if she isn't she will run around and around the cage until you take her out. Well, my dad had this female that would sit still and even raise her tail, every time she was put into the cage, even if she wasn't in heat. My dad named her "The Whore".

Hey, they've got rubber mats on the railroad crossings in Oshkosh, too.

With 17 miles on the odometer I'm going to stop at this fast food place for breakfast. I take a seat by a window, like I always do, so I can keep an eye on my bike. There is a non-English speaking teenage boy with the belly of a man out front. He has a water hose in his hands and he's supposedly spraying the sidewalk off. I'm going to eat a hurried breakfast and get out there before he drenches my bike. I rush out and sure enough he's getting my bike all wet. The light over this kid's head is only about 40 watts. I say something to the kid, and he says something to me. It's probably a good thing that we don't understand each other.

I'm on my way again, with clean…wet…tires and wheels.

I'm four miles north of Oshkosh and it's 73 degrees. I have a 5 mph tailwind, YES…! You heard me right, a tailwind…! And in Wisconsin…! Unbelievable…! It must be because I'm leaving. The sky is cloudless, not in the usual way. It's neither blue nor gray but rather an absence of color.

As I ride along there is sweat dripping from my forehead.

In the fence rows there are cobwebs covered with dewdrops that sparkle like pearls as moisture drips from them in the early morning sunlight. The dandelions have all turned to seed now. They are just puffballs on the end of a hollow straw.

It's 9:00 in the morning, as I ride through Neenah/Menasha. It's 80 degrees out, already and there is a lot of humidity in the air. I'm afraid it's going to be a hot one, today.

At 9:42 a.m. I have 40 miles in as I ride on flat terrain, but the temperature continues to climb. It's 82 degrees as I ride through Appleton. The perspiration is running off me like a leaky faucet.

I'm three miles out of Kaulauna and it's 86 degrees. It's pretty damn HOT and humid out here. My clothes are saturated with sweat already this morning.

I have about a 5 mph crosswind as I ride through Wrightstown.

A BIG dog is chasing after me, it's nipping at my panniers. Even if it's hotter than hell out, when a BIG...barking...gaping-mouthed...dog comes after me...I pick up my pace considerably.

I ride in 100 plus degree weather in California all the time, but we don't have all this stinking humidity.

I go through the small town of Wrightston. You know you're in a small town if you miss church on Sunday and the preacher sends you a get-well card.

There is a small, very small...fire station in Greenleaf. I sort of expect to see a Dalmatian in the window. Dalmatians were called firehouse dogs back in the stagecoach days. Horse theft was so common that the stagecoach drivers would string a hammock between two stalls at night, and sleep behind their horses. But, if the driver owned a Dalmatian, he could sleep in a hotel because the Dalmatians protect the horses. The spotted dogs guarded the firehouse and kept the firemen company during their long, boring waits between fires. The horses are all gone from the fire stations now, but the Dalmatians aren't. Thank God, some traditions are carried on.

It's HOT today. When it got up to 100 degrees in the San Fernando Valley, where I live, I'd ride over the Santa Monica Mountains and in about one hour I'd be down at the Ocean...where it's always at least 20 degrees cooler. And the scenery's always a lot nicer at the beach.

Thirst seems to be a problem for me. No matter how much I drink, I can't seem to quench my thirst today. The sun's rays and the clinging humidity are drawing rivers of sweat from my body. I feel as though I'll be thirsty for the rest of my life. The inside of my mouth has turned to cotton, and I'm craving cold liquids, (like beer). A nice cold beer will push out my thoughts of girls, maybe. I was never in the service so I missed out on all their sex training films. Sex was on my mind a lot when I was young. My dad never had any Playboy magazines lying around. And I never once saw my dad hug or kiss my mother...or as matter as fact...even hold her hand. All I had was the Sears and Roebuck catalog (the lady's underwear and swimsuit sections were the best). I would look up every dirty word I could think of in the dictionary. When I was growing up, you never saw any risque words in print or in the paper or anywhere except in the dictionary or on some bathroom walls. The best magazine I found was *National Geographic*. I'm sure young boys have used it for years to get a look at the human anatomy, thanks to the pictures of the life styles of the still primitive civilization.

I remember the first X-rated movie I ever went to. Back then there were no X-rated movie houses. We would find out by word of mouth where there was going to be a movie. Pay the man at the garage door $5.00 to get in…and sit or sometimes stand…in someone's garage and try to see through the thick smoke to the screen. The best part, was for your $5.00 you also got all the beer you could drink.

I have between a five to 10 mph tailwind and it's very warm. Warm…Hell…! It's Damn Right **HOT**…! It's 90 degrees.

I stop at a small store in Lark to get something to drink and to pick up some well-packaged junk food. I'm as dry as dust. My mouth feels like it's full of unbaked cookies. As I sit on the front steps of the general store, sweating buckets, drinking out of the half-gallon carton of milk I bought…two kids…probably nine and 12 years old…come racing up on their stunt bikes. They jump off their bikes and let them crash down in the gravel. As they walk by me, the oldest one says, "Aren't you kind of old to be riding a bike?" I say, "I don't think so (I believe that bikes are one of those things that shouldn't be wasted only on children) just how old do you think I am?"

He replies, "23".

With a smile that wraps halfway around my head I thank him. I finish my milk and fill my water bottles. It's time for me to hit the road again.

As I ride through Denmark, a Fire Siren goes off. I immediately look around for a fire truck, then I realize that it must be noon. As I recall, all the small towns in the Mid-West blow their sirens at noon.

Today the temperature and humidity are both in the nineties. I think Summer in Wisconsin is an experiment that didn't work. I have a five to 10 mph cross-tail-wind.

I seem to be riding a little faster on this golden thread of road that connects me with the rest of the world. Of course, 23-year-old kids ride much faster then 46-year-old kids. I pass an empty farmhouse on the outskirts of Corners. Its screen door is banging in the wind and weeds are growing in the corn stubbles next to the house. As I slowly ride by I'm wondering, did the occupants die from the heat exhaustion? The temperature must be high enough to boil human blood today.

It's 1:04 p.m. I have 80 miles on the odometer and it's 92 degrees. I have between a five to 10 mph tailwind as I ride out of Stangelville. I see patchwork views of fields with farmhouses and barns in every direction.

There is this huge tank, out in the field on this farm. It's made out of the same material as the silos, but it's about four times larger in diameter. It's only about 15 feet tall. I don't know what they would use it for, but I'll find out.

As I ride through Ellisville a car goes around me with cherry-bomb-glass-packs on. They sound like the ones I use to have on my first few cars.

I have about a 20 mph crosswind, now, it's slowing me way down. I think the wind is blowing in off Lake Michigan. It's so HOT and humid it sucks all the energy out of you. I just saw a hunting dog chasing a rabbit and they were both walking.

I just spotted this guy out by his mailbox. He's more than tall. He's huge. He's a bear of a man. His neck's bulging, his chest could fill out two ordinary men, and his massive biceps match most men's thighs. Anyway, seeing as there is one by his barn I'm going to stop and ask him what the big tanks are used for.

Well, it seems that farmers who raise pigs have these tanks. They store the pig manure in them. This produces methane gas, which they use to heat their houses with in the wintertime. Sounds like a bunch of shit to me.

Seeing as how it's 7:20 p.m. I think I'll spend the night in Kewaunee then take the ferry across Lake Michigan tomorrow.

As I ride into town, I can see a ferry docked off to my right. I'm not sure if the ferry is leaving today or tomorrow. So, I ride over and find out. As I ride up the roadway there is this guy standing in the road with a walkie-talkie. He's got more hair growing under his nose than he does on top of his head and he's tall enough to play ball for the *Boston Celtics*. Actually, there's no hair on top of his head. I figure that's probably because no hair can grow at that altitude. By the way, I once looked at a chart on weight ratio according to your height. I figure my weight to be about perfect, according to the chart (if I were normal, which I know I'm not and I wouldn't want to be) but I should be about a foot taller. I stop to ask this guy when the ferry was leaving. He says, "It's leaving in less then 10 minutes…and…if you want to be on it you could leave your bike with me and I'll load it while you run over and buy a ticket." So I grab my handlebar bag off and let him have my bike. I run over to the ticket office, and tell them that I need a ticket. They say you're too late. The car ramp is already pulled away. I explain to them that I have a bike…not a car…and it's already loaded…so they hurry up and get me my ticket. I barely caught the ferry by the skin of my teeth. No sooner do I set foot on the ferry than we were on our way. I really would have liked to have got on the ferry early enough, so I could change out of my sweaty, bike clothes, and get into more comfortable street clothes for the crossing. Well, there's not much chance of that with my bike below deck…somewhere…and we're pulling away from the dock before I can even sit down.

I'm getting off the ferry at 7:28 p.m. I've crossed into the *Eastern Time Zone*. I'm in Michigan. I'm really on the East Coast, now.

For some reason, as soon as I get off the ferry and find my bike, I check my odometer to see if by some miracle it has advanced the 60 miles it was across Lake Michigan. But, it still reads 96 miles. Unfortunately, the miles on the ferry don't count. I'm sure I'll put on a few more miles today before I'm able to find a motel.

It's still 80 degrees out. The lengthening of the shadows tells me it's time to look for a motel. It's 7:50 p.m. and I've ridden 102 miles today.

Well, I find this motel on the outskirts of Ludington. It's $53.00 for the night. The most I've paid for a room yet. It's not a great room, but I guess it's all right. There is no place around close to eat, though. At least I'm spending the night in Michigan instead of Wisconsin. It's my first day back on my tour and I'm already ahead of my "tentative" schedule.

It was basically flat all day today, especially crossing Lake Michigan.

*   *   *

*Statistics for **DAY TWENTY** Monday, July 3, 1989..*
102 miles of riding today, 13.4 average miles per hour for today, 2,252 miles of riding in twenty days, 113 average miles of riding per day.

Day Twenty-One

From Ludington, Michigan
To St. Louis, Michigan

It's 7:30 a.m. and it's the Fourth of July. I guess I'd better get cracking. I leave the motel at a little after 8:00 a.m. It's another beautiful, sunny day.

About one mile beyond the motel there is a beautiful Ramada Inn. I would have stayed there...if I had known about it.

A long...shoulder-less...yo-yo ribbon of asphalt...which has a lot of traffic this morning...the most I've had on my tour...so far...separates Ludington and Scottville. You know, it never fails...when there is a lot of traffic...there is no shoulder to ride on. Actually, there is about an eight-foot wide gravel shoulder (which makes things even worse) for some unknown reason, motorists expect me to ride in the loose gravel, which is impossible.

Boy, I hope this town up here has a place to eat breakfast, I'm starved. I didn't go out for dinner last night because the closest restaurant to the motel was about two miles away and I didn't want to ride or walk to it.

Aha...! There is a little truck stop. I'm stopping.

It's 9:00 a.m. as I leave the restaurant. I was sweating all the time I was in there, and it wasn't just because of the beautiful waitress. It was because it's so HOT and muggy already this morning. I had to keep taking napkins and wiping my forehead off while I was eating...so sweat wouldn't drip in my food...which probably wouldn't have hurt it anyway. It had the consistency and taste of axle grease...awful stuff.

I believe I could actually sit in the restaurant and eat and lose weight. Explanation: water or perspiration weighs about eight pounds per gallon.

I'm sure I didn't eat more than two pounds for breakfast. As much as I was sweating, by the time I finished breakfast, I should have been about three pounds lighter. They didn't have an air-conditioner or ever a fan on in there. I guess they like it hot.

It feels very warm out already. I check the thermometer and find that the temperature is. It's only 73 degrees out, but the humidity is terrible. I have a 5 mph headwind that actually feels quite good. (It's not too often you'll ever hear me say anything good about a headwind). My jersey is soaking wet. I'm surely glad I took a shower this morning.

As I ride by a church its bells are ringing. It's not Sunday, so I figure it must be because it's the Fourth of July. I wonder if I'll be anywhere I can see some fireworks tonight.

It's 9:33 a.m. I have 10 miles on the odometer as I ride through Scottville. I have a 10 mph crosswind out of the north which…if it stays that way…will turn into a tailwind…after I make a turn 30 miles up the road and start riding south.

An old…old…man is hobbling out of the bushes next to the road. He looks to be nearly a hundred years old. He's weathered and worn but his eyes are sparkling out of his wrinkled face. His dirty white, gray-streaked beard reaches almost to his waist. His patched clothes hang on him making him look like a scarecrow. I nod to him as I ride by.

This road is what I would call table flat. It's actually flatter than some of the pool tables I've played on.

My jersey is made out of a material that's supposed to draw your perspiration away from your body…to the outside…where it will dry off by the breeze blowing over it. It's always worked well back in California. I could ride in 100-degree weather and stay dry. But out here, with all this humidity…it's a different story. The breeze can't evaporate the perspiration fast enough. I look like a drowned rat, with a helmet on…if you can imagine that.

I stop at an extraordinary beautiful lake in Walhalla. It looks like it would be a nice place for a picnic. I stop to put some sun-block on my big nose…but…as long as I'm stopped…I might as well put my sunglasses on seeing as how I'm riding straight into the sun.

It's still very flat out here, so far. But the heat is getting hotter and the humidity is getting thicker. It's 78 degrees.

I'm experiencing huge patches of brilliant white flashes in the eastern sky. One minute they're there and the next they're gone. I can't imagine what it could be. It's not lightning, and the flashes are much larger than a plane. As I ride closer, I can finally identify it. It's a large flock of white birds flying in a harmonious pattern.

I'm riding on a two-lane back road. It's so quiet out here. All I can hear is the whisper of the wind as it flows past my ears, and the occasional buzz of a bee. Why, I'll bet it quiet enough out here to hear a mouse pissing on a cotton ball.

The road is relatively well maintained, but it doesn't make any allowances for all the hills. I see a wayside picnic area up ahead. It's 10:18 a.m. and I'm going to stop and see if there is any water and I'll take a little break. At this stop, I see that the entire floor of the forest is covered with ferns.

There is an elderly couple sitting at a picnic table. As I lean my bike against a nearby tree, the gentleman comes over and starts asking me all about my tour. His face is coffee-colored and criss-crossed with a million tiny wrinkles. His hair is bleached rust red by the sun and is as thick as wool. A rather pleasant looking gentleman. His wife, on the other hand, has a nose and eyes that are a little too large. At first glance she sort of resembles a cow. One of her legs is a little shorter than the other, which causes her to limp as she walks. She has a dog on a leash, or maybe the dog has her on a leash. It's pulling her over to the water faucet where it takes a drink and sits down in a puddle of water before she's finally able to get it to come over by me. You know that there is absolutely nothing in the world more friendly than a wet dog. She can't control the dog at all. I believe that some people own pets, and some pets own people. She thinks the dog is amazing because it catches frogs and brings them back to her. I'm thinking, "BIG DEAL." After I finish filling my water bottles, they go back to their table and get a cold coke out of their cooler for me. I thank them and sit down to drink it.

I'm on my way again.

As I ride by this Fire Station the sirens start blowing and a fire truck comes screaming out of the station...right in front of me! It scares the shit out of me!

It's not as pretty along the edges of the road as it has been on previous days. It's still green but there are not as many flowers and I'm starting to see more garbage in the ditches, the farther east I ride. A van, covered with stickers from almost a hundred different attractions, blows it's horn and goes around me. It's the couple from the wayside. They wave to me as they speed off.

I just turned south on Route 37, so I have a 10 mph tailwind, now. Route 37 is a brand-new road that's as smooth as a baby's butt.

Oops...! There is a Dairy Queen...! With 30 miles in I've got to stop. I haven't ridden past a Dairy Queen, yet. I had my usual, a peanut butter malt. I just love'em.

It's 11:28 a.m. and the heat is intense. It's 82 degrees but it feels much hotter. It feels hot enough to liquefy the black top. I ride through Baldwin and find that there is a lot of traffic on the road, mostly campers…which makes me a little uneasy. I've heard of a touring cyclist who got killed by a camper. What happened was that the camper's steps, which stick out about a foot…were left down. The driver, not being aware of this…came too close to the cyclist…and mowed him down.

There isn't a cloud in the sky and the sun is shining, toasting everything it touches except for the little yellow flowers that are all along here. The river I'm paralleling must be popular for canoeing because I've already ridden past several canoe rentals. I've been on several river rafting trips in Central California, but I truly love canoeing. When I lived in Wisconsin, I owned a yellow fiberglass canoe…which I named "My Yellow Submarine."

I recall some great trips my son and I took. We would throw the canoe on top of my car and go way up into an Indian Reservation in Northern Wisconsin. We'd unload it, put it in the river and ride the rapids down. Sometimes, we would go for days at a time, just floating down the river…stopping to make our meals along the way and camping out at night. It was great. As I recall, we could make our way down the river for three or four days, without even seeing as much as a car or house or any civilization at all. We caught fish and fried them up. We shot squirrels, cleaned and cooked them over an open fire. My son was only about 10 years old at the time, and I must say, he was a very good sportsman. Many, many times going over the big rapids we would capsize…and my son…not being able to reach the bottom, (and even if he could have the current was too strong for him to stand up) would float down the river for a half-a-mile or so before the water slowed down enough to allow him time to grab onto an overhanging limb or something and hang on until I could get to him. He never panicked. Not once. He was a good kid, and he still is.

When we got through the rapids and the water was calm, we could just float along, quietly…coming within a few yards of deer drinking out of the river. We watched beaver as they cut down trees. I especially remember this one night when we could hear all this stomping around outside our tent. I slowly unzipped the door flap and a buck snorted and took off. Now, if you've never heard a buck snort…up close…at night…let me tell you, it'll scare the shit out of you.

Then there was this one morning we crawled out of our tent and went over to get our socks, which we had hung over a branch because they were soaking wet…and…much to our surprise…they were frozen stiff. I must say we had some good times. I really believe it was a good learning experience, for both of us.

I have a 10 mph tailwind, as I cycle alongside the rivers…streams…and lakes of Michigan. With fields of green grass and ditches full of flowers, many thoughts run through my head.

You know, winning a race or getting a very good time on a time trial, is an exciting thing for me…but it's sort of like getting a new car…the excitement wears off long before the payments do. But, having a close relationship with someone is something that will last a lifetime.

I just rode through the little town of Lilley. I'm riding along, on this traffic-free country road…that's winding its way through a dense forest with little fingerlets of sun pointing out trees, now fallen and covered in a brilliant green moss surrounded by tall ferns. Wild flowers line both edges of the road, and butterflies glide from one blossom to another. The birds are singing beautiful melodies to me. I say to myself, "This is better than sex." But it doesn't take long until I snap out of it and come to my senses. Nothing is better then making love with someone you're in love with. I think I had better call my girlfriend tonight.

Just out of Brohman there's a little pond off to my right full of blooming…cantaloupe-size white and yellow lily pads…stretching as far as I can see. There are dragonflies hovering over the pond that has an algae-covered bottom. In the heat of the day, the dragonflies rest on the surface of the water. I guess so their wings won't catch on fire.

You know, if you live in a city as big as L.A. long enough and never get out, you start to believe it's an all right place to live. But, when I get out here and see all these beautiful places, I realize that there is much more to life.

I work with a guy who was born in L.A. and has lived there all his life. As soon as he got out of High School he got a job at *Rockwell* and he's been there ever since, for 29 years now. If you were to ask him, he would say that L.A. is the best place in the world to live. Why…? Because he hasn't been anywhere else.

When I tell him about some of my weekend bike trips to Santa Barbara or San Diego (both about 100 miles from L.A.) he tells me that he's never been there. I guess if you've never been more than 30 miles from where you were born, it might seem like a good place to live. If you don't have anything to compare it to, what you have is as good as it gets. I'm surely glad I don't live my life like that. I've had a lot of totally different kinds of jobs and I have never been sorry that I moved onto the next one.

I guess L.A. is all right if you like smog…heat… earthquakes… gangs…pollution…high rent…high rises…high insurance…concrete… and $100,000.00 fixer uppers (those are the houses that need a lot of work, before you can even move in). Isn't it a scary society when we have to pay to keep our names out of the phone directory? Right now, the only thing that's keeping me in L.A. is my job, and that's not a very good reason to stay. I've always believed it's better when you can choose a place to live, rather than having to live somewhere out of necessity. After seeing all this beautiful country on this tour, I've decided that life is too short to stay where I don't particularity want to be, just because of a job. I think I've done my time in the BIG CITY, and it's time for me to get out.

I'm riding along on a nice little old tree-lined country road with a 10 mph tailwind. Off to my right there is an old house with a broken screen door. A BB gun is leaning against a tree that has a rope (from which a boy is swinging) tied to a limb.

There is a lot of traffic out here, now. It's 1:35 p.m. I have 55 miles on the odometer as I stop in White Cloud to get something to eat. It's 85 degrees. Before I go in, anywhere...I always take off my helmet...and...of course...my hair is usually soaking wet. I walk into this eating establishment...drenched from perspiration...on this clear...HOT...sunshiny day...the waitress comes over...looks at me...and ask if it's raining out.

I get back on this country road which is getting a little rough. The edges of the road are full of tall shade trees, which are probably centuries old. The filtered sunlight is drifting down, ever so slowly...through the lacy fernlike leaves of the smaller trees...onto the forest floor...which is covered with pine needles. The sweet fragrance of pine and a 10 mph tailwind more than make up for the rough road.

I just rode by a sign on a bank in White Cloud that says it's 91 degrees out, and it's 2:55 p.m. The faster I pedal, the more I sweat. The heat waves are rising up off the road like butterflies. I stop at a roadside park to get something to drink. Sweat is trickling into my eyes as I take a drink of water. The water must have a lot of iron in it, because it tastes like a mouthful of raw pig iron. One thing about riding in the United States, you can drink the water, most of the time.

It's awful HOT out (92 degrees). It only takes a few miles for the water in my plastic bottles to warm up. God, I wish I had a cold beer.

I just turned east off Route 37 onto Route 82.

I don't think I could have picked a better time of the year to take this tour (except for the heat). Spring and summer are perfect times of the year, with all the twigs budding. The scents of wild flowers are following me everywhere. There are some little yellow flowers all along the road's edge, even a few that I know the names of like the Black-Eyed-Susan.

I'm taking on warm water like an old steam engine. Let me tell you, riding out here under the HOT sun, I just might be cooking some of...if not all of...my brain cells.

If I drink Coke, Dr. Pepper, 7-up or any kind of soda, it has to be just right. The coke has to be cooled just enough so that there's ice floating on top. Not frozen completely, but with some ice floating on top. So when I tip it up some icicles flow into my mouth…then I can push them around with my tongue until they melt.

At 80 miles I stop in Howard City to call my daughter back in L.A. Again, she isn't home.

Off to my right there's a horse standing up to it's belly in a rust-colored stream. The water is muddy, but it's still an unforgettable sight. Riding along slowly, I see that the tall grass right alongside the road is moving in odd directions. I have to stop and find out what's making it move that way. Oh neat…! It's a batch of young rabbits. There are five or six running through the grass…!

In Howard City I turn north on Route 46 for a couple of miles, into a 5 mph headwind. Soon, I'll turn east again and ride toward Amble. It's cooled down a little bit, it's only 85 degrees.

There are huge fields of wheat or barley, all through this area. Barley soup. Of course, I can eat it…although it's a little salty…but for the most part I like my grain made into beer.

I remember when my dad was farming. He really had to watch the weather closely. He needed at least four days of warm, dry weather, to get a crop of hay in. The first day he would mow it down. The next two days he would rake it into rows to dry. Then, on the fourth day, he would bale it and put it up in the barn. If it were to rain on the hay before he got it into the barn, it wouldn't be much good. That's what they mean when they say, "You've got to make hay when the sun's shines." Also, if the hay weren't dry enough when he baled it, it would get so hot in the center of the bale that it would start on fire. Every year, several barns would burn to the ground, because of this. Today, it's much safer and easier. They cut and crimp and put the hay into rows, all in one operation. The crimping breaks the stems so it will dry out faster. Then, they bale it the very next day.

I ride gently down a twisting road that enters into the Main Street of Lakeview. Lakeview consists mainly of one street. I stop at a small store and buy some Gator-aid, peanut butter cups and an ice cream sandwich.

I'm on the road again. On the road again, I just can't wait to get on the road again, seeing things I may never see again. (I get carried away once in a while).

I have a five to 10 mph tailwind as I ride out of Lakeview. For the last ten miles I've been riding on a beautiful new road, with about a two foot wide shoulder. It makes it easy to let my mind wonder.

Idle Thoughts;

When I was a kid, I asked my dad where calves come from. He said the cow's go out in the tall grass out back of the barn and find them. I remember looking for hours and hours day after day trying it find a calf. I guess I should have asked my mother, after all, she was a registered nurse. She might have told me. I learned a lot about sex from my mother, even though she didn't know it. I'd better explain. When she wasn't around, I would sneak upstairs and look through her nursing books. That's where I learned about the birds and bees. If it were left up to my dad to tell me I would probably be a bird watcher today.

I remember once, when I was a little older…my dad told me…that anytime an animal was about to have a baby…it would go to the furthest corner of the fields…away from the buildings to be alone to have its young. In the spring of the year, when most animals are born…when it was raining…I used to walk with my dad to the furthest corners of the fields and he would pick up the new born lambs, and carry them back to the dry warm barn. Of course, the mother would always follow. Cows and pigs would also go to the furthest corner possible and have their young. Later, I remember going out as a kid and watching a calf being born. I believe it's an experience everyone should have. I also recall this one time my dad really got upset with me. That's when I brought a newborn pig home. You see, when you take a newborn away from most sows they get furious, by instinct. They will kill dogs that get too close. My dad later told me about a farmer he knew that had his leg chewed off by a protective sow. So, from then on instead of bringing home the bacon, I stuck to bringing the lamb's home.

    Seeing all this grain growing out here reminds me of the time when my dad threshed oats. It's too bad, but that's something that's been lost to modern times, forever. Everybody combines oats now. Granted, threshing was a much harder and slower way to harvest oats, but it had its good points too. It was a good way for all the neighboring farmers to get together and drink beer without catching hell from their wives. Now, my dad never drank alcohol at all. So there was never any around the house for me to sample. But, at good old threshing time, the horse-tank in the milk house was always full of cold bottled beer. I still remember the very first beer I drank. I had to push the blocks of ice to one side and stick my arm down into the ice cold water…clear up to…and past…my shoulder to retrieve a bottle. God, it was COLD. I'd grab one and rush off to the haymow (where I wouldn't get caught) to drink it. I remember it being the worst stuff I had ever tasted…but I forced the whole bottle down anyway. Needless to say, since that time…I've acquired a taste for it. To this day I don't think my dad ever knew I took that bottle of beer.

    Oh…! Oh…! That's the end of my brand-new road.

    I can honestly say that I've never done drugs of any kind. Neither my dad nor mother smoked or drank or did drugs. I guess once, at a drive-in when I was a kid…I had a few near beers. Oh, in my seventh and eighth grade of school I used to smoke cigarettes, secretly. I didn't have any money to buy them, so I stole them. I remember one time I had an opened pack of cigarettes hidden out in the pasture…so my parents wouldn't find them…under a dried out cow pile. Well, guess what, it rained. The cigarettes got all wet, not to mention a little brown. It didn't matter to me; I took them upstairs in my little hideout above the granary, and spread them all out to dry. The next day, I lit one up. It tasted a little shitty but, what the heck…they were too precious to throw away.

My mind is freewheeling right now. More thoughts: I've been around a lot of bicycle racers and, they'll do almost anything to cut down on their bike weight. They buy these really thin latex, inter-tubes. I mean they are as thin as a condom. They are so thin that there only good for short races, the air escapes right through them…and within a couple of hours they're flat. In my opinion, if they want light tires, they should get the biggest tires they can find, and fill them with helium.

It's 6:59 p.m. I have 110 miles on the odometer and I'm four miles east of Six Lakes. I have a 5 mph tailwind and it's 83 degrees.

There's a red-winged blackbird…! I haven't seen one of those suckers for quite a while. They really are beautiful birds with the red on their wings glistening in the sunlight. Off to my right is a huge potato farm. The weather today is picture perfect and we…my bike and myself…seem to be gliding along effortlessly.

I stop at a roadside park in Cedar Lake, to get something to drink and to take a quick leak. Well, I'm not actually going to take a leak in the Lake. Although, No…! I'll rush over to the restroom. Thank God for urinals. I'd better explain that. Have you ever rushed into a restroom without paying much attention to the sign on or around the door…and then…as soon as you get inside…a thought crosses your mind…did I or didn't I read the sign properly? I suppose if someone screams…you're probably in the wrong one and…if they don't, it really doesn't matter. If I'm not sure, the first thing I look for is the urinal. They are a wonderful invention. I mean, where else can you piss on the wall and not get into trouble? Of course, it does have a few disadvantages. Like when you're standing in front of one reading the writings on the wall and there's someone standing in the urinal next to you doing the same thing and he starts to laugh, with his pecker in hand, and he pisses all over your foot.

There is a relatively large lake here and, with no wind…the lake is as smooth as silk. The mirror-like surface is recreating the beauty of the surrounding trees. The stillness and peace are broken only by the distant call of a loon, (sounds like a scene out of *"On Golden Pond."*) As I stand here quietly admiring nature, I spot a doe and her fawn slip out of the shadows at the far side of the lake. They carefully walk down to the edge of the lake to get a drink. On this side of the lake the wild flowers look almost golden with the sunlight on them.

There are a few pesky skin divers (mosquitoes) in the shady spots.

It's 7:49 p.m. and I'm near Vestaburg. I have clear skies and not a breath of wind. After years of listening to the jackhammers of so-called progress in L.A., out here it's amazingly quiet and still. I'm riding through scenic farm county with the sun at my back, projecting a shadow far ahead of my front wheel on the road. The old saying is true, it doesn't matter how fast I ride…I still can't catch my own shadow.

When I was planning my itinerary, I thought I might want to ride at night…once in a while…but I haven't yet…except for a little in Montana. And I probably won't. I don't want to miss seeing any of this fabulous country of ours.

It's 8:34 p.m. and foggy. It's cooled down to 70 degrees. I've ridden 132 miles so far today and it is time to check on a motel room here in St. Louis. I get a room at a Travelers Inn. It's not the greatest place on earth, but they do have an indoor pool.

Today's ride has been hot, but wonderful just the same. The backcountry roads through Michigan are basically flat. Oh, there were a few little rollers in the morning…but for the most part…it was flat and nice riding.

I finish showering and I walk over to a Bob's Big Boy that's right across the street. I have a big turkey sandwich with some fries and a banana split for dessert. I think I will walk the streets for a while. This is interesting…there are two barbershops on one block. One has a sign that says, "Haircuts $6.00". And the other one has a sign that reads, "We Fix $6.00 Haircuts."

I recall when I was in High School…men got their hair cut in a barber shop…and ladies got theirs cut in a beauty parlor…the way God intended it to be. Best of all, you didn't need an appointment. Anyway, I would go to this barber in Berlin. He was an old man and he had the shakes, but he was quite good at cutting hair. What he would do was, hold his clippers in his right hand and he would put his left hand around the back of your neck, and you would shake right along with him.

Well, I'm back at the motel now. It's 11:30 p.m. I guess I had better hit it.

*   *   *

*Statistics for **DAY TWENTY-ONE** Tuesday, July 4, 1989.*
132 miles of riding today, 13.9 average miles per hour for today, 2,384 miles of riding in twenty-one days, 113 average miles of riding per day.

Day Twenty-Two

From St. Louis, Michigan
To Sandusky, Michigan

I woke up at 6:20 a.m. and I'm finally getting out of bed at 7:05 a.m.

One hour later, I step out of the motel door and walk through the very loose gravel...pushing my bike...to the street. It looks as though I've stepped into the twilight zone or into a cloud. A steamy haze seems to be getting thicker and thicker. The morning light can hardly penetrate the thick...wet...low-hanging fog. Being in no hurry to get on the open road, I'll just cut my way through the heavy fog in town and stop at the first restaurant I come to.

It's 70 degrees as I leave the restaurant. The morning mist is as thick as the soup was in there. Mist, Hell...! There is a wall of fog so thick that all the cars have to have their headlights on. I put on the belt beacon (a flashing, yellow light) I bought for night riding.

I have a 10 mph headwind as I ride on the shoulder of the road for safety reasons. I notice that the hairs on my arms are covered with little droplets of water. And so are the spider webs in the tall grass alongside the road. Some of them are just spectacular.

I didn't see any fireworks last night, except on television. The closest fireworks were in Saginaw, which is about 30 miles away. There are fireworks or gang wars in West L.A. almost every night.

I can't think of a better way to celebrate the Fourth of July (The Independence of America) than by riding across it. Years from now if someone were to ask you how you spent the Fourth of July of 1989, would you remember? Did you sleep late, or watch a ball game on TV? How did you spend the day? One thing's for sure, I'll always remember how I spent mine. The United States has always been special to me, but this makes it a little more special.

It never fails, when there is no shoulder, or poor visibility, there's always a lot of traffic. It's not that hot, but it's very humid. I'm dripping like a leaky faucet again this morning.

A little trivia here. St. Louis, where I spent the night last night, is the geographical center of Lower Michigan. I know because it says so on there City Limit sign.

There are a lot of huge trucks going by. They must be hauling an awful lot of weight because they have a lot of axles and wheels under them. Most so called "Big Rigs" have 18 wheels. I just saw one with 30 wheels. I'll get a picture of one, if I can find one that's stopped.

There is still a lot of morning mist in the air. The early morning light is barely penetrating the fog. There seems to be an unusually large amount of traffic on this road. Birds are mysteriously appearing out of the foggy sky. One appears, then another, seemingly out of nowhere. They appear much like a drop of ink would suddenly appear on a piece of paper. One second it's not there, and the next second it is.

I notice a lot of churches throughout this area.

I'm in my middle chain-ring down on my drops. I could do just fine without all this humidity and headwind. When all these big trucks, coming from the other direction…go by me and their gust of wind hits me…it almost stops me dead in my tracks for a second.

All through this part of the country, there are huge grain elevators alongside the road, usually next to railroad tracks. I see a lot of used cars sitting in people's yards in Breckenridge with, "For Sale" signs on them. It reminds me of these two guys I overheard talking in a bar in L.A., once. One was trying to sell the other a car. He was living in the car, out back of the tavern. He tells this guy that he would sell it to him for $100.00. The other guy says, "Does it run…?" The first guy says, "Heck No…! If it ran, it wouldn't be worth anything." The other guy says, "What do you mean…?" First guy, "Because if it ran, somebody would steal it, for sure."

It's 10:06 a.m. I have 20 miles on the odometer. as I ride through Merrill.

I'm riding along here with the early morning dew still glistening on the grass. This one particular flower catches my eye, so I stop. I lie my bike down and walk back to take a better look at it. It's a beautiful wild flower…standing all alone…as if to say…here I am blossoming just for you. I can smell it's wonderful fragrance. It smells like sweet perfume. I put my hands around it and gently feel it's soft…smooth…petals. Hmm…Makes me think of my girlfriend.

I can see the humidity hanging in the air. You can see the air in L.A. too, only it's a different color. It's sort of a reddish-brown. Most people refer to it as smog, which is a word derived from smoke and fog. I recall talking to this black man in a bar in L.A. once. He said, "You talk about smog, I was a white man when I moved to L.A."

The sun is trying really hard to break through the fog. It's cleared up enough now that I can take my belt beacon off.

Riding into Hemlock, I spot this house on top of a hill. It's square and has green shingles. It's looking down the hill with big white-curtained eyes.

I lock up my brakes as a rabbit runs across the road right in front of me.

There is an Arby's in Shields where I get something to eat. It's high noon, when I leave Arby's.

My ride from Shields to Saginaw wasn't greatly inspiring, except for the little flower. The fog was heavy and the shoulder of the road disappeared as the traffic grew heavier. Saginaw is a very big city. I've heard that some parts of cities are beautiful, like the parks that they try to fix up to look like the country. I believe that cities are where most men seem to spend most of their lives doing what they hate.

I'm riding on a road that doesn't have a shoulder and the road just made a turn for the worse, I have a 10 mph headwind now. It's 84 degrees and I have to stop and rest for a minute. There's still no shoulder on this road and there is a lot of traffic and it's very humid out. Other than that, it's a beautiful day.

The wind has changed to a 15 mph head-cross-wind as I ride out of Richville. I stop to do a little repacking hoping to cut down on the wind resistance a little. I put my air mattress and sleeping bag inside my panniers. It's hard riding today because of the crosswinds and humidity. It seems as though death…taxes…and afternoon winds are all inevitable.

At 60 miles I stop to take on water at a little roadside park. It's a beautiful spot, with a river twisting its way through the trees and lush grasslands. The damp forest, which would normally be cool from the shade of the trees…is humid and stifling HOT. As I fill my water bottles, I can hear a cloud of swamp vampires swarm over me. Did you know, if you were to kill one, a hundred more will come to it's funeral. I fill my water bottles and ride out of there…in less then five minutes…with no fewer than ten mosquito bites…! I'm on the road again. Even a mosquito doesn't get a slap on the back until she starts to work.

*   *   *

There are a lot of huge Big Rigs going by me, now. I don't worry too much about them though, because I believe professional truck drivers are the best drivers on the road. They are on the road every day…and…if you do anything every day…you're bound to get better at it. At least that's what I tell my girlfriend.

I drove Big Rigs cross-country for about a year, between marriages. I think it would be a hard way to make a living, if you're married. I mean, we only got back to our home base once every six weeks…for preventive maintenance. And that was only for the weekend. Most wives require more than preventive maintenance.

I was very lucky all the time I was driving truck. I never got a ticket. By the way, did you know that when you drive cross-country…if you were to get a ticket…you not only get one from the State you are driving in…but you also get one from the Federal Government. When trucking, you have to keep a log, which is an official record. If I was to write down that I was in Kalamozoo at 6p.m. and I get stopped 100 miles down the road an hour later, I would get a ticket for speeding.

    I always drove with the CB and a radar detector on. I considered myself a good driver. I only had one little mishap…and until right now…I've never told anyone about it…not even my co-driver. Here's what happened. My co-driver wanted to go into a *K-mart* store to get something, so I pulled up to the front door and dropped him off. Then, because…at the time…I had only been driving for about a week…and I didn't want anything to go wrong because I really enjoyed driving…so I drove way out in the back parking lot to turn around…where there weren't any cars to worry about. I watched ahead of me and proceeded to make a large turn. Well, I heard this "Crunch" and looked out my side window. Much to my surprise, here's this big…tall…double lamp light post…leaning at about a 45-degree angle. I looked around to see if anyone saw what I did. No one did, so I backed away from the lamp. I took a quick look at the trailer from the driver's seat, and it looked all right…like nothing had happened. So, I pulled around front and waited for my co-driver to come out, keeping one eye on the leaning lamppost. A few people started to gather around it, then someone went inside and got the manager to come out and look at it. He walked right by my truck. I was really sweating it, and praying for my co-driver to hurry up and get out here. Well, he finally did, and as I pulled out the driveway, I watched out of the corner of my eye as the lamp came crashing down to the ground. It landed with about as much noise as a bull moose makes in rut season. My co-driver said, "What was that?" I said, "I didn't hear anything," and hurried onto the open road.

Now, I've heard that some people don't like truck drivers because they think they drive too fast. Let me tell you. Fast drivers are not bad drivers. Truckers have to drive fast if they want to make any money, and that's what they are out there for. Most truckers get paid by the mile. Just to make it simple, lets say they get 10 cents a mile. If they were to drive 50 mph they would be making $5.00 per hour. Then, if they were to drive 70 mph they would be making $7.00 per hour…so…how can you blame them for driving fast?

There's another reason why people don't like truckers. They sometimes tend to get right on your rear bumper. Well, here's what I have to say about that. It's very hard for a fully loaded Big Rig to get his speed up. I mean that he has to go through 21 gears to get up to the speed limit. Then, he has to shift down on every little grade in the road. Let's say he's going up this grade, trying to keep his momentum up…and here's this Sunday driver…just a poking along. I mean, if you want to poke along and enjoy the scenery, get yourself a bike and really enjoy it! Of course, the truck can't pass on a hill…so…naturally…he gets as close as possible to the car…mainly because he wants to keep his momentum up. I mean, they don't get right behind you and lay on their air horn, even though you may deserve it. If the guy in the car had any courtesy at all, he would speed up and get out of the way. Now, let me tell you something else you may not know about truckers. On an eight-lane freeway, like some Interstates are, eighteen wheelers (Big Rigs) are only allowed to drive in the lane farthest to the right. They can only use the second lane for passing. Big Rigs are not allowed in the two left lanes, at any time. So, it seems to me, that cars should stay in the two left lanes, when there are trucks around, out of courtesy.

*   *   *

It's 3:19 p.m. I have 70 miles on the odometer as I ride through East Dayton.

I've talked about truck drivers…now…let me tell you what I think about women drivers. They are not bad drivers either. It's just that most of the time they're so unpredictable. One thing you can always count on though, even if there is no traffic coming they absolutely…positively…won't drive over that centerline when they go past me. I don't know exactly why. Maybe they think that, if they were to venture over that painted line…in the middle of the road…they would mysteriously fall off the edge of the world.

As I ride into Kingston it's 87 degrees.

I recall one night when I was driving a Big Rig in eastern, West Virginia. Of course…being at night…it was hard to spot the Bears (Police Officers).

Well, this voice came over my CB

It was a Smokey (another word trucker's use for Police Officers).

He said, "Hey Midwestern…! How fast are you going?"

(There was a sign on the back of my trailer that said it belonged to Midwestern).

I answered back and said, "Double Nickels." (55)

He replied, "You better get out of the way then, because there's a trailer that's about to run you over."

I ride into Elmer at 5:29 p.m. and I have a 10 mph headwind. Seeing all these big-rigs keeps reminding me of my truck driving days. Usually, when your co-driver is driving, you're in the bunk sleeping. Except when you're all slept out and you're in a good-sized town. Then, you normally climb into the passenger's seat and casually glance down at the female drivers. From the passenger's seat you can get an excellent view of things. Most girls will smile at you and occasionally one will wave. Others will show you a little more of their cleavage. And still others will pull their skirts up as high as possible, if they are not there already. I'll never forget this one day when my co-driver woke me up and told me to get in the passenger seat and take a look, so I did. This young girl was driving down the road with a smile on…and that's all she had on. By the time I woke up three truckers had her blocked in. There was a truck in front and one in back of her, and we were on the left of her. By this time all the truckers in the vicinity had their CB's on and were telling each other to get up here and take a look for themselves. Actually, it was quite funny.

*   *   *

I'm stopping at this implement dealer to take a picture of my bike leaning up against this huge tractor. I'm thinking, strange how a young boy can drive a hundred-and-forty-thousand-dollar vehicle all day but he isn't allowed to drive a car on public roads. I also think the state government has their drinking laws all wrong. They should put the age limit on the other end. What I mean by that is, they should control the older drinkers before they start fooling around with the younger ones. There are several reasons why I believe this.

1) Older people can drink a lot more then younger ones because they've had a lot more practice.

2) Older people usually have more money and can afford to drink more.

3) Older people have a lot more reasons to drink.

4) When older people have too much to drink they tend to make fools out of themselves. For instance, a drunken 55-year-old man somehow thinks he has a chance of taking home an 18-year-old girl. Whereas, an 18-year-old boy that has too much to drink…throws up…gets sleepy…and goes home to bed.

OK. What age limit do you think should be put on the old folks…? 35…? 45…? 55…? or maybe 61…? Yea…! that sounds good. At age 61, no more alcohol for you. Unfair, you say. Well, that's what state governments did to the young people. They picked a number that sounded good to them and said, "Yea…! 21…21 sounds like a good number. No one can have any alcohol before the age of 21. We don't care if you're married…a parent…or a soldier fighting for our country. It just doesn't matter. The law is the law. I've heard many kids say it's just not fair and you know what? I think they are right.

All right, I've talked about truck drivers and women drivers.

What's else…? How about bicyclists?

Some people think bicyclists are "Assholes" for riding out in the road as far as they do. Let me put it this way…bicyclists have the same rights…and have to obey the same rules as cars and trucks do.

The laws in most States say that bicyclists have to stay as far to the right as "safely possible." On the open road I always ride just to the right of the white line on the far right edge of the road. If I were to get over any farther, I would be in all the glass and rocks and other debris on the shoulder of the road. I would get a flat immediately. Cars don't realize that we can't always ride on the far right of the road. We have to watch out for all kinds of things…like…for instance…drain grates. A bike tire will drop right in most of them, sending you flying over the handlebars.

Now, riding bikes in town is a whole new ball game. This is where motorists get the most upset at us. When there are parked cars on my right and moving ones on my left…I prefer to ride closer to the moving ones. Given a choice, I would rather get hit by a car traveling in the same direction and about the same speed as I am…than to run head-on into an unmovable object.

For one thing, the moving cars can see you. People getting out of their parked cars don't look behind to see if there is a bicycle coming before they open their door. Think about it…you probably don't…either. Anyway, if they fling open their door…right in front of you, you're going to end up in the hospital. I know. I'm talking from experience. It also wrecks your bike. And you know what else? The guy that caused the accident gets out of it scott free. In fact, most of the time you end up paying to get his door fixed…! At least, if I ride out in the traffic and get hit…the guy driving the car (if he stops) will at least get a ticket.

With 97 miles on the odometer at 6:08 p.m. I check on a motel room in Sandusky. The motel has a lounge and a restaurant in it, all for a $38.00 price. And I get a free continental breakfast in the morning. It's a really nice room, too. I rode 97 hard miles today, riding into a 10 to 15 mph headwind most of the day.

I'm showered and all cleaned up, it's 7:10 p.m. and I'm going to go downtown and get something to eat. I really pig out at this restaurant. I have soup…a salad…the main course and dessert…and a couple of beers.

I'm going to bed fairly early tonight. I've got a real mess in my panniers to straighten up in the morning. I've got to repack, and rebag and reorganize all my stuff.

I tried to call my daughter a couple of times, but she wasn't home. I'm going to keep trying, other wise she just might call out the *National Guard* to hunt me down. She's a good kid.

*   *   *

Statistics for **DAY TWENTY-TWO** *Wednesday, July 5, 1989.*
97 miles of riding today, 11.9 average miles per hour for today, 2,481 miles of riding in twenty-two days, 113 average miles of riding per day.

Day Twenty-Three

From Sandusky, Michigan
To London, Ontario

It's 7:30 a.m. and I'm going to get up now. First, I'll go over to get something to eat and then, I'll pack my panniers when I get back.

As I walk over to the motel restaurant and have their complimentary breakfast, I can see that it was a night of zero visibility. I go in and eat french toast and drink hot coffee. It's actually quite good, and there is a lot more than I expected.

There is a pay phone just outside my motel room so I use it to call my daughter. It's 8:30 a.m. here (I forgot that it was only 5:30 a.m. in California) so, naturally, I wake her up. She's a little pissed, but she'll get over it. I tend to piss her off a lot, anyway. When I'm done talking to her. I start to walk back to my room when the phone starts ringing (just like it always does). Now, the operator isn't a personal friend of mine, so I just keep on walking.

It's 9:00 a.m. as I start to ride. The fog is slowly lifting and the sunlight is filtering through the mists. As I pedal down the road, only the weather is gray. It's actually another beautiful day. The sun's just breaking through the fog...or haze...or whatever you want to call it. It's quite warm. I don't know what the temperature is, but I'll check in a minute. It looks like its going to be a nice day for my ride.

What is today, anyway...? Tuesday or Thursday...? Let's see, Monday, Tuesday, Wednesday. Well, I guess it's Thursday.

Hey...! Gas here is $1.09 for regular, and $1.06 for unleaded...! In L.A. unleaded is always more expensive than regular.

It's 75 degrees out and I'm riding on an old concrete road. It has about an eight-foot wide gravel shoulder and it's broken up pretty good, I mean pretty bad. Where they've re-black-topped over the concrete, it's much better. There is still no shoulder, though. Luckily, the traffic not too heavy as I ride through the small town of Carsonville.

There is no breeze at all this morning and the trees and shrubs are all drooping dead still in the humidity. It's still overcast and hazy as I pedal through the morning. I'm sweating a lot, and I mean a lot. I'm not complaining though, it's still a beautiful day and it's surely nice not to have to fight a headwind.

I ride past a large house in Port Sanilac. It's very similar to the one I lived in back in Buck Creek, Indiana. When I was in grade school, I remember my dad holding me upside down over the upstairs balcony and tickling my feet.

I also recall my two brothers and I would go out in the yard, which had a lot of huge maple trees. We would hide behind these trees and have Rock Wars. We would throw rocks as hard as we could at each other. This one time I got hit in the forehead and was knocked out cold. I remember seeing stars. Now let me tell you, stars are best seen at night.

It seems a little cooler riding now.

I shall not soon forget the scene that greets my eyes as I look upon Lake Huron. Its forested cliffs line the lake and its waves tumble over its rocky bed far below. I have a 10 mph crosswind now…coming in off the lake…from my left side. The rising sun has warmed the dull overcast sky. Bright rays of sunlight are breaking through the open spaces in the scattered clouds.

There are a lot of nice homes and cottages all along here. All the homes are on the lakeside of the road, except when the road gets too close to the lake…then they are on the other side. There are a so many beautiful trees along here.

It's 10:56 a.m. I have 20 miles on the odometer and I'm going to stop in a restaurant here and have another breakfast.

I love breakfast but this food is ordinary...with greasy sausage and high prices...and the waitress is unpleasant. And, to top it all off...I'm getting hassled in here by people traveling in motorhomes who can afford to travel at a six-miles-per-gallon rate. I pay and leave.

*   *   *

Riding out of town along a high bluff that overlooks Lake Huron, I go through green forests of pine and leaf-waving aspen...birch and maples...whose branches almost meet over this little old country road. There is no shoulder at all and the road is pretty heavily traveled. The good drivers pull over a little and go around me, with anywhere from two to four feet between them and me. There are these kids in a pickup truck, with a bumper sticker that reads, "Gas, Grass or Ass, Nobody Rides for Free," who decide that they want to get as close to me as they can, missing me by a distance equal to their intelligence. I feel my heart miss a beat as they honk their horn...flip me the one finger peace sign...and shout obscenities at me as they speed by. They pass with less than an inch between my handlebars and their fender. I'm so pissed. I give them the international signal back. I really try to control myself. This is the first time on my tour I've resorted to this particular hand signal. It's not a very smart thing for me to do. For one thing, I'm grossly outnumbered. Besides that, they could just wait for me to go by and run me over the next time. But worst of all...it brings me down to their level...and that's not the level I want to be at. I realize now that, it's not what happens that's important, but how I react to it is important.

For the most, part the countryside is nice and green out here. I haven't seen any wildflowers, for quite a long time. Well, there have been a few...small yellow ones...the same kind I've been seeing all along.

I'm only about a quarter mile from Lake Huron, but there are such thick woods and vegetation...I've only seen the lake three or four times...so far. This part of the country has enough moisture for the dense hardwood forests the broad-leafed trees, common to this cold temperate region, to flourish.

I love to peer between the houses along the shore to see the boats...yards...and flowers. I watch the people...glad that I'm not taking out the garbage...painting the house...digging in the garden...or cutting the grass. I'm delighted to be smoothly pedaling along on my bike, humming to myself. I still have a lot of traffic as I ride in 78 degree temperature into Lakeport. The road has a rather good (two foot wide) blacktop shoulder now.

It's 11:44 a.m. and, apparently, I've just ridden through Birch Beach. I mean, don't blink or you'll miss it. A sign at the outskirts of town says that it's the home of 243 friendly people and one Grouch. You know you're in a small town when nobody uses their turn signals because everybody knows where everybody is going (except me).

I sure hope they'll let me ride across the bridge going into Canada.

There is a lot of pollen floating around in the air. It almost looks like it's snowing out. This fuzzy pollen sticks to my beard and eyebrows once in a while. But, I'm on vacation and I refuse to put my glasses on. There are beautiful cattails flying past me in the ditch and beyond them are grass...cattle and woods of maple...birch...hemlock...aspen...spruce, and fir trees.

I have between a five to 10 mph crosswind now. Well, I guess it's closer to 5 mph. It's 12:47 p.m. and I have 40 miles on the odometer. I'm ready for a stop at a McDonalds on the outskirts of Port Huron, to take a leak and get something to drink. I'm about as dry as my bank account is on April the 15th.

* * *

There is a sign that says, "No Pedestrians or Bicycles" at the bridge that I have to cross to get into Canada. Now, I'm wondering just how am I going to get across. A gentleman, from Customs (driving an escort van), flags me down. We put my bike in the back of the van and he takes me across the bridge. It's a very high iron bridge. It has arches as high as a rainbow. At least this way they don't charge me a toll. I stop at Customs, just across the bridge. Now, I have never smuggled anything in my life. So why...then...do I feel an uneasy sense of guilt on approaching a customs barrier? As I walk in, there is this shapeless woman...with a Mona Lisa smile...looking at me as if I have a booger hanging out of my noise. She looks as though she might have been pretty ten years ago. She's managed to pack her Bartlett pear-shaped hips (one of the dangers of being too computer friendly, I'm afraid) into what...she hopes...is a pair of mean jeans. The first thing she asks me is, "Do you have any Mace?" Maybe she thinks I might have some for spraying at dogs or something. I don't know. She then asks me where I'm going and for how long? She's looking me over as if she would love to examine my teeth and hooves. Then, she asks me to step into her office. I thought great...now she wants to have sex with me. The next question is, "How much money do you have on you?" Now, I think that's kind of personal. We aren't that close...yet...but I don't want to argue with her. I realize that I have to take into consideration that females are overly curious animals, anyway. Next, she asks me why I'm riding out here, because today and tomorrow, are supposed to be the two hottest days of the year (it's 89 degrees). I tell her what I'm doing and ask her if I'm allowed to ride my bike on 402, which is the main highway here. She tells me I can take it for about five or six miles, then get off at Airport Road.

It's 1:36 p.m. and I'm in Ontario, Canada. I feel good...! It's the pull of another country...a country I'm just beginning to explore.

*   *   *

I start riding on 402, another one of these times when they've turned a nice little old country road into a wide gash of a superhighway, a multiple-lane carrier of the nations goods. Of course, they don't allow bicycles to ride on it, not as if I would want to, anyway. Not with its speeding cars and trucks zooming past, coming within a foot or so of my left shoulder. Somehow, they call this progress. They bulldoze all the nice trees and roller coaster hills down...and turn them into a straight...flat...boring interstate. I wouldn't ride on a road like this even if it were legal. And here's this sign again that says, "No Pedestrians or Bicycles." I figure this probably means the same thing in Canada as it does in the United States. So I'll get off just as soon as I can.

I'm three miles east of Point Edward and I have a 10 mph crosswind from my left. There's no doubt about it, it's Summer. It's hot...really HOT...90 degrees. When I marked my route out on my itinerary, I planned on traveling the secondary back roads and here I am with a super highway unrolling ahead of me like toilet paper. There is a sign "Monitored by Aircraft." Why is it that whenever you see that sign you always look up? And, of course...the sky is always empty. I see reflected heat, floating about eight inches above the road. Ah...! There is an off-ramp. I'm going to get off this superhighway and pedal south, until I find a little old country road.

I'm six miles east of Sarnia riding on Route 7 now, a much nicer road. There are a lot of motels all along here. Gas is 54.5 cents for regular and 53.5 cents for unleaded. Super unleaded is 56.9 cents a liter.

These service stations bring back memories of when I was a kid and I would ride my bike over the rubber hoses to ring the bell and when the attendant came out...I rode off...! FUN...!

This is a nice road, with about a four foot wide blacktop shoulder.

There are a lot of farms out here with wheat or rye...I don't know which it is...but there are huge fields of it. There seems to be a lot more farming here than there was in Michigan. Pigs smell the same here as they do in the United States.

Here's another one of those little roadside Churches for the traveler. I'm not stopping at this one. My Church is in the open air. That's where I feel closer to God, more so than I would in a building. I see a lot of brick homes around here, not just the old ones, but the new ones are brick, too. This is a beautiful road.

With 60 miles on the odometer it's 2:33 p.m. as I ride through Reeces Corners, Hmmmmm…Reeces Corners, Reese's Peanut Butter Cups…I wonder if there's a connection? I have between a five to 10 mph tailwind. Nah…! I'll take that back. It's only about a 5 mph tailwind at the most. There is very little traffic on this road.

I just lost my good shoulder. I have about an eight-foot wide gravel shoulder now, which is useless to me.

All Right…! There's a robin…! That's the first one I've seen this year.

The ranch houses out here are set on top of knolls, sheltered by groves of oak and Douglas fir. They seem to be surveying their crop lands.

As soon as I find a place to eat, that's exactly what I'm going to do.

These wheat fields remind me of an old joke I just have to share with you. These two guys had been friends for a long time and they were on vacation in wheat country. There were good crops all around them. Harry took his pipe from his mouth and pointed to one of the fields and grunted, "Nice crop of wheat." Five hours later, when they were seated by their campfire…Bill broke the silence and said, "It wasn't wheat, it was rye." Then he rolled up in his blanket and went to sleep. The sun was well up when Bill woke the next morning. He looked around but Harry and his gear was gone. Then he found a note under a stone at the foot of the nearest tree. It simply read, "Too much argument in this camp."

*   *   *

As I ride through Warwick it's 3:14 p.m. I have a 5 mph wind that keeps switching around. I'm riding over an overpass of a two-lane divided road. It has an eight-foot wide gravel shoulder on it…just like this one.

I see another red-winged blackbird. I know the names of about as many birds as I do plants. The corn throughout this area sure looks like it needs rain.

I have 80 miles on the odometer and it's 91 degrees. It's 3:59 p.m. as I ride out of the hot, sunbaked town of Adelaide. There is not a living thing to be seen. Even the lizards (if there were any) have all disappeared. The pastures smell like cattle…silage…grass…and wet hay…which remind me of my spring days on the farm in Wisconsin.

Cattle seem to have a good life. They are always eating. If they are not eating, they are chewing their cud. And if they are not eating or chewing their cud…they are lying down…resting up…so they can eat and chew their cud some more.

There are heat waves that look a lot like water crossing the road. As I wheel past one farm after another, in this heat, I'm visualizing a soda fountain or a root-beer stand…or at least a lemonade stand alongside the road. But all I see in the sun's glare are dry fields and a road that seem to go on forever.

There's a little coffee shop in Hickory Corner where I stop to replenish my fluids.

I'm leaving the coffee shop now. They move very slowly in there, I guess to avoid wasting energy. All I had was a ham and cheese sandwich and some iced tea.

I'm about to mount my bike when I discover that I left my computer on while I was in the coffee shop. So I'll have to calculate my time and average speed tonight.

I ride past this barn that has the owner's last name on it. It's the last name of a cheap friend of mine. He's so cheap that when we would go camping and a hot shower would cost 25 cents and a cold one was free…he would always take a cold one. I've heard other people say that he's so cheap…he uses both sides of the toilet paper.

It's 5:24 p.m. and I have a 10 mph tailwind as I ride out of Poplar Hill.

A north wind is carrying in the smell of pigs. This is definitely pig country.

My tires are buzzing over some very roughly textured asphalt as I ride through the small village of Lobo. The village has been turned inside out by all the road construction. I'm thinking to myself...if you think only a woman's work is never done...you know very little about highway construction. This is a hard road to travel, from its grooves to its gravel. I've been riding on this poor excuse for a road for more than five miles now, and I can't ride on the shoulder because it's loose gravel. I'm finally to the end of the road construction. I've ridden through six and a half miles of this shit...with deep grooves...running at all different angles. It wasn't any fun at all.

I'm rolling along fairly well with a 10 mph tailwind. It's cooled down to 85 degrees.

Shell gas is 51.9 cents for unleaded and 52.96 cents for regular and 54.9 cents for super formula.

*   *   *

It's 7:17 p.m. and I've ridden 114 miles today. I'm ready to get off Route 2, in London. I stop and check on a motel room. There's a gentleman sitting behind the counter having a conversation with himself. As he stands up, I can see that his head and stomach are perfectly round, just like a stick man's. He says that he doesn't want to let me have the last available room without a reservation. So, he yells to his wife in the back room. She comes out. She's a breastfully flat (wait a minute...that's a contradiction). Anyway, she doesn't have much of a figure or head of hair. You know, it's hard to let your hair down when it's that short. Anyway, they argue and finally agree to let me have the room for $38.00. It's a small room.

I'm going to get cleaned up and check the neighborhood out before dark. I walk over to Browns Chicken and have a chicken dinner. The girl behind the counter asks me if I want french fries or taters, I tell her to give me the taters. The chicken...taters and a coke...cost $6.61. Very expensive, I'm thinking...for a fast food place. O Yea...! They didn't put ice in my drinks, either.

Out walking the streets, I check out the prices of things. Gas is about 52 cents a liter…24 cans of Coke are $6.99…a liter Big Gulp is 69 cents at a 24-hour 7-11 store. Two liters of milk is $2.45. That seemed a little high to me. They have a Radio Shack, and a McDonalds and a Dairy Queen. It looks about the same here as it does in the United States. They have a 24-hour Post Office in the 7-11 store. I think I'll get some of my stuff and mail it back home.

Well, I mailed some of my excess weight home. The girl behind the counter was new at her job and she didn't know what she was doing. So, I ended up looking up the prices for her. I think I used the right chart. It ended up costing $5.10 to mail my stuff.

I'm going into the Dairy Queen for a peanut butter malt…just like I always do. I just love them. The girl behind the counter says she's never heard of a peanut butter malt. I ask her if she has any peanut butter. She looks around and finds some, so I tell her how and she makes me a peanut butter malt. Their malts…well…they are actually shakes…are $2.00 apiece. Everything else, hamburgers and sundaes and so on are between $2.77 and $3.00 apiece. A lot more then I've been paying in the United States.

I'm back at the motel now. This room smells like a whorehouse, Oops…! I mean I've been told they smell like this. I wouldn't know myself. I had a friend who was so dumb that he thought a cathouse was a place for sick cats. On second thoughts, maybe he wasn't so dumb.

*   *   *

Statistics for **DAY TWENTY-THREE** *Thursday, July 6, 1989.*
114 miles of riding today, 14.1 average miles per hour for today, 2,595 miles of riding in 23 days, 113 average miles of riding per day.

Day Twenty-Four

From London, Ontario
To Niagara Falls, Ontario

It's Friday, July the 7th, I believe. I leave the motel at 8:25 a.m. and head for a McDonalds that's only about a block away. I have their so-called big breakfast, an Egg McMuffin and coffee. The coffee is so thick that the sugar floats on it, so I'm getting a large diet coke to wash it down with. My breakfast costs $6.50…a little expensive…but things seem to cost more in Canada. At least they gave me the exchange rate in McDonalds which is 15 cents on a dollar.

The only place I've really been ripped off on my tour…so far…was at the motel I stayed in last night. They charged me $2.00 more than it should have been, and they didn't give me the exchange rate. Oh, Well. I have a clean rag to wipe my chain off with now. Anyway, if that's the most I get ripped off on this tour, I'll be very fortunate.

I couldn't find any big motel, like a Super 8 or Holiday Inn or Ramada Inn or any other major chains like that. So, I stayed in a little love-nest motel. That's probably why I got ripped off.

It's overcast and 76 degrees, and I have a 10 mph tailwind. There is about a two foot wide blacktop shoulder on this road, but it's pretty badly broken up so I'm riding right on the white line at the edge of the road. There is a lot of traffic today, but I guess it's not any worse than riding in L.A. The humidity must be very high because I'm sure sweating up a storm this morning.

All the ditches are freshly mowed throughout this area. It smells GREAT…! A lot of the farms out here have these little individual family cemetery plots, with four of five gravestones. Some are fenced in with wrought iron fences, which are covered with vines and flowers that...more than likely...bloom throughout the summer months and way into the fall

Gas in London is 49.9 cents a liter. I don't know why I'm so concerned about the price of gas, my vehicle is muscle and beer powered.

I have a 5 mph crosswind as I ride into Thamesford. I'm out in the country now and there's nothing but good smelling farmland all around me. Freshly tilled dirt has its own distinctive smell. Maybe it's a smell that only farmers can appreciate. I used to be a farmer and I just love the smell of it. It brings back some good memories. I remember my dad plowing the fields and me running behind in the furrow and collecting fishing worms. I also recall as a kid...after...or even in the rain...at night...my brother and I would go out in the yard and collect nightcrawlers. I would hold the flashlight and coffee can...and he would pick the long...skinny...slimy...

disgusting things up. They looked sort of like baby snakes, and to this day…I HATE SNAKES…!

Most of the corn out here is about four to five feet tall. I haven't seen any wildflowers for quite some time. The pastures are all green which makes for a good grazing area for the large herds of cattle.

I'd say about 90% of the houses in this part of Ontario are made out of brick.

I have between a five to 10 mph tailwind that's a little bit off to my left now. I'm surprised…! I have some rollers today. Yesterday it was pretty flat all day. It's only 10 a.m. but it's rather warm out, 86 degrees.

At 10:36 a.m. with 23 miles in I ride into the town of Woodstock, the Dairy Capital of Canada. Riding through Woodstock is like cycling back in time. It's an old town that looks like it's been unchanged for a hundred years, except for the traffic and paved streets. The whole town would make a good *Norman Rockwell* painting.

Seven miles out of Woodstock…near Eastwood…I ride on another speed bump road. There is a Texaco filling station in Eastwood selling gasoline for 51.9 cents a liter. I guess I'm accustomed to seeing gas prices quoted by the gallon, so 50 cents looks like it's cheap. But…actually…it's expensive. It's about $2.00 a gallon, considering the exchange rates and all.

My stomach tells me it's time for lunch at 11:24 a.m. I see a small restaurant and go in for a malt…a coke…and a raisin pie a la mode. It cost me to $5.00. All the restaurants I've stopped at in Canada serve fairly warm water and pop, without ice.

Every few miles I ride past a sign that says, "Pick your own Strawberries." Now I haven't actually seen any strawberries but I can smell them. As I stop to take a picture of a newly painted barn I can't help but notice that there are sure a lot of horse ranches throughout this area. I'm riding over small hills…past old…farmhouses…vineyards…and small villages that rest on the hilltops. As I ride past one ranch after another, I see a lot of horses' asses…which only means that the wind is blowing in the right direction. Beads of sweat are dripping off the tip of my nose.

This river I'm riding over, just east of Paris…reminds me of when I was a kid. My brothers and I would go swimming in the Pine River, which was right across the road from our farm in Poy Sippi. Pine River is a spring-fed trout stream, which makes it one of the coldest rivers in Wisconsin. We didn't care, we would walk up the riverbank, until we came to a place that wasn't too deep. Then we would wade out into the middle of the river…through knee deep muck…occasionally reaching down and grabbing a handful and flinging it at each other. The middle of the river was the best place for swimming, the current was strong enough that it washed all the muck away and left a nice sandy bottom. We would splash around for a while then wade back out through the thick black muck. When we reached the bank we would splash water on our feet and legs to rinse the muck off. One of us always carried farmer matches with us…I don't know why…it couldn't have been for cigarettes. Anyway, we discovered that putting a hot match to the leeches that clung to our legs was the best way to get them to drop off. Ugh…!

I have a 10 to 15 mph tailwind, off to my left side. As long as I'm moving it doesn't seem too hot…but as soon as I stop…the sweat just pours off me. This is definitely riding in rolling terrain again. It's not too steep, but it's rolling all right. Oh Shit…! Nothing…absolutely nothing…smells worse than a chicken farm…! Especially in this 90-degree heat.

I'm picking up the smell of strawberries now. Much better than chicken shit.

There are a few yellow wildflowers along the road. The July sun is shining bright as I ride over a hill and down into a little country town. I stop at a general store that looks peaceful and inviting in the sunlight. I'm going to get off this iron horse of mine for a while. As I walk into the general store, a grandmotherly woman behind the counter snaps her head around so quickly her earrings are a blur. She seems surprised to see me, much like a kid who's just had an icicle dropped down the back of his neck. I buy a liter of milk and two bananas from her. Then, I go out front and eat them.

It's 1:51 p.m. I have 60 miles on the odometer and I have a 10 mph tailwind as I ride out of Copetown. Up ahead the sky has turned a milky...sort of soiled-looking...overcast. Maybe it's just the humidity hanging in the air.

I'm taking a picture of a huge hospital in Hamilton for a couple of reasons. One, because it's laid out differently than most I've seen and two, because my girlfriend works in a hospital.

Riding right in downtown Hamilton, I don't notice the wind...too much...but I do notice the heat. It's 92 degrees. I'm allergic to any weather over eighty. It makes me break out in a sweat.

There are a lot of vineyards and orchards all along this road. People are out in the orchards, picking cherries. There are huge vineyards of grapes, and one orchard after another of peaches, cherries and apples. They virtually have every kind of fruit imaginable in this area.

It's 3:53 p.m. as I stop at a Dairy Bar in Lincoln. I have a coke and some apple pie a la mode.

There are signs all along here advertising "Pick your own Cherries." The average price seems to be $10.00 for six quarts.

I can just see Lake Ontario in the distance from here. I guess later in the day I'll get a much better look at it.

Gas is 48.5 cents a liter in Vineland...but..."Who Cares...?"

Aah...! Wonderful farm smells...! Blowing in from the northeast is a delicate breeze laden with the essence of freshly spread manure. There are literally hundreds of acres of grapes between Jordan and St. Catharine's. And all the cherry trees are just loaded with cherries.

At 5:25 p.m. I have 100 miles in and I'm near St. Catharine's. I make a turn here so now I'm riding straight toward the lake and I have a 15 to 20 mph headwind. The temperature has dropped to 83 degrees and the afternoon sunshine feels toasty without being overwhelming.

Out on the side of the road is a sign that reads: "Raspberries and Rhubarb." When a farmer has Row Crops...whether it is grapes...beans or corn...he is always judged by the straightness of his rows. I look down the long rows of grapevines near Niagara-on-the-Lake and notice that Lake Ontario appears to be higher than the road I'm riding on.

A young lady...I say young...because they all look young to me anymore...went very slowly around me. She's wearing a baseball cap and driving a '82 ketchup-red Corvette. She peers out of her window at me as though she had just discovered glass was transparent. I nod and smile back at her.

I have a 10 mph tailwind and it's cooled down to 79 degrees.

I just took a picture of a Canadian Fort, Fort George. I'm thinking now isn't that a good French name. Speaking of France, I'm riding past a winery. It's the third winery I've ridden past in the last five miles. It's a good thing I'm not a drinking man.

It's 7:44 p.m. and I'm riding through Queenston snapping my camera away like a mousetrap. I think I'm taking more pictures of the beautiful countryside than a busload of Japanese tourists would. I'm in second gear, battling with some very hilly terrain here in Niagara Falls, but it's cooled down to a pleasant 76 degrees now.

It's sure pretty out here. I'm riding on *Niagara Parkway* and it's been one big beautiful park for the last 10 or 15 miles. It's 8:12 p.m. and I've ridden 132 miles so far today.

I stop to check on a motel room in Niagara Falls.

I go into a Days Inn lobby and what do I see? A sign hanging behind the desk, which reads, "We'll make you feel right at home." Well I didn't ride more than 2,000 miles so I could feel right at home. Besides, I don't like the looks of the guy behind the counter. He's got eyebrows as black as a raven's wings and he's as hairy as King Kong's armpits. So, I exit and ride on over to a Travelers Inn, which is right across the road. As I walk in, I notice two signs hanging behind their counter. One read, "Kids $9.95. Not a bad price...I figure...if you want one. The other one reads, "Why not spend your second honeymoon here? Twenty percent discount if you're with the same wife." Now, I like a place with a sense of humor so I talk to the young lady behind the counter. She has bluebird-blue eyes and a smile you could see from an airplane.

I take the room which costs $66.00 for the room plus another $10.00 deposit for the key, which I thought Sucked. They don't have any rooms downstairs, so I have to carry my bike up two flights of stairs. That Sucks.

After putting my stuff in my room I go to get some ice and the ice machine doesn't work. That Sucks.

I walk clear down to the office and ask them where I can get some ice and they tell me that I have to go to the restaurant next door and ask them for it. That Sucks.

They have a shuttle bus running to the Falls, every 15 minutes from here. I know that if I were to take the shuttle I would want to stay downtown for quite a while so I ask at the front desk, when the last shuttle returns to the Motel. She says, "I don't have any idea."

That Sucks, too.

Anyway, I walk back over to the Days Inn, which has a nice restaurant. Another reason I checked into the Travelers Inn instead of the Days Inn, is because of some creative advertising. It advertises shuttle service to the Falls. But now I find out that the *Park Service* runs the shuttle service...not the motel. For the most part, what I've discovered about advertising is that it's a way of making you think you've longed all your life for something you've never heard of before.

I still have to walk down the road a couple of blocks to catch the shuttle.

The motel I'm staying at has an outside swimming pool and this Days Inn has a heated indoor pool. I think I might have made the wrong choice. Oh, Well...! In a hundred years none of this will matter...anyway. I walk in the door of the restaurant at 9:50 p.m. and they're closing at 10:00 p.m. I ask if I can get their special. They have a steak and a baked potato special for $7.99. I have that and coffee. I also try a Canadian beer. So now my dinner ends up costing me $12.99 instead of $7.99. After dinner I walk back to the Travelers Inn and have another beer...just to see how much it cost...its $3.02. Quite expensive but it's very good beer.

One thing's for sure. It would cost too much for me to get drunk here. I think I'll take tomorrow off and go to the Falls. I walk back to the office and pay for another night.

I'll probably sleep in tomorrow, then walk over to Days Inn and get their special "All-You-Can-Eat" breakfast. I don't know how much it is...but I know how much I can eat...so I'm going over there no matter what.

I'm going to stay up and watch a little television...call my girlfriend...then hit it.

*   *   *

*Statistics for **DAY TWENTY-FOUR** Friday, July 7, 1989.*
132 miles of riding today, 13.3 average miles per hour for today, 2,727 miles of riding in 24 days, 114 average miles of riding per day.

My Day Off

Niagara Falls, Ontario.

It's 7:21 a.m. Saturday, July 8th. It's my day off, but I think I'll get up anyway. It's an absolutely beautiful day.

They didn't give me a receipt for my room for today, so I go down and check on that. As I walk in the lobby, there is an overdressed old man holding hands with a much younger…what I presume to be…second wife. They tell me at the office that there is a three and a half-hour tour today, leaving at 9:00 a.m. going to the Falls and all over town that cost $13.00. So I say, "Great sign me up."

I have to rush over and eat breakfast before the tour starts. Days Inn has their All-You-Can-Eat Buffet Breakfast which suits me fine. It's $7.55 plus a tip. One thing I've discovered about Canada…The food is terrible. I have two cups of coffee and some french toast, that is as hard as leather. I can't even cut it with a fork or my butter knife. The bacon is half-done and soggy…and when I try to eat it…it sticks to the roof of my mouth.

It's time to go on the tour now. It's an absolutely perfect day. The sun is shining bright, and it must be 70 or 75 degrees out already. The tour guide tells us that this is the clearest day they've had all year. He says that it's been raining or foggy for quite some time.

It's just a perfect…crystal clear…day today.

Our tour guide is telling us how expensive things are around here. He says that when he goes down and fills his car up with gas and gets a pack of cigarettes, it usually costs him around $45.00. He tells us that minimum wage in Ontario is $6.50 per hour. He goes on to say that thirty years ago before they had all the motels around Niagara Falls, you had to stay in a spare room in someone's house which usually cost around $2.00. And, now...if you were to stay in the exact same room (which they now call a Bed-and-Breakfast) it would cost you $120.00 a night. Talk about inflation.

We stop in a little gift shop and I notice that the film for my camera cost $6.32 (I bought mine in California for $2.30 a roll). I get a fountain coke. It's $1.46. As I check out the prices of other things. I discover that a pack of cigarettes is $4.25. A liter of gas is 51 cents, which is about $2.75 a gallon in American money.

It's 12:30 p.m. and I'm back from the tour. It was a really good tour. It went to the Falls as well as other places throughout town. I'll probably catch a bus and go back to the Falls tonight. They have colored lights on them and it's supposed to be spectacular. The park overlooking the Niagara River in front of my motel is part of the same park I was riding through yesterday. It's 36 miles long, with a bike path its entire length. It also has an 18-hole public golf course that costs $20.00 to play. It's a beautiful self-supported park with the tours being its main support.

It's 1:00 p.m., a good time to go over and have a few beers and then catch a nap. Just for your information...the difference between a nap and sleeping is that when you're sleeping you're under the covers...napping is done on top of the covers.

Well, it's 4:30 p.m. I had a few beers and took my little nap. Now I'm going to go down to see what this town is like at night. I take the shuttle downtown and ride on the biggest Ferris wheel I've ever seen. It's got 40 seats that'll seat up to eight people, each. It's 185 feet in diameter.

Seeing as how I have today off I think I'll write my girlfriend a letter.

I go to four stores and I can't seem to find an envelope in this town. I can find plenty of post cards, but I prefer sending a letter instead of a post card. Here's my reason behind that. Let's say your sitting at home and the mail comes. You go out into the scorching L.A. heat and retrieve this post card, with a beautiful picture of the snow-capped mountains on it. Or, if you happen to be somewhere that's cold...there is no doubt about it, you'll get a post card of a sunny beach scene with naked bodies. I mean, have you ever seen a post card with an ugly picture on it? Then, when you turn it over, what do you almost always see? "Having a wonderful time, wish you were here." Now, let's pick this apart. Of course you're "having a good time." You're on vacation while they are at home working. But, do you ask how they are? No...! Now for the last part, "Wish you were here." Now, you know that's an outright lie. If you wished they were here, you would have taken them along in the first place. Maybe I'll call my girlfriend instead.

I'll tell you one thing...for the price of food around here...if a guy takes a girl out for dinner, he damn well better get laid.

I stop in a grocery store to get a liter of milk and some Reese's peanut butter cups, one of my favorite health foods. While I'm in the store a guy comes in and gets some cigarettes. It seems that they sell cigarettes in packs of 15 for $2.55. *Wonder Bread* isn't priced too badly. It's $1.35 for a loaf.

On the tour I took to the Falls this morning, the guide was bragging about how good the hot dogs were at this place right across the street from where I'm staying. So, I walk over and get one. Well, a hot dog and a coke came to $4.85 and the thing was tough and so hard it squeaked like rubber bands as I chewed on it...! Maybe they like them like that...but I don't.

Ho, Well...! I'll be back in the good old United States tomorrow.

As I walk back to my motel rain clouds are forming over my head. It may rain tomorrow, but it was a perfect day today.

Day Twenty-Five

From Niagara Falls, Ontario
To Newark, New York

Arising at dawn...I pack my bike...fold and re-pack my map.

It's 7:00 a.m. and it's time for me to roll out.

It's another beautiful day, the sun's shining and it's clear and 66 degrees out.

I have aspirin...throat lozenges...and some cough drops...all mixed together in a plastic bag, to save room. I've heard some horror stories about Border Crossings, so I'm dumping them all out. It seems that if pills aren't in their original packing, they question them. This could hold me up for hours and sometimes even days. I talked to a guy last night who's fiancee works at the Border Crossing. She told him that it doesn't matter what you look like...if her supervisor says search a car...they search it. Sometimes they even tear the door panels off and when they're done they don't put anything back together, they just leave it all torn up and it's up to you to get it fixed. It seems that when you're at Customs you have no rights at all. She said that some people have tried to collect as much as $500.00 for damages Customs did to their car, without any success.

Well, here I am at *Rainbow Bridge*. Customs is right on the other side of the bridge. It's a toll bridge. It costs me 10 cents to cross it, to get back into the United States and that's the best deal I've ever had.

It's 7:15 a.m. as I coast into Customs.

Yahoo...! I shout to no one. It's 7:22 a.m. and I'm back in the good old United States. Contrary to the rumors I'd heard Customs was a snap. It just goes to prove that sometimes the things we fear the most turn out to harm us the least.

An American-made McDonalds draws me in like a magnet. As I slowly down hot coffee and eat greasy burgers and fries, I realize that McDonalds is as American as apple pie. I'm as happy as a kid at Christmas time. I'm even thinking about sliding down their slide. I can put away my old badly creased maps of Ontario and open a new one of New York...the last state I'll be riding in on this tour. It almost smells fragrant, like fresh bread, as I let my imagination run wild about the roads I'll be riding on in the upcoming days.

Although I hate to, I leave McDonalds.

Well, I believe Canada and the United States are as different as night and day. I thought Canada would be the highlight of my tour, but it wasn't. It was a great disappointment to me. I saw fewer wildflowers and more flies in Canada than I have anywhere. There's one good thing I can say about Canada though...they do make some good beer. A bit expensive...but good.

Wildflowers are wagging their colorful heads in the breeze as I ride by.

I'm so happy, I could sing the National Anthem, if only I knew all the words. It's going to be a wonderful day. This land is my land, this land is your land, from sea to shining sea.

It's 8:23 a.m. I have 10 miles on the odometer. Sunday morning church bells are ringing as fruit falls to the earth with a thud. I just can't tell you how good it feels to be back in the United States.

As I ride through Colonial Village the birds and I are singing Hymns this beautiful Sunday morning. The way I see it...with God being everywhere...I can worship Him anywhere. I prefer to worship Him riding through the beautiful forest He created...instead of in a man-made structure.

* * *

Have you ever noticed how men are perfectly happy when they're all dressed alike...like at weddings...in church...and at funerals...even their own. Women, on the other hand...are not pleased...to say the least...if they look anything like anyone else. Does this mean that they are more creative or just that they are not happy having their clothes stamped out with a cookie cutter, with everyone looking exactly alike? Maybe, there is a little rebel in each and every one of them. If so, I have to applaud them for that. Anyway, as I ride past this graveyard I can't help but wonder…what if these graves were to be dug up lets say…in a hundred or a thousand years? Much like we're digging up Indian and Egyptian graves today to see how the people lived back then. One thing's for sure, they won't be able to tell much about the male population. Because everyone from a farmer to a city slicker to the President of the United States will all be dressed exactly alike. Now, the ladies of our time will show some individuality. They'll find that they preferred different jewelry and clothes. Thank God that they'll be decomposed, so they won't discover all the makeup. But, I'm sure they'll discover a few wigs…some inch and half long acrylic fingernails…some unusually long eyelashes and some false teeth. But what I think what'll puzzle them the most are the two lumps of silicone stuck to some of the ladies chest bones. That stuff won't decompose, you know. So, I've decided…that when I die…even though I'm a perfect male specimen without any silicone parts, I would like to be cremated. I don't want to take up any space on this land…and being the good Christian that I am…I know my spirit will already be in Heaven.

* * *

I have a 10 mph tailwind. A light breeze is bending the willows, and patches of sky overhead are a brilliant blue. This morning is absolutely beautiful. There are a lot of dairy farms out here. As I ride by this one farm, I can smell the fresh hay and hear the cackling of a hen that has apparently just laid an egg and is informing the world about it. And there are lots of wild flowers along the road again…I don't know why…but I didn't see many in Canada.

At 9:31 a.m. as I pedal into Lockport. I have to stop and take a picture of the *Historic Erie Canal Locks*. A sign here tells me that they were finished on

October 26, 1825 and its 363 miles long. I'm not a historian, I consider myself to be more of a nature lover. I like beauty in its natural state. Again, I am reminded of my girlfriend.

There is no wind at all now...well maybe a 5 mph tailwind at the most. I don't know, but Lockport and Gasport might not be the best places in the world to live. I've seen an awful lot of funeral homes around here.

I haven't seen any big trucks on this road yet, maybe that's because it's Sunday.

There are a lot of blue wildflowers all along the road.

I have 40 miles in and it's 10:21 a.m. as I stop at a busy restaurant with a family atmosphere. I mean the place is packed. There must be at least forty people in this little bitty country restaurant. I notice that there are a lot of people in here with their Bibles open...with passages underlined and highlighted. I wonder if they took the time to do this themselves or did they buy the Bibles already that way?

I know now why it's so busy. The food is great and the sourdough toast I'm having for breakfast is outstanding. I leave the restaurant at 10:47 a.m. There is a bike path here...somewhere...that I can ride on. It's 82 degrees. I have a 5 mph tailwind as I ride into Middleport.

I'm a true believer in that a 3,000-mile bike tour is more than a vacation. It's an experience that can...and probably will...change my life forever. I can honestly say that I have not enjoyed life as much as I have in the last four weeks.

As I ride into Medina, the sun is bright and there is no wind or clouds in the sky. It might get really hot today...but one thing's for sure...it's not going to rain.

I'm riding on a brand-new road...with a four-foot wide...blacktop shoulder. It just doesn't get any better than this. I see a sign outside a church located next to an ice-cream parlor. It reads, "Stop in and try one of our Sundays-They're Free." I went to a church once where they didn't pass a collection plate or charge anything for the preaching...and let me tell you...it was worth it.

Friday night, when I got to my motel in Niagara Falls, I washed my clothes out in the sink…wrung them out in a towel…turned the heat down to low…hung them on the hot air vent to dry and this morning (Sunday) they're almost dry. I don't know if it's the humidity or what, but it sure takes them a long time to dry out.

I'm surely glad I stayed over a day and saw Niagara Falls. It was well worth it. It's beautiful out here today and there is very little traffic.

There is this stray dog that's been following me for the last 2 miles. I think he wants to be my friend but he's afraid to come too close.

*   *   *

I'm riding on the so-called *"Erie Canal Bike Trail."* Actually, it's an old grass and dirt wagon train trail, which it's more suited for even today. I enjoy riding on rural roads, but this is overdoing it a little. It's scenic and all right for a short distance, but if I were to continue riding on this trail it would take me a year to get across New York State. Besides, I'm a little afraid of running over snakes, especially the black ones. They scare the hell out of me. There is probably one of those long "Phobia" names for this, I'm not sure.

All of a sudden…I hear this crashing in the brush…followed by a low…rumbling growl. I stop immediately and look through the brush. What do I see…? A Saint Bernard with a snake in it's mouth…! When the dog spots me, it drops the snake and stares at me. At this point I'm not sure if I'm more scared of the dog or the wounded snake. Luckily, three kids sitting on a fallen tree, call for "Buster", and he goes to them. As I approach the kids, Buster is standing there scratching his back on a tree limb. Even though they all look alike, I'm soon to find out that only two are brothers and the other a neighbor. One of the boys has a slingshot made out of a forked stick and a strip of inner tube hanging around his neck. They ask me numerous questions like; "You mean you've ridden that bike all the way from Seattle…?" "Don't you get tired…?" "Where do you eat and sleep…?" "Are you running away from home…?" "Isn't it dangerous…?" "How far are you going…?" "Why are you doing it…?" "How many miles do you ride a day…?" "How many flats have you had…?" and so on.

I tell the kids that I have to get back on a paved road. And they say that they will show me a quick way to get off the bike path and back on the road. So, I ride with them until they cut down this steep bank. Here I have to get off and walk down with both my brakes locked up, and it's so steep and the grass is slick. My foot grip is a solid gob of mud. I have to put my bike in front of me, and sit on my butt and slide down. Once I get down, the kids tell me which way to go and they go their way and I go mine. I know good will eventually come out of the bad. My way is through a tunnel. The wet walls of the tunnel drip constantly on me as I ride under the Erie Canal.

Anyway, I'm finally back riding on Highway 31, now. I probably rode four or five miles on that dirt trail. It was a scenic route but that was far enough for me.

There is no wind at all.

I stop and get myself a Pepsi although I can't seem to quench a thirst with sugar drinks. There is nothing better then a cold beer and a ride in the country to satisfy me.

It's 12:50 p.m. I have 60 miles on the odometer as I ride through Fancher. I have between a five to 10 mph tailwind and it's 83 degrees. Above and off to my right, ropes are singing in their pulleys on a flagpole. The flags help me to determine the wind speed. The road is relatively flat as I ride along at a comfortable 13 mph pace.

There is a sign at a farm that says, "Black Raspberries, pick your own, Soon."

Riding through small villages…and through fields of deep green…I can smell all the smells of the season and be aware of all the changes. I feel like I'm getting younger every day. I'm not going to stop riding until I get old, and I won't get old until I stop riding.

My, what a wonderful day it is. I always feel great when the wind is at my back. I am just out of Holley, the sweetness of unseen honeysuckle wafts through the afternoon air like a warm fog. There is no wind at all.

I have a flat tire. But Hey…! What the heck…! If things don't go wrong once in a while, how am I know when they are going right? I sit down on a curb in Brockport and pull out the limp tube…replace it with a new one…pump it up and I'm back on my way in less than ten minutes. Not bad, I'm thinking to myself.

There is a lot more traffic now, but it's no problem because I still have a four-foot wide blacktop shoulder and there haven't been any Big Rigs all day.

I make another stop at a little Deli. Tony…the guy behind the counter…is short and stocky…like a pit bull…with black hair and a bushy mustache. I'm really pigging out. I order a large Coke…a large peanut butter malt…and a cheeseburger with fries. I eat about $7.50 worth of junk food. It's good junk food though, and it fills me up.

As I leave the Deli I have between a five to 10 mph tailwind.

Well, it's a five to 7 mph tailwind. Somewhere in that vicinity, anyway. One thing is for sure, it's 87 degrees. I have 83 miles on my odometer as I ride into Rochester.

The river running through town has a mucky bottom and is a color somewhere between that of wet sand and chocolate milk.

I probably have about a 5 mph tailwind now. It's a little hard to tell in town. I'm in downtown Rochester. Thank God, it's Sunday. There is little traffic and that's just fine with me. Riding through, what I call, an industrial wasteland, isn't enjoyable for me. The sweet scent of hay fields and vineyards and pine forests is replaced with the pungent odor of refineries and sewage plants and chemical works. Buses and semis roar past me with their occupants sealed in a protective shell of steel and glass. As they travel along in their world of chrome and plastic…in their air-conditioned coffins…with exhaust pipes, I'm sure they are not even aware of all the pollution they are creating. I happily ride out of town. The river is running under the road, and the wind is blowing over it. There are fantastic and new sounds everywhere. I even heard a horse fart. In Macedon I pause to admire an old stone bridge with an algae-green stream flowing below. There is a beautiful little waterfall that can only be seen if you stop and look through one of the arches of the bridge.

With 114 miles in at 5:57 p.m. I'm just outside of Palmyra, and the first big truck of the day goes around me. WOW…! I have a surge of adrenaline and an accelerated heartbeat as a sparrow flies right into me.

I ride over the tar-filled cracks in the road. It sort of sounds like I'm riding over sticky flypaper.

Further along the road, the farms around Port Gibson are beautiful, with clean white houses…red barns…rows of outbuildings…granaries…pig barns…chicken coops…tractor sheds…and tool sheds all brightly painted.

There is a sign, just across the ditch. Well, there are actually two signs. One reads, "Newark One Mile." The other reads, "Nelleys Bar and Grill, Topless Waitress." An arrow is pointing toward Newark. I'm figuring, "What the heck…!" I could use something to nibble on, I mean a bite to eat. So I'm following the arrows. At the edge of town there is another arrow, so I follow it to another and another. Now, Newark is only a two-street town and I follow the arrows around these two streets, (twice). I haven't yet found any Topless Bar and Grill…! So, I stop in the only filling station in town and ask where Nelley's is. This big man with a monk-like bald spot that's slowly spreading across the top of his head laughs and says, "There isn't any place called Nelleys and there never has been. We just put those signs up to get people to come to our town." Well, I guess the joke's on me.

It's 6:45 p.m. I've ridden 122 miles today. I check into a motel room in Newark. I had a quite an easy day today…with a 10 mph tailwind most of the way. The first half of the day was quite flat and the second half…from Rochester on…was a little bit rolling…but not too bad.

Well, I did it again today. I burnt my big nose. Oh, well.

Newark looks like a little bitty crossroads town to me, but there must be something here because it has a big Sheraton Hotel in it.

* * *

I walk downtown and get some Tang and cinnamon rolls for tomorrow morning. I'll probably eat a couple of them tonight. I can't resist good food.

I stop at the Corner Tavern on my way back to the motel for a couple beers. It's been a bright day…so…as I walk in the darkness of the bar I almost fall over a stool. I might have walked right by a glass sitting on the bar, but my timing was perfect. As I sit there…thoroughly enjoying my beer…a soft sound behind me makes me turn around. A girl…a remarkably pretty girl…with long brown hair curling around her ears…is standing there. She's got rather timid-looking dark blue eyes. Her face is flushed a little with embarrassment as she returns from the bathroom, (where women go to do whatever they do). It's easy to see that she isn't wearing a bra and to be frank…she doesn't need one. She's really making her dress look good. Of course, she would look good in whatever she wears. As matter of fact…she would look good…wearing nothing.

She's young and she's lovely. She sits down next to me and asks me if I have a light. Now…I don't smoke…but I immediately say, "Yeah," thinking I just might have one. It's certainly worth a look, and who would say no at a time like this…? The bartender sees me going through my pockets and kindly hands me a book of matches. As I light her cigarette, she gently wraps her hands around mine. They're as warm as toast. Although I know that babies aren't made this way, it's as close as I've come for quite some time. I stare at her ring finger, trying to see if she's carrying any gold. As we talk, I feel good...I have all the right answers to all her questions. We eat hot dogs. After she finishes eating one in front of me, I feel even closer to her. We drink beer...lots of beer. We eat Pizza and drink more beer. She tells me that she loves men that drink from a glass and not a bottle. After she tells me that most girls around here get married before they are eighteen...whether they're pregnant or not...she rests her hand on my thigh and softly whispers to me, "I love your rippling thigh muscles". She asks me where I'm staying...and I give her my room number...just because I like women. I think they are fascinating. Besides, I'm only a few days short of the end of my tour and maybe...just maybe...I'll get lucky. Now I'm not an adulterer...maybe a fornicator which sounds even worse. Oh, Well.

I'm back in my room now. I listen to the weather report and eat a cinnamon roll. I stay up until well after 2:00 a.m. I sort of feel like I did at Christmas time when I was waiting for Santa Claus to come.

Well, she never came. I guess if you don't expect anything you'll never be disappointed. I must admit that I was a little disappointed when I finally crawled underneath fresh sheets, to sleep alone.

*   *   *

*Statistics for **DAY TWENTY-FIVE** Sunday, July 9, 1989.*
122 miles on riding today, 13.3 average miles per hour for today, 2,849 miles of riding in 25 days, 114 average miles of riding per day.

Day Twenty-Six

From Newark, New York
To Sangerfield, New York

I awaken on Monday, July the 10th, and I turn on the television to see if I can catch the weather. I missed it last night.

At 8:35 a.m. I leave the motel, mount my bike and head on down the road. It's overcast and pretty warm out already this morning (80 degrees). I have a strong 20 mph crosswind, from the right, which will be great after I make a turn…about 20 miles up the road.

I'm carried along by the soft, sweet fragrance of two-foot high roadside flowers. They are a lot of blue wild flowers swaying in the breeze. I'm pedaling hard but I'm making very slow progress with this wind. It's like swimming upstream against a heavy current.

I know I'll never see Rose again, but I've already thought about her about a million times. As I stare into these flowers I still see her smiling face.

There are a lot of wildflowers all along the edge of the road and huge green pastures beyond that. It sure is beautiful country. Riding along in this rolling terrain, I notice an owl perched as if it's an extension of a fence post. Right out here in the light of day, its brown mottled feathers are all puffed out and its ears are alert and pointing skyward.

I'm rolling through the sleepy little town of Phelps. It's been a long time since I've seen a town with diagonal parking on main streets. There is cloud cover all over the sky, for which I'm grateful. It's 81 degrees now and, if the sun comes out from behind the clouds, it's going to be a scorcher.

As the road bends southeast I have a bothersome 25 mph crosswind blowing against me and it's continuing to slow me down. There is nothing worse than being forced into one of my lowest gears, on flat land...pushing my hardest on my pedals...only to reach a ridiculous slow speed.

This is the strongest crosswind I've had yet. Every so often I see a giant tree lying uprooted, blown over. I'm down on my drops just pedaling...not thinking...just pedaling. In spite of all my efforts, my average speed is constantly dropping. That's all right though, I'll get my reward as soon as I get to Geneva and make my left turn, then I should have a nice tailwind.

The road just changed directions as sharply as a rabbit. That was a very...very...hard 14.66 miles I just rode. I have a 15-mph tailwind now. Yes a tailwind...!

At 10:30 a.m. I am ready for breakfast in Waterloo. I walk into the restaurant, the hostess leads me past a bouquet of flowers that are slumped over a pitcher on a table, way back in the corner of the room. This table is as far away from everybody as possible. I don't know if it's because I look like a drowned rat, or because I smell like one. As soon as she leaves I get up and take a window seat. It's really a super hot and muggy day today. I order a hot cup of coffee...then wonder why, as sweat from my nose drips into the cup. I order buckwheat pancakes, because they are supposed to be good for me, although I can't figure out why. If they are supposed to be so good for me...why do they smother them in butter, and bring you hot syrup to pour all over them? I try to cut into them with my fork, notice...I say try. It's impossible...! When I finally get a piece cut with a sharp knife I try to stab it with my fork, another impossible feat. I have to slide my fork under it...like a forklift, and hoist it up to my mouth. So much for health food. Looking into the coffee grounds at the bottom of my cup I figure it's time to go.

I'm on my way again. It's as hot out here as the inside of a baker's oven on a June night in New Orleans. It's just a HOT, muggy, July day as I ride out of Waterloo. It is a very steamy 91 degrees already and this morning and the humidity weighs a ton. Unable to penetrate the summer haze, the morning sun hangs over Seneca Falls much like a harvest moon.

This countryside is downright beautiful. It looks like scenes from *"Gone With the Wind,"* with huge groves of trees that appear to date back to the beginning of time, providing shade for the plantation-style mansions. Old houses with front porches...upstairs and down, remind me of New Orleans. Massive gate posts, some of them masterpieces of brick or stone...guard long...sweeping driveways...compelling my eyes to look and see.

I have at least a 20 mph tailwind, now. It's hotter this morning than any time I've experienced on this tour yet. I'm breathing heavily and just a dripping with sweat. The sweat on my forehead is trickling into my eyes...dripping off the end of my nose onto my mustache...then seeping into my mouth as I ride. It's so hot and humid that my jersey is soaking wet, even though I have this 20 mph tailwind. It seems that the faster I pedal, the more I perspire. I have to stop often and wipe some of the sweat out of my eyes.

I'm struggling up this hill, in second gear...dripping like a leaky faucet. I have to wipe the sweat out of my eyes, again. The mercury has reached ninety-two, and I'm sure the humidity matches or exceeds that. It's hotter than Africa...!

A line of hot red skin that runs across the bridge of my nose is peeling today.

The green countryside and the downhills coax me ever onward. I have at least a 20 to 25 mph tailwind now. I am forced to take breaks more frequently and to drink much more water. I sure hope I can find a bar tonight so I won't dehydrate.

As I ride through Auburn, the blacktop seems to vibrate in the heat, and the water I have in my water bottles is hot enough to brew tea. I've come to the conclusion that bicycle touring is the ultimate full-sweat...full-body workout.

Humid heat waves are boiling up, turning dusty tractors into shimmering distortions. I'm riding on a roller coaster road. It's HOT and humid, but, I figure…after riding this far…I should be in good enough shape to handle anything.

This is a wonderfully smooth, lightly traveled blacktop road that snakes its way through the countryside. It's like riding on a giant roller coaster. I'm going to call this the Peak-to-Peak Highway. I climb up 1,000 feet…then coast down 800 feet…then up another 500 feet…and then down again. There are few…if any…flat spots on the road. But the beauty of the forests…the wildflowers…the quiet farms and lush green meadows…combined with the wonderful breathtaking views…make riding a pleasure. Even though I'm perspiring like a cold beer on a hot day.

I think the last time I sweat this much, I was in bed, and I can't remember that far back.

"Oh, YES I CAN…!"

I'd better call my girlfriend tonight.

It's 1:25 p.m. as I stop at a Deli for some much needed lunchtime shade in Skaneateles. I often wonder why is it that most restaurants have these little bitty holes in their pepper shakers? Is pepper that expensive?

Here's something I've learned about food.

There are four basic food groups;

1) food that causes heart attacks;

2) food that causes cancer;

3) food that causes strokes;

4) and food that's bland but harmless, unless you choke on it.

So I say, eat and drink what you want…whenever you want…and as much as you want. Just remember, most dinosaurs ate plants (healthy food) and they're all dead. Ninety-nine percent of the people who drink milk die before they're a hundred.

I know that malts are not a vegetable, but I believe they are just as good for you. I believe that the secret is in how you chew your food. You should chew your food thoroughly. Get in the habit of counting your "chews" before you swallow. Allow 5 for vegetables...10 for meat...20 for bones...30 for gum and 40 for fruitcake.

I'm coming face to face with a little known fact (at least to me anyway) that New York State is NOT...FLAT...!

This tour has rewarded me with many...many...miles of dramatic beauty. Off to my right are small houses clinging to a hillside, like droplets of water on a leaf. And to my left are tiny Monopoly houses on a valley farmland.

It's 2:40 p.m. I have 60 miles on the odometer and it's cooled down to 82 degrees. I have a 10 mph tailwind as I ride through Marietta.

I'm in second gear climbing a hill that makes men out of boys and heroes out of grandfathers. And, to make things even worse, my gears aren't working very well. They are jumping in and out. I'm taking on water like an old steam engine as a double clutching truck slowly passes me.

*   *   *

Mikey, my friend...told me that there weren't any hills in New York. I'm not too sure about that. I've been in second gear for an awfully long time now.

Let me tell you a little about Mikey. Most cyclists' hero is Greg LaMond. Mine is Mike Pielate (Mikey). We've worked together at *Rocketdyne* for six years.

When I first started riding, I had a $100.00 Sears...Free Spirit...bike. When I rode I wore walking shorts, and a tee shirt and tennis shoes. And I weighed about 224 lbs.

Mikey, on the other hand had a $1,000.00 bike. He's skinny, and races in the *U.S.C.F. (United States Cycling Federation)*. He trains every day. He does intervals on hills I can't even ride up.

I'm 15 years his senior.

It would be easy for Mikey to make fun of me, or simply have nothing to do with me. But, he's not that kind of a guy. He has always encouraged me. When I would ride 7 miles to work, he would say, "Great Job, Harold" Now, 7 miles isn't even a warm-up ride for him. We're good friends and we still ride together once in a while. I've improved quite a lot in the last few years. Mikey's only about twice as fast as I am now. When we're out riding and come to a big hill…he usually takes off and rides hard to the top (to get a good workout) then he always comes back down…and rides up again with me.

He's tops in my book.

He lived in New Jersey for 15 years and he told me that there weren't any hills in New York. Well, there may not be any hills here, but there are a few mountains. Maybe he meant New York City.

This #@&%#! road is just one hill after another. I'm really starting to hate roads with names like…Hillcrest…Highland…Mountain High…North Pass…Mountain Ridge…Mountain Gate…Ridge Crest…Summit Road…Summit Crest and Lookout trail. This kind of road may have great lookouts but they really aren't much fun to ride on.

It's hotter than a June bride out here. I'm saturated from head to toe with sweat. Even my riding gloves are wringing wet.

I have a slight downhill as I silently glide through the quiet little village of Amber. I'm getting an exciting new view around every corner. This is the first time, since I was a kid that I've seen kids with shoes with the toes out.

There seems to be a glitter coming from my spokes as I roll along. Does it sound like I like downhills…? You bet your sweet ass I do. The terrain and I continue to roll. From each hilltop, all that's visible are more hilltops…with the next town sitting atop the highest one in sight. As I ride along in this warm climate, I can hear the electric wires humming overhead and each time I pass a utility pole, the tone of the hum changes.

There is little, to no traffic on this road. All I see ahead of my front wheel is another hill. But there are some spectacular views all around me.

Off in the distance I see a large bird…maybe an eagle…on the very top of a tall tree. I stop to see if I can identify it. With a flap of it's monstrous wings, it takes off…gliding like a small piper cub and coming to rest in a tree on the edge of the woods beyond the meadow where I first spied him. There he sits, with wings folded at his side. A massive and impressive sights even at a thousand yards. I watch and watch, reluctant to go on while he still sits there. But, it's obvious he's in no hurry to fly again, so I'm going to ride on.

I have a 15 to 20 mph tailwind as I ride out of Vesper.

The, (what I thought would be flat) grasslands of New York State, are pretty damn hilly. I know my plan was to ride as much as possible on back and secondary roads but I wish I had stayed on Highway 20. This #%@Z! road is nothing but one hill after another. I would like to stop, but I'm so sweaty, I'm afraid that if I stop to rest, here in Tully, I'll rust.

It's 4:13 p.m. as I stop in a little grocery store to get some milk to drink in Apulia Station. It's 84 degrees. I drink a quart of milk and eat a couple of Reese's peanut butter cups. Um, Umm, Good…!

Sweat is dropping off the end of my nose as I lick the salt-water from my upper lip. I can smell the rain and hear a lot of thunder, now. I'm riding under a two-tone sky where the low clouds to the south are growing darker and darker. Only about a half-mile away it's darkened and I see a lot of lightning. And here comes the wind. I don't think I've ever seen it blow so hard. A blast of wind just bent the trees down and turned up the pale white underside of the leaves. It's bending small trees into bows and snapping them like buggy whips. It's a loud, cracking storm. The thunder sounds like empty barrels rolling down-stairs, and they're long stairs and the barrels bounce a good deal.

I have 80 miles on the odometer and between a 25 to 30 mph tailwind as I ride out of Apulia. Whenever there is a thunderstorm brewing the wind always picks up. But I have to keep pedaling forward, just like the hands on a clock. After all, if they are not moving forward, what good are they?

This two-lane blacktop road is quite scenic, and relatively well maintained. But they sure didn't make any allowances for all the hills. I'm riding up this hill so slowly…in low gear, I can just barely keep my balance. I realize that we all have our ups and downs but this is ridiculous…! I'll make it though. I haven't walked my bike yet, and I won't. It's against my religion.

I finally made it to the top of that hill. Now, ever so slowly…I'm climbing another one…in low gear again. This is not a leisurely ride in the park. I'll do it once, but I resolve, never to do this road again. If I were to do this tour again, I would stay on Highway 20. I sure wouldn't take this #%@Z! road. I don't know what grade this hill is…but…with a 30 mph tailwind…it's still taking all I've got to get up it.

Just a little ways over to my left it's pouring down rain. I'm going to stop at the first motel I come to. Of course, that might be quite a ways. There is no civilization around these here parts. Only a few houses that are being lived in and many empty ones and vacant lots.

The afternoon has welcomed me with rain showers, I guess to make sure I'm not lacking in humidity. Unfortunately, the rain jacket I have leaks in a hard rain. The waterproof material is supposed to breathe…to push my perspiration out from the inside…but not allow rain to penetrate in from the outside. Maybe I've got the damn thing on inside out. The mountains are dripping raindrops, just to let me know who's the boss. I can see the rain coming and I ride as fast as possible, looking for some kind of shelter. I go through a hard rain now toward a porch. I push my bike up onto this covered wooden sidewalk then shake some of the water off me, much like a dog. The sound my tires make on the wood is awesome. This sort of reminds me of a time when I was riding with a girl on a pier in California. She said it was as much fun as a vibrator, and you don't need batteries.

*   *   *

As I slowly push my bike down the wooden walkway past false-fronted abandoned buildings, I come to this small old Post Office. I would guess it to be about 150 years old, about the same age as an ex-wife collecting alimony lives to be. I go inside and about two minutes later the sky drops its entire load of water. Sheets of rain descend, thunder claps...and lightning crackles.

To pass the time during the storm, I go inside the Post Office and chat to the owner. His name is Elmer. He's a neatly dressed man well along in years, with a Greek face and fine wind-lifted white hair and a clipped white mustache. His wife is old and looks even older...all the same...she is a very nice person. I drink a half-gallon of milk, which I purchase in the combination grocery...hardware...Post Office and home (they live upstairs). This is definitely a one-store town. The thunderstorm rages overhead, shaking the Post Office ceiling. As the wind picks up...the lights start blinking...then they go off all together.

I pull out my road maps. But, to find out where you are going...you must first know where you are...and I don't. The couple running the Post Office says they're retired and are running the store just to keep busy. I tell them that they look too young to be retired. I'm lying, but I know it'll please them. The gentleman gets a flashlight and we look at my maps. We discover that I have made a wrong turn...back the road aways...and I shouldn't even be on this road. But I am, so they help me pick out the best route back to Highway 20...where I should have been all along.

At 5:42 p.m. the sky has stopped falling and the wind has almost stopped blowing, so I'm on my way again. It's sprinkling a little. I know now that it's better to ride in the rain in my shirtsleeves and shorts...because a shower from the sky almost always feels better than the shower of sweat caused by the combination of my rain gear and the humidity. The only exception is when it's a cold rain.

Leaving New Woodstock, the hill continues to climb...as I do in my lowest gear. I continue to ride through a near rain forest of ferns and big leafy trees just dripping from the afternoon's rain. The sunlight makes crystals out of the raindrops on the tropical looking shrubs.

There is nothing but hills...hills...hills...and more hills. I'm getting pretty damn sick of hills. I have to look at the bright side though, the temperature has dropped about 10 degrees after the rain, and the air smells fresh and clean. It's a lot different from the air in L.A., which you don't only smell but you can see, as well.

Riding along out here, I can smell the pine trees...the new-mown hay...the wildflowers...and the smell of freshly plowed dirt. The birds were gurgling, instead of singing. Ain't it great to be alive and well...!

I'm five miles east of Sheds at 6:25 p.m. The rain has stopped but the hills continue. It's been uphill ever since I left the Post Office. Elmer, at the Post Office, told me that there were two major hills that I would have to climb before I got back to Highway 20.

You know, light from the sun travels at a rate of 186,000 miles a second, but that's no big deal...it's downhill all the way.

It's been a very rough day so far. The roads are wet and the earth is soggy from the recent rain. The country smells wonderful after the storm, and the sun's slowly casting its pink glow on the hills. I'm not even to the major hills Elmer was telling me about, but I'm in low gear again. These hills make the streets of San Francisco pale by comparison.

I haven't had a bike with S.I.S. shifting that's shifted worth a shit, yet.

I'm trying to distinguish the shallow puddles from the potholes.

Civilization seems far away. It seems a though I'm the only man left on earth. It's so peaceful. Sometimes I'm glad for the company of silence…It makes for a perfect situation for thinking. Sometimes the nicest sound I hear is no sound at all. There's still a faint smell of rain in the air.

I have between a 5 to 10 mph tailwind. The rain has washed the air clean, and patches of blue sky appear overhead…the birds are beginning to fly out of the woods and rabbits are coming out of their holes. The sun, which has been absent all afternoon has come out in full force to light my way. All I can hear out here is the humming of my own tires and the many…many birds singing to me. Sometimes it's really nice to get off the beaten path if there aren't a lot of hills. I always take the scenic route, although sometimes by mistake.

It feels like it's cooled down a little, and the wind has almost stopped. It's beautiful out again. The sun…, everything…, and me are shining. I'm spinning along this road riding toward West Eaton, listening to the grass grow. A true bicycle tourist is never in a hurry to get anywhere. Quiet country roads are what cyclists live for.

I can hear this bell, way off in the distance.

A little deer just ran across the road, right in front of me. Now it's turning around and running back like a streak.

The bell I hear is a cowbell. The cow is standing next to the fence by the road.

There is a little gray in the sky now, with little rays of hope shining through. It's 7:41 p.m. I have 110 miles on the odometer as I ride out of Madison. The hills have smoothed themselves out into rolling dairy farms. This is my favorite kind of ride. The momentum of one downhill swoop propels me up the next rise. The land and road roll on and on like an endless sea. I'm spinning along like the wheels of a well-greased machine.

I ride along, listening to the birds singing.

I stop to observe the wildflowers…not only to look at…but also to see them…up close. I hear the whispering uproar of butterflies in an adjoining meadow. Slowly, with the lengthening of the tree shadows, I mount my bike and roll on.

*   *   *

I'm at a crossroads, which has a run-down motel on one corner…and a Steak House (that's out of business) on the other corner. There is a liquor store across the street and a tavern, kitty corner across from the motel. There is a sign on one corner that says Singerfield, one mile. I don't actually like the looks of this motel, so I'm going to ride on into town and see what's there. I ride for about a mile and a half and I don't see any motels. So, being tired…and knowing that it's getting late…I reluctantly resort to asking this weather-worn gent setting on his porch…where all the motels are in town. There is an old dog lying at his feet, retired just as I imagine he is. You know, it's amazing how most dogs look like their owners. They are both half asleep, have the same color hair, and almost the same length noses (I believe the dog's is a little shorter). He speaks from the side of his mouth and tells me that there is a hotel in town…but the best place to stay…is at the motel at the crossroads. So, I beat it back there and walk into the office dripping wet, stepping on a soggy doormat. The proprietor is a fat, toothless man in a sleeveless shirt. He is kind enough to give me a cup of coffee and a room for $22.00. It's not too bad of a room, except for the fact that it doesn't have any air-conditioning.

I've ridden 118 very hard miles today. I did a lot of hill climbing…I mean a lot of hill climbing…! I've been wringing wet most of the day from sweating as well as the rain.

*   *   *

I've shaved and showered and I'm pretty dehydrated from all my hill climbing today. I think a beer will do me some good, so it's off to the local pub for a tall one or two. As I walk in the bar there is a band playing but nobody seems to be listening. The bartender is a stocky man with a healthy stomach hanging over pants that are cut off below the knees. He has a wide belt that struggles to retain his stomach. He's definitely a fellow beer drinker. While I sample the local beer, I look around a bit. There is a ten-point buck trophy above the door. A gallon jar of pickled pig's feet and hard-boiled eggs is on the back bar. A sign behind the bar reads, "Beware of wife." And at the pool table…in the middle of the room…is one tough-looking broad. She has sleek legs…wears a tank top over her ample size boobs. She's wearing cut-offs that have the absolute maximum of strategic cutting. In the smoky atmosphere, all eyes in the bar are fixed on her as she bends over to shoot pool. If I could be arrested for my thoughts, I would probably be in jail right now. I undress her in my mind…as I suspect every other man in the bar has already done. As I watch her, I can see that she's not a good shot…but that doesn't matter. She's still manages to beat every one she plays. That's because they really don't care much about the game, they just want to watch her play. They know good entertainment when they see it. Most men are not as dumb as most women think they are.

HAROLD IN LOVE

Seated next to me at the bar is a short, balding man with a spare chin. He has something sticking out of the side of his mouth, it looks as though it might have once been a cigar. He asks me if I have a match, I tell him that I don't smoke. He says, "That's the trouble with today, nobody smokes anymore. It's hard to find people with matches." I say, "They probably all died of lung cancer". There are several rough and rowdy women slumped over in a booth with their heads on the table. They lift their heads every once in a while and talk to each other. I can catch only bits and pieces of their conversation. One of them mentions that she likes whip-cream. The other says she prefers chocolate syrup, because it's harder to lick off. Then the jukebox starts and all I can hear is the music. By the time the music stops they have both got up and gone into the bathroom. I think I've learned a lot about women over the years…but…for the life of me…I don't know why they always go to the bathroom two at a time. By this time the guy with the chewed-up cigar is totally obnoxious. He's one of these, who…just add liquor…becomes an instant asshole. He's mumbling something about one woman and that was enough for anyone…and one-half would be even better. I would have liked to slip a king-size rubber over his head, but I'm always polite to people bigger than I am.

A few stools down they are talking about work and women. All they have is little 6-oz. beer glasses (what I call shot glasses). Before the bartender could return with my change, my glass would be empty again. You've got to understand, beer is like potato chips, and nobody can have just one. Well, he finally gets tired of filling my glass, so he goes into the kitchen and comes out with a pint mug just for me. We're both happy now. He says that the 6 oz. glasses were for normal people, not me. I order a steak sandwich and fries, and a few more beers. Last night I was drinking beer brewed in Rochester; tonight I'm drinking beer brewed in Utica. It's their local beer, and it's pretty good stuff. I leave the tavern and walk over to the liquor store and get myself some Doritos corn chips and a quart of milk. That sounds like a good combination to me. I take them back to my motel room and finish them off.

I leave the windows wide open because it's quite warm out and they have screens on them. Right outside my front window there is a bug zapper that keeps sizzling bugs all night long. There are no flies or mosquito's in L.A. I believe the smog kills them off. As I sit on the john and relax...I notice a small...neatly penciled...poem directly in front of me on the door...it reads: Some come here to shit and stink, some come here to sit and think, but I come here to scratch my balls and read the writings on the walls. Anyway, as I'm sitting here I wonder whether Kevin Costner or Dan Haggerty (now that John Wayne is in Hillbilly heaven) would be the right actor to play me in the movie version of my tour.

I try to call my daughter, and of course, she isn't home. It's 11:00 p.m. and I'm going to fall into a self-satisfying sleep now, as a moon as new as an egg is resting in the weatherless sky above the hills.

*   *   *

*Statistics for **DAY TWENTY-SIX** Monday, July 10, 1989.*
118 miles of riding today, 12.9 average miles per hour for today, 2,967 miles of riding in 26 days, 114 average miles of riding per day.

Day Twenty-Seven

From Sangerfield, New York
To Hyde Park, New York

At 6:00 a.m. I get up and walk over to get breakfast. The morning has dawned with a clear sky and not a breath of wind…or a cloud in the sky…and the sun's up and shining bright. It's just another perfect morning.

I'm walking over to a small truck stop for breakfast. I order the usual: potatoes…eggs…toast and bacon…and of course…my coffee.

The waitress, who looks to be in her early thirties has perfectly molded legs. She has nice rounded…firm buttocks…her breasts are ample, and well-shaped. She has short red hair (by the way, did you know that redheads are rusty blondes) and a wide smile. She's wearing the usual waitress/cook outfit, which proves it isn't what you wear, but how you wear it. She looks good. She's soft spoken, and I caught a whiff of her faint, but very pleasant perfume as she cuts up with a trucker sitting next to me at the counter. He has gray hair the color of dried-out moss and a sharp little chin that juts out from his toothless mouth. His Adam's apple is bobbing like a cork as he talks. He's wearing denim…hat…jacket…pants…boots…and probably even underwear. The waitress is talking about Joe. Everybody in the Truck Stop agrees that Joe's death took them by surprise, because nobody knew he was alive. Another trucker, with salt and pepper hair that's thinning considerably and eyebrows that flare out like the wings of a butterfly, also mentions that his truck runs about as well as our government.

There is a group of farmers sitting at a table. One is wearing a cap that's very ratty and salt-crusted. He's licking at his mustache and drinking coffee. I guess they are sitting around having their morning meeting. They are smoking cigarettes and drinking coffee. A half dozen men and all wearing the same kind of clothes…baseball caps…long-sleeved shirts and cowboy boots. They don't have much to say. Early-rising men not only don't talk much to strangers, they barely talk to one another. Breakfast conversations are usually limited to a series of grunts.

I'm glad I walked over here before I started riding. There are a lot of rough-looking guys in here, and I would have looked a little bizarre walking in here wearing my bicycling clothes.

It's 7:18 a.m. as I slip my feet in the stirrups of my iron horse, and it's time for me to hit the trail. I ride along, watching the sunrise and the wheat fields turn to a brilliant butterscotch color against a blue sky, yielding me an awesome display. There seem to be a dozen shades of yellow and about twice as many shades of green. The fragrance is intoxicating. It smells like perfume to me. The road is straight as far as my eyes can see. The land and the road and I am rolling…rolling…just a rolling along. I've been on the road for one half-hour and I haven't seen anyone, yet.

This stupid bike isn't shifting very well this morning.

I'm riding on a scenic, lightly traveled backroad of America. Only once in a great while do I see a house. And when I do see one it has a yard that looks like a putting green. Every hillcrest reveals another postcard view of lush green fields…some with beautiful horses with flared nostrils…standing next to white painted fences…watching me roll past. My overwhelming sense of it all…though…is quiet…with no cars…no voices…and no wind. Then, all of a sudden…I hear this scratching on the blacktop just behind me. Now, I've heard this sound before so I immediately pick up my pace, then I look around. The dog's tongue is flopping up and down, dripping with saliva as he digs his paws into the blacktop. I don't know if this local hound thinks I'm a bird…raccoon…or possum…but he sure seems to enjoy chasing me down the road. Lucky for me, he seems to be all bark and no bite. There have been more dogs chase me in New York State than anywhere else on this tour.

No two of my days are ever alike, since both the weather and the terrain are constantly changing. Some of the hills are strenuous but the road surface and the spectacular scenery make it quite enjoyable all the same. I mention this because I'm climbing another hill and passing green farmlands with wonderful trees in the fencerows.

That Mikey's so full of shit. According to him this is a supposedly flat grassland. But it's pretty damn hilly. I'm in second gear, climbing another BIG hill.

When I was leaving the motel this morning, I met this man and his son. He was wide and square at his shoulders as if he'd forgotten to take the hanger out of his shirt. He and his son both had what I call electric hair…wild and curly. It wasn't quite blond and it wasn't quite brown…more of an applesauce color. They both had touring bikes. I talked to them for quite a while. They were riding from Rochester to New York City.

It's 69 degrees out this morning. It's HOT and I sweat a lot when I climb these hills…then…when I go down the other side…it's pretty damn cool.

I just rode up a killer of an uphill followed by a short downhill. I'm in low gear on this hill…but it's beautiful country…and I get a lot of time to enjoy it…crawling along at a four miles per hour pace.

I would say walking (and I don't mean hitchhiking) would be the best way to enjoy everything. But it sure would take a long time to walk across America. Maybe horseback riding would be the next best way, but not for me. I like to look at horses. I believe they are beautiful animals, but I'm not too fond of riding them. Besides, I like to do things under my own power. So it seems to me that biking is the best possible way (at least for me) to see the real United States.

There is no wind at all as I ride into West Wenfield. It's not quite as humid today as it was yesterday, which makes it nice.

This hill and I continue to climb through a forest with its lush green grass, and pine trees. I'm embraced by a quiet peacefulness, free of noise and exhaust fumes. I stop to lie down on a bed of pine needles. The smell of the pine is sweet. As I lie here in the cool shade, I close my eyes and think about pleasant things. Like the spring rain...a newborn calf...running horses...and fields of tall grass. And of gently rolling terrain, with long sweeping curves. The road, in my mind...seems to curve around forming into the figure of a beautiful lady's body with all the hills in the right places. Sometimes you just have to close your eyes to see. I'm admiring the beauties of Nature. I adore Nature and I enjoy life. Here I am, sounding romantic again. I think I had better call my girlfriend tonight.

I slowly sit up, and I watch a narrow brownish stream forming a ribbon in a sea of grass. It's a nice little stream snaking its way through the thick underbrush with its water running over the stones, collecting in little pools behind mossy rocks and trickling between them into lower pools. I could stay here all day, but I have to get going.

I figure that for every uphill there is an equally sized downhill...if that's the case...I have a lot of downhills coming. The mountainous nature of this terrain makes riding a little difficult, to say the least.

For miles now, there have been no power lines or billboards. Just trees...rocks...water...bushes...and the road. I love Rural America. All I can see from the top of these roller coaster hills, are more rollers.

As I ride along, a giant picture is stretched out before me. I can see the deep valleys that seem to cross each other in every direction.

The sun is out and the sky cloudless. It's a beautiful day and I intend to savor it. The creeks and rivers are running a muddy brown, too thin to plow and too thick to drink. They are so different from the clear mountain streams of Washington and Montana, but beautiful just the same.

I have a 5 mph tailwind. It's 9:30 a.m. and I've ridden 28 miles so far today.

I stop at Burger World, in Richfield Springs for another breakfast. I'm as hungry as a horse. By now, I'm wide-awake and ready to taste some of my day's fuel. There is a fine-looking girl sitting at the counter. She's got black hair and rosy red cheeks. She's plentiful without being plump and is wearing blue jeans…age-worn to maximum comfort…and a red-checked shirt. As I eat, there are five women sitting at an adjoining table, jabbering in two different languages. One is a spitting image of her mother. She's tall and boney. Not a good-looking girl, but being young has one advantage, she doesn't have anything cluttering up her mind. One is a short…dark…pudgy woman and she's wearing lots of religious jewelry. I swear her purse is big enough for a mugger to hide in. Another one has her face so thickly talcummed it's almost a dead white. Her layers of nail polish are chipping like paint on an old barn. I overhear one say, "What…? She isn't married but she has a child?" The young girl spoke up and says, "Yes, but it's a very little one."

I leave Burger World. I had a good carbo-loading meal. Well, maybe not so good. I had a fried baloney sandwich and a root beer float. I believe that most people have their morals all wrong. They eat for an alternative reason. I eat what I eat because I love good deep-fried food, and I feel wonderfully healthy.

Everybody in there was complaining about the humidity we had yesterday. It's not too bad today. At 10:07 a.m. It's 73 degrees as I ride out of East Springfield.

It's nice to be out here riding along in the crisp morning air, with no additives. The air smells a lot different out here than it does in L.A. I get all the smells, the good ones and not so good ones. The smell of fresh air…pine trees…new-mown hay…wildflowers…the smell of freshly plowed topsoil…especially right after a rain. I also get the not so good smells like a skunk or chicken shit…pigs and manure freshly spread on the fields. All this you miss when you are in a car. Ain't it great to be alive and well…!

I'm riding on highway 20, through Otsego County. It's full of dairy farms and fine old houses. I'm impressed with the natural beauty and charm of these wide-open spaces. Portions of the road are hilly…much like a roller coaster…over and over again…and some of the hills are really tough ones. I'm climbing a second gear hill right now. This is where the serious bikers don't ride Harleys but pedal twelve, fourteen and twenty-one speed Cannondale…Trek…and Paramounts.

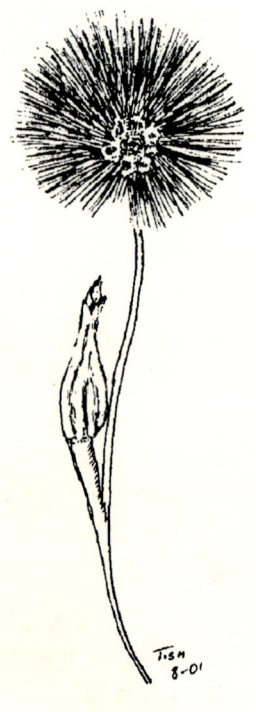

It's wonderful to see unspoiled villages and wooded hillsides…and dairy…grain and vegetable farms. In other words, farms surrounded by farms.

How different it is living a dream, from just dreaming it. This is definitely a tour of a lifetime. I enjoy being out here in nature, riding on uncluttered roads. If I look off to the south of me, I can see the blue summer skies filled with low-lying cotton-ball clouds that are almost totally obstructing some of the hills. The wind is very calm. I think I'll stay dry all day today. I'm just filled with the gladness of being alive. I'm atop one hill, with forest behind me and open land in front of me. There are gooseberry bushes and asparagus in the fencerows. And, on the other side of the fence, is a garden and a watermelon patch…then, even beyond that are more fields and woods. I feel like I'm at the top of the world looking down on all creation. I love to stop to pick some dandelions, hold them to my lips and blow gently and watch the tiny dark chutes float free of their fragile mooring.

This is ideal biking weather. My energy surges as I move through this countryside aromatically filled with alfalfa and clover. Oh…! The joys of cycling…! It's Thursday morning and there isn't much traffic. I have a 10 mph tailwind as I ride through Sharon Springs. This is where I turn south on route 10.

Each road has it's own particular memories. My pedals turn slowly through one of the most beautiful counties my eyes have ever rested upon. I'm in no more of a hurry than the clouds floating overhead. Riding opens my mind to thoughts. Ahead of my front wheel are silent green farmlands with small farms and pastures and mountainsides of maple and fir and alder and wet green moss. As I ride along, I study cloud patterns and the flight of birds. A northeast breeze wafts by me bringing a strong smell from a distant pig farm. I am amazed that I take my fresh country air far too much for granted.

The breakfast I had back in Richfield Springs was so good I can still taste it.

I stop to photograph a golden breasted meadowlark. There seems to be one on every other fence post.

A big, shiny new car, that...by its bumper sticker...I suspect...belongs to a Jehovah Witness. It looks out of place as it whips past very close to me. The driver is eating and driving. I suspect he's driving down the endless runway with his cruise control on but his brain in neutral. I wonder if it has occurred to him that he has even traveled through this beautiful country...or if he had seen anything at all. A passenger is clicking a camera through a closed window. I'm sure that the noise of the engine and soundproofing of the passenger compartment prevents them from telling whether the birds are singing or not.

I guess the entertainment of their trip occurs on the inside of the windshield, and later in photos. I see something dive into the ground. I slow for a woodchuck hole, then gradually resume my speed. I can't help but smile to myself as I roll along on two wheels.

At 11:36 a.m. I have 50 miles on the odometer and I'm nine miles south of Sharon Springs. I have a 15 mph tailwind and I'm still riding on rolling terrain.

There are tiny, familiar-looking dots up ahead on the other side of the road. They are rapidly taking the form of cyclists heading my way. Riders in the distance are unmistakable to me. I can't see the pedal motion at first, but I can see a short, body with legs that don't quite reach the ground. Basically, I'm a quiet person. (But I don't mind rattling off into this recorder). I don't consider myself to be a very entertaining conversationalist so I think I'll just pedal right on by and wave to them. Besides, I'm getting a little tired of telling stories about the few strange or scary incidents of my travels…when the real story lies in all the quiet…special moments in between.

But, they're flagging me down. As I coast in, I discover that they're a group of ten touring bicyclists. They're a young group of 4-H'ers riding their bikes from New York City to Rochester. They're riding 160 miles in a week. They're led by two college professors, one of whom…I found out…has written an unimportant textbook. He's about middle height…but the thinness of his body…and the length of his legs…gives him the appearance of being much taller. They have a lot of questions for me. The first of which is:

"Where did you start from and where are you riding to?" Followed by, "Are you a professional rider or a teacher?"

I tell them that I'm an amateur, which simply means that I'm doing what I'm doing for the love of it and not for fame or money.

"How much rain have you run into?"

I told them that I've only had a few sprinkles, and that I don't even bother putting rain gear on anymore. Instead, I just get wet, because I know I'll dry off quickly enough as soon as the sprinkles stop.

"How do you feel after riding 3,000 miles?"

"I feel the best I've ever felt in my life."

"What was the hardest part?"

"Getting up in the mornings."

A beefy young guy with a face as red as a fire hydrant asks me,

"Does your ass ever get sore?"

I say, "You bet my ass does, even with space age padded cycling shorts it still gets sore."

Then one kid asks me,

"How old are you?"

I tell him that age is just a number, you're as young as you feel. Then I chuckle to myself, because I've always wanted to say that but the occasion has never presented itself before.

Then one kid asks me,

"How does Washington State compare to New York State?"

I say, "You can't compare any two states. It would be like trying to compare apples and oranges, which is better?"

Then one of the leaders asks me if I could give them any advice.

I say, "Sure...! Don't push yourself. Ride at your own pace, no matter what it is. Everybody rides at a different pace." I tell them that I don't ride fast, just far.

Then the other leader asks me,

"What have you got out of your tour?"

I have to think about that one a minute. Then I answer by saying, "I will always remember the adrenaline rush as a dog chases me...and the memories of hearing the rain fall on my helmet and seeing the first robin of the spring...the education of it all. I tell them not to settle for the ordinary. There is only one way to find out if you like something, and that's to do it. I go on to say, "Ride your bike all the way across America some time. It's something you'll never forget. You'll love it. There is never a dull moment. It'll give you a new lease on life." I say, "Use the talents you possess. The woods would be very silent if no birds sang except those that sang the best. How little we realize the privileges we enjoy. We must always have old memories and young hopes." And with that we wish each other good luck, and we go our separate ways.

*   *   *

It's past lunchtime and I'm still lunchless so I stop at a McDonalds in Cobleskill.

At 12:37 p.m. I leave good old McDonalds. I have a 15 mph tailwind and it's 82 degrees. I stop in Howes Cave to call my daughter. No luck.

Higher and higher the road climbs hanging to the mountain edge as if it were tacked on. All I can see is the sky and clouds. It's almost like flying. I guess I'm not in Kansas anymore, Toto. I've just ridden up a mile long, second-gear hill.

As I ride along this country road, my mind starts to wonder. I'm having daydreams about night things, in the middle of the afternoon. You know, when you're working and rushing around, you don't have time to experience the creative side of your brain. That's why I believe you have to get away from it all and just be by yourself from time to time. As I chest, I mean crest the summit, I stop to take a sip (of Tang). After stopping on the peak, I pedal on...sort of gliding my way over the smooth curves. Down the road I can see a dense forest that I'll be entering into shortly. Then as I slap, snap back to reality...I realize I'm riding along the last leg of my tour, into the foothills of the Catskill Mountains. It seems that when you try not to think of something, you tend to...you tend to...think...of it more.

I think I'd better call my girlfriend tonight.

I learned to travel, now I travel to learn. I believe that if you absorb enough parts from enough places you'll create your own whole. Home and work seem to be a thousand miles away, (actually they are 3,000). I'm as free as a bird. Ain't Life Grand...!

Wheeling over the countryside, I find plenty of time to observe the view-a-rama of rolling countryside, dressed in early summer green and newly opened wildflower accessories. All this looks as though it was professionally landscaped, and I guess it was. All the peaks and valleys were landscaped by the same person.

Our maker said that we should place more confidence in Him and He will take care of us. What a promise, and how little we appreciate it.

I'm effortlessly pedaling closer and closer to Middleburgh, through rolling country with fields of grain stretching to the sky...on ranches that are far apart. A tailwind is propelling me through even more spectacular scenery now. I'm getting more pleasure in just one month of riding than I could in a whole lifetime in a city.

God's shining on me. It's amazing how good I feel when it warms up a few degrees. I'll bet it's always warm and sunny in Heaven…and I know there aren't any cars there.

Calves with their tails stretched out are running around their grazing mothers who chew their cud and watch as I ride past.

I recall reading the Berlin paper when I was in High School and all that was in it was *4/H* and *Future Farmer of America*…and *Boy Scout* news…School Board meeting and Town Council meeting…and of course…the Church service schedules. It seems as though more people who moved away from Berlin subscribed to the local paper than people that lived there. I often wonder why…? Do you suppose that they want to see if they had made the right move?

At 1:26 p.m. I ride through the pleasant…old…sleepy…little town of Middleburgh…nestled in between two green mountain ranges. There's a dog sleeping right in the middle of the street. This town definitely has character. Most towns of this size have at least one bakery and I sure could use a cinnamon roll.

I've been living in the big city way too long. It's been years since I've seen a little boy playing with a puppy. You know you are in a small town if someone asks you how you feel and spends the time to listen to what you have to say. They are not just trying to make conversation. I thank God for all the small towns and the people that live in them. It's a great way to live. It's America as far as I'm concerned.

I'm riding along on the wings of a friendly 10 mph tailwind. I roll down into a ravine of this absolutely beautiful valley. Roadside wildflowers are as abundant as crops. They cover the slopes, and their scent fills the air. Weathered gray barns and farmhouses are set out amongst the valleys and bluffs. It's so beautiful out here. It looks like a *Hamms* commercial.

I've fallen in love. I've fallen in love with this wild, beautiful country of ours and everything it contains. It's the kind of love people dream of having with other people...selfless and free of doubt...reverent and everlasting.

Boy...! I sure could use a peanut butter malt.

I have at least a 15 mph tailwind as I freewheel along past cornfields waving in the wind. With 70 miles in at 2:00 p.m. I stop in Franklinton and try to call my daughter again...Of course, she isn't home.

I'm getting an extremely fast, pleasant, wind-blown downhill ride here. A 20 mph tailwind pushes me along as fast as lightning around blind curves but, Hey...! Life is a daring adventure or it's nothing...!

It's weird what comes to your mind when you're on a bike all day.

I'll explain, I was just thinking.

Why do they call tall people tall?

Short people are called short.

And what's the opposite of short?

That's right, Long.

So there are short people and there are long people.

At least, that's what my girlfriend says.

I'm freewheeling along on a brand-new road just out of Livinstonville.

Riding downhill, on a brand-new road like this one...with a 20 mph tailwind...is great...! This is the way cycling is supposed to be...!

A trivia question here;

When they state that a mountain pass is so many feet above sea level. Which Sea are they talking about? The sea level of the Atlantic and the Pacific Oceans are different. Otherwise, they wouldn't need locks in the Panama Canal.

This is great...! In a single day's ride I can pedal through a fragrant pine forest, beside breathing waterfalls. Undistracted from the sights...sounds...smells...of the country around me...birds can be heard but seldom seen among the spring leaves. The breeze in the trees is one of the prettiest sounds there is (when it's coming from the right direction). I have all this, and without an admission price. Traffic is keeping to a trickle on this new road that's as smooth as glass. I'm spinning along with the efficiency of a good Swiss watch. I really enjoy the rhythms of bicycling. The sounds of my bike tires on the road and the wind as it rushes past my ears makes me feel like I did back when I was a kid still in my single-digit years. All things are beautiful in the sight of children and of God.

I have never seen things more beautiful than I have on this tour.

I've just ridden up a monster hill followed by a very long…very nice…enjoyable descent. The warm afterglow of accomplishment I get after every climb makes it worth the effort. I feel the excitement of a downhill and my adrenaline is flowing as I lean to round another curve.

I have a 15 mph tailwind as the road and I try to stay on top of a ridge. The hillsides are so steep and thick with oak trees, I feel as if I'm following a trail through the misty treetops.

After another long climb I'm relieved…the kind of relief a swimmer feels on coming to the surface after a long, deep dive. On the top of this hill is another impressive view of a green carpeted forest. I stop to take a few deep breaths of the pine-scented air before I head on down the other side of the mountain.

At 3:16 p.m. I stop at a drug store that advertises pie and ice cream, in Preston Hollow. Like a youngster, I'll skip the vegetables and go right for the pie. I'm having a coke and apple pie a la mode. The same gentleman that fills the prescriptions here also makes ice cream sodas. He's a tall chap with a black cloud of hair.

It's 87 degrees as I pedal through what seems to be an endless wave of green trees, just south of Durham. I certainly am aware of the tailwind…even though its push isn't enough to do much…but it offsets some of my wind resistance.

I've seen no fewer than 20 'Deer Crossing' signs today. I believe there are a lot of deer in this part of the country. For the last sixty miles I've inched my way up mountain passes and rolled down thickly wooded hills to green valleys far below. It's almost like biking through the folds of a loosely draped blanket.

Overhead hawks are enjoying thermals. They, too…are flying free…not even flapping their streamlined wings.

Life couldn't be better.

As I ride out of South Cairo I have 100 miles on the odometer and it's 4:18 p.m. and 90 degrees and I have the same 15 mph tailwind, that helped me ride the first fifty miles today. Gravity has helped me the last 50 miles pulling me downhill ever since I got on Highway 145.

As soon as I ride out of Catskills I come to the *Rip Van Winkle Bridge*. It's a beautiful bridge. I would like to stop half-way across and take a picture but that's impossible. The bridge is too narrow and there is too much traffic. The view of the river is impressive. A fishing boat is leaving a slow V in the shining water far below.

The sun is dropping a notch lower, coloring the clouds. As soon as I get across the bridge the road starts out as a succession of gentle dips…then…all of a sudden…it climbs up toward the sun.

The sunlight is filtering its way through the thick forest. The scenery is spectacular and the terrain is rolling now. I believe I became a nature lover when I saw so much of her in the raw.

I'm wheeling southward through a forest over roads that dip and swoop through tunnels carved through the forest. As I pedal along, the afternoon sun casts bars (bars, I like that word) of light across the road to spotlight my way, mile after mile of my favorite type of terrain.

A little more hill-climbing here and then at 5:10 p.m. I stop in a deli in Germantown. It's 83 degrees as I enter and sit at the counter. I get a twinkle in my eye as I watch the young lady behind the counter. She's dressed in all white and looks as pure as the driven snow. Her hair is the color of polished pecans and is fresh from the curling wand, as it drops in loose coils. Her breasts are pressed full against her uniform, casting shadows to her waist. A golden cross swings gently high on her long throat. I ask her if she knows how far it is to New York City. I want to ride far enough today, so I'll be sure to get there tomorrow. She says she thinks it's about

50 miles. Another girl sitting at the end of the counter says it's 100 miles. I guess neither one knows for sure.

I leave the deli. I had a butterscotch malt and a large coke and some beautiful thoughts in there.

For some reason there are an awful lot of State Troopers on this road. The road here follows the Hudson River, more or less. There are gentle hills as I ride through woods where the sun is streaming down to the clean forest floor.

Ha...! I hear a helicopter. I haven't heard one of those since I left L.A. It sort of reminds me of home.

Most of the time the beautiful, dense forest blocks my view of the river. But, once in a while...I get a glimpse of a small...spring-fed pool that's nestled in a tangle of vines and brush. I'm riding along through a thick forest in semi-darkness. I only occasionally get a glimpse of the sun overhead through a lacework of branches. My eyes are searching the semi-darkness as sunlight dances off the tops of the trees.

I come across this Kodak moment that's too good to pass up but the sun can't cut its way through the canopy of trees. The flash comes on, so I don't expect it to turn out. The sun is always shining somewhere.

I've grown fond of touring. I enjoy the uncertainty of touring. I like the ever-changing unknowns. Touring is my private joy.

Oh...! The joy of being out in the mountains and in the woods all day...! The trees make a nice windbreak. With 125 miles in it's 6:44 p.m. and I'm going to stop and call my daughter, again.

I'm on my way again. She wasn't home. She's never home. I have a 10 mph cross-tail-wind that's pretty much blocked all the time by the trees. It's 7:08 p.m. as I pedal up a hill just south of Rhinebeck, I notice a Church with a sign out front that reads, "It is never the wrong time to do the right thing." So, I thank God for this good life. The trees around the church are huge with massive trunks. They look sort of like columns to the roof of Heaven.

Now I'm not a religious man…or maybe I am…I'm not sure. I've noticed that "born again" Christians don't go around telling people that they are born again. Well, I'm not ashamed of it…I'm a born again Christian…and I'm proud of it. I'll have to admit that I'm doing a little backsliding, but I'm not a hypocrite.

I ride bike once in a while with this married man. Now, he's a church-goer and he has the Bible verses to prove it. The extent of the verses I know is John 3:16. Anyway, he and his wife not only go to church every Sunday but they both teach a Sunday School class. He loves to preach to me as we ride along. Then, at the end of the ride he suggests that we all go to a titty bar for a beer. Now that's what I call a hypocrite.

I just climbed to the top of this long hill, which makes me feel as good as I do when church is letting out.

Another passage has just come to me, "The path of rightness being narrow, but broad is the road that leadeth to destruction." Now everyone interprets the Bible differently. To me this sort of renders against riding on Interstate.

I can't believe how thick the vegetation is all along this road. There is moss hanging overhead in most of the trees. I can just imagine seeing Rip Van Winkle tucked beneath one of these ancient oaks, hopelessly entangled in the dense undergrowth.

I'm just waiting for an opening that has enough light so I can take another picture. I just can't believe it. All along this road the woods are so thick and there are vines hanging from all the trees. It seems a little eerie, yet beautiful just the same.

By the way, "Do you know what's green and hangs from trees?"

"Monkey Snot…!"

I stop to call my daughter, again.

She's still not home.

It's 7:51 p.m. the black-leafed trees are waving and fluttering in a slight twilight breeze, making dancing silhouettes against a darkening sky.

I've ridden 141 miles today, and I'm going to check on a Super 8 motel in Hyde Park. Now I know Hyde Park is famous for something. I think it's the home of Franklin D. Roosevelt. I take the room at $36.00 for the night. A shower is the first order of business. Then I watch a little television and take a walk downtown.

The King and Queen are both closed, (Burger King and Dairy Queen). The only places that are open are two really fancy restaurants. The kind where you have to wear formal evening dress…you know…like undertakers wear. I certainly don't feel like going to either one of those places so I'm going to walk over to a little deli. I get a turkey sandwich and a quart of milk…some chips and a small apple pie…and some little chocolate cakes. I'll save some for in the morning, maybe.

Walking back to the motel, I look up and as I absorb the beauty of the sunset over the trees, I feel an immense sense of calm settle over me. At the same time the moon spans over the treetops like a silver wheel, emitting beams of light. I believe the moon must be closer than New York City, because I can see the moon but I can't see N.Y.C.

It's 11:33 p.m. as my head hits the pillow with wonderful thoughts.

*   *   *

*Statistics for **DAY TWENTY-SEVEN** Tuesday, July 11, 1989.*
141 miles of riding today, 14.1 average miles per hour for today, 3,108 miles of riding in 27 days, 115 average miles of riding per day.

Day Twenty-Eight

From Hyde Park, New York
To New York City, New York

It's 6:00 a.m. July 12. I'm going to get up now.

I go to the lobby and I'm greeted by a wonderful aroma.. Great…! The coffee is nearly finished perking. I have a cup, then another and yet another. It's as free as it is at an A.A.meeting. There is only one thing better than a hot cup of coffee in the morning. Boy, you've got a dirty mind. They also have some bread and jelly on the counter, so I make myself a jelly sandwich. A jelly sandwich, this reminds me of a fellow worker who was constantly complaining about his lunch. It seems that he had jelly sandwiches in his lunch every day. One day, I said to him, "Why don't you tell your wife to make you something else for lunch?" He said, "My wife doesn't make my lunch, I do."

The guy behind the front desk looks a little strange. His eyes are really close together. Actually, his head looks like it might have been run over by a truck. His whole head is streamlined…flat…except for his ears. The only thing I can imagine is that when he was a baby, his parents pulled on his ears trying to widen his head…which didn't happen. Instead, he now has a flat head and enormously large ears.

Anyway, I ask him, "How far is it to New York City?"
He says, "It's about one hour."
I say, "It'll take me more then an hour because I'm riding a bicycle."
So, then I ask him, "How many miles is it?"
He seems uneasy, much like a man committing adultery. Then he speaks slowly, as though he is rearranging his thoughts…and says,

"Oh…I'm…not…sure…I know very little about bike riding…and I really don't care to have it explained to me. It's 50 or 100 miles, I'm not sure. I've never heard of anyone doing it by bike."

I say, "It's the same distance, if you do it by car or bicycle." He's a lot of help. I don't know, maybe he didn't understand my California accent.

I washed my gloves out in the sink, and dried them on the heater last night. They were beginning to smell quite raunchy.

At 6:42 a.m. I wheel my bike outside, climb on it and turn its wheel into the unknown. The day is sunny…warm…and crisp like it is in the early fall. It's only 58 degrees out. It's really quite nippy riding in the shaded areas.

There is no wind at all this morning. There is however, a stream of cars pouring down this worn-out road and my comfortable shoulder of blacktop has come to an abrupt end.

Suddenly, a spectacular view from the top of a small hill stops me. Old stone fences…farmhouses…and villages seem to make quilts out of the rolling farmland. A stream that runs right under the road looks gorgeous, glistening in the early morning sunlight. It's delightful to see little minnows gliding upstream through its gurgling, clear water. I'm thinking that this is a perfect way to end my tour.

I ride through Poughkeepsie and stop to eat a mini-apple pie, one that I bought last night. You know that I owe my happiness to avoiding certain foods, like wedding cakes. I'm a firm believer that you should have to renew your marriage license every year. I believe marriage is much like a hot tub, it's not so hot after you get used to it.

At 8:13 a.m. I have 18 miles on the odometer as I roll through Fishkill (great name, huh…?) long before most folks are up.

Roads are not always smooth for bicycles, especially…on the shoulder…where I try to ride whenever possible. I'm riding on a really rough shoulder, here, just to keep from getting killed. There are an enormous number of cars. It's just an endless stream of cars and trucks. On the shoulder there is a flea market of rusted nuts and bolts…giant black carcasses of truck retreads...license plates...pieces of wire...V-belts...nails...beer cans...glass...gravel...and various car parts...not to mention the cracks...grooves...and holes in the road. As I maneuver around deep potholes gravel pops from under my tires. I'm sure I'll more than likely get a flat tire, but that's still better than getting killed.

LITTERED ROADSIDE

One thing I've learned on this tour is that there is no such thing as flat land. It's either uphill or downhill.

Once again, I notice a lot of small, blue…wildflowers blanketing the edge of the road.

On most vacations, tourists (myself included) tend to eat too much. We sit in our cars most of the time…or lie out in the sun. None of which is good for you. We get overweight…lazy…and burnt. We usually feel worse after the vacation, than we did before it. It's quite different on a bicycle tour though. I am constantly exercising…so I naturally get in better shape as this vacation progresses and I feel better. A 185-pound man (me) riding at a moderate pace (fifteen miles per hour) expends somewhere around 600 calories an hour. This gives him license to guiltlessly eat whatever he wants as he travels. On this tour, my average day's ride is 115 miles…which…at a moderate pace…means I burned around 5,000 calories a day. So, I'm obliged to eat and drink as much as I choose.

I've been riding on rolling terrain for the last 20 miles and I have a 5 mph tailwind.

I see a deer down in the woods. In the lush green…overgrown forest…the deer really stands out. It looks almost red, instead of brown. By the time I get my camera out, the sun on the horizon is only giving me a silhouette of the departing deer. So, I capture the picture in my mind. I've seen a lot of beautiful things on this tour that can only be captured with the naked eye.

I can't believe it…! I'm paralleling the Hudson River, so…I thought it would be flat or even a little downhill…(after all, rivers always run downhill) but it isn't. My map makes it look like it's a direct and easy route, but my map lies. It's nothing but a series of never-ending dips and climbs.

I'm so tired already this morning. I'm going to have to talk to Mikey when I get back to L.A. I'm going to ask him when the last time he was here, because I'm sure they've added a few hills since he's been here.

I round a corner just south of Mckeel Corners and run smack into a solid mass of green. Now, I've never seen a rain forest but I can imagine it looking somewhat like this. Tall green trees with Spanish moss hanging down from the limbs like long, graybeards. There are green ferns and vegetation everywhere.

At 9:00 a.m. I ride out of Nelson Corners. I keep turning the cranks in granny gear. These hills are getting a bit wearing and they are really starting to take a toll on me. I'm sure that if I were to make an elevation chart of this terrain it would look like the waves of my heart beat on a heart monitor.

Tall trees shade the road like a giant green awning. I'm riding through a maze of green with tunnel vision…as the moss-covered trees tower above me. The road looks like a tunnel cut through a giant hedge. There is a small sign that says the *Appalachian Trail* crosses the road here.

I have a 5 mph tailwind and the trees continue to line the sides of these two narrow lanes of asphalt. I only occasionally come to an opening, where I get a view of the Hudson River.

As I pedal through this quiet avenue of peaceful…natural skyscrapers…the thick forest only allows little sunlight to penetrate. I like peeping into the forest where a ray of sun spotlights a leaf, or a limb. I ride along, realizing that I am just admiring nature and doing it no harm.

I'm accomplishing things now that I never thought I possibly could. I realize now that it was all cycle-logical that I was always capable of accomplishing these tasks. It's just that I've been in a slump…for the past 30 years.

I don't think there is a better feeling than to be free and healthy.

I honestly believe that long-distance cycling is just as much mental as it is physical, if not more so. I didn't ride all that much before I started out on this tour. I wasn't in the greatest shape. But this is something that I really wanted to do, so I did it. I think it's all in the attitude you have.

On most car vacations you travel as fast as you can from point (A) to point (B) so you can start your vacation when you get to point (B). On a bicycle tour your vacation starts right away. Riding from point (A) to point (B) is your vacation…you don't have to wait until you get to point (B).

I think you have to make your ride as enjoyable and fun as you can. If you don't enjoy riding, you're going to have a lousy time. I can honestly say that I enjoyed every minute of my tour even though I swore at the hills a lot.

With 34 miles on the odometer I stop at a marvelous overlook of the river near Peekskill (figure that name out) to rest and eat my *Ding-Dongs*. My eating habits on this tour are pretty much the same as when I'm at home. And I planned it that way. You see, I didn't want to make any big changes and risk getting sick. So, I eat out at junk food places, just like I do at home. I didn't eat any *Power-Bars* or drink any *Body-Fuel*. I just put some Moon Juice (*Tang*) in my water just so it would taste a little better. I never eat what cyclists are supposed to eat. Instead of eating pancakes for breakfast, I eat biscuits and gravy. I pretty much eat junk food all the time. My idea of something really good is chicken fried steak: To make it you take a piece of beef…pound the hell out of it…dip it in egg and flour…pop it in a skillet with bacon grease and fry it up. Take it out, throw in some flour and milk and salt and pepper and you've got some gravy. Add a piece of toast and lots of butter, and a glass of cold milk. And I can't help but lift my eyes to heaven and say a word of praise to Our Lord.

As I ride through Montrose there is no wind at all, but the heat and traffic are increasing. It's 72 degrees. I have to ride on this #%@Z! shoulder, dodging chuckholes all the way. It's full of cracks…and potholes…and rocks…and glass. I just can't believe all the rubbish along the road. There are some things I might expect to see…like broken fan belts…or glass. But just how come there are drive shafts…mufflers…tail pipes…brake disk and shoes…even brake drums…shirts…pants…shoes? I've even seen underwear on the shoulder.

* * *

Cars, pickups and giant twin-trailer semi's fly by me doing their own versions of the 55 mph speed limit. I don't want to think of what might happen if one of their retreads shredded at seventy-miles-per-hour as it passes me. Just the turbulence created behind them is almost enough to set me in a tailspin. As I prepared to have my name in the paper...in the obituary section...I imagine it would read something like this, **Harold Wagoner** (or Howard Wagner because people have misspelled my name all my life and they'll probably misspell it on my monument as well). A 45-year-old free spirited young man, who defines himself as "Not an expert at anything, but enjoys everything" blah...blah...blah...blah...he was an average American male...six feet...with very little hair on his head and a threatening pot belly. He was drawn to challenges like moths to a porch light. Survived by two ex-wives who already have everything he ever owned. One thing is for sure...I won't be remembered as an intelligent man who failed in life.

At all the bike races I've attended they have different age groups: 16 to 18...18 to 25...25 to 45...and 45 to death. Well I'm 45 but I still have a lot of things to discover. And this certainly isn't the Highway to Heaven. I believe that somewhere beyond the horizon there has to be a force more powerful than people controlling my destiny.

*   *   *

If I can find a place to eat, I'm ready for a good breakfast now.

At 10:30 a.m. I stop for breakfast in Croton-on-Hudson. I guess...by now...you've figured out that I'm not exactly what you would call a health food nut. I figure, if it isn't deep-fried in grease, it isn't real food.

When I get hungry at work, I usually go to the vending machine and get a Reese's peanut butter cup. Mardy, who is one of those... disgusting...skinny...count every calorie...health nuts...says to me, "Why don't you eat a yogurt bar instead of that junk?" Well, I've tried those rotten-tasting fermented-milk concoctions they call yogurt and I detest them more than anything.

Anyway, as I sit there...thoroughly enjoying my peanut butter cups and Pepsi, Mardy is eating a nasty mixture of alfalfa sprouts...tofu...wheat...shredded zucchini...sunflower seeds...and a few other questionable ingredients...which he then washes down with a few swallows from his can of guava-apricot-papaya-banana-peach nectar.

I explain my way of thinking to him. You see, I would have to eat about 20 yogurt bars to get the same amount of nourishment as I get eating just one Reese's peanut butter cup.

*   *   *

It's a little bit overcast now, which makes it nice for riding.

You know, it's gratifying to me just to know that I can pack up my panniers and with a minimum amount of planning...take off on my bike to an undetermined destination for an indefinite amount of time...and enjoy it.

One thing's for sure...this isn't the best road in the world. It has an ever-increasing river of traffic on it.

As the hills become higher and the climbs longer and steeper, the woods are getting thicker. I stop to catch my breath at the top of this especially steep hill. There is a jungle-like growth of flowers...trees...shrubs...and hanging moss. As I look into the lush forest, I can see some moss-covered rocks, hiding in the shadows of the trees. There is moss growing on everything. When I was in the Boy Scouts, I didn't believe that moss only grew on the north side of trees and...right here...is living proof of it. Moss grows on the shady side of things and that could be any side.

There is no wind but there are some very tough hills on this road. There seems to be no end to them. It's just one hill after another. I just ground my way to the top of this hill in my bottom gear. I'm riding past the town of Ossining's cemetery. I'm convinced it must be where they put all the cyclists that didn't quite make it up the hill.

At 12:28 p.m. I have 60 miles on the odometer as I ride into Hasting-on-Hudson...I have a 5 mph breeze from my right, which is blocked by trees 90% of the time. One thing's for sure...I'm not out of the woods or hills yet. I just grunted my way up another bothersome hill. I'm riding along on the white-painted line now because the road has no shoulder. It's like riding on a long balance beam.

Most of the time the beautiful trees obstruct my view of the river.

Everyone I've talked to and everything I've ever read about people who have done a Trans-Continual bike tour, say it's much harder than they expected it to be. I've found it to be just the opposite. It's much easier than I had expected it to be.

Back in the Midwest, where they grow the majority of the crops...it has to rain two or three times a week...or there wouldn't be any crops. So, naturally...I expected to get wet a lot. Well, for some reason, I didn't. It only sprinkled on me a few times on my whole tour, and it didn't sprinkle hard enough for me to bother with putting my rain suit on. I put it on 3 times, just because I had it. There was a couple of times it really came down but I was under cover. Once I was in a Post Office and another time I was in a bar.

Off to my left I can see a water tower with "Yonkers" painted on it. Well, I'm really disappointed now. After my three-thousand-mile-plus trek, on my Trek...I expected to see a big sign that read, "Welcome to the Big Apple, Harold." Or maybe they would present me with the key to the city that won't unlock anything. But No, there wasn't even a sign to let me know that I'm in New York City.

CONSIDERING
RE-ENTRY

I just struggled up another second gear hill, in Yonkers. Yonkers, I'm afraid my tour is really funneling down. The streets here are clogged and dangerous. It seems like everyone is double-parking.

At 1:12 p.m. I ride through Manhattan on Broadway Avenue. It's 77 degrees. There is a small, compact black man on the sidewalk with a gasoline-powered leaf blower. Those of us who like to breathe nice clean air despise them. They are noisy and stir up more dirt than a Kitty Kelly book, and there's always blue-black smoke pouring out of them.

The fire escapes slashing down the sides of the buildings look like giant spider webs.

It's really interesting to people-watch as I ride along. There is a lady with her hair caught up in a knot and her skirt's a maxi, revealing only a few inches of her ankle above her worn-out tennis shoes. And there's a man standing toe to toe with her and he's shaking his finger like it's got a angry bee on it.

I ride around cars double-parked…with people sitting in them reading their newspapers. Broadway certainly is a traffic-choked street. The air's saturated with diesel fumes and it's burning in my lungs. I just hate the smell of BIG Cities.

Talk about noise pollution, I swear these #%@Z! New Yorkers can't drive without one hand on their horn. (Don't sugar coat it, Harold.) If manufactured noise isn't an offense against human nature, I don't know what is.

As I see it now, the biggest problem in this city isn't the gangs…it's the taxi cab drivers. They drive completely crazily and they don't care about anyone. They are absolute maniacs…! I'm now convinced that when someone say's "Stick it where the sun don't shine," they're talking about The Big (Rotten) Apple.

I've seen a few of the "I Love New York" bumper stickers on cars in Los Angeles. I say, if you love something, then that's where you should be. On second thought…I guess it's all right to love some place and not live there…but it's not all right to live in the United States and not love it.

I try to believe in the best in people. Yes, once in a while I'll run into a two-legged rat…but on the whole…people are usually friendly…and good to me. New York City is one exception. They drive by me…missing me by inches…with one finger on their horns and the other up in the air. No wonder they drive all over the road, it probably wouldn't even bother them if they dented their cars by hitting me.

Picture this: Here's this guy standing on the corner, with a black trench coat on that goes almost to the ground. He's as thin as a rail, narrow-faced with an oversized pointed nose. He's standing there with his head leaning forward, looking at the ground. His Adam's apple is bobbing up and down his extra long neck. He has a bald spot almost the size of his head. He looks like a vulture to me.

It'll always be a mystery to me, how there are millions and millions of people on this earth, and no two are exactly alike.

At 2:46 p.m. with 73 miles in, I ride into Central Park. It's warmed up to 80 degrees. I can see that this town is like a nervous hive of bees. I ride through the streets of the Big Apple, and, at every crosswalk...pedestrians cross directly in front of my path...even when I have the green light.

Huge cement trucks with snarling bulldogs on their hoods barrel down on me at breakneck speeds. Buses cut me off in a display of right-of-way. And cab drivers are turning the asphalt streets into a free-for-all.

I believe New York is a very unfriendly city. It's a jungle out here. I think there is more here than meets the eye. I believe the people of N.Y.C. have to be prisoners of war.

All day the riding conditions have grown worse. The increased population as I approach New York City is only part of it. The most noticeable thing to me is that the roads, carrying a heavy traffic load...aren't any wider. I know that heavy traffic doesn't improve the disposition of drivers and I feel a definite resentment by many of the motorist at my presence on their roadway.

As I ride past St. Patrick's Cathedral a swarm of people cross the street...against the light...right in front of me. Some of them are wearing beepers. Let me tell you what I think about beepers. Whether they are real or counterfeit, they are the most common way for insignificant people to impress other people with their high professional and social values.

It seems that traffic signals mean nothing in Manhattan. I have a red light and people are blowing their horns at me.

I veer to the left to avoid hitting a big, fat pedestrian who has stepped into the intersection while chewing away on a huge pretzel, paying no attention at all to the traffic. It hasn't taken me long to figure out that the law of the jungle rules on New York's streets. Most, and I say most...pedestrians yield to cyclists...cyclists to taxis...taxis to buses...and buses to garbage trucks and only the quick and strong survive.

I've seen a few New York messengers. And they didn't look like Nelson Vails, the bicycle messenger in "*Quicksilver.*" Vails actually did work as a messenger in N.Y.C. He also got a silver medal for cycling in the Olympics.

If I were to describe a typical messenger, he would be a young... unshaven man...with long hair. His bike would be rusted and bent and the handlebars would be wrapped with electrical tape. His rims would have oversize knobby tires.

As I ride past the *Empire State Building* the only way to see out of this concrete canyon is to look upward past the skyscrapers.

It's 3:25 p.m. I have 79 miles on the odometer as I ride into Union Square...it's starting to sprinkle a little bit. A delivery truck goes around me and speeds down the avenue, with no regard for his or anyone else's life. By the smell of his exhaust he must be burning shit for gas. People are running around like rats in a granary.

I wonder, is it true that none of these buildings have thirteenth floors because of superstition?

As I ride through *Washington Square* in Manhattan, a New Yorker...with blood in him...waves to me. On second thought, he probably isn't a New Yorker.

There is an old black gentleman. His skin so black that it's difficult to distinguish his features. He's as black as his own shadow. His shirt matches his face, wrinkled and out of shape. I feel sorry for him as he stands on the asphalt beneath a blue cloud of exhaust.

I just got my first glimpse of the twin towers of the *World Trade Center*.

At 4:35 p.m. I'm at *Battery Park* in Manhattan. I would like to stop and walk around a little, but I know it would be a mistake leaving my bike unprotected in this neighborhood.

I think I'm in one of the worst neighborhoods in this city. The streets are especially bad. I want to ride across the *Brooklyn Bridge* so I get on the ramp to cross it. I don't see any signs anywhere restricting bicyclists but as soon as I get on the bridge I can see a walkway in the middle of the bridge, where foot and bicycle traffic are supposed to be. Of course, by this time it's too late for me, I'm already on the road and there's a high fence between the sidewalk and me. Cars and taxis and trucks are flying by me with one hand on their horns and the other out the window with their middle finger extended...hollering obscenities at me. A woman just yelled out her window at me "All you bums should be shot." Now I know where the people are that would actually hurt a fly. I know I'm in the wrong but there is nothing I can do about it now. I remember, as a child, walking across the high beams in our barn. Well, this is much worse. I feel as out of place as a Sand Hill Crane in a chicken coop. The traffic crossing the *Brooklyn Bridge* is the worst I've ever seen. I get nervous, just thinking about it now.

I just made a wrong turn off Atlantic Avenue in Brooklyn, but I think I'd better not stop to ask directions or backtrack. I consider backtracking recycling, and I'm not ready to be recycled yet. I'm sure this is not the best part of town, all I can see on the street are abandoned and stripped cars...and jagged walls with collapsed roofs...and piles of junk. Everything is covered with graffiti. Black people with nothing to do, turn their heads toward me like sunflowers turning toward the sun. I ride through a bunch of kids playing baseball in the street. I remember, as a kid, playing baseball. The one thing I didn't understand was why I was always the last one to be picked to play on a team. I knew I wasn't the best player but I didn't consider myself to be the worst, either.

There is a group of about ten teenage black folks (that's southern for young gentlemen). One is pointing at me with a finger the size of a zucchini. Now, I'm thinking that this is not the best place in the world to be. I just want to be invisible. These streets are filled with unfriendly traffic and people.

There is a slight drizzle and it's sort of gray-black out.

New York City is one place that's changed my attitude, fast.

As I ride past rotting buildings and vacant lots filled with refuse...boarded-up stores and pushers on the make...I would like to stop and take some pictures but I have more common sense than that. I'm riding through a neighborhood in Queens, where it's not safe to stop, let alone take a picture.

I believe that if you ride in New York City, you have to follow these common sense safety rules;

1) Always ride at least 60 miles-per-hour.

2) Always keep your money in a safe place, such as Switzerland.

3) Never make eye contact, this is asking to be mugged. In the New York court system, a mugger is automatically declared not guilty if the defense can prove the victim has a history of making eye contact.

I'm riding on 150 St. in Brooklyn, through a neighborhood of burned-out buildings. I'm thinking that the local kids must have a hard time just staying out of jail…and not get a record…let alone try to graduate from high school.

This road is so rough…it looks like it's being prepared for resurfacing, but it's not. It's just one #@%Z! road. I'm probably only about a mile from the air terminal but I have to watch out so I don't hit a rock or pothole in the road and crash. I just saw a store sign that boasted: Police Locks…Door Locks…Window Gates installed. The sign is badly faded but it's painted red, white, and blue. Says a lot for this part of our country.

I know today I've ridden over some of the worst roads in New York City, and probably in the whole world.

I'm at the *John F. Kennedy Airport* terminal, now. How good it is to be alive, I'm thinking as I inhale deep lungful of carbon monoxide. There is no single event to account for my . . . luck. No, not luck. I don't believe in luck, but guidance getting through N.Y.C. I didn't have any visions. God didn't make an appearance. But, somehow…I've made it through the streets of New York City unharmed and I'm so happy I could dance on my own grave.

I wasn't exactly sure of when I would get to J.F.K. in N.Y.C. so I didn't buy my return flight ticket ahead of time and it's a good thing I waited, because I'm here two weeks earlier than I thought I would be. And there is no way I would stay in this town for two weeks. After riding through it I've discovered that I don't like it very much. I go in and see if I can find a flight to L.A. soon.

It's 6:45 p.m. and it's 75 degrees out. I've ridden 101 miles today, and I'm in the terminal at J.F.K. Airport. I push my bike in, so I can keep an eye on it while I stand in line to get a ticket. If I find a long line…I find it somewhat pleasing…because somebody else has already done some of the waiting.

I'm finally at the head of the line and I tell the girl behind the counter that I want a ticket to L.A. She says, "Will that be one way or a round trip ticket?"

I tell her, "One way, thank you."

She tells me that I can get on the next flight to L.A. but "Last minute tickets are grossly over priced."

I say, "How much are we talking about here?"

She says, "It'll cost you $588.00 for a one way ticket…plus…$30.00 for your bike…plus…$10.00 for a bike box."

I say, "Yea…! That's really expensive all right, how much would a ticket cost…if I were to take a flight back tomorrow or the next day instead of today?"

She says, "It'll be the same price."

So, I say, "Well, then give me a ticket." I dislike being here (N.Y.C.) more than anyplace.

By the time I get my ticket, it's only a half-hour before the plane leaves…so I tell her that I don't know if I have enough time to take my bike apart…and box it. She tells me that she needs my bike in 10 minutes or less, or it won't make it on the plane. I tell her that there is no way I could get it ready in 10 minutes. She says, "Bring your bike over here and I'll help you with it." I couldn't believe it, a friendly person…in New York City. So she put the box together, while I took my handlebars and panniers off my bike. We boxed it up really quick and sent it on its way. Next, I have to make out tags and put them on my panniers.

I say, "You saved my life."

She says, "No big deal."

I wish she had said it a little differently.

I was hoping I would have enough time to clean up a little and change into my street clothes...and maybe even get a bite to eat...and have a few beers...and call my daughter...before I had to get on the plane. But it just didn't work out that way. My daughter probably wouldn't have been at home anyway.

As soon as I get seated, the plane takes off. I suddenly realize that a chapter of my tour, and of my life...has come to a close.

*   *   *

*Statistics for **DAY TWENTY-EIGHT** Wednesday, July 12, 1989.*
101 miles of riding today, 9.9 average miles per hour for today, 3,209 miles of riding in 28 days, 115 average miles of riding per day.

My Flight Home

I want to get out of New York City in a New York minute and…Praise the Lord…I'm on my way to California. It may be the land of fruits and nuts but that's better than rotten apples. I have a seat on the airliner next to a young lady. Now I know that I have to smell like a man who bathes only on leap years. The plane seems warm to me and as I sit here quietly, I actually begin to steam. I smell bad enough dry…but wet…I'm sure I could drive a lame skunk out of its hole at forty yards. I'm feeling lower than a snake's belly, but there is nothing I can do about it. And to make it even worse my wet skintight…shiny bike shorts…make me look like I have a coat of black paint applied from the waist down to just above my knees.

The young lady curiously asks me. "Just what are those shorts made out of?"

I answer and say, "*Spandex*, which is actually melted money." She smiles.

I'm flying at 620 miles per hour, about 600 miles an hour faster than I traveled eastward. As I look down from the airplane window, I can't believe I rode all that way. I ask Judy, (the lady sitting next to me) if she has ever ridden a bicycle?

She says, "I sure have. I ride my bike to campus once in a while. I once read a book called, *Biking Made Easy for Imbeciles* and it actually turned out to be a very good book, once I got past the hard parts."

Then, I ask her if she had ever thought about riding across the United States?

She says, "I can answer that in two words, im…possible."

In a mere five hours we're somewhere over Colorado. We're crossing the jagged backbone of the Continental Divide. I've discovered that the hills are a lot easier at 31,000 feet. Twenty-eight days of biking flashes by in six hours with no sensation of travel at all. Air travel is fast with no adventure…no challenge…no sweat…no fun…no cows…no farmers…no hills…no sense of accomplishment and no memories. I honestly believe now, that if you really want to see the real United States, you have to ride across it on a bicycle.

I feel very good. I took seven weeks off work, and it only took me four weeks to complete my tour.

It was sprinkling, and dark, when I left J.F.K. As soon as the plane got above the clouds, the sun was shining. We flew over a thick cloud cover, over all of the eastern United States, and most of the western states as well.

As we fly west at this time of evening, we see the sun that keeps setting on the horizon of clouds…for a long…long time.

I'm taking a lot of pictures of it. Judy thinks that I'm just wasting my film…trying to get a picture with the sun almost down. I assure her that I'm not…because there isn't any film in my camera anyway. She smiles again.

Once in a great while there is a break in the cloud cover, and I can see lights from farm houses far…far below.

Now, I have to agree that airline food isn't the best food in the world but I couldn't believe it. Judy couldn't eat all of hers. I mean, I could easily eat five or six portions the size they give us.

The further west we go, the darker it gets. As I look down, there are blankets of clouds beneath me…with only an occasional clear spot…where I can see some ground lights.

A little off to my right…and below the plane…there is a lightning storm. It's the first time I've seen lighting from above. It's kind of neat.

As I arrive at L.A.X. at 10:30 p.m. it is three hours later than when I left J.F.K. There is a three-hour time difference, so the flight actually took six hours.

I guess I went from a primitive way of transportation, (the bicycle) to the most modern way (the airplane), but...when I step off the plane my legs are stiff and achy. That never happened on my cross-country tour.

I try to call my daughter. Again, she isn't home, so I'm going up to a tavern in the airport terminal. After all, I believe birds should fly and men should drink. I'm carrying my handlebar bag...with my camera and tape-recorder...all my notes...and all the film...so it wouldn't end up in Salt Lake City or some other ungodly place. I also want to carry it so my film wouldn't go through the X-ray machine. I've heard it's not supposed to be good for the film. I'm sitting here calling my daughter every once in a while, to see if she's home, I want her to come and get me. Of course she isn't. I stay in the tavern until it closes, at which time it's obvious that my daughter isn't going to be home at all.

Seeing as how I've had quite a few beers and it's dark I think I'll go down and get my bike...put my panniers on...and ride to the first motel I come to and stay there for the night...then ride on home in the morning.

As I walk toward the baggage area a strange feeling comes over me, much like the feeling you get when you walk up to your locked car and see your keys in the ignition. I have visions of missing panniers and a mangled bicycle frame. When I get there, my panniers and bike aren't there. My first thought is, "Oh Shit...!" Somebody stole my bike and panniers while I was sitting in the tavern for those three plus hours. I immediately go to the baggage claim window, to see if they have any idea of what happened to them. A young lady that looks as though she has just stepped out of a mayonnaise jar checks and tells me that I got it to the airport terminal in New York City too late for them to put it on the same plane I was on. So, they were going to put it on the next available flight to L.A. which would be tomorrow. Well, that made me happy and sad at the same time. I'm happy because nobody had stolen it, but sad because it's not here.

Well, I still need a ride home, and my daughter isn't around so I'm thinking I'll just have to make the best out of a bad situation. So I say to the young lady, "Great, just how am I going to get home now? I planned on riding my bike home."

She says, "You were going to ride your bike all the way to Chatsworth. That's 25 miles from here."

I say, "I know it's a long way but I was going to try to make it anyway."

She says that they will arrange to take me home in an airport shuttle van.

I say. "All right. But how am I going to get my bike?"

She says that they will deliver it to my apartment, as soon as it arrived tomorrow.

So, I get on the shuttle and go home. When I'm getting off the shuttle, I discover that I had left my handlebar bag somewhere. I think about it for a while and figure out that I've probably left it in the tavern at the airport. When I first got to the tavern, I put my bag on a stool beside me…then…when it got busy I had to put it down on the floor…beside my stool. Then when I left…after a few…actually quite a few…beers…I must have forgotten all about it. Being the last person to leave the tavern made my chances of the bar help turning it in fairly good. The very first thing in the morning, as soon as the tavern opened…I called them…and thank God they had found it. So I jump in my car and head right down there to get it. I mean, everything of any importance is in that bag.

As long as I'm at the airport I'll go over to see if my bike has arrived yet. I talk to the manager and he says, "We're sorry but it's not here yet, but because we said it would be here today…and it isn't we'll reimburse you for the shipping of it. They had charged me $30.00 to send it, plus $10.00 for the bike box. So, he wrote me out a check for $40.00 and said that they would deliver it the next day. When the box arrived it was damaged. I checked inside and discovered that the odometer was missing. I called the claims department and they reimbursed me for that. Interesting, isn't it, how I can have a whole 28 days of uncomplicated travel on my bike…with only myself to count on…and how 24 hours of dealing with advanced technology can be so complicated.

The End
Of a perfect vacation.

Epilogue

There is no way I can explain all the wonderful experiences I encountered along the way.

I took a lot of pictures trying to capture some of the spectacular scenery. Of course, my photographs don't do the scenery justice. Maybe if they were Three-D it would have helped. There is just too much beauty to capture in a photo. I recorded things. Putting words down on paper, or on a tape recorder, is a very dull substitute for seeing the images.

Other things I can't describe satisfactorily, and I'm not sure anyone can…are the incredibly wonderful sounds and smells you encounter on a bicycle tour.

Like:

The gentle sound of rain drops falling on leaves.

The sound of rain as it pounds out a rhythm on my helmet.

The sound of a small stream as it trickles over rocks.

The sound of my heart pounding as a quail suddenly flies up not more than two feet in front of my wheel.

The sound of my heart pounding as I struggle to climb an especially long…steep hill.

The sound of the ever slightest breeze gently blowing through the trees.

The sounds of the wind blowing through the grass, fence and telephone lines.

The sound of a pine cone…acorn…and even something as small as a leaf falling to the ground.

The sound of a bee, a cricket and a frog.

The sounds of crows crowing and cows mooing and of woodpeckers and the squirrels sending out their warning.

The smell of the rain .
The smell of new mown hay and grass.
The smell of pine trees and leaves.
The smell of fresh air and the not so fresh air.
The smell of wildflowers and country gardens.
The smell of freshly tilled ground.
And all the farm smells.

These are just a few of the things I'll always remember. Long after the beauty of specific images has faded, in my memory I will marvel over them for the rest of my life.

I believe that once in everybody's life time there comes a moment too big to be missed. Judging from the stories I've heard on my tour, many people miss out on that moment. They tell me things like, "I've always wanted to do this, or that, but it just never worked out." What I really think happens is that the bluebird of paradise whispers into their ears tempting them to loosen up…take a chance…come join in on the fun…live a little. But the fear of failing…or looking silly…causes them to shoo the bird away.

Everyone should have his or her dream and live it to the fullest.

I believe that, twenty-five years from now an old…baldheaded…graybearded…seventy-year-old man will be chuckling at the memories of his youthful adventures and he'll still be planning new ones.

I would like to say Thanks.

Thanks to the Dixieland band that showed up in a park in Washington to play just for the fun of it.

Thanks to the rough-looking man in the large dump truck, for not blowing his air-horns at me while I stood there straddling my bike through a green light…daydreaming…watching a beautiful girl cross the street.

Thanks to whoever planted the marigolds along Highway 2, not content with only making a small patch of land beautiful…but also for putting a sign up that read, "Flowers, Have Some."

Thanks to the old dog that came and sit quietly beside me on the steps of a country store, while I drank a quart of milk. I was honored that he selected me to share his silent company with.

Thanks to the flat-chested young lady that stood her ground while a policeman wrote her a ticket for indecent exposure.

And a very special Thanks to Rose.

Afterword

After being home for a few days now, I realize that I haven't worn a shirt with buttons, or a belt or brown socks, in over a month. It's just not cool to wear colored socks when you're cycling. As I sit here reflecting back on my tour, I'm thinking of ways that I might have improved on it. I know now, a lot better than before…what to take along and what not to. I took a lot of stuff I really didn't need. But, what the heck…it was my first tour…and how was I to know? It just goes to prove, experience does have its advantages.

I made a few mistakes. I should have called my girlfriend. I thought about it many, many times during my tour but I never called her.

People often ask me,

"Would you do the trip again?"

I answer and say, "Absolutely, but it wasn't a trip it was a tour."

They ask, "Would you do the same route again?"

"Yes, it was a very good route".

"Would you do anything differently?"

"Sure I would," but, at the time I did my tour, it was the right way for me. Things are constantly changing in my life…and yours too…I hope. I can honestly tell you, that I'm glad I did the tour…alone. I had a lot of time to think about things, and to quietly enjoy nature. I learned a lot about myself, what I'm capable, and not capable of doing. I had no idea that I could ride my bicycle 115 miles a day, for 28 days…and still feel great. I mean, if I would have had the time…there is no doubt in my mind…that I could have ridden back to Seattle, and enjoyed it. I now believe that the ultimate tour (for the average biker) is across this great country of ours. A coast to coast bicycle tour is a dream of millions of bicyclists. It's a plan for thousands and an achievement for hundreds. I say, don't abandon the idea of riding a two-wheeler from the Pacific to the Atlantic because only a few have done it. The tour is within range of nearly anyone who has the time…the ambition…the bicycle…the stamina…good sense…and good planning. I'll always appreciate the experience of bicycling across North America. I wouldn't trade it for anything.

I'm in much better shape now, than I was when I started my tour. I ate everything in sight on my tour and I still lost 10 lbs, which is great. I now weigh 184 lbs. but I'm 6 feet long, so that's not too bad. Before my tour, my blood pressure was 140 over 95, now its 120 over 75. If it starts to go up again, I'll know it's time for me to take another tour.

Conclusions

I'll always be grateful that I had the chance to bicycle across this beautiful country of ours. It was the most fun I've ever had with my clothes on. And I'm glad I did it alone…not for a cause…or for fame…or to win a bet or a race. I never really wanted anyone to ride with me. With somebody else I knew there would be a lot of friction. I'm not a man who takes to people easily. I'd want to do one thing and they'd want to do another. There was no small talk or distractions on my tour. It was just me…my bike…my thoughts…and the road. It's in situations like this that I do my clearest thinking. Solutions dissolve problems…relaxation replaces stress…and each hill climbed represents another personal obstacle overcome. During times in my life when I can't see the forest for the trees, my answer often lies in pedaling out of the woods alone. When I return, I not only have a fresh outlook on life but I also have more self-confidence. Accomplishing something on my own is the only way to gain the confidence I need to set and attain even higher goals.

There is just no way I can tell you the whole story. There is only one way to truly understand what I'm talking about and that's to:

"Do it by yourself. For yourself…!"

About the Author

Born in Indiana on the 16th of November, 1943. His mother was a registered nurse, his dad was a farmer, just like his dad and grandfather were. His childhood days were spent on a farm. When he was in the fourth grade the family moved to a dairy farm in Wisconsin. This is where he got into *Cub Scouts, 4-H* and the *FFA (Future Farmers of America)*. He also joined the *Boy Scouts* and eventually become an Eagle Scout.

He went to Berlin High School. Then moved to Kansas where he drove Big-Rigs cross-country. From there he moved to California and worked as a machinist for a large Aero Space company. After his bicycle tour he purchased a RV and for the last ten years of his life he's been traveling across the United States and enjoying life with his friend and wife "Tish". In his travels he has picked up numerous part time seasonal jobs. From busting crabs in Northern California to being a cashier at Wal-Mart and K-Mart stores in Florida and Wisconsin. He's worked at True Value hardware stores in Cal.ifornia and Wisconsin. Other seasonal jobs have included State Park Systems in Florida and California. He has also been a National Park Ranger in Utah. He's what they call a full time RVer (a snowbird) who travels in the north in the summer and the warm south in the winter, as far south as La Paz in Baja. His hobbies are kayaking, bicycling, fishing…and enjoying life.

Printed in the United States
805100002B